Business Innovation

FOR DUMMIES®

Business Innovation

FOR

DUMMIES®

by Alexander Hiam

WILEY

Wiley Publishing, Inc.

Business Innovation For Dummies®

Published by
Wiley Publishing, Inc.
111 River St.
Hoboken, NJ 07030-5774
www.wiley.com

For general information on our other products and services, please contact our Customer Care Department within the U.S. at 877-762-2974, outside the U.S. at 317-572-3993, or fax 317-572-4002.

For technical support, please visit www.wiley.com/techsupport.

Wiley also publishes its books in a variety of electronic formats. Some content that appears in print may not be available in electronic books.

Library of Congress Control Number: 2010926833

ISBN: 978-0-470-60174-7

Manufactured in the United States of America

10 9 8 7 6 5 4 3 2 1

WILEY

About the Author

Alexander Hiam's career integrates business and creativity in unusual ways. His work has included business strategy, high-tech entrepreneurship, new-product development, branding, naming, negotiating, and consulting — often in the role of innovator or generator of new ideas and approaches.

He's also taught thousands of managers innovation and creativity skills through his workshops and idea-generation retreats, as well as through his authorship of study materials such as *The Manager's Pocket Guide to Creativity* (HRD Press), *Creativity By Design* (HRD Press), *Creative Roles Analysis* (Trainer's Spectrum), and *The Entrepreneur's Complete Sourcebook* (Simon & Schuster).

Alex's professional focus on business innovation and how to lead it is balanced by his interest in the arts. He shows paintings, collages, and photographs and writes fiction — his favorite being fantasy adventures for young adults. In this book, he harnesses his creative imagination to the task of helping others be more creative and successful in their businesses, whatever those might be.

Alex's clients include the U.S. Coast Guard (he helps keep its leadership training innovative and at the forefront of management practice) and a lengthy list of companies, government agencies, nonprofit boards, and more. He's helped the U.S. Senate work on its collaborative problem-solving skills and brought new assessment tools to the finance department of the City of New York. His creativity exercises are used by top ad agencies to help their staff be more open to fresh ideas, and he shares his enthusiasm for innovative branding with students at the Isenberg School of Management at the University of Massachusetts–Amherst. Alex likes to help others achieve their creative potential and find fresh options and solutions.

Alex's other *For Dummies* books address his fascination with innovative approaches to marketing. He is the author of *Marketing For Dummies,* 3rd Edition, and *Marketing Kit For Dummies,* 3rd Edition (both from Wiley).

Dedication

My wife, Deirdre Richardson, suffered through lengthy writing sessions for nearly a year, and still managed to maintain a positive, encouraging attitude about this book — thereby serving as a perfect role model for what it takes to support a creative process from beginning to successful end!

Author's Acknowledgments

I have lots of exciting ideas, but sometimes I need a little help disciplining them into proper shape for implementation. That's why I'm so appreciative of the fine editorial team at Wiley that worked on this book with me, including acquisitions editor Stacy Kennedy, project editor Elizabeth Rea, copy editors Christine Pingleton and Kathy Simpson, and technical reviewer Lisa Gundry. It takes a team to do anything worthwhile. It helps when it's a really good team!

I also want to thank my associates and clients at Trainer's Spectrum, who provide me so many great suggestions and also, on occasion, the honest feedback that helps get the wrinkles out of my thinking.

Publisher's Acknowledgments

We're proud of this book; please send us your comments at http://dummies.custhelp.com.
For other comments, please contact our Customer Care Department within the U.S. at 877-762-2974,
outside the U.S. at 317-572-3993, or fax 317-572-4002.

Some of the people who helped bring this book to market include the following:

Acquisitions, Editorial,
and Media Development

Project Editor: Elizabeth Rea

Acquisitions Editor: Stacy Kennedy

Copy Editors: Christine Pingleton,
Kathy Simpson

Assistant Editor: Erin Calligan Mooney

Senior Editorial Assistant: David Lutton

Technical Editor: Lisa Gundry, Ph.D.

Editorial Manager: Michelle Hacker

Editorial Assistant: Jennette ElNaggar

Cover Photos: © Andy Ryan/Getty Images

Cartoons: Rich Tennant (www.the5thwave.com)

Composition Services

Project Coordinator: Lynsey Stanford

Layout and Graphics: Kelly Kijovsky

Proofreaders: John Greenough,
Bonnie Mikkelson

Indexer: Sharon Shock

Publishing and Editorial for Consumer Dummies

   Diane Graves Steele, Vice President and Publisher, Consumer Dummies

   Kristin Ferguson-Wagstaffe, Product Development Director, Consumer Dummies

   Ensley Eikenburg, Associate Publisher, Travel

   Kelly Regan, Editorial Director, Travel

Publishing for Technology Dummies

   Andy Cummings, Vice President and Publisher, Dummies Technology/General User

Composition Services

   Debbie Stailey, Director of Composition Services

Contents at a Glance

Introduction 1

Part 1: Making Your Mark as an Innovator 9

Chapter 1: Taking an Innovative Approach to Work................................... 11
Chapter 2: Creating an Innovative Career Path 33
Chapter 3: Leading with Creative Vision 45
Chapter 4: Innovating in Sales and Marketing.. 67
Chapter 5: Being an Innovative Strategist 79

Part 11: Stimulating Your Creative Side: Thinking in New and Different Ways 99

Chapter 6: Getting Juices Flowing in Brainstorming Sessions 101
Chapter 7: Mastering Advanced Brainstorming.. 121
Chapter 8: Going Beyond Brainstorming 143
Chapter 9: Turning Problems into Opportunities for Innovation................. 159
Chapter 10: Going Shopping for Innovations 171
Chapter 11: Coming Up with Creative Combinations.................................. 183

Part 111: Applying Creativity and Innovation to Daily Challenges 197

Chapter 12: Delivering Fresh Presentations and Proposals........................ 199
Chapter 13: Negotiating Creative Win–Wins 219
Chapter 14: Innovating to Save Costs... 231

Part 1V: Implementing a Major Innovation 245

Chapter 15: Managing the Development of an Innovative Idea 247
Chapter 16: Spreading the Word to Diffuse Your Innovation....................... 261
Chapter 17: Protecting Intellectual Property 275
Chapter 18: Building a Business Around Your Innovation 295

Part V: The Part of Tens 309

Chapter 19: Ten Creative Ways to Boost Your Career................................ 311
Chapter 20: Ten Tips for More Innovative Meetings................................... 317
Chapter 21: Ten Ways to Stimulate Your Creative Genius 323
Chapter 22: Ten Tips for Better Implementation of Your Ideas 331

Index 339

Table of Contents

Introduction *1*

    About This Book 1
    Conventions Used in This Book 2
    Foolish Assumptions 3
    How This Book Is Organized 4
        Part I: Making Your Mark as an Innovator 4
        Part II: Stimulating Your Creative Side: Thinking in New and
          Different Ways 5
        Part III: Applying Creativity and Innovation to Daily Challenges 5
        Part IV: Implementing a Major Innovation 6
        Part V: The Part of Tens 6
    Icons Used in This Book 6
    Where to Go from Here 7

Part 1: Making Your Mark as an Innovator *9*

    Chapter 1: Taking an Innovative Approach to Work **11**
        Tapping Into Your Own Creative Force 12
          Generating more ideas 12
          Identifying your biggest barriers to creativity 14
          Taking advantage of your biggest enablers of creativity 16
        Constructing Your Creative Place 18
        Introducing Creative Practices to Your Daily Routine 21
          Balancing tight and loose activities 21
          Freeing yourself to daydream 22
          Pursuing interesting questions instead of letting them pass by ... 22
          Cross-training the body to strengthen the mind 23
        Seeking Broader Experience 24
          Finding ways to challenge yourself 24
          Taking personal risks 24
          Spending more time with people who aren't at all like you ... 25
          Seeking the company of innovators 26
          Getting out of your personal and career silos 27
          Supporting inquisitive behavior 27
          Learning from innovation mentors 28
        Becoming a Leading Innovator 29
          Making your creativity and drive visible to higher-ups 30
          Stepping up to development teams and roles 30

Chapter 2: Creating an Innovative Career Path.....................33

Seeing Your Career as an Adventure 34
Breaking through the barriers to career change 34
Making opportunistic moves.......................................36
Counting Up Your Transferable Skills and Experiences.........37
Seeking Opportunities to Innovate...39
Moving Toward Growth..40
Encouraging your own personal growth.....................40
Targeting growth areas in your current organization....................41
Taking advantage of fast-growing cities.....................41
Serving the fastest-growing age groups 42
Tapping into international growth 42
Inventing Your Next Job 42
Proposing a new position for yourself 43
Generating freelance and consultative work..............43
Developing entrepreneurial career options 44

Chapter 3: Leading with Creative Vision 45

Visualizing the Possibilities for Innovative Leadership..........46
Setting ambitious goals..46
Encouraging others to envision change too...............48
Knowing when innovation is required 50
Getting to Know Yourself as a Leader.......................................51
Identifying your leadership orientation......................52
Zeroing in on your leadership style 54
Adjusting your style to fit the situation 54
Adapting the classic styles for faster innovation 56
Putting orientation and style together........................58
Developing Your Leadership Skills 59
Seeking feedback..59
Working with a mentor...59
Seeking varied leadership experiences.......................59
Managing the risks of innovation................................60
Projecting a Positive Attitude 61
Expressing both hopefulness and optimism 62
Being pragmatically creative.......................................62
Going for that positive ripple effect 62
Putting All Your Leadership Skills Together.............................63

Chapter 4: Innovating in Sales and Marketing 67

Making an Inconspicuous but Powerful Impact 67
Assessing (And Violating) the Norms 68
Finding abnormal ways to accomplish your goals 69
Communicating in a different way...............................69
Violating social norms on purpose..............................69
Avoiding the cost of a sales call..................................70

Committing to a Creative Approach 71
    Writing your creative brief 72
    Coming up with the first round of creative ideas 73
Narrowing Your Focus to Find Sources of Creative Advantage 75

Chapter 5: Being an Innovative Strategist 79

Thinking Big by Planning to Re-create Your Business 80
    Shifting from more of the same to creative planning 80
    Including a mix of traditional and creative
        elements in your planning 81
Ensuring a Healthy Strategic Cycle 82
    Phase-shifting in strategic time 83
    Influencing strategy from the bottom up 83
Investing in a Family of Innovations 84
    Being tough on underperforming projects and products 84
    Making your next strategic move 85
    Deciding how big a strategy to pursue 86
    Including customer value in your strategy 87
Managing Your Product Portfolio 88
    Riding a best-selling product to the top 88
    Understanding the life cycle of each product category 88
    Mapping your product portfolio 90
    Planting enough seeds to make sure something grows 92
Seeking Strategic Partnerships 92
Mastering the Art of Change Management 94
    Enlisting the eager believers and excluding the hopeless cases ... 94
    Making the destination visible to all 95
    Managing resistance during the change process 96
    Watching out for snap-back 97

Part II: Stimulating Your Creative Side: Thinking in New and Different Ways 99

Chapter 6: Getting Juices Flowing in Brainstorming Sessions 101

Identifying Opportunities for Group Creativity 102
    Calling for help with a problem 102
    Inviting questions for consideration 104
    Building on suggestions 104
In or Out?: Issuing Invites to the Brainstorming Session 104
    Deciding how big to make the group 105
    Excluding people who squash the creative spirit 105
    Including people who contribute needed knowledge 106
    Adding people who bring unique perspectives and styles 106
Planning the Creative Process 106
    Deciding how much creative distance you want to travel 107
    Budgeting sufficient time 107
    Deciding how many sessions to run 108

Preparing for Your Role as Facilitator 108
    Practicing your questioning and listening skills 109
    Guiding the group away from negative dynamics 109
    Controlling your nonverbal signals 110
    Becoming familiar with the challenge at hand 111
Mastering the Core Brainstorming Methods 112
    Warming up the group 112
    Using Osborn's brainstorming rules 113
    Introducing variations to improve results 114
    Considering additional creative processes 117
    Wrapping it up 117
Being a Brilliant Participant 118
    Contributing great ideas 118
    Being an informal leader and cheerleader 119
    Overcoming your own creative timidity 119

Chapter 7: Mastering Advanced Brainstorming 121

Going the Distance to Cash In on Creativity 122
    Critiquing the results of your brainstorming 122
    Doing more research based on first-round questions 124
    Being persistent 125
Focusing Your Brainstorming in Creative Ways 125
    Stimulating a shift in how people think about the topic 125
    Fighting design fixation 126
    Sharpening the view with narrower problem definitions 127
    Breaking the problem into smaller problems 128
Visualizing for Creative Success 129
    Introducing visual reference material 129
    Using imagery to stimulate the mind's eye 129
    Sketching ideas rather than describing them 130
    Building solutions from standard geometric shapes 131
    Storyboarding an idea 131
    Making small-scale models 132
    Using sticky notes and a wall for your brainstorming 132
    Drawing a mind map 133
    Combining research with mind mapping 134
    Using mind-mapping software 135
    Clustering ideas and suggestions 136
    Producing insights and proposals from your mind map 136
Maximizing the Power of Team Thinking 137
    Using index cards and the nominal group technique 137
    Using pass-along brainstorming 139
    Generating ideas from random words 141
    Working individually, too! 141

Chapter 8: Going Beyond Brainstorming .143
  Using Customer Input for Inspiration 143
    Organizing a focus group.. 144
    Asking customers to fantasize about their ultimate product 145
    Inviting customer input, both critical and creative...................... 145
  Redesigning Processes 146
  Taking Advantage of E-Mail.. 148
    Including a provocative question or situation............................ 148
    Designing your e-mail for thoughtful consideration 149
    Holding an e-mail contest for best idea 150
    Engaging in creative e-mail conversations 150
  Crowdsourcing for New Ideas... 151
  Going Deep for Intuitive Insight... 153
    Using naturalistic decision-making.................................... 154
    Going back to nature 154
    Asking a wise elder 154
    Using soothsaying techniques 155
    Being inventive... 156

Chapter 9: Turning Problems into Opportunities for Innovation 159
  Seeing Problems with a Fresh Eye.. 159
    Framing problems as creative opportunities............................. 160
    Postponing the decision to allow time for creative thought........ 161
    Using creativity prompts 162
    Approaching problems with optimism and hopefulness 162
  Applying Analytical Problem-Solving.. 163
    Using Dewey's problem-solving process 163
    Performing a payoff analysis 166
  Engaging Your Creative Dissatisfaction.................................... 168
    Recognizing the opportunity to be creative............................. 169
    Considering the opportunity costs of not innovating.................. 170
    Applying intuition along with logic.................................. 170

Chapter 10: Going Shopping for Innovations. 171
  Exploring Your Industry's Trade Shows.................................... 171
  Crossing Boundaries for Good Ideas 173
    Visiting the wrong trade shows 173
    Talking to outsiders... 174
    Seeking out cross-training opportunities 175
  Benchmarking Industry Innovators 175
    Studying upstarts and startups....................................... 175
    Interviewing innovative job candidates.............................. 177
    Seeing what businesses are boasting about............................ 178
    Taking a positive approach to evaluating possibilities 178
    Checking for alignment with your competencies..................... 179

Sourcing from Innovative Suppliers 179
  Evaluating suppliers based on their creative momentum 179
  Asking your suppliers for free consulting 181
  Bringing your suppliers together to brainstorm 181
Going to the Experts for Help 181

Chapter 11: Coming Up with Creative Combinations. 183
Finding Inspiration in Successful Creative Combinations 183
Finding Innovative Combinations of Your Own 185
  Revisiting classic combinations for quick wins 185
  Brainstorming combinations with one of your core products 186
  Recombining fundamental innovations 187
Combining Problems with Solutions 189
  Finding problems similar to your own 189
  Looking for problem themes 190
Getting Resourceful in Your Search for Combinations 191
  Pairing things that nobody thinks should go together 192
  Playing with words to find unexpected combinations 192
  Imitating without violating intellectual-property rights 193
  Combining a customer want with a solution you can sell 193
Seeking Unusual Information 193
  Casting a broad net 194
  Seeking weak signals 194
Trying Unusual Forms 195

**Part III: Applying Creativity and
Innovation to Daily Challenges 197**

Chapter 12: Delivering Fresh Presentations and Proposals 199
Building the Credibility You Need to Be Creative 200
  Sizing up your audience and context 200
  Providing enough structure to reassure the audience 201
  Engaging the audience 202
Finding Your Unique Insight 202
  Starting with research 203
  Incubating the facts until a fresh perspective pops out 204
  Brainstorming for insight 204
  Avoiding fixating on the first big idea 206
  Outlining a strong framework for your presentation 206
Making Your Point with the Five Tools of Creative Presentation 207
  Incorporating sources and facts 208
  Engaging the mind's eye with good visuals 209
  An analogy is like a newly cleaned window 210
  Telling tales 211

Branding Your Message with an Appropriate Look and Style.............213
    Matching tone and style..213
    Creating a visual signature 213
    Repeating your auditory signature.................................215
    Controlling your body language 216

Chapter 13: Negotiating Creative Win–Wins 219

Turning Conflicts into Creative Opportunities 219
    Identifying conflicts with rich potential for innovation.................220
    Reframing the disagreement to introduce
        creative problem-solving 221
    Signaling your good intentions to create buy-in..........................222
    Beginning the dialogue with easy win–wins..............................222
Assessing Everyone's Conflict Styles.........................223
    Identifying the natural collaborators 223
    Reassuring the competitive negotiators.........................224
    Making sure that your own style is consistent with your goals... 224
Bridging the Gaps to Form an Ad Hoc Problem-Solving Team 225
    Sharing your own interests and issues first 225
    Building a creative problem-solving team 225
Transitioning to Solution Brainstorming..........................226
    Making sure that everyone knows it's safe to share ideas...........227
    Suspending judgment.................................227
    Facilitating brainstorming when participants are hostile 228
Identifying and Refining Win–Win Ideas 228
    Agreeing that some ideas hold significant promise 229
    Working the top three ideas until one emerges as best 229

Chapter 14: Innovating to Save Costs 231

Avoiding the Creative Frost Effect..........................231
    Boosting creative determination 232
    Avoiding pessimism about the future...........................232
    Trying a clean-slate approach.................................233
Focusing on the Biggest Cost Categories 234
    Identifying spending categories.................................234
    Focusing on major sources of error or rework.....................236
Learning from Others..................................236
    Sending out your scouts 236
    Reviewing examples of cost-cutting measures elsewhere...........237
    Asking around 239
Using Savings-Creation Methods from Idea to Implementation 239
    Finding out where the losses really are 239
    Generating effective cost-cutting ideas...........................240
    Evaluating cost-cutting proposals 241
    Implementing cost savings 241

Part IV: Implementing a Major Innovation 245

Chapter 15: Managing the Development of an Innovative Idea.....247

Planning the Innovation Process 248
    Being flexible about the design 249
    Clarifying the goal 249
    Communicating early, often, and widely 250
    Emphasizing long-term benefits...250
    Monitoring the results...250
    Building strong implementation teams..250
Innovating in Teams 251
    Maintaining momentum through the
        four stages of the team's life..251
    Tapping into diverse contributions by team members 252
    Finding your strongest team role 253
    Determining what the team leader needs to do...........................254
    Considering a skunkworks to protect
        your team from interference...254
Building Development and Implementation Networks.........................256
Launching the Innovation..257
    Emphasizing planning, preparation, and refinement 258
    Promoting the project..259
    Projecting the rate of adoption..260

Chapter 16: Spreading the Word to Diffuse Your Innovation 261

Strategizing to Spread Your Innovation..261
    Identifying potential adopters..262
    Finding out how fast your innovation will spread 264
    Setting the strategic parameters...265
    Targeting those early adopters 266
Designing Your Media Mix for Maximum Diffusion...............................268
    Aiming for intelligent, sophisticated buyers 268
    Emphasizing personal media in the early days 269
    Adapting your marketing to the inflection point 271
Priming the Pump with Freebies 272

Chapter 17: Protecting Intellectual Property....................275

Determining and Keeping Track of Your
    Intellectual Property Assets 276
    Deciding what merits protection..276
    Assessing the value of your intellectual property......................277
    Keeping track of the protective steps
        you've taken (or need to take) 278
Copyrighting As Much As You Can 279
    Adding copyright protection to your work 280
    Getting copyright protection when you're not the author..........281

Protecting Your Brands through Trademark..281
  Ensuring that your brand is trademarkable..............................282
  Applying for a trademark in the U.S. and elsewhere....................283
  Increasing your chances for trademark approval 284
  Establishing your rights by using your mark..............................284
Pursuing Patent Protection 285
  Searching for existing patents...286
  Budgeting the cost of filing a patent..287
  Considering foreign patent protection..289
  Filing a provisional patent 289
  Assigning or licensing your patent rights....................................290
Protecting Trade Secrets..290
  Taking reasonable precautions..291
  Enforcing a trade secret...292
Keeping Your Records, Writings, Plans, and Designs Secure..............292

Chapter 18: Building a Business Around Your Innovation 295

Doing Your Development Homework 295
  Researching and refining your idea and market........................296
  Deciding whether to proceed with your innovation 296
  Protecting your intellectual property 297
Writing a Winning Business Plan..297
  Design the cover, title page, and table of contents 299
  Write the executive summary 299
  Write your market analysis 300
  Prepare a company description..301
  Write a description of your innovation..301
  Describe the organization and management of the business 302
  Summarize marketing and sales 302
  Present your service or product line 302
  Explain your funding needs...303
  Prepare your financials 304
  Prepare an appendix of supporting documents 305
Funding Your Innovative Venture 305
  Pairing up with venture capitalists..306
  Locating angel investors 307
  Obtaining loans 308
Selling Your Inventions..308

Part V: The Part of Tens 309

Chapter 19: Ten Creative Ways to Boost Your Career............311

Look for Opportunities to Stand Out 311
Share Your Enthusiasm for Innovative Ideas..312
Look for Emerging Problems You Can Help Solve 312
Look for Emerging Opportunities You Can Surf.....................................313
Do Something You Really Enjoy 313

Consider Working on Commission...314
Build Two Careers at the Same Time...314
Study 315
Volunteer 315
Champion Someone Else's Good Idea...316

Chapter 20: Ten Tips for More Innovative Meetings 317

Ask for Original Information and Ideas......................................317
Reorganize Your Meetings, Not Your Staff.................................318
Re-solve Old Problems..318
Use a "Sideways Thoughts" Board 319
Pay Close Attention to Body Language..319
Control Routine Topics Tightly 320
Control or Exclude Spoilers 321
Brainstorm at Least Once a Month 321
Ask for Multiple Alternatives 322
Meet Somewhere New and Different..322

Chapter 21: Ten Ways to Stimulate Your Creative Genius 323

Persist, Persist, Persist 323
Work on BIG Problems..324
Rotate among Three Knotty Problems 325
Eat Ideas for Lunch...325
Work on Your Self-Talk 326
Correct Your Mental Biases 327
Nurture a Secret Project..328
Cross-Train in Art 329
Do Art Projects with Your Kids 329
Start or Join an Inventors' Club 330

Chapter 22: Ten Tips for Better Implementation of Your Ideas 331

Develop Your Team First...331
Plan for the Worst 332
Account for Each Project Separately 333
Document Failures..334
Differentiate Owners from Workers 334
Communicate 335
Avoid Burnout..335
Resolve Conflicts (Don't Avoid Them) 336
Know When to Persevere 336
Know When to Quit 337

Index *339*

Introduction

*I*nnovation means so many things: new-product development, new brands, new ad campaigns, new Web sites, new production processes, new designs, new strategies, new solutions to persistent problems, and a great deal more.

Truth is, you need to innovate to succeed in your working life. The creative, forward-thinking people are the ones who make their mark and get ahead. It's often risky to try new things or propose new approaches, but it's even more risky to play it safe and close your mind to creative change. If you don't take the lead as an innovator in your workplace and your field, you can be quite sure that somebody else will.

Businesses need to innovate too — and by *businesses,* I mean any organizations where people work, including startups, small businesses, big businesses, government offices and agencies, schools, hospitals, theaters, museums, temples, and churches.

My work has brought me into all these workplaces and many more. It's so rewarding to help people create their own, better futures by teaching and facilitating the challenging process of innovation. It's the most fun work I've ever done, except, I suppose, when I'm the innovator myself and am creating a new product, building a new business, or producing something innovative just for pleasure (such as a new art exhibit). Without innovation, work would be a dull, thankless routine. With it, there's a reason to get up and rush to work each morning. Innovation gives us energy, and it gives energy to our workplaces as well, allowing them to grow and prosper instead of stagnate and fail.

About This Book

There's a great need for innovators. In fact, that's really all we need right now. People who resist change and don't want to discuss new options and ideas are of no use to the world today, if they ever were. We humans are the innovators. Innovation is what separates us from all other life forms on this planet, and what creates the social and economic growth that we need to nurture to prevent future economic meltdowns.

Your career, wherever it may be today, will accelerate if you pay more attention to how you contribute ideas, manage their development, and spearhead their implementation. Whether you work as a lone inventor, an enthusiastic entrepreneur, or a salaried staffer who insists on finding the time to contribute to new initiatives, your innovativeness stimulates your own career and contributes to the healthy growth of the organizations and people surrounding you.

In working with tens of thousands of employees all across North America, I've found that many of us working stiffs already know the basics of how to brainstorm ideas. Sure, I could show you many more advanced techniques, but I assume that you've already been exposed to the basics and feel confident about how to brainstorm, either alone at your desk or with a small group in a conference room. But here's the other statistic that I've gathered in my travels as an author, educator, and consultant: Basic brainstorming and its variants take place regularly in very few workplaces.

There you have the paradox of innovation in business: Everyone knows how to generate fresh new ideas, but nobody uses these techniques. As a consequence, most decisions are made without anyone examining a full set of creative options. Many opportunities to innovate are lost, and usually nobody even realizes that an opportunity has passed by.

So you see, I have a personal agenda in writing *Business Innovation For Dummies.* I want to help you and others actually use the incredibly powerful tools and techniques of innovation. I want you to try being an active, practicing innovator. Give it a try for the next week or two. If you like it, extend the experiment to a month. If that works for you, try being an innovator all year. I'm pretty darn sure you'll get hooked for life, and your life will be far richer for it.

Conventions Used in This Book

When you're reading this book, be aware of the following conventions:

- ✔ Whenever I introduce a new term, I *italicize* it.

- ✔ Any information that's helpful or interesting but not essential appears in *sidebars,* which are the gray-shaded boxes sprinkled throughout the book.

- ✔ Web sites and e-mail addresses appear in `monofont` to help them stand out. When this book was printed, some Web addresses may have needed to break across two lines of text. If that happened, rest assured that I haven't put in any extra characters (such as hyphens) to indicate the break. When you use one of these Web addresses, just type exactly what you see in this book, pretending that the line break doesn't exist.

Additional conventions that you should be aware of are my uses of three terms that appear often in this book: *innovation, creativity,* and *brainstorming.*

✔ **Innovation** is applied creativity or creativity for a purpose. It involves creative generation of new ideas, designs, plans, and so on — and then it involves the development and refinement of those ideas and their implementation. Sometimes, innovators need to bring their inventions to market, putting on their sales hats to finish the process. At other times, the end user is within the innovator's own organization. Still other situations may involve spreading an innovation to society to benefit public health or for some other worthy cause. Whatever the goal, innovation has a practical purpose that aims to create value by changing something in the real world, not just in the imagination.

✔ **Creativity** simply means coming up with fresh ideas, designs, or solutions. It's often the result of intuitive "aha" insights but also can come after careful analytical study of a topic. Artists are often creative, but not always. Businesses sometimes do creative things, but less often than artists do. Everyone working in business, however, can and should do some creative thinking every day. This book shows you how to weave more creativity into your work, and how to profit from the benefits of having fresh ideas and new perspectives to offer to your workplace and field or industry.

✔ **Brainstorming** refers to the broad range of structured techniques for idea generation. Alex Osborn, a cofounder of the giant advertising agency BBDO, coined that term back in the 1940s, and it's become a generic term that almost everyone uses. It's cumbersome to say *idea-generation techniques,* so people say *brainstorming* instead. Osborn had a specific technique in mind when he first used the term, however, and if you want to follow his specific brainstorming rules, see Chapter 6.

Foolish Assumptions

I assume that you're intelligent (not a foolish assumption, given what I know about my past readers). But although I believe that you're intelligent, I assume that you don't have all the technical knowledge, practical experience, and encouragement and support needed to come up with creative insights or innovate with success in your workplace. Everybody needs some help when it comes to innovation. You'll find lots of helpful methods and ideas here.

I also assume that you're able to adapt the techniques and examples in this book to your own situation. The methods I cover are very broadly applicable. Have faith that you can adapt them to almost any situation. Sometimes, it might take a little creativity, but I'm sure that you're up to the challenge of making innovation happen wherever you are!

Further, I assume that you're willing and able to switch from being imaginative and creative one moment to being analytical and rigorous the next. Innovators need to take both perspectives, depending on the challenge at hand. Sometimes, you need to compare options and reject the weakest. At other times, you need to suspend judgment and open yourself to fresh ideas and possibilities. Knowing when to be open and when to be tough is part of the art of being an innovator. Try to be aware of which role you're taking at any particular moment so that you can switch from creative to critical thinking as each situation requires.

Finally, I assume that you'll not only work on your own creativity and innovation skills, but also will encourage others. It takes lots of people to make the world a better place.

How This Book Is Organized

This book is organized in parts that I describe in the following sections. Check out the table of contents for more information on the topics of the chapters within each part.

Part I: Making Your Mark as an Innovator

The expression "to make your mark" is interesting because it suggests two different things. Making a mark means making an impact or a difference by doing something that other people remember and appreciate. Also, your mark means your personal stamp or brand, so making your mark means more than just making a difference; it also means being remembered or known personally for what you do.

In Part I, I show you how to apply your creative energy in ways that benefit both your organization or workplace as a whole and you as an individual pursuing your own career. Whatever your line of work, the chapters in this part help you bring more reactive energy and innovation to what you do on a daily basis so that you open your career options and see more and better possibilities for yourself. I show you how to step up as a leader of innovation before diving into the specifics of bringing the power of innovation to sales, marketing, and strategic planning.

There are many ways to make your mark as an innovator. I can't wait to see what you'll do next!

Part II: Stimulating Your Creative Side: Thinking in New and Different Ways

Innovation has to start with a novel idea. People with better ideas rise to the top, floating their organizations and associates up along with them. That's the force of a strong creative idea, and to generate more of them when and where they'll do the most good, read this part with care!

Part II is an essential primer on how to run a productive, effective idea-generating session, as well as a deep toolbox full of powerful creativity techniques. It also focuses on ways to turn a specific problem or crisis into a great opportunity for forward progress and innovation, because problems are often perfect opportunities for introducing modest proposals based on your radically new ideas.

Also in this part, I share one of the secrets of successful innovators: You can often find existing innovations and bring them into your workplace or product line without the full cost and trouble of developing them from scratch. These *found innovations* are extremely important in the business world, and this book is the only one I know of that addresses them. Finally, I really let the cat out of the bag by sharing an even deeper secret of top innovators: You can create breakthroughs by combining two or more good existing ideas or designs. Inventing something entirely new would be nice, but it's actually amazingly difficult. More often in business, innovations are the result of clever combinations of other people's breakthroughs, with just enough originality to make them unique.

Part III: Applying Creativity and Innovation to Daily Challenges

Innovators often focus on really big goals: develop a best-selling new product, patent a winning new design, or create a new business model that produces runaway profits. Major breakthroughs are great, but they don't come along every day. What should you do in the interim to keep your creative edge and continue to make your mark in small but significant ways?

This part helps you apply innovative thinking and methods to some of the common challenges of daily work. I show you how to create compelling, memorable presentations and proposals that sway people's minds. I also show you how to apply the power of innovation to conflict resolution and negotiations; the force of creative thinking can easily sway the outcome in new and better directions.

Finally, I tackle an unpleasant but essential reality of business life: the need to find ways to cut costs. Budget cuts are usually performed with a very dull knife. I'd much rather equip you with a creative mind and an ability to turn budget problems into opportunities for improvement.

Part IV: Implementing a Major Innovation

Usually, you won't be able to work alone as an innovator. It takes a team at the very least, and this part shows you how to form and run effective development teams to bring your innovation to life. In Part IV, I dive into the art and science of spreading the word and getting people to trade their old ideas, habits, and shopping patterns for new ones. I also focus on the ownership of inventions, designs, and expressions of ideas — the so-called *intellectual property* that people continually sue about in courts around the world. You probably need to study intellectual-property laws and practices to be a savvy innovator, avoiding trouble and taking advantage of the many benefits and protections that the law affords.

Part V: The Part of Tens

I have so many exciting tips and ideas that I want to share with you, and this part contains 40 of them. Each pointer in the Part of Tens is a useful technique that didn't find a home in one of the main chapters of the book but probably ought to find a home in your approach to building your career, managing the creative process, and implementing the innovations that will make your mark visible for all the world to see.

Icons Used in This Book

Look for these symbols to help you find valuable information throughout the text.

This icon alerts you to points in the text where I provide added insight on how to get a handle on a concept.

This icon points out mistakes and pitfalls to avoid. Whatever you do, don't skip these paragraphs!

Any information that's especially important and worth remembering gets this icon.

This icon points out real-life applications of the theories of creativity and innovative business practices.

Where to Go from Here

The beauty of *Business Innovation For Dummies* is that you can skip to any part, chapter, or section, depending on your needs. You can certainly read the book from cover to cover, but you don't have to.

If you're about to plunge into a meeting or work session in which you really need some fresh ideas or insights, you might try making Part II your starting point. Flip through the chapters to find something you can try right away. There's nothing quite as satisfying as a fresh list of 10 or 20 helpful ideas to get you going, and the chapters in Part II can certainly deliver that many, if not a great deal more.

If you're thinking more broadly about your working life and how to pump it up with new energy and momentum, start with Chapter 1, and read as many of the chapters after it as you can. The book makes a good self-study workshop that will certainly change your approach to work if you give it half a chance.

Part I
Making Your Mark
as an Innovator

The 5th Wave
By Rich Tennant

"I think Dick Foster should head up that new project. He's got the vision, the drive, and let's face it, that big white hat doesn't hurt either."

In this part . . .

What will people remember you for if you leave your current job next month? Will you leave a legacy behind? Will you leave something that people will name after you or hold up as an inspiration for those who follow? I hope so! It's important to make your mark wherever you go by contributing not only your effort, but also your good ideas. This part helps you engage your work in creative, proactive ways by being a source of innovations of all sorts.

Whether it's a marketing challenge, such as redesigning a brand's logo and look, or a strategic challenge, such as deciding how to achieve greater success next year than last, your career is made up of your contributions as an innovator. Step up to a leadership role in innovations of all kinds. It's rewarding to be part of the solutions to problems and one of the architects of the future!

Chapter 1

Taking an Innovative Approach to Work

. . . .

In This Chapter

▶ Engaging your most powerful personal asset

▶ Providing yourself a place to imagine

▶ Introducing daily creative practices

▶ Broadening your experience

▶ Benefiting from creative mentors

▶ Leading and succeeding through your innovative initiative

. . . .

Creativity is often thought to be the exclusive province of artists. This misconception gets a lot of people in trouble. Unless you spend a portion of every working day being creative and opening yourself to the possibility of innovation, you and your employer or business are going to be stuck in the past instead of creating the future!

As you open this book, you also need to open yourself to fresh ideas and curious questions. Innovation taps into the creative and intuitive side of your mind — the so-called right-brain activities that are essential to the arts and invention. But innovation in a business environment (and in government and nonprofit workplaces, too) needs more than creative thinking. It also requires you to enlist the enthusiastic support of others and to push ahead with plans that turn your ideas into reality.

Being creative in your work means bringing a special spark to it and recognizing that things are going to change — so why not be the one who dreams up and then spearheads innovations?

You can bring positive change to anything and everything, from products and work processes to customer complaints or resource shortages. Conflicts and disagreements are wonderful opportunities for innovation because they reveal the various limitations and tensions that are holding people back in your workplace. Also, any special project — whether it's a major presentation, a new planning cycle, or a move to a new location — is a great opportunity to innovate. Whenever you face a new responsibility or problem, put on your innovation hat. This chapter shows you how.

Tapping Into Your Own Creative Force

I define *creative force* as the power to create that flows through all of us. This definition is important because it takes a stand on a pair of perennially controversial issues:

✔ Some people say that creativity is a rare skill, but in my experience, we all can (and should!) be creative in our approach to our working lives. Creativity may come a little more naturally to some than others, but trust me on this: You will benefit substantially from nurturing your creative force and adopting creative practices.

✔ Creativity isn't really about play or games. You need to approach it with respect because it's a powerful thing — perhaps *the* most powerful thing. Life is a powerful creative force; each birth brings a unique new being to life. The world is inherently creative, and so are you. You can and should tap into the power of this creative force.

You can see the power of creativity each time a successful innovation changes lives and the world. Creativity is an extremely powerful asset. When you use your natural creative power to innovate in your own life or to bring innovations to the lives and work of others, you're quite capable of changing your world.

The fact, however (and it's a somewhat sad one), is that most people never fully realize their creative potential. Most of us don't tap into the strength and power of our own creative capacity — let alone the additional capacity of those around us. Here are several proactive practices that can help you engage your creative force more fully than most people do.

Generating more ideas

Make a habit of thinking about possibilities. A simple way is to start with your own needs.

Imagining innovations to meet your daily needs

We think about needs constantly. I need coffee to get going in the morning, for example. Someone had a similar need and invented a coffee maker with a built-in timer. In thinking of the next breakthrough in coffee making, I start by considering my needs. I don't mind my home-brewed coffee, but really, I prefer to have someone at a good cafe make me a cappuccino or latte from Italian espresso beans. This leads me to the idea of a coffee cart that would drive around my neighborhood and provide me a fresh-brewed gourmet coffee as I get into my car on the way to work — or maybe as I get out of my car in the parking lot before going into work. Aha! I haven't even had my coffee yet, and I've had an innovative idea! It's going to be a creative day.

Recognizing great ideas

Another good way to boost your creativity is to simply take note of creativity around you. People are surrounded by creativity and innovation but usually pass by it without taking special note. Recognize that you need the stimulation of other people's creative thinking. I collect good examples, rather the way an art collector gathers fine paintings. When I see a clever new product, I admire the insight of its inventor.

I also keep an eye out for creative advertising. Ad agencies have so-called creative departments full of wacky people whose job is to dream up something clever. Sometimes they actually do, and their example can inspire you to try new approaches to your own daily challenges.

Why start yet another memo or staff e-mail with a boring subject line when a catchy headline might make your point more creatively? Maybe you'll send out an e-mail to your staff with a subject line like "Breaking news: There *is* such a thing as a free lunch!" as a way to entice everyone to come to a lunchtime training session in your department. If you use that headline, of course, you'll have to actually deliver lunch for free, which may not be in your budget. But maybe you could get creative and ask the newest restaurant in your area if it would like to take advantage of an opportunity to provide samples of its fare to a group of local professionals. That way, you won't have to find cash in your budget for that free lunch. There's always a creative option, if not two or three.

Holding out for more options

Perhaps the simplest but most powerful creative practice is to insist (to yourself and to others) that there must be more choices. Creativity expands your options — but only if you realize that more options are better.

Imagine that you're being held captive in a locked basement, and your captor gives you a gruesome choice: You may either shoot yourself and die quickly (a loaded gun is provided for this purpose), or you may wait while the basement is flooded and then die slowly by drowning. Which option do you choose? If you say "Neither," you've taken the creative approach to this problem, but you were given only two choices, so it's up to you to create more options. Have any ideas? I know that it's hard to think under pressure, but please hurry up; your captor has snaked a hose down into the basement and is about to turn the water on. . . .

What did you come up with? Here are a few options I thought of:

- Find the toolbox (there's always one in a basement, right?), and use a screwdriver to remove the hinges from the basement door.

- Shoot the gun at the main electrical line (there's one coming into a breaker box in most basements) to start a fire, setting off the fire alarm, which is required in most building codes and, if you're lucky, is linked to a central dispatcher.

- Get your captor talking at the basement door (before he turns the water on), and shoot him through the door.

- Shoot the hose with the aim of breaking it and pushing the end out of the basement.

- Try to trick your captor into coming into the basement (perhaps by saying that you choose to shoot yourself, but the gun is jammed, and can he show you how to fix it?); then escape while the door's open.

- Find the master valve that controls the water to the building, and turn it off. (There's usually one in the basement.)

This mental exercise may seem to be far removed from your workplace challenges, but it's really not. Most of the time when there's a budget crunch, for example, senior management fails to ask for ideas before resorting to the axe. Suppose that someone says, "We've got to cut the budget, so decide which of your five staffers to lay off." You ought to stop and look for alternatives before you pull the trigger on anyone's job. There's always another way.

How about retaining all five employees but shifting them to four days a week, or looking for ways to conserve energy and materials instead of cutting staff? A brainstorming session with your staff might produce many practical ways to cut the budget without laying anyone off. It's worth a try. A little creative thinking can make a bad situation much better than it looks at first glance.

See Part II of this book for lots of techniques and tricks that can help you generate more options.

Identifying your biggest barriers to creativity

We all have the potential to generate imaginative insights and ideas, but most of the time, we don't. Why not? The biggest reason is that we're hemmed in by numerous barriers to creativity, especially at work.

Knowing your creative enemy

Studies show that the following are major barriers to creativity in the workplace:

- ✔ Lack of time and opportunity
- ✔ Criticism by others
- ✔ Strict, stern, or critical supervision
- ✔ Rigid policies, rules, procedures, or practices
- ✔ Exhaustion or lack of regular sleep
- ✔ Pessimism and negative thinking
- ✔ Lack of diverse experiences and inputs
- ✔ Either–or thinking that keeps people from exploring multiple options
- ✔ Lack of support for new ideas and approaches from your boss or colleagues
- ✔ Not knowing how to apply your creativity to your work
- ✔ Self-censorship due to lack of confidence, uncertainty, self-doubt, shyness, or other reasons

When you recognize your own barriers, you can take steps to reduce their power over you. If peers are negative thinkers who dismiss ideas out of hand, for example, do your creative thinking out of range of their negative comments. If you're under too much time pressure to think creatively about problems and needs, give yourself a creativity break: Get away from your desk, and spend a lunch hour walking and thinking without the pressure of constant interruptions.

Also, don't let self-censorship get in your way: Allow yourself to generate many ideas without concern for quality. Every barrier can be countered with a simple strategy that reduces its influence, at least long enough to allow you to generate some insight. For more help identifying your barriers, try taking the Personal Creativity Assessment created by yours truly (published by HRD Press and available on the Web site that supports this book, www.supportforinnovation.com).

Being alert to your stylistic strengths and weaknesses

Your *creative style* — the way you approach challenges requiring innovation — can also be a barrier to creativity because some people naturally prefer a structured, planned approach to a looser or more intuitive approach. Structure and planning are excellent for developing and refining a concept after you've come up with it, but they get in the way of initial insights. If you like to do things in order, value neatness, and feel most comfortable working from a specific plan, you'll find it difficult to switch to a freestyle, imaginative approach.

To switch your style and come up with fresh new ideas, think of creativity as a form of play. When you play, you let go of normal inhibitions and open yourself to possibilities, proving that you're capable of making creative leaps of the imagination, even if your normal professional style is stiff and structured.

Turn to Chapter 15 for more help on dealing with the limits (and corresponding strengths) of your specific creative style. If you aren't sure what your creative role is, visit www.supportforinnovation.com to test yourself and find out which stages of the *innovation cycle* (the process of generating, developing, and applying or commercializing an insight) are your strongest and weakest.

Bringing your creativity to practical, routine tasks

It may seem that innovation has to be about those major, once-in-a-lifetime ideas. Not so! There are a thousand small breakthroughs for every big one, and you'll never come up with a big idea unless you build your creative muscles by coming up with a thousand small ones first. Do things in new ways, and look for better approaches every day. (For specific tips on how to apply creativity in daily challenges, read Chapters 11, 12, and 13.) Also check out the sections "Constructing Your Creative Place" and "Introducing Creative Practices to Your Daily Routine," later in this chapter.

Taking advantage of your biggest enablers of creativity

A *creativity enabler* is anything that stimulates your creativity. Common enablers include a good night's rest, a change of scene, a good example of imaginative thinking, a cup of coffee, exercise, and a walk on the beach (or anywhere that's relaxing, open, and natural). Also, anything that makes you laugh enables creative thought. You may have other more personal enablers too, such as a creative mentor you can talk to, a favorite place, or a hobby that helps you relax and get "in the zone."

Visual images enable creative thinking because creative insights are often visual in nature. Too often, people approach work from verbal or quantitative perspectives. In fact, many challenges posed by employers and bosses are barriers to creativity, rather than enablers, because of the way they're presented. If you reframe the question around some visual exercise, however, you can convert it to a powerful enabler of innovative ideas.

A great way to stimulate your own creative thinking is to collect a few simple visual images; clip them from magazines or pull them out of the library of symbols in any handy word processing or design program. Then challenge yourself to use each image to come up with an idea by analogy.

Figure 1-1 shows how you might set up a visual challenge for your imagination if you want to come up with a new line of clothing that could boost sales for a clothing manufacturer or designer. Try your hand at it right now (because practice helps boost creativity). Can you come up with any fun ideas for new clothing brands? Do any of the symbols suggest possible brand names and concepts?

When you've tried this exercise yourself, look at Figure 1-2, where I've exercised my own imagination with this challenge. Are all my ideas likely to become million-dollar successes? I doubt it, but maybe one of them will.

It's important to avoid self-critical thinking when you exercise your imagination (see "Identifying your biggest barriers to creativity," earlier in this chapter).

Figure 1-1:
Use this
form to
come up
with ideas
for new
lines of
clothing (or
substitute
a product
category of
your own
choosing).

Symbol	Brand name	Tag Line, Positioning

Symbol	Brand name	Tag Line, Positioning
	**Heavy Duty**	Clothes that work for you (Traditional work clothes)
	**Refrain**	Helping you hit your high note (Attractive, professional business casual)
	**Take One**	Getting it right the first time (Stunning outfits for first dates)
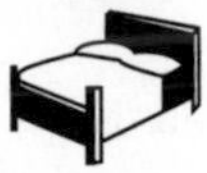	**Back to Bed**	Comfortable garments for a busy world (Casual, relaxing; the closest you can get to pajamas without actually wearing them)
	**Continuing Ed**	Clothing for the student in all of us (Adult version of popular "tween" styles)
	**Family Planning**	Watch out or you might start something (Sexy night-out clothing)
	**Diner Designer**	Making Americana Chic (Contemporary versions of styles from the 1930s and '40s)

Figure 1-2:
Examples
of ideas
for lines of
clothing,
suggested
by visual
images.

Constructing Your Creative Place

Does your workplace encourage creative thinking? Probably not. I visit a lot of workplaces at big and small businesses, nonprofit organizations, and all sorts of government agencies, and in my experience, fewer than 1 percent of them are naturally creative spaces. This is a problem, because people need innovation at work, but the spaces they work in make it hard to create.

A creative space needs to do the following:

- ✔ Make it easy to focus on an important challenge or task without interruption.
- ✔ Offer control of the physical environment, including configuration of desk and chair, lighting, layout, decorative elements, and sounds.

✔ Offer varied and interesting inputs, including visual, verbal, and other sensory inputs.

✔ Make people feel very comfortable, focused, and able to come up with good ideas.

To stimulate creativity, your workspace should *not* feel cluttered or crowded, or make you feel frantic and stressed by constant interruptions and emergencies. Unfortunately, this is just what most workplaces are like! It's up to you to fight back by defending a place and/or time in your day where you can be creative and open to possibilities. Some people can't achieve a calm, creative state of mind in their workplaces and have to resort to taking walks or retreating to a favorite coffee shop or park during their lunch break, but ideally, you can build a creative environment at work. Here are some ideas you can try:

✔ Post a sign asking not to be disturbed during certain times so that you can focus and think.

✔ Use a desktop lamp, shade, hanging cloth, or hinged freestanding screen to give yourself some control of your lighting.

✔ Clear the decks! Keep the cluttered pile of paperwork out of sight in a drawer or cabinet so that you're truly able to focus on one important problem at a time and not always be reminded of other tasks.

✔ Introduce something playful to your workspace. Rotate tactile puzzles and windup toys through the space to give you a different kind of stimulation than you usually get from work, or post humorous cartoons to inspire your imagination.

✔ If possible, introduce low-volume mood music of your choice (but of course, you'll have to keep it quiet enough not to disturb anyone else's concentration).

✔ Introduce something living, such as a potted plant or a vase filled with gravel, water, and spring bulbs.

✔ Display pictures of people who encourage you and believe that you are creative and brilliant. If this doesn't sound like your spouse or children, put their pictures out of sight when you try to come up with breakthrough ideas, and select a mentor instead. If you don't have a creative mentor, elect someone famous to fill the role. A picture of Albert Einstein really does make you smarter. Try it if you don't believe me!

✔ Keep a scrapbook or screensaver file of beautiful art, nature photos, travel photos, or other images that help you feel removed from work and your usual routine. Open the folder and scan the images when you want to take a creative turn.

Building your personal studio, shop, or laboratory

If you want or need to step up the innovation level with long periods of creative work, you may need to go beyond making small adjustments to a conventional workspace. You may need to configure a real studio, lab, or workshop for yourself, where the entire space is set up and equipped to support the creative work you have in mind. Consider these possibilities:

- An inventor working with electronics needs a place to do electronic engineering (requiring a computer running specialized design software), plus perhaps a place to mock up circuit boards and another place to mock up the actual equipment that the circuit boards go into. Depending on what you're working on, this workspace could be a fairly simple refit of a two-car garage or a very expensive high-tech laboratory requiring the help of a venture-capital investor or an employer with a large research-and-development budget.

- A marketer working on ad campaigns and Web sites needs a very different sort of space — a studio with a flip chart for brainstorming, a computer with graphic design software and large display screen, and perhaps a round table for laying out examples of competitors' materials or holding group brainstorming sessions.

What kind of creative space do you need? Ask yourself this question and then do as much as you can (given your current resources) to create your own creative space.

It's important to find simple ways to protect your creative focus, whether by designating a space or a time to work on innovations, or both. Every workplace I've ever visited has had an official policy of being innovative, but because this goal is rarely translated into a work environment that's good for innovative thinking, it usually comes to nought.

A perfect workspace or place is very helpful, but in truth, much of what goes on when you innovate takes place deep inside your head. It's possible to stimulate breakthrough thinking by using your computer as a resource. Look up other people's work, and seek inspiration on the Web. Create a computer desktop with resources that you find helpful in your creative thinking, such as helpful computer programs, templates, and (especially) file folders of examples. I like to gather visual images that inspire me. They could be clever inventions, inspiring landscapes, or any other images that catch my eye and stimulate my imagination.

Also consider creating a playlist of music that you've selected because it helps you think clearly and creatively. (My creative playlist includes all the Bach cello concertos, which for some reason are amazingly good for stimulating creative thought.) You may also want to organize a bookmark folder of interesting Web sites for doing research to support your creative thinking or stimulate new ideas. Plugging into the facts, ideas, and designs of hundreds of other people is a great way to power up your imagination. (You can find a selection of inspiring images and examples at www.supportforinnovation.com.)

Introducing Creative Practices to Your Daily Routine

When I get called in to help an organization become more innovative, it's usually because something has gone wrong and the organization needs a big breakthrough idea in a hurry. Generally, I find that it has no creative routine, meaning that I have to get it from 0 to 60 creative miles an hour in a hurry — a task that's barely possible and usually quite a challenge. If you want to get in good cardiovascular shape by running, you don't enter a marathon as the first step. You start jogging every morning and work up gradually to long distances. It's really the same with creativity. Daily practice makes it easy to come up with the ideas you need, both big and small, when you need them most. If more people introduced creativity into their daily routines, they wouldn't need me to rush in and run creative retreats. They'd simply have the ideas they needed when they needed them! This section covers simple ways to develop a positive habit of creativity.

Balancing tight and loose activities

A *tight activity* is one that has strict parameters or rules and little room for variation or creativity. Business values tight activities because they produce consistent performance. McDonald's makes every burger exactly the same way, for example; that's part of its success formula. Also, it's important to enter accounting records accurately, using the same accounting system all year long.

Most of what people do in workplaces consists of tight activities. But tight activities put the right brain to sleep and reduce creative thinking. They need to be balanced with some loose activities.

A *loose activity* has little or no structure and no obvious right answer. It invites — in fact, requires — you to make things up as you go. Drawing a connect-the-dots picture is a tight activity; drawing a freehand picture of your own is a loose activity. Riding your bike, walking, or jogging a set route is a tight activity; exploring a new route is a loose activity. Learning a choreographed dance routine is a tight activity; choreographing or improvising your own dance is a loose activity.

What loose activities do you like to do? Make a list. Try to do at least one a day.

Freeing yourself to daydream

Mixing some loose activities into your normal routine of tightly controlled tasks is helpful (see the preceding section), but it doesn't guarantee break-through ideas because it still keeps you highly active. If your day is pro-grammed with so many responsibilities that you can barely catch your breath, you have no time for creative thoughts to percolate.

I have an acquaintance who's an inventor. His output is largely creative. Every now and then, he patents some brilliant new invention that he's spent months thinking through. The rest of the time, he does a lot of thinking. His favorite places to work are hammocks and couches. He likes to close his eyes and lie back, letting a problem float around in his imagination until something clicks into place in a new way. It may look like he's napping. The only way you know that he's not is that every now and then, he writes another brilliant idea.

I'll bet that daydreaming on a couch is a very different approach to work from yours. If you're too busy for your imagination to get a thought in edge-wise, you're going to have to take a timeout in your daily routine. Even ten minutes of gazing at the sky or walking through a flower garden may be enough to free your mind and allow creative thoughts to form. Your right and left brains compete for dominance, so to let your creative right lobe do its thing, you have to shut the logical, organized left lobe down at least once or twice each day.

Please note that this daydreaming has to take place before you get too tired for either side of your brain to do good work. If you work hard all day and then collapse on a couch in front of the TV, you won't do any creative thinking, because you'll already have used all your energy for thought. Build some day-dreaming time into the early part of your day, when you're still fresh enough to do good creative work.

Pursuing interesting questions instead of letting them pass by

When you make a point of mixing some loose activities (see "Balancing tight and loose activities," earlier in this chapter) into your daily routine, and also find time to relax and let your mind wander or daydream now and then, you'll find that your naturally inquisitive nature starts to express itself. You'll be increasingly curious, and you'll be able to tackle interesting questions, both practical and impractical (and either type is fine for stimulating innovative thinking).

It's terrible to be too busy to take an interest in questions such as these:

✔ Why do we always do it that way? Isn't there any better alternative?

✔ Do you think someone's already solved this problem, and we just have to find out what they did?

✔ Why do we divide the work the way we do? Could it be divided up differently?

These questions are traditionally called "dumb questions" because they set aside our knowledge and experience; they get us to examine our assumptions and start all over with an open mind. Make a habit of asking dumb questions and exploring possibilities. Every innovation starts with a simple question. Ask enough questions, and you'll find that you've seeded a lot of exciting innovation.

Cross-training the body to strengthen the mind

The mind and body are inextricably linked. You can't do good creative work when you're tense, irritable, sad, or depressed, and you can't sustain creative effort if you're ill, weak, or tired. The body needs to be in reasonably good shape and feeling fairly well for you to come up with good ideas. Therefore, you need to tend to your physical needs and adopt healthy practices to achieve your full creative potential. Exercise and healthy living are important to innovation.

In addition to keeping you healthy, exercise can broaden your thinking and strengthen your creativity if you seek out new experiences through your exercise regime instead of always doing the same thing day after day. Try to pick up a new sport, join a class you've never taken before, or work out with a new group of people to build training and ongoing learning into your workouts.

Trying a new sport or acquiring a new skill is very much like trying to invent something. You can expect lots of early failures and a feeling of naïveté or even ignorance, followed (if you persist) by the growth of competence and a growing feeling of mastery. This experience helps you feel good about being naïve and ignorant — something that you need to practice to avoid self-censorship and fear of failure when you try to be creative at work.

Seeking Broader Experience

Wide experience helps you innovate because, as I explain in Chapter 11, creative concepts often come from the combination of knowledge about apparently unconnected things. It's important to get out of your world and explore other people's worlds so that you can draw on a breadth of knowledge and experience too.

Finding ways to challenge yourself

When people ask me what they can do to become leading innovators in their field, I always suggest that they study or work in some other field for a while. If you work in the insurance industry, go take an evening course on geology, art history, or microbiology; anything that you're completely ignorant of will do the trick. Within a few weeks, you'll be seeing your own field or work quite differently, I promise.

Studying another culture and its language is a great way to stimulate your thinking. Taking up a new hobby can also do the trick. I've met a lot of entrepreneurs who built their hobbies into successful businesses. But there's no one best way to ensure that you have a rich and varied range of knowledge and experience. Follow your nose, and let your curiosity be your guide. Being open to new challenges that interest you is a really great way to build your creative power. It gives you more inputs from which to create innovations, and it makes you flexible and hardy enough to be a champion of your innovation as well.

Taking personal risks

Innovators don't mind failure, but they aren't gamblers. They take calculated risks that have a reasonably high chance of success. To increase your rate of creativity and produce more innovations, you need to avoid making wild or irresponsible gambles, but at the same time, you need to avoid playing it safe, worrying about what people will think or what will happen if you fail. These sorts of thoughts can sabotage your efforts at creativity.

A lot of interesting research shows that successful innovators, entrepreneurs, artists, scientists, and other highly creative people tend to be very open to new experiences and ideas, and have a strong feeling of *self-determination*. Self-determination's psychological meaning (similar to its political meaning) is the feeling that you can individually decide your own fate. People who are self-determined

✔ Have a sense of being in control of their lives.

✔ Tend to listen to their own ideas and instincts instead of always doing what others tell them or what convention says.

How do you gain the strength of will and self-reliance that highly self-determined people instinctively have? You can strengthen these qualities by not worrying about the risks of being wrong or embarrassing yourself if you offer a suggestion that doesn't work; tell yourself that you can come up with better approaches if you keep trying. Regulating your self-talk is a useful technique, especially when you combine it with a daily habit of open, creative practice. See Chapter 9 for specific ideas you can use to adopt a more optimistic, creative personality or strengthen the creative personality you already have.

It feels risky to stick your neck out with an opinion, option, or design of your own, but that's just what business needs and what *you* need to do to have a successful career today. Practice self-determined, creative behavior until you begin to feel comfortable with the risks of being wrong and having your ideas shot down. I never worry that one of my suggestions will be shot down because I have confidence that I can always come up with more.

The nice thing about tapping into your creative force is that the more you use it, the stronger it gets. You may run the risk of being wrong now and then, but there's one risk that you never need worry about: You'll *never* run out of ideas! If one is shot down, just launch another, and another, and another. . . .

Spending more time with people who aren't at all like you

Diversity is the fertilizer of innovation. Diverse experiences and acquaintances give you a diverse range of inputs and ideas to work with. Many successful innovations actually arise from pairs or teams of people whose cultural and intellectual backgrounds are very different. Opposites react. Take advantage of the learning and ideas you get from talking with people whose experiences are very different from your own.

On the flip side of the diversity coin, people who share your background and experiences are easy to be with, but they tend to shut down your creativity. Comfortable social situations are actually barriers to innovation. When all of a company's managers are from the same background (or are the same gender or race), the company tends to stop innovating and eventually runs into trouble.

Mixing it up for sustained success

My dad was a really good investment analyst and had a great eye for strong management teams. I once asked him why he pulled all his clients out of the stock of a particular company when others were still rating it as a buy. In response, he pointed to a photo of the board of directors and said, "Notice that they all look alike? There's no diversity in their management team. I'm concerned that they're riding on their laurels and don't have new ideas." He was right, and some years later, the company went into bankruptcy. That company was called Stone & Webster, and it was founded by my dad's grandfather, Edwin S. Webster, along with his roommate from the Massachusetts Institute of Technology, Charles Stone. Therefore, it was hard for my dad to sell off the stock, but he knew that a lack of diversity was bad for business.

Seeking the company of innovators

If you don't spend time with creative people, you'll have a hard time being creative yourself. The problem is that most of us work with people who aren't creative (or who *seem* not to be creative).

Fewer than 10 percent of people are naturally highly creative, so your odds of bumping into someone who is naturally very creative are fewer than one in ten. Actually, the odds are worse than that in most workplaces, because hiring tends to emphasize qualifications and experience, not creativity. Even worse, of these few rare highly creative people, more than half hide their creative light under a bushel because of pressures to conform to a less creative, more conservative stereotype of what an ideal employee ought to be.

I once met a successful corporate chief executive officer who presented himself as a very cautious, conservative, dark-suited man at work, but on the weekends, he hybridized new varieties of day lilies. His secret creative passion helped nurture his natural innovativeness, and I think it kept him open to new ideas and strategies for his company. I thought it was a shame that his employees never saw this side of him, however, and I urged him to become more of a creative mentor by sharing information about what he did outside the corner office.

If you find yourself surrounded by people who don't seem to be creative, seek out the company of some new friends, role models, or mentors. Most cities have inventors' and entrepreneurs' clubs, and I recommend attending a meeting now and then to pick up some of the positive energy these groups always have. Creative energy flows across any and all boundaries, however, so you can get just as much energy from attending a fiction-writing workshop as you would from attending a more business-oriented event. Be broad-minded about your search for creative peers. Why not volunteer to help design and build sets for an amateur theatrical production? Anything creative and fun will do the trick; it doesn't have to be directly related to your profession.

Getting out of your personal and career silos

Experts on organization design use the term *silo* (from the tall grain silos of traditional farms) to describe workplaces where people are isolated into groups based on their functions. It seems efficient to have all the salespeople in one place doing sales and all the accountants in another place doing accounting. Why should they ever intermingle? If accountants are concerned about an increase in the discounts given out by salespeople, however, what can they do about it except perhaps complain to headquarters? If the two functions had some overlap, accountants and salespeople might naturally chat about such a trend and come up with an insight of value to the company.

Organizations do best when they don't have tall silos in which groups, teams, divisions, subsidiaries, or functions are isolated from one another. You also benefit from getting out of your silo, and you should try to get out as often as you can, even if your employer doesn't make it easy to do so. Try one or more of these ideas:

- ✔ Take a rotational assignment in another location and/or function.
- ✔ Wander into unfamiliar parts of your workplace to find out what the people there do.
- ✔ Take a class or workshop in a field you know nothing about.
- ✔ Read another profession's magazines or blogs instead of your own.

Any of these activities will help you mingle with people who work in different silos, exposing you to fresh thinking and ideally building your cross-silo network of professional acquaintances, too.

Supporting inquisitive behavior

An advantage of finding and spending time with creative people is that you can encourage one another's creativity. I use the term *inquisitive behavior* to describe the general approach of asking questions and stimulating creative thought. Inquisitive behavior is the same in every field. It gets you thinking about creative possibilities by asking *open-ended questions* (questions that don't have any clear right answer).

When someone from your creative peer group or your workplace asks an inquisitive question, encourage creativity by taking the question seriously and helping that person come up with possible answers. Also try asking inquisitive questions yourself — the more the better, especially in traditionally noncreative settings like staff meetings.

Here's an example of inquisitive questions you might ask in a meeting addressing the practice of offering customers discounts to close the sale:

- ✔ **Inquisitive question:** Why is it called *discounting?* What are the origins of that term?

- ✔ **Insightful answer:** Roman merchants would place extra product to the side of a pile being counted and offer to throw in the extra if the buyer purchased the counted pile at the asking price.

- ✔ **Possible creative response:** Stop discounting the price, and return to the practice of offering extra free merchandise instead. That way, customers continue to pay the list price, and they hold more inventory of your product, delaying the time when the competition will have an opportunity to try to take the customer away.

Inquisitive questions can lead to new solutions, as this example illustrates. Without an inquisitive question or a few, a staff meeting on the topic of discounting would simply focus on how big a discount to give. With inquisitive thinking, that same meeting can explore alternatives to straight discounting.

That said, think about the normal staff meeting and what would happen if someone asked, "Hey, what do you think the origins of the word *discount* are? Where'd it come from?" Most likely, the boss or someone else in the room would quickly say, "Would you please stay on topic? We aren't historians; we're salespeople." Oops — so much for inquisitive thinking. Be careful not to shut it down, and if someone else tries to, shut him or her down by saying something like this: "Hold on. Let's give the question a chance. Sometimes, the strangest questions produce the most useful answers."

Learning from innovation mentors

To find a good *innovation mentor* (someone who can help you learn how to innovate and create), look for a person whom you find to be personally inspiring and who thinks you have a lot of untapped potential.

It's best to find a mentor who doesn't supervise you or have any other formal relationship with you, whether professional or personal, so that your mentoring relationship is the only way you relate. That way, you can focus 100 percent on discussing your career path, your current projects and challenges, and your ideas and how to move them ahead.

Also try to find people who have implemented an innovation by heading a team that brought about a major change or by starting a company or launching a new invention. Anyone who has brought about something new will have lots of helpful insights into the challenges of building momentum and implementing a new idea.

Mentoring is growing more common, but in most organizations it doesn't focus on innovation. Work to find a mentor who's been a successful innovator in the past and can share insights on invention, creative branding, novel business strategies, implementation, or other important innovation topics. Also try to make yourself available to *mentees* — people with less experience than you who would benefit from having access to your ideas and pointers. What goes around comes around, as they say, so by mentoring others, you may be more likely to be mentored yourself! (For more on how to set up and run productive meetings with your mentor or mentee, check out Chapter 3, and see my notes on the topic at www.supportforinnovation.com.)

Becoming a Leading Innovator

Tapping into your personal creativity allows you to become a successful innovator, because creativity is the fuel of innovation. You need to make a practice of imaginative thinking so as to have the creative power you need to fuel your own innovative career, as well as to fuel the innovations you bring to your work and workplace. That's why business innovation begins with a sustained effort to live a more creative life. An innovative approach benefits you in many ways:

- ✔ Helping you adapt to changing circumstances as you build a successful career

- ✔ Making you stand out from others, even if they have more formal qualifications or experience than you do

- ✔ Enriching your work by making each day a fresh, engaging experience rather than a boring routine

- ✔ Enriching your life by keeping your mind and body vital, flexible, and healthy

I've read a great many studies showing that people with an open, creative approach to life tend to live longer, rate themselves as happier than others, and have better luck avoiding major illnesses. They also tend to have more successful and profitable, as well as personally fulfilling, careers. There are a lot of reasons why you want to try to stand out as an innovator!

Making your creativity and drive visible to higher-ups

Many people are hesitant to offer suggestions or take initiative in their jobs, especially if they're relatively young or inexperienced, or don't hold a position of power and authority. It's a mistake to self-censor and hold your ideas back. How else are you going to stand out? How else are you going to get to do interesting new things? I hope that over the coming year, you'll develop a reputation for being an exceptionally innovative and interesting person who stands out from your peers because of your creative ideas and willingness to tackle new challenges.

Many people fear that their competence will be questioned if they appear to be too creative or bring up too many suggestions (some of which inevitably will be ruled out as impractical or — dare I say it? — dumb). Competence and creativity are two separate things, and you can show your competence by doing careful work and following through on commitments. If you're also bubbling over with ideas and enthusiasm, that's a bonus that doesn't detract from your competence; it adds another dimension to your workplace personality.

Another concern many people have is that they don't want to be viewed as criticizing their boss or their employer as a whole. Okay, I agree — you don't want to get stereotyped as a malcontent. But that has more to do with *how* you present your ideas than with *whether* you present them. If you frequently make disparaging or negative comments ("It's stupid how we keep doing X and never come up with a better way," for example), you'll certainly earn a negative reputation. Instead of voicing criticisms, offer suggestions. Say "What if we replaced X with Y?" instead of "X doesn't work well."

Everyone (especially senior managers) likes innovators for their useful stream of positive suggestions. There's a world of difference between innovators and complainers. If something bothers you, take your complaint to your creative space (time, place, or virtual place; see "Constructing Your Creative Place," earlier in this chapter), and turn that complaint into several alternatives. Then voice your positive suggestions instead of the negative-sounding complaint.

Stepping up to development teams and roles

A great way to gain innovation expertise and show that you have lots of creative energy and initiative is to volunteer to help implement a positive new change. Most workplaces have at least a few committees, teams, or work groups that are tasked with solving a problem or handling a difficult transition. Because these assignments are temporary, they draw on volunteers who do double duty, helping the team as well as covering their normal duties. Many people think that you'd have to be insane to take on an extra task voluntarily, but I think you're insane if you don't. It's the perfect opportunity to test your innovation skills and demonstrate your resourcefulness and drive. Make something new happen in your workplace at least once this year — preferably before you finish reading this book.

If you have any trouble with people who resist the new and blame you for their problems, check out Chapters 9 and 13, where problem-solving and conflict-resolution strategies can help you deal with those naysayers in your workplace who don't like innovation. Chapter 3 has resources for leading a project team, should you be lucky enough to be put in charge. And Chapter 18 covers how to take an idea and run with it on your own as an entrepreneur, should you decide that it's time to go out on your own and build your own business.

Chapter 2

Creating an Innovative Career Path

· ·

In This Chapter

▶ Breaking out of the mold: Pursuing an adventurous career path

▶ Making diverse work experiences add up to an impressive résumé

▶ Exploring ways to grow your career

▶ Creating your own job opportunities

· ·

*H*elen Keller famously wrote, "Life is either a daring adventure, or nothing." If given the choice, I'd opt for an adventure, but in truth, most people wobble down the middle, somewhere between nothing to write home about and a real adventure. This chapter will make sure that dull fate doesn't happen to you!

Aside from avoiding boredom (or should it be spelled bore-*dumb?*), the pursuit of career adventures ensures that you achieve your full potential by enriching your skills, experiences, network, and knowledge base. And these days, if you hadn't noticed, there aren't any stable, guaranteed career ladders to climb, so if you want a great career, you have to invent it for yourself.

I coauthored a bestseller called *Adventure Careers* back in the 1990s. At the time, I wanted to help people discover meaningful work and avoid dull, cookie-cutter career paths, and from the hundreds of e-mails we got, our readers seemed very excited to find that they had creative options beyond the standard want ads. In retrospect, however, there turned out to be another benefit to their quest for unique, exciting work adventures: Now they're all grown up and hold positions of leadership in business, nonprofit, entrepreneurship, and government sectors. Their early adventures made them successful by teaching them to be more flexible and innovative than their less adventurous peers. What I learned is this: *Varied, exciting work experiences create the innovators and leaders of the future.*

This chapter will help you chart an innovator's course from where you are right now toward a more dynamic and enriching career that engages your imagination and drive to the fullest. There are practical things you can do to make your career more dynamic and find more opportunities to innovate. Start with a different view of your career; then follow through by seeking opportunities that fit your existing vision of what you'd like to do.

Seeing Your Career as an Adventure

A good rule of thumb for innovators — or anyone, really, who wants to live an interesting and fulfilling life — is to always be doing something that makes a good story. What does that mean? It means that if you have to answer a question like "What have you been up to?", or you find yourself writing that proverbial letter home (or maybe today it's a blog), you instantly know what you want to say because it's a fun story that people will find engaging.

For example, as a sideline I've been working on a series of young-adult fantasy-adventure novels for a few years. When asked why I'm doing this, I simply tell the truth of the matter, which is that my eldest daughter, when she first went off to a sleep-away summer camp, wanted me to write her every day. I couldn't think of what to say, so I started writing her a story, and by the end of the summer she had a large pile of cards and a desire to see what would happen next. So did I, so I turned them into a book (see www.thestoryof drift.com for details, if you're interested). That's what's called a *back story* in fiction writing — background information that helps bring a character (or in this case, a book) to life. You need to accumulate interesting back stories too, so that you, as a character in a résumé, come to life and so that your résumé develops three-dimensionality that other résumés lack.

The way to develop an interesting character in fiction is to put the character in a challenging situation and see what he or she does. How will your character get out of trouble this time? It's really that simple to write exciting stories, and it's that simple to develop a rich, varied, and innovative career, too. Just put yourself in a new and challenging situation, preferably one you've never been in before and don't feel qualified to handle, and then see how you do. I guarantee that despite a few tense moments, you'll come through just fine in the end. The hero of the story always does!

Breaking through the barriers to career change

If you go from school to an entry-level job in a field and then work your way up, perhaps getting some additional training along the way, you soon find that you have greatly narrowed your options. Giving up on your field and starting all over again in another would mean giving up the salary level you've achieved, as well as having to compete against younger entry-level employees. Many people feel that they're trapped by their own career success and can't change direction. The main barriers you run into if you try to do something creative or different are

✔ Practical financial barriers associated with taking a cut in pay or benefits

✔ A credibility problem when you try to talk a new employer into hiring you to do something you don't have much experience doing

✔ A lack of self-confidence arising from your lack of traditional qualifications and experience

✔ Possible age or other forms of discrimination if you don't fit the mold of the typical applicant

Of these four barriers to doing something new and different, three are largely external, and one is internal: your own confidence issues and concerns. Tackle that one first because it's more fully in your control and also because it has considerable influence on the other three barriers.

In my experience, you can often overcome the initial resistance of potential employers by exhibiting a really positive, can-do attitude. Wise employers know that they can teach skills, but they can't develop good attitudes in people; they have to hire for that quality.

Have faith that if you believe you can and should do something new to broaden your experience, you will eventually find an employer who agrees and likes your positive attitude and enthusiasm. This person may be a rare employer, but keep searching until you find her. She's not only your next boss, but also a potential mentor for your innovative career, because she understands the value of diverse experiences and values a creative approach.

If you're locked into an expensive lifestyle you can barely afford, finances are something you need to work on right away. They can be improved only incrementally, so get started immediately, and work on them for the next six months to a year. Here's what to do:

✔ **Reduce your carrying costs.** These costs are the regular (monthly or quarterly) expenses you have to cover to pay your bills. Get rid of expensive vehicles, appliances, memberships, and leases. Most households can cut their routine bills by about 20 percent without any major changes in lifestyle.

✔ **Chip away at credit-card bills, and stop using all credit cards at once!** If you can't afford it on a debit card, don't buy it, period. (That goes for automobiles too. If you can't afford to buy a car with cash, don't buy it. Your career is much more valuable in the long run than your ride.)

✔ **Move to a less expensive home.** Most people's largest expense is housing. Keep in mind that transportation is often the second- or third-largest household expense, so try to move somewhere in or near a major metropolitan area offering lots of work, study, and volunteering options, plus public transportation if possible.

Also consider sharing an apartment or duplex. Often, this approach can cut your living costs by 30 percent to 50 percent.

✔ **Take care of yourself.** Good health is a money saver, whereas illness is financially debilitating. Exercise, healthy eating, avoidance of alcohol and drugs, and early bedtimes add up to real savings in the household budget and free you to focus on developing an interesting, innovative career. (In fact, healthy habits are a bigger financial factor than health insurance, because an illness prevented saves, on average, a lot more than a year's worth of health insurance premiums.)

Make do with a smaller place and a less expensive lifestyle, and keep yourself healthy and fit. The goal is to see how small a percentage of your income you have to spend each month to cover the bills. If you can begin to get ahead of your costs and run a substantial surplus, you can reinvest that personal profit in an innovative career. In other words, invest the extra cash in yourself!

Making opportunistic moves

When you work on your financial and emotional health, and no longer feel trapped in your current position (see the preceding section for tips on how to do this), you're ready to answer the door when opportunity knocks.

Speaking of opportunity knocking, you can get more information on the topic of finding an exciting dream job at the Opportunity Knocks Web sites: `www.knocks.com`, where you can reach President Wendy Terlwelp for personal branding and career coaching, and `www.opportunityknocks.org`, where hundreds of interesting job openings in nonprofits and charitable organizations are posted.

You can find lots of similar services on the Web by searching for interesting job openings and career boards where openings are posted. Type "finding a better job" into your favorite search engine. Also check out Monster (`www.monster.com`), Employment Spot (`www.employmentspot.com`), and CareerBuilder (`www.careerbuilder.com`).

Moving toward growth with your current employer

The most obvious opportunities are the ones closest at hand. If your current employer has any interesting new opportunities, consider making a move, even if it's a *lateral move* (at the same pay level) or a *downward move* (at a lower pay level). The level is less important than the momentum of a position. Momentum means growth and future potential, and you should always be looking for and moving toward where the momentum is. If your employer is cutting back in most areas (as many are), chances are that there's still one area in which hiring is going on because of an urgent need to increase staff. Try to shift to a position — any position — in that growth area. Whatever it entails, it will expose you to some cross-training and teach you some skills that are of growing economic value.

Working your networks for opportunities

Your personal and professional networks are great sources of opportunity. If you hear that someone is looking for somebody to do something that interests you, get in touch with that person, and find out more about the opportunity. Take a "why not?" approach to such opportunities, and see whether you find them interesting.

Taking on short-term and volunteer projects

A great many short-term, part-time projects are available. Some pay well; others, such as internships and volunteer work, not so well. I think it's good to be doing one such short-term project at all times, even if you're holding down a full-time job. The breadth of experience you gain and the rich professional network you build add up to a lot of benefits from those side assignments.

I've worked with hundreds of successful entrepreneurs, and more than 95 percent of them had extraordinarily adventurous early careers characterized by many, diverse projects and positions. The richness of experience you gain from varied work adds up to a better ability to innovate in the future, whether you do it as an employee, a freelancer, or a business-building entrepreneur.

Counting Up Your Transferable Skills and Experiences

When your aim is to climb a fixed career ladder, you need to accumulate a series of ever-higher positions within a specific field. A traditional résumé tells the story of such a career climb by listing job titles and responsibilities by year. First, you may have been an assistant; next, a junior manager; then a department manager . . . and so on. Your career is unlikely to consist of a straightforward climb up a fixed ladder, but your résumé probably still looks like that's what you're trying to do. This format is the traditional approach to résumés and the one that most people follow.

A better approach is to create a list of the competencies you've gained through your varied work experiences, and make note of how each experience contributed to specific competencies. (I might note that I gained leadership skills through my work on the boards of directors of numerous nonprofits and my coaching of youth soccer teams, as well as any management positions I held in my formal, paying work.) Where have you picked up leadership skills and experiences? Making a list may help you prove that you're qualified for an exciting new paid opening or volunteer opportunity.

Drawing on experience to design a retro speedboat

Ross Hartman took a few engineering courses in college but has no formal training or experience in *naval architecture* — the engineering and design of boats. That hasn't stopped him from parlaying his practical experience as a builder and his rusty knowledge of engineering into an exciting startup business that makes speedboats styled after classic cars of the 1950s and '60s, such as the Ford Mustang. His business, Dana Levi Boats (www.danalevi.net), employs a naval architecture firm to produce construction blueprints and retains a boatyard in Florida to create the molded fiberglass hulls, but the design concepts all flow from the founder's imagination and pen. Like many inventors, he had no formal training in the industry but had enough imagination, and enough general skills, to shake up the industry with something fresh and new.

After you document your experiences and how they add up to skills and qualifications, you're ready to write a modified résumé. You can (if you think it necessary) keep the format looking traditional, but make a point of noting the specific transferable skills you gained under each job listing. Also add part-time and volunteer jobs, as well as any major projects you worked on for full-time employers. Listing such experiences separately helps you tell your story better.

If you're dealing with an open-minded or nontraditional interviewer, consider reformatting your résumé as a table. Down the left side, list jobs and projects (as in a traditional résumé). Across the top, label the columns with specific skills (such as Communications, Leadership, Design and Invention, or Software Programming; see Figure 2-1). Then fill in cells appropriately to show how and where you gained experiences in each of the columns. This tabular format makes clear sense of a diverse set of job experiences, helping potential employers see how you've been working steadily on core skills, even though you've done it across numerous jobs and projects.

As Figure 2-1 shows, you can organize seemingly disconnected experiences into a coherent description of your core competencies. (To prevent confusion, limit the number of competencies to five.) At the top of this résumé, you can state a work goal or desired position that relates to the competencies. At the bottom, you can summarize the competencies that your various experiences demonstrate. The summary of your competencies should align with the requirements for the job you're seeking. Check job descriptions from employers to make sure that you're using this competency résumé to tell your story in a way that makes it obvious to potential employers that you have the needed experience and competencies, even if you haven't done the specific job you want to apply for.

Competency Resume
Onawa French
Goal: A leadership role in marketing or communications

Jobs and Projects:	Experiences by Category:			
	Leadership	*Communications*	*Marketing*	*Design*
Sales Representative, FBM, 2010	Team leader for annual sales conference planning and management.	Sales and service for 40+ core accounts.	Helped select new products and suppliers.	Redesigned sales materials, created interactive Web site.
Girl Scout leader 2009–10	Mentor and supervision for teens, weekend trip planner and chaperone.	Organized regional conference.	Prepared outreach program in three counties.	Created regional Web site.
Team leader, branding project, Mayfair Stores, 2008	Formed team, ran team meetings, managed subcontractors.	Presented plans and results to executive committee meetings.	Prepared project budgets and projections for marketing plan.	Naming, logo design, advertising programs, Web site design.
Assistant Store Manager, Mayfair Stores, 2006–7	Supervised floor staff, trained and put in charge of conflict resolution.	Prepared weekly store reports to HQs, represented store at neighborhood development meetings.	Volunteered to draft annual marketing plan for 2007.	Prepared window displays for holiday season, designed circulars for newspapers.
Intern, French Catering, 2005	Mentored under Cincinnati Entrepreneur of the Year.	Coordinated bookings by phone and e-mail, scheduled staff.	Wrote a press release picked up by local papers and TV.	Redesigned menu and brochure, updated Web site.
Summary	*Team leadership, staff supervision, supplier management*	*Selling, customer service, public speaking, reports, plans, conferences*	*Product selection, outreach, PR, planning*	*Web, print, window, and logo design*

Figure 2-1:
A com-
petency
résumé in
tabular
format.

Seeking Opportunities to Innovate

As you search for interesting opportunities (including projects at your regular workplace, volunteer jobs, and short-term or part-time jobs), favor those that encourage some form of creative expression. It takes creativity to

✔ Organize a fund-raiser for a nonprofit organization.

✔ Develop a solution to a challenging problem in your workplace.

✔ Redesign a workplace process to save money or improve quality.

Anything that isn't "by the book" may be a good opportunity to express yourself. Tackle extra assignments or new jobs with an innovative spirit, and make an effort to do something new and innovative in each job and project you undertake. The big-picture idea is to treat everything you do as an opportunity to make your mark as an innovator. Of course, this goal is easier to achieve if you select jobs and projects for their creative potential and avoid ones in which you'd be expected to follow a set of instructions to the letter.

If you type "creative work" in a search engine, you'll come up with lists of so-called creative jobs, such as ad design, software design, and painting (not house painting, but painting for gallery sales). These careers can be creative, of course, but the lists miss the key point: Creativity and innovation are important in a great many careers and jobs, not just those in the arts. Engineering is creative. Managerial leadership is creative. Business strategy is highly creative, which is why I tend to run a strategic planning retreat in much the same way that I run a creative branding retreat, with lots of idea-generation activities to open the mind to possibilities. If your current job doesn't permit you to innovate, start searching for another job today. There are lots of them. What makes a job creative and innovative is a desire on the part of management to be creative. If the members of the senior management team understand that they need fresh ideas to grow and prosper, they'll probably value your initiative and ideas.

Moving Toward Growth

As you pursue your innovative career, make a point of pursuing growth. Growth takes several main forms:

- ✔ Your own development of knowledge, skills, credentials, and relationships with a wide range of interesting and accomplished people
- ✔ Growth areas (such as a growing department) within an organization where you work
- ✔ Economic growth in specific regions and sectors

Encouraging your own personal growth

Your personal growth is the most important dimension of growth to keep in mind as you navigate your career options. Make a point of learning and developing at a high rate to keep yourself sharp and up-to-date as an innovator.

If you use the competency-based, tabular résumé format illustrated in Figure 2-1, it's easy to see where your holes are and where you could use more experience. Create a large, for-your-eyes-only, and very detailed version of a competency résumé to help you decide which opportunities or experiences to pursue next.

Targeting growth areas in your current organization

Keep in mind that in organizations, there are generally stagnant areas you want to avoid and exciting areas where growth is taking place. Go where the growth is, even if the jobs aren't as stable and well-paying as more traditional ones. In the end, growth wins out over stability every time.

A biological analogy is helpful: Visualize an established business as though it were a giant plant. Somewhere down at its historical base is a solid old trunk of dead wood, while up in the leafy branches is fresh green growth. Some people are naturally suited to positions in the trunk. That's fine for them, but their careers are going to be dull and stagnant because they favor stability over growth. Keep in mind that new skills are developing and the seeds of new enterprises are growing at the flexible ends of young, leafy branches, not down at the base of the old tree. The branches are where new ideas and new technologies are being tested, and where new market opportunities are being pursued.

To take advantage of the growth areas of your employer, join task forces working on new ideas or implementing new technologies. Also see whether you can help with the sourcing or development of new products. And if your employer opens a new office or expands into a new market, be the first to volunteer for the challenging (and perhaps risky) assignments out there on the frontier of your business's growth. That's where you get the opportunities to innovate and problem-solve, and it's where you gain the skills that will make you an appealingly innovative candidate when you next apply for a desirable job.

Taking advantage of fast-growing cities

Give some thought to geographic and demographic growth trends. In the United States, Los Angeles, Miami, and New York are adding people faster than other large cities, making them good areas to work. For the absolutely fastest rates of growth, however, several small cities top the list, including Round Rock, Texas; Cary, North Carolina; and Gilbert, Arizona. If you work in any of these cities, odds are that your career will grow faster than elsewhere in the country, and more opportunities will open up to you. If you're stuck in a low-growth or shrinking area, bite the bullet and move to a fast-growth area right away. It's really, really hard to have a successful career outside a growth area.

If you look at social statistics for the United States, you'll see that Hispanics (a diverse set including people of various Latin American national origins) are a large and fast-growing category. Businesses and services of interest to Hispanics are going to have a leg up because of this population growth. Similarly, the smaller but even faster-growing category of people who identify themselves as multiracial or biracial is reported to be the fastest-growing group in the United States, perhaps presenting interesting opportunities to innovators who can think of ways to serve this group's needs. Ideas, anyone?

Serving the fastest-growing age groups

If you slice the population by age, you'll find that one particular age bracket is growing faster than the others. Which one? It varies by country. In slower-growing, highly industrialized countries like the United States, Canada, Great Britain, and Japan, it's the elderly. People over 85 are the hottest growth sector of these mature economies, believe it or not. In less-developed countries with faster population growth, teens or young adults often make up the fastest-growing group. Clearly, economic opportunities for innovators differ, depending on whether population growth is centered in the elderly or the young of a country. In one case, innovations in education are greatly needed; in the other, healthcare and elder care are hot areas.

Tapping into international growth

Study your country's growth patterns, and make sure that your work is of importance to some growing group, whether defined geographically or by social or population statistics. Also be open-minded about international opportunities. Right now, enterprising young adults in the United States are mindful of the fast economic growth in China and India and are looking for opportunities to tap into these hot international economies.

My son Paul, who graduated from college last year, entered the U.S. job market during the trough of a deep recession. His solution? He got a job teaching English at a Chinese university and headed off for a year abroad. He'd studied Chinese in college, fortunately, so his job search wasn't confined to the United States.

Inventing Your Next Job

Most people search for work. That approach reflects a noncreative view of work in which you assume that someone else has to create your opportunities for you, and all you do is apply and hope to be selected. In an innovative career, you turn that assumption over and think of your next job as something *you* will create.

Proposing a new position for yourself

Take a good look at your own organization or any other that you know something about and have access to. What does it need? Where are its biggest problems and opportunities? If you were in charge, what new position would you want to create and fill with an eager innovator like yourself? When you have an idea in mind, write it up (use the same format for job descriptions that the organization does) and then send a cover letter and your new job description to an appropriate contact. There's a chance that your proposal will be picked up and you'll be hired to do the job you so thoughtfully crafted. It's certainly worth a try.

If you think imagining a new position, writing the job description, sending it in, and getting hired to fill it seems unlikely, think about what consultants do to make a living. I've done a fair amount of consulting, often because I've talked some executive into listening to my proposal telling her what I think I can do to help her company out. In other words, to get hired as a consultant, I had to persuade someone that there was a need for me. It's commonplace for consultants to do this, but nobody else in the job market ever does. Take it from an old consultant: The best jobs are always the ones you invent for yourself.

Generating freelance and consultative work

If your proposal to create a new job opening for yourself (refer to the preceding section) doesn't get accepted, think about freelance consulting instead. For every permanent new position, there are dozens of short-term, project-oriented opportunities. I've learned more from my consulting experiences than from any full-time job I've ever had. Consulting is fun. Well, not fun like a vacation in Cancun, but fun in the way that exciting, high-pressure performances are fun. Tackling a tough project on a deadline is always a challenge, and challenges bring out your innovative best, right?

To find freelance and consultative work, keep in mind that 90 percent of consultants are hired by someone who already knows them. You need to work your professional network to find out what's needed and who to talk to.

Join professional organizations in your area, whether that area is defined by geography, a professional field, or (preferably) both. Attend meetings, especially if a sit-down meal is in the offing. I'm not saying this because I like free food (although I do!) but because the best networking happens when you get a chance to sit and share a meal with a group of people who share a professional interest. Meals last long enough and are relaxing enough that you can strike up real conversations and make new friends.

After you zero in on some opportunities for freelancing, present yourself promptly and professionally. The early bird gets the worm, so don't delay, wondering whether you're the right person. Pick up the phone or get on e-mail and make contact right away, preferably early in the workday. Then dress yourself, and your résumé, according to professional custom in the business or industry in question, and set up a face-to-face meeting as soon as you can. Beyond that, there isn't much of a formula.

It's probably best to avoid fancy sales pitches. Just be yourself. Ask questions; offer suggestions; smile; and say that you think you can solve the problem, whatever it is. See whether the potential client will offer you a contract, and if it does, agree to start right away. Eagerness wins the most contracts in the consulting game. Inflexibility and a demanding, arrogant approach lose the most contracts.

Developing entrepreneurial career options

Most of the really creative people I know have started at least a few new businesses, theater groups, dance companies, charities, or other organizations. The interesting thing is that the majority of these people don't call themselves entrepreneurs and have no intention of starting the next big business. They just have good ideas that seem to need an organization, so they start calling people up, and soon, they've gotten another organization off the ground. They may do this work entirely in their spare time outside a 9-to-5 job, but still, it's probably the most meaningful and exciting thing they do all year.

I recommend this approach. Start something small in your spare time, and get others to help you grow it into an established entity with a life of its own. Who knows? Maybe it will grow large enough to take the place of your regular job, but even if it doesn't, it will give you lots of great opportunities to strengthen your creative skills.

Chapter 3

Leading with Creative Vision

. . . .

In This Chapter

▶ Defining an innovative goal to motivate your team

▶ Exploring your leadership orientation and style

▶ Building leadership experience

▶ Setting the right tone for hopeful creativity

. . . .

*T*he world needs innovative leaders. Okay, sure, sometimes, in some places, what's wanted is stewards who protect tradition and prevent change. The emperors of ancient China decided to close their kingdom off from the outside world and stop things from changing, and they succeeded for a while — but innovation continued beyond their borders, leaving them so weakened that they lost control and were overthrown. In the end, it's always better to be on the side of innovation.

Fast-forward to today, when the need for innovative leadership is urgent. When leaders forget that they're supposed to be creating helpful new ways of doing things, the economy slides toward ruin. Innovative leadership is the fuel of healthy economies and societies.

You need to be an innovative leader. It's the one universal trait in any and every successful career, whether in or out of the business world. I train a lot of leaders with a wide range of competencies. A U.S. Coast Guard officer obviously knows things that a bank manager doesn't, and vice versa. But every leader needs to know how to support and direct the work of others — and, periodically, to spearhead innovative changes.

This chapter bumps up your innovative leadership skills a few levels by addressing the ways you challenge your team and how you adjust your leadership style to help your team innovate effectively.

Visualizing the Possibilities for Innovative Leadership

It's natural to focus on making sure that everybody's at their desks or workstations, has something to do, and is doing it at least moderately well. But supervising the details of your team's work is only one small part of your leadership responsibilities. You want to get everyone oriented and working on the right tasks before you run out of energy so *you* can look up and think about the future while they work. *Leadership* means, most simply, creating positive momentum toward a good goal or objective for the future and making sure that everyone is moving in that direction.

You can think of your leadership job as having two main parts that you can visualize as a house with a triangular roof. The house represents the current activities that need to be coordinated, and the triangular roof turns the house into a directional arrow pointing upward. The roof is created by the sense of purpose and direction of the leader's vision. When you visualize positive change, you provide an overarching structure that gives meaning and energy to the daily grind. And when you make your goals ambitious and encourage innovative pursuit of them, you get everybody fired up about working for you.

Setting ambitious goals

Your vision needs to be ambitious. Don't settle for just keeping things going or making do. That's boring, and it doesn't contribute much to the group you're leading. What use is a vision that lacks vision? Here are some examples of good goals for innovative leadership:

- Double sales over the next two years.
- Upgrade to cutting-edge equipment and modernize the entire organization.
- Cut costs by 25 percent.
- Prevent accidents and achieve 100 percent safety.
- Find or develop a best-selling product to grow the business.
- Find a solution to a major problem so that the group can move on.
- Launch a major ad campaign that boosts sales and builds brand image substantially.

The main point to keep in mind is that leadership vision has to have a creative element to it. You *imagine* a better future; then you help your group make that vision real. How do you go about imagining a better future? You might try starting with the simplest but perhaps the most powerful technique for innovative thinking: the creative thinking process illustrated in Figure 3-1. Often termed the *Wallas model* after Graham Wallas, who formalized it in his book *The Art of Thought* in 1926, it was first described in 1921 by Henri Poincaré, one of the most creative and important mathematicians of the 19th century.

Following is Poincaré's journal entry describing one of his most important contributions to mathematics. What's interesting is the creative process and how it works:

> *"For fifteen days I . . . sat down at my work table . . . I tried a great number of combinations and arrived at no result. One evening, contrary to custom, I took black coffee; I could not go to sleep; ideas swarmed up in clouds; I sensed them clashing until, to put it so, a pair would hook together to form a stable combination. By morning I had established a class of Fuchsian functions. I had only to write up the results which took me a few hours."*

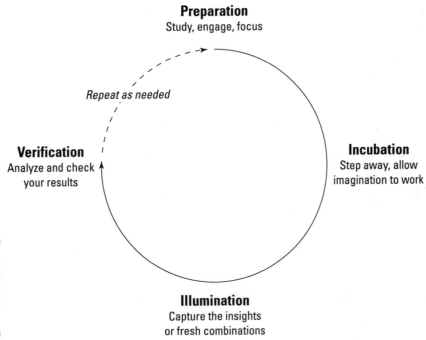

Preparation
Study, engage, focus

Repeat as needed

Verification
Analyze and check
your results

Incubation
Step away, allow
imagination to work

Illumination
Capture the insights
or fresh combinations

Figure 3-1:
Poincaré's
creative
thinking
process.

As Figure 3-1 illustrates, Poincaré's process is comprised of four steps:

- **Preparation:** The essential first step for Poincaré (and anyone wanting to achieve a breakthrough idea) is to become deeply engrossed in your challenge. Hard, unrelenting effort, often without immediate results, is essential. Notice that Poincaré put a lot of focused effort into his invention. You need to focus hard on the question of what your leadership vision should be. Give yourself time to study your situation, and clarify your priorities before announcing what your goal is.

- **Incubation:** As arduous as preparation can be, it's unlikely to produce an "aha" breakthrough unless you then introduce a period of incubation, in which you let the problem sit in your subconscious while you rest; do something else; or think about it in an unstructured, casual manner.

- **Illumination:** Make sure that you feel a real sense of excitement about the idea. That way, your idea will excite others too. A creative insight usually falls into place quite suddenly, instead of bit by bit, the way a logical step-by-step solution to a problem will.

- **Verification:** Check your idea or theory by testing it in the real world, such as by making a prototype. Testing your design or theory sometimes produces unexpected results, allowing you to return to the drawing board and refine your thinking.

By the way, Poincaré's creative thinking process can be applied to many types of problems and design challenges, so it's worth practicing until it comes naturally to you.

Encouraging others to envision change too

When you lead, you need to demonstrate your commitment to innovation by being creative yourself and by having a vision of a positive future. In addition, you need to ask your team members to suggest ideas of their own. Your overarching vision of future improvements creates a gap between the present and the vision, and everyone can and should put creative energy into trying to fill that gap. The innovative leader doesn't keep tight control of the creative thinking; she shares the responsibility and fun of innovating with the entire team.

Researchers have compared the behaviors of leaders who create innovations with the behaviors of those who don't. The findings are clear and helpful: You need to lead in ways that encourage your entire group to be thoughtful and outspoken in the pursuit of improvements and new ideas.

Table 3-1 is a checklist you can use to make sure that you're acting in ways that stimulate innovation and produce breakthroughs. (For details on the research behind this checklist, see the article "How Leaders Influence

Employees' Innovative Behaviour," by Jeroen P.J. de Jong and Deanne N. Den Hartog, in *European Journal of Innovation Management,* Volume 10, Number 1, 2007, or visit www.creativeforce.org for a more detailed checklist.)

Table 3-1	**Checklist of Innovative Leadership in Action**	
Do You Use This Leadership Behavior?	*Leadership Behavior*	*Explanation*
	Role-modeling innovative behavior	Acting creatively to stimulate creative behavior in others; exploring opportunities, generating ideas, and championing their development.
	Providing intellectual stimulation	Increasing employees' awareness of problems; stimulating them to rethink old ways of doing things; challenging them to think of ideas.
	Stimulating knowledge diffusion	Organizing information sessions; encouraging learning, informal communication, and sharing of knowledge.
	Providing vision	Providing a sense of direction, overarching goals, and general guidelines.
	Consulting with employees	Asking employees their opinion before making decisions; checking with people before making changes that affect them; incorporating some of their suggestions.
	Delegating	Granting employees enough freedom and autonomy to encourage ownership of their work.
	Supporting	Showing enthusiasm for new ideas and providing tangible support for their development; not penalizing new ideas.
	Providing feedback	Offering direct feedback and/or arranging for others to give feedback to provide employees responses to their ideas. (Feedback should be positive and aimed at helping improve an idea, not shoot it down.)
	Providing recognition	Paying attention to new ideas and the people who offer them; offering praise or awards for innovative behavior.

(continued)

Table 3-1 *(continued)*

Do You Use This Leadership Behavior?	Leadership Behavior	Explanation
	Providing rewards	Offering financial rewards for successful ideas and applications. (The pressure of being paid for ideas, however, can make employees less creative and more cautious, so be careful not to rely too heavily on financial incentives.)
	Providing resources	Making the necessary time and money available to employees to develop and implement their ideas.
	Monitoring	Avoiding monitoring employee time and activity too tightly, but generally keeping track of how things are going, especially with the development and implementation of new ideas.
	Assigning interesting tasks	Matching employees with work they like and find motivating; offering complex, interesting tasks; rotating task assignments.

None of the activities in Table 3-1 is hard to do. The trick is to realize that they're important. The checklist can be your toolbox of innovative leadership actions. Dip into it by using at least one of these actions a day, and you'll have an innovative group, company, or team that will pursue your vision with enthusiasm.

The basic concept behind all the activities in Table 3-1 is job enrichment, in which the supervisor makes sure that each person is working on interesting challenges that engage a range of his or her abilities. Everyone has the ability to innovate, but few managers build innovation into the work their employees are doing. When you find ways to challenge people to generate and apply new ideas, you find — ta-da! — that they're amazingly innovative after all.

Knowing when innovation is required

Innovating is a lifestyle. You need to make it a part of the regular routines of your workplace, so really, innovation should be on the agenda every day. Sometimes, however, innovation is truly essential and has to be the number-one priority. When should you, as a leader, drop everything and make creativity and innovation your priority all day long?

The trick is to know which *strategic phase* you ought to be in. Should your organization focus on efficient production or creative searching? Consider the following:

- ✔ **Efficient production** is what you do right after you've implemented one or more innovations and want to profit from them. You scale up by getting everybody to do his part accurately and quickly — which adds up to cheaply when it's done consistently. Efficient production is repetitive in nature and rewards consistency. It's the order of the day until you sense that you're beginning to lose the creative edge and it's time to change over to something new.

- ✔ **Creative searching** is what you do when you know that you'll need to make major changes soon, and you want to come up with or find the right set of innovations for the future. This book should be your business bible during the creative searching phase. Let things run themselves by routine as you focus your leadership time and energy on innovating.

Some organizations (especially the ones with big budgets) try to be in both phases at the same time. It's important, however, to emphasize one over the other. You can't really balance efficient production and creative searching. They each have their own, quite opposite, demands. Both strategies are important at all times, but one should be dominant.

Usually, it works well to use a *punctuated equilibrium* approach, in which you have a routine of efficient production for some months or years, punctuated (or interrupted) by an intense phase of creative searching, followed (when you find the right innovation) by scale-up to another phase of efficient production. You, as the innovative leader, are responsible for deciding which phase is appropriate and leading accordingly. (See Chapter 5 for more help with your strategies and plans.)

Getting to Know Yourself as a Leader

Many leaders assume that the most important things to focus on are the group they'll be leading and how to manage it. Leadership courses start at the opposite end of the spectrum, however, by challenging leaders to study *themselves* instead. Good leadership requires good self-leadership, because unless you know yourself pretty well, you won't be able to self-manage to the high degree needed to be effective.

The most important thing to know about yourself as a leader is what your approach looks and feels like to the people you lead. For starters, does your team think you're an active, involved leader or a distant, uncaring one? This question gets at *leadership volume,* or the amount of leadership presence you provide.

Often, you may think that you're providing enough leadership when actually, you're so busy with your own work that you aren't present for your team, and they think you're remote and unavailable. Be careful to keep the leadership volume turned up loud enough that your entire team can hear you. Don't be so distant that team members aren't sure whether they really *have* a leader!

The kinds of activities listed in Table 3-1 need to make up a large part of most of your days. Otherwise, your leadership won't really be visible to the people you're supposed to lead. I think the following expression is a great reminder: Leadership is *action*, not position.

Identifying your leadership orientation

It would be nice if all you had to do was get the volume (or amount of leadership) right, but of course, it's not that simple. You also need to know which of two fundamental orientations to use at any given time (and by the way, because they're fundamental orientations, you need to be consistent in your use of one for some time instead of jumping erratically between them). To identify your basic leadership orientation, ask yourself the following questions:

1. **Do I focus on doing things consistently and carefully?**

2. **Do I find routines boring and dull?**

3. **Do I take pride in perfecting my skills?**

4. **Do I get the most enjoyment out of trying new things?**

5. **Do I insist that employees and team members do things correctly?**

6. **Do I insist that employees and team members try new approaches?**

The following sections explain what your answers to these questions indicate about your leadership orientation.

Maintenance orientation

If you answered yes to questions 1, 3, and 5, your default orientation is toward maintenance, and you'll find yourself a natural for the strategic phase of efficient production. You're probably particularly good at keeping a successful business or operation going smoothly and well. This maintenance orientation will tend to reduce the amount of creative thinking and experimentation you do, however, and will make it more difficult for you to lead innovation and change. You'll need to make a conscious effort to change your orientation to allow innovation to happen.

Innovation orientation

If you answered yes to questions 2, 4, and 6, you probably didn't answer yes to the others, because people usually favor one or the other orientation. Your orientation is creative, and your tendency is to look for new ideas and approaches. You ought to find it fairly easy and natural to adopt innovative leadership techniques and to inspire others to become more creative. Your weakness may be in persisting long enough with one idea to bring it fully through development and refine it into a profitable routine.

Can you master both orientations?

As I expect that you've already figured out, you need to be able to shift your orientation and not be stuck with just one approach. Knowing your basic orientation helps you understand not only your strengths, but also your weaknesses.

A maintenance-oriented leader is great at keeping things running smoothly and doesn't get bored with the pursuit of efficiencies during scale-up, but he may tend to forget about creativity and fail to lead the way to the next big thing. Maintenance makes sense only as long as what you're maintaining is worth it. At some point, you need to trade it in for a new model.

The innovation-oriented leader is a natural when it comes to finding the next great idea and working on it, but she begins to lose focus and get bored just when the innovation's kinks are finally ironed out and it's time to profit by using it efficiently.

Which is your strength: innovating or maintaining? Whichever it is, know your strongest and weakest qualities, and make a point of hiring people who can help you with both. I'm a natural innovator myself, but my business partner, Stephanie, has a maintenance orientation. She's really good at making things hum along efficiently, and she keeps a close eye on plans and budgets, which means I can spend most of my time imagining. Sometimes, when her orientation fits the strategic phase we're in, she takes the lead. At other times, I step forward (with a new product I've designed, for example) and take the lead as we change our product lineup or try a new business model. If it works, I turn the reins over to her to fine-tune it and make it run profitably.

I've found that I'm so strongly oriented toward innovation that it's hard for me to change my own approach and be a good maintainer, so I rely on someone else to help me cover the other orientation. Most people are less extreme in their orientation, however, and can teach themselves to switch from one orientation to the other more easily than I can. It's up to you to decide whether you can cover both basic leadership orientations yourself or you need a partner to help you.

Zeroing in on your leadership style

Your *leadership style* is the approach you take toward the people and tasks involved in achieving your leadership goals. Everyone has a leadership style, but (just as with basic leadership orientation, discussed in the preceding section) most people aren't very aware of what their style is.

What leadership style do you seem to have in the eyes of your team members? Do you delegate often — perhaps too often, because you're too busy to help them figure out how to do their work? Do you tend to talk and think about the work itself, but ignore the humans who do it and their often all-too-human problems and concerns? Or are you very empathetic and aware of people problems, but not very good at planning and structuring the work?

To find out what your leadership style is, consult Figure 3-2. It asks you two questions outside the four-box grid. These questions are called *forced-choice* questions because you have to pick one of the two possible answers. When you've chosen your two answers, go to the cell where they intersect on the grid, and read about the style that corresponds to your choices. There are four main leadership styles, and one of them probably is your default (the one you turn to most often):

- ✔ **Instruct:** You give an employee clear information about what to do and where, how, and why to do it. Then you make sure that you are available (or someone else who understands the work is available) to correct and answer questions.

- ✔ **Coach:** You assign projects or assignments that build on and develop employees' skills while you provide both instruction and support to help the employees rise to the challenges you've set.

- ✔ **Relate:** You listen and use your empathy to understand what employees are concerned about and help them feel better about their work.

- ✔ **Delegate:** You recognize that an employee or team is ready to take on more responsibility, and you reduce your level of supervision and challenge that person or team to do larger projects independently.

Adjusting your style to fit the situation

The leadership grid in Figure 3-2 is the gold standard of leadership training because most experts agree that it's important to learn to adjust your style to meet your team's needs. Often, one person may need one style of leadership, while another has a different need. When I run leadership workshops and retreats, I spend a good amount of time helping leaders practice adjusting their style to different people and situations. You can work on this skill on your own by always remembering to ask what you think people's task-structure and human-support needs are and then picking the style that matches those needs, per the grid in Figure 3-2. In the next section, Table 3-2 provides more details about how to use each of the styles well.

B. Do you:

Treat employees with empathy, consideration, and personal support?	*RELATE* *Encourage and* *support*	*COACH* *Improve skills* *through practice*
Expect employees to take care of themselves?	*DELEGATE* *Expect people to* *be competent*	*INSTRUCT* *Explain what* *to do*

A. Do you: | Expect employees to complete an assignment without close supervision? | Give clear, specific, instructions and check performance often? |

Figure 3-2: Answer two questions to see which of the four styles you favor as a leader.

Your leadership style is a really important factor to get a handle on, because you need to know what your default style is — the style you exhibit when you're not really paying attention to leadership style. You also need to know how to use alternative styles and when it's in the best interest of an employee or the entire team for you to switch to a different style.

Effective leadership often comes down to knowing which style to use when. After surveying the styles outlined in the preceding section, you may find that you're instructive by nature. This default style enables you to explain an assignment clearly or to give clear, prompt performance feedback so people know how well they're doing. But you need to recognize that people don't always need instruction. Leadership is more than that. Sometimes, you need to switch styles and lend a considerate, empathetic ear; that's what the Relate style is all about. At other times, the issue may be that someone is more than ready to be trusted with a more challenging assignment, so you need to switch to the Delegate style.

Coaching is a mix of instructing and relating. It's both informational and supportive. When you coach, you put effort into helping the person feel good and try hard. You also put effort into designing the right tasks with a good level of challenge and supervising employees as they learn to master new challenges.

Coaching is a great way to develop your team's capabilities, but it's a lot of work. You have to turn your leadership volume up higher than with the other three styles. So don't feel like you have to coach all the time.

The reward for coaching well is that you eventually develop your team's capabilities to such a high level that you can delegate to the team and turn your leadership volume down even more — but not off, because you still have to stay in regular touch. A good reminder is to tell yourself, "Delegate, but don't abdicate."

Delegating is the ultimate goal of your developmental leadership, but whenever you introduce an innovation and need to get your team members up to speed on it, switch back to coaching until they've gotten the hang of it and you can delegate again.

It's important to get good at the day-to-day leadership of people and their work, because that gives you and your team an edge when it comes to innovating. People work better, and have more energy and enthusiasm for creativity and change, when they have competent leadership. Without it, they worry and feel defensive about their work, and they aren't open to change or willing to innovate. (If you want to take a leadership-style assessment and get more help with being an effective leader, visit www.tspectrum.com and purchase a copy of StratLead Self-Assessment, an inexpensive way to evaluate your leadership style.)

Adapting the classic styles for faster innovation

The classic leadership styles defined in Figure 3-2 — Instruct, Coach, Relate, and Delegate — are based on a model that came out of studies of well-established organizations, such as large factories, where change was gradual and most people weren't actively engaged in innovation. As a result, the standard ways of thinking about leadership style tend to ignore creative and innovative leadership behaviors.

Table 3-2 shows how each of the four classic managerial leadership styles can be expressed as two different sets of leadership behaviors, depending on the orientation you need: conservative and maintenance-oriented or creative and innovation-oriented.

Try this metaphor on for size: Think of the basic leadership styles as ways of gardening. A focus on maintenance is like weeding, watering, and harvesting the garden, whereas a focus on innovation is like planting and developing new plant varieties.

Table 3-2	**Leadership Styles for Maintenance and Innovation Phases**	
Basic Leadership Styles	*Maintenance Focus*	*Innovation Focus*
Instructive/ Directive	Document standard operating procedures. Establish rules and norms. Impose schedules, quality standards, and other measures of efficient performance.	Set challenging goals. Communicate needs and constraints. Provide processes and criteria for improvement. Teach creative thinking and innovation techniques.
Coaching/ Developmental	Mentor and coach to raise competence levels. Offer cross-training opportunities and other chances for professional development. Pair new with experienced people for on-the-job development and training.	Facilitate brainstorming and problem-solving sessions. Create participative suggestion systems. Protect innovators with incubator or skunkworks structures (covered in Chapter 15).
Relational/ Concerned	Support good workers when they're having temporary problems. Listen to concerns, and show that you care. Make a point of getting to know all team members or employees so that you can count on having good communication with them.	Avoid being critical of suggestions, ideas, and questions. Answer questions with questions to stimulate thinking. Encourage creativity by role-modeling right-brain activity and conversation. Seek unique perspectives, and invite each person to share his unique thoughts and diverse experiences, because these are good sources of fresh insight.
Delegational/ Trusting	Review performance less frequently as people learn to be better self-managers. Give employees opportunities to take on new responsibilities and work toward promotions.	Share the responsibility for coming up with new ideas and approaches. Allow people to run with their ideas and see whether they can make them work. Empower project teams to test and develop worthy new ideas.

The most important thing to know about your leadership in terms of its impact is whether you're maintenance- or innovation-oriented. Whether to orient yourself toward running the existing business efficiently (maintenance) or innovating effectively to change it (innovation) is the most fundamental decision you need to make whenever you find yourself in a leadership role.

Putting orientation and style together

As an innovative leader, you'll often be asking your team to come up with or implement creative new ideas, solutions, or designs. Whatever each person's specific duties are, everyone has one assignment in common: Contribute to the effort to innovate! Figure 3-3 is a diagnostic grid that you can use to figure out which style to use and how to use it to keep your team members innovating productively. Answer the two questions outside the four-box grid and then go to the cell where your answers intersect.

Figure 3-3 helps you get both your orientation and your leadership style correct, at least on the macro level (you may need to adjust style for specific people, however). As Figure 3-3 shows, you should delegate as a general style only when your entire team is flexible and eager to take on responsibility or when you're ahead in the innovation game and can be efficiency-oriented for a while. Otherwise, you need to use one of the other three styles and turn up your leadership volume by putting more effort into communicating with and guiding your team.

B. Is your team:

Resistant, inflexible?	*RELATE* *Encourage and support people as they learn the new routines*	*COACH* *Guide people through the development of innovation*
Energized, flexible, resilient?	*DELEGATE* *Allow people to take the ball and run with it as they profit from the innovation*	*INSTRUCT* *Stimulate innovation through hands-on facilitation and clear direction*
A. Is your organization:	Ahead of competitors, innovative?	Challenged by competitors or other external concerns?

Figure 3-3:
Answering the questions helps you adjust your leadership to the creative context.

Developing Your Leadership Skills

Innovation is, by its very nature, taking a leadership role. You can't innovate from the back of the pack. You have to be out in front in your thinking — and your *doing* — to make exciting new things happen. So the pursuit of leadership skills and resources should always be on your personal agenda.

Seeking feedback

The most fundamental difference between great leaders and bad ones is that great leaders seek and welcome feedback. They ask questions like "How am I doing?" and "Is there anything else you need from me to do this project well?" Then they listen to the answer with an open mind and a smile, ask clarifying questions, thank the contributor for her feedback, and *act on it right away*. If you let them, your team members will help you become a better leader.

Working with a mentor

A *mentor* is someone with the experience, skills, and supportive attitude needed to help you figure out how to succeed. When someone offers to mentor you, it should feel like an honor. If nobody asks, you might try asking someone whether he'd be willing to mentor you. What's involved? Meeting every now and then so your mentor can ask you how things are going, offer advice, and ask probing questions to help you figure out what to do next.

Mentors who have invented or implemented major innovations themselves are the best, because they already know the ropes and can give you advice born of real experience. If you aren't familiar with how to work with a mentor or your mentor isn't sure what's involved, you might want to consult an inexpensive booklet and assessment tool I wrote called *Mentoring for Success* (published by Trainer's Spectrum; see www.tspectrum.com/mentoring_success.htm). I highly recommend finding a mentor who has innovation experience and can help you by giving you sage advice and encouragement throughout your career as an innovative leader.

Seeking varied leadership experiences

Mentors are very important to success as an innovator, because they contribute the benefit of their experience. As the old saying goes, however, there's no real substitute for your own experience. If you want to be a successful innovator and an effective leader, make a point of trying a wide range of roles and assignments. Don't typecast yourself.

Even if your technical or professional knowledge is fairly narrow, go ahead and try your hand at leading a professional team or volunteer project outside your specialty. The experience will definitely enhance your innovation and leadership skills. In fact, the experiences that take you far from your comfort zones are always the most meaningful in hindsight. Don't be afraid to try new things! After all, this is exactly the kind of courage you'll need to give your team when you lead the way toward innovation, so you'd better have plenty of creative courage of your own.

Managing the risks of innovation

Innovation entails risk. After all, the majority of new ideas fail to come to fruition. As you push ahead, full of enthusiasm, you may discover that an idea isn't as practical as you first thought, or perhaps someone else is developing a competing approach or design that will prove even better than yours.

So is innovation worth the risk of failure? Actually, yes. If you don't innovate at all, you're bound to fail. Your failure may be gradual, but you can be sure that you'll become increasingly out-of-date, and being out-of-date is what dooms businesses to bankruptcy and people to unemployment.

You run a risk of failure when you do nothing at all. The goal of innovation is to improve over that baseline risk. Without innovation, you'll gradually fall out of style or out-of-date. With innovation, you have an improved chance of staying up-to-date and also a chance of getting ahead of the pack!

As a leader with an innovative vision, you need to be alert to a wide range of risks, and ready to duck and weave to avoid them should they come up in your firm:

✔ **Technological changes can blindside you, so keep an eye on technology.** Assign several people (or more, if you can) the duty of staying up-to-date on major advances in your own industry or field and in any others that might share underlying technologies.

✔ **Financial investments can turn into risky gambles if a development project proves to be costly.** Many good inventions drive their founder out of business before some bigger company with deeper pockets picks them up and makes a success of them. Ouch! Be careful to scale your investments appropriately. It's a mistake to risk so much on a new product that failure could drive you out of business. If you can, scale the initial launch down to a level of risk you can manage; if not, find a bigger partner to help.

✔ **Protect your ideas as much as is practical.** The longer you can keep others from imitating your invention, the more profitable it will prove to be. (See Chapter 17 for how-to advice.)

✔ **Manage your business tightly and well.** Your ability to weather the risks of the innovation phase of your business strategy is determined in large part by the strength of the last efficiency phase, where you had the chance to profit from a stable business for a while. During this profitable period, you need to save up reserves for when you'll need them in the next major innovation effort.

Knowing that you'll need to reinvent your business formula gives you the foresight to build your own war chest of useful assets — including financial savings, valuable assets such as buildings that can be resold, expensive equipment needed in R&D (that's business-speak for *research and development*), savvy staff trained in new technologies, and helpful business relationships with other leading innovators — to get you through a major change.

Projecting a Positive Attitude

If you started at the beginning of this chapter and are feeling a little intimidated by all the talk of leadership skills and actions, take heart. There's one thing you can do that I guarantee will make up for a lot of errors or missteps in every other aspect of your leadership. Leaders who maintain a strongly optimistic and positive frame of mind are able to build and maintain innovative momentum, even when things go wrong. It turns out that a realistic optimist is far better at stimulating creative behavior or at leading a team through a tough implementation than any other kind of leader!

There's a lot of research supporting the importance of optimism at work. It's actually one of the few things that most experts agree on. Optimists are more creative and innovative, more motivated, and more satisfied with their work. They also live longer, healthier, happier, and more successful lives. Entrepreneurs need to be reasonably optimistic to succeed.

Keep in mind, however, that optimism can be taken too far. At its extreme, optimism can produce overconfidence and a lack of realism. Your goal should be to be realistically optimistic, with a positive, can-do attitude but also willingness to admit that a strategy isn't working and to change directions if need be!

Expressing both hopefulness and optimism

Before I get into the specifics of how to add optimism to your leadership approach, I need to mention that researchers sometimes distinguish between hopefulness and optimism. Why? Well, *hopefulness* is indicated by a generally positive attitude about the future. If you believe that you'll somehow come up with creative solutions to any major problems that get in your way, that's termed hopefulness. It's good — just as good as optimism, which has a more specific definition.

Optimism is defined as taking personal ownership of good events ("My leadership helped the team find a new way to market our products," for example). It goes along with the opposite approach to bad events. Instead of taking the blame for them, optimists tend to say things like "Our first two attempts to bring our products into new markets failed because luck just wasn't with us and our timing was off."

Probably the literal truth is somewhere in the middle: You deserve some of the credit for a good event and some of the blame for a bad event. But if you emphasize blaming yourself for bad things and avoid taking any credit for good things, you'll be debilitated by the belief that you aren't likely to succeed. You can improve your self-talk by focusing on evidence from past experiences that encourages you to try again. When you make a habit of talking in positive ways about the past, you not only convince yourself that you can make good things happen in the future, but also convince your team members that they can be successful innovators.

Being pragmatically creative

It's important to aim for a positive attitude that supports innovation, so you may want to think about what that means for you. A pragmatic approach to optimism may be your best bet. Don't just say, "Oh, it's okay; we don't have to do anything; things will get better on their own." That's an unrealistically optimistic view and goes along with feelings of personal lack or responsibility and even helplessness. A pragmatic optimist says, "Things don't look so good right now, but I'll bet we can figure out a good way to deal with this problem and even find some hidden opportunities in it."

Going for that positive ripple effect

When you're in a positive (optimistic and hopeful) frame of mind, you tend to spread that positive attitude to others. It spreads quite naturally, both through what you say and through the way you act. Positive statements indicate that you're

✔ Hopeful about finding solutions to problems

✔ Enthusiastic about the possibility of discovering, creating, or inventing something new

✔ Open to ideas and options and interested in learning something new

Positive people express their optimism through their body language. They have

✔ A buoyant stride and energetic movements

✔ An open, relaxed posture

✔ An interested facial expression when others are making suggestions

If you find it hard to sound and act like an irrepressible optimist, you may need to revitalize your own attitude before you go around sharing it with others. It's a happy fact of leadership that you have an obligation to be in a positive, energetic frame of mind.

Take the time to figure out what rituals and lifestyle changes you need to make to come to work each day full of optimism and energy so that you can naturally role-model and spark that kind of energy for your whole team. Adopt an exercise regime during lunch hour, for example, if it gives you positive energy.

On days when optimism just isn't there, and you feel down, stay away from your team if at all possible. Go out and recharge yourself before you interact with your team members so as not to contaminate their attitudes. The leader's attitude spreads more powerfully and rapidly than anyone else's, so take advantage of the leverage your attitude has over other people — and please don't make the all-too-common mistake of amplifying your bad mood by sharing it at work!

Putting All Your Leadership Skills Together

Figure 3-4 uses the metaphor of a house to show what it looks like when you put your leadership house in order. It begins with the foundation, which is your attitude — the positive, hopeful feelings that you spread to give your team the energy and enthusiasm it needs to persist in the pursuit of a successful innovation (see question A in Figure 3-4).

The interior of the house, where you and your team dwell every workday, is defined by the support and structure you provide as a leader who understands the effective use of the Instruct, Coach, Relate, and Delegate styles (see question B in Figure 3-4).

The roof, which provides an overarching purpose and direction to your team's work, is sustained by the vision of the future you articulate as an innovative leader (see question C in Figure 3-4). Notice that I've divided the roof into three possibilities to reflect three main options for your leadership vision. You may choose to

✔ **Discover** the next big innovation (appropriate to the innovation phase of your business's strategic cycle).

✔ **Focus** on implementing it efficiently (appropriate to the efficiency phase of your business's cycle).

✔ **Problem-solve** if something comes up to interrupt one of the preceding (appropriate when a major new threat arises and you have to change direction to cope with it).

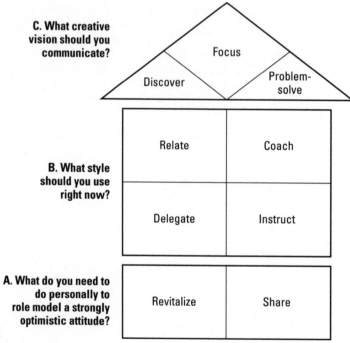

Figure 3-4: Inhabit your leadership house.

That's pretty much it. Innovative leadership can be summed up with this simple diagram. It means that you need to integrate three levels of leadership. On the fundamental, emotional level, you need to keep your team energized with a positive, optimistic attitude. On the practical level of daily work, you need to provide clear instructions, along with the right level of support to keep people feeling challenged and interested in their work. Finally, on the highest level, you need to periodically remind everyone of why you're all working so hard — because of the excitement of trying to grow larger, do better, or overcome some major obstacle and achieve your vision of a better future.

Chapter 4

Innovating in Sales and Marketing

In This Chapter
▶ Gaining competitive advantage by breaking unwritten rules
▶ Taking steps to ensure creativity throughout the marketing process
▶ Finding creative advantage in all five main marketing areas

reativity in marketing means wild or crazy advertising to most people. That's not really what I have in mind in this chapter, although sometimes a creative ad, Web page, or sales presentation is just what you need to grab attention and close a tough sale. But really, there are many more fundamental and important places where you need to innovate as a salesperson or marketer. Creativity often matters most and makes the most impact in ways that are subtle or even invisible to the average customer.

This chapter helps you find ways to innovate in sales and marketing so as to gain share and make history in your market. You start your break from the pack by finding creative ways to violate the norms of your industry and market. The chapter also helps you develop a creative approach to sales and marketing by working on a creative brief and identifying your creative advantage.

Making an Inconspicuous but Powerful Impact

Creative marketing is virtually impossible to spot unless you're a real expert, but it has more impact than any other kind of marketing does. A creative strategy might be as simple as deciding to focus on a different type of product from your more traditional competitors.

Your marketing strategy can get creative in the way that it talks about benefits — the things that the product does for or gives to the user. If most of your competitors design products and write ads with one benefit in mind, you can try to redefine the market by focusing on another benefit. Quality may trump style, for example. Or maybe you'll choose to emphasize reliability over speed or cost over service.

Consider the example of Under Armour, now a successful marketer of athletic apparel, but just a few years ago, the company was seeking U.S. Small Business Association funding and struggling to launch a new business. Its concept was to make a tight-fitting, moisture-wicking T-shirt for high-performance sports. The product strategy was innovative because leading sports-apparel companies focused on the outerwear, not the underwear.

Under Armour sells mostly on the basis of performance. Its clothing really does wick sweat away and helps you stay cool, thereby helping you perform better. Major sports-apparel brands like Nike, Adidas, and Puma compete as much on the basis of fashion as performance. In fact, 90 percent of sports apparel is sold to people who don't wear it for its intended use and therefore are buying it for fashion reasons. So Under Armour's approach is radical in the sense that it goes back to the roots of its industry by selling clothing to people who are looking to perform better, not just to look fashionable.

Because it had a performance edge, Under Armour was able to price relatively high and avoid deep discounting. As competitors rushed to offer similar products, Under Armour faced more price competition, but it responded by continuing to innovate. Right now, the company is marketing a new line of mouth guards that prevent jaw clenching and therefore save energy for athletic performance. Offering something that customers can slip into their mouths that will actually make them stronger is a creative idea. Under Armour is an upstart, but so far, its continuing innovation has helped it gain share from giant rivals. It will be interesting to see whether it can continue to be a market innovator — and continue to outsmart the Goliaths that compete against it.

Assessing (And Violating) the Norms

Many innovations take place in, or need to be communicated through, the sales and marketing functions. In fact, marketing is driven by innovation. You have to refresh your advertising, Web strategy, and product offerings continually, or you'll soon be left behind by more innovative competitors. This chapter shows you how to *effectively* innovate your approach to sales and marketing to boost visibility and impact for your campaign.

Finding abnormal ways to accomplish your goals

Marketing arose, in point of fact, as a creative way to avoid having to make personal sales calls to sell something. It costs less to sell something by mail or on the Web than in person. You may be able to continue this trend by finding new ways to cut the costs of sales and marketing activities without hurting the results! Are sales calls the norm now in your industry? If so, can you find a way to eliminate them? You might decide to combine a richly informative Web site with excellent tech support via e-mail and phone, plus a library of short streaming videos on your site or on YouTube (www.youtube.com) to take the place of traditional face-to-face sales and support.

Alternatively, if there's no personal selling in your industry right now, you could be the first to reach out and shake your prospects' and customers' hands. The point is to do something different. Innovators attract attention in marketing. Copycats don't.

Communicating in a different way

A great way to violate the norms is to advertise in a medium that none of your competitors uses. Radio has been abandoned by many marketers, so maybe you could do a fun retro radio ad with old-fashioned sound effects and a campy voice-over. Or how about being the first in your industry to pull out of the traditional (and probably expensive) trade shows and sell business to business (B2B) exclusively over the Web? Maybe you can do something simpler, like making a how-to video that you give away for free on YouTube. The point is, if you communicate in a novel way, your message is more likely to stand out from all the rest.

Violating social norms on purpose

Sometimes, the norms you face aren't business norms (like how to distribute or advertise); rather, they're more fundamental norms. Social norms are the rules within a society about how to conduct yourself. They dictate, among other things, these rules for display of emotions:

- ✔ Which emotions are considered good and bad
- ✔ How you're supposed to feel in a particular situation
- ✔ How you should act when you experience a certain emotion

Think about the power of those unwritten emotional rules. If you display anger in a public setting in Japan, you'll be frowned upon and probably won't close your deal. If you don't get angry when your sports team loses in the United States, people will think you don't care. Different emotional rules apply in different cultural settings. Now, what happens when you intentionally build a violation of an emotional rule into, say, a TV ad or a *Candid Camera*–style YouTube video?

Whenever you violate an unwritten rule about appropriate emotional expressions, you attract a lot of attention. A whole lot. Somebody having a meltdown in the middle of the mall will be noticed by every single person in that mall. So if you want to create an attention-grabbing ad, consider a script or story line involving someone who violates an emotional rule — someone who's too angry, happy, or even depressed. Drug companies have learned that if they run TV ads showing people who look really, really sad, they get a lot of viewers and strong recall of the ads, which works great for depression medications. But if you want to sell something to happy people, show someone over-the-top happy — irrationally, inappropriately happy. Violating the social norm guarantees memorability.

Avoiding the cost of a sales call

If you rely at least partially on a sales force or sales representatives, you're giving away between 10 percent and 20 percent of each sale to pay for people to wear out shoe leather on your behalf. Salespeople are key to making complex sales when their expertise is used to select the right items or design the right service program. In many cases, however, you can create a Web site that explains the options and presents the choices to customers more clearly than all but the best of your salespeople can do. It's hard on salespeople but easy on your budget to reduce the use of sales calls and substitute an expert-system Web site instead.

In addition to providing information and advice, salespeople remind customers to place orders. Showing up with samples and order forms is a good way to get the attention of a store buyer or a purchasing agent at a company. But you can often substitute a mix of e-mail links to new Web catalogs, traditional mailings of catalogs and sales fliers, telephone calls, and other arm's-length communications.

A good rule of thumb is to substitute three or more arm's-length communications for one sales call to have equal impact. If sales aren't sufficient, add two or three more arm's-length contacts. A regular B2B customer may need to be reached by e-mail, mail, or phone once every week or two throughout the year.

Committing to a Creative Approach

It's easy to keep doing pretty much what you've done in the past. Even when you print a new catalog or run a new ad campaign, it may in truth be very similar to the last one. Are you truly innovating?

Researchers find that successful innovators do one thing more than other people do: *They decide to be creative.* The decision to seek a creative approach is the first and most vital step in innovation. So please repeat after me: "We *will* be innovative in our approach to marketing." Good! Now start looking for your next creative breakthrough.

To inspire you, Figure 4-1 is an interesting example of a creative sales and marketing approach. You can see what appears at first glance to be a large billboard or maybe a mural. Actually, it's a reverse mural, made by cleaning the grime off the cement wall of an underpass. The unusual ad was created with the product it advertises: Green Works, a natural but (obviously) powerful cleaner made by The Clorox Co.

Figure 4-1:
A mural made with the cleaner it advertises.

A creative ad campaign is just one of the ways you can innovate in sales and marketing. Many of the most successful innovations involve the product itself.

What do you do with your patio furniture when you're not using it? The furniture company JANUS et Cie created the Obelisk, a modernist sculptural thingy that sits elegantly in a corner, looking like an alien might hatch out of it. Rather than an alien, it hatches fancy outdoor armchairs and a table. The design is a combination of sculpture and furniture. (Chapter 11 explores the power of creative combinations; check it out to come up with clever designs of your own!)

You probably haven't seen the Obelisk on a friend's deck or patio because it's quite expensive, but if the concept is good, other furniture makers will probably create knockoffs by using less expensive materials and variations on the original form. (See Chapter 10 for details on how to safely modify innovative concepts and introduce them in versions of your own.)

Writing your creative brief

A *creative brief* is a written description of the target customer and the desired behavior you want to stimulate in that customer, as well as any background information and concepts or ideas that might help the creative department of an ad agency come up with something that will do the trick.

The creative brief was developed to help give informational support, creative insight, and strategic context to the writers of ad copy, but it can be applied more broadly than that. You can also use it to help focus the creative design efforts of product developers, packagers, and other members of the marketing team or to help your sales representatives design a winning trade-show booth. It's also very helpful as a starting point for Web-page design, product-demo videos, and really almost anything else you may do in marketing.

The creative brief helps give focus and momentum to the creative process. Keep it brief enough to review easily during writing or design (three to ten pages). Here are the components of a good general format that you can use when writing one:

1. **The strategic playing field:** Describe your current position in the market, major competitors, trends, and opportunities. Use a *SWOT* analysis (that's *strengths, weaknesses, opportunities,* and *threats* in the market), and show a *perceptual map* (a graph laying competitors out on two major dimensions of customer attitude, such as economical versus expensive or rugged versus stylish). Then summarize the strategic situation. You might say, "Upscale homeowners are looking for innovations in patio and deck furnishings, but the market is surprisingly traditional, which gives us an opportunity to innovate."

2. **Your target customer's profile:** Describe the users of your product as specifically as possible, including not only who they are, but also how they think and feel about the product when buying and using it. Include a profile of a target customer and even a photo, if you can find an appropriate one. You might show a well-dressed, successful-looking middle-aged couple standing on a large deck behind a gorgeous suburban house.

3. **Your goal:** Describe what you want your creative work to accomplish in customer behavior (such as what they will buy, when, and how). Your goal might be "Convince condo owners with small decks that they need compact sculptural stacks of deck furniture."

4. **Your message:** Very simply, in a single sentence, state what you want to communicate to target customers (see Step 2) to get them to buy (see Step 3). Your message might be "Clean, handy, and elegantly stored in plain sight — all the furniture needed to stage a deck party or watch the sunset with your special someone."

5. **Creative input:** This includes any interesting tidbits of information or suggestions that might help the creative process, such as quotes from prospective customers or fun facts, and several starting ideas that might lead to even better ones with some work. You might include pictures of NASA-designed compact seats and engineering specifications on the durability of high-tensile molded plastic furniture in outdoor settings.

6. **Schedule and constraints:** What's needed, and when do you need it? Here's where you summarize the business side of the project and identify specific outputs (such as a brochure for retailers to use, a point-of-purchase display, an educational video, or a Web-page design). Also identify any constraints, such as budget limitations, that need to be considered when evaluating creative ideas. You might mention that market research established a limit to what your target customer is willing to pay for porch and patio furniture.

Your creative brief helps stimulate creative thinking and also channels it toward a specific business goal. In other words, it ensures productive innovation in marketing. (For help deciding who should work on the project and how to get your team to generate good ideas, see Chapter 6.)

Coming up with the first round of creative ideas

It's never too soon to use your imagination! As you work on a creative brief (refer to the preceding section) or just generally think about how to innovate in marketing, try to generate some ideas. Good or bad, they're all helpful because one idea always leads to another.

Consult the chapters in Part II for help in coming up with creative ideas, or just start jotting down your ideas now. Remember that when you violate a marketing or general social norm (on purpose), you often come up with something that has impact and stimulates interest.

Following is a warm-up exercise that involves generating a creative starting point for a new ad campaign. It will get your imagination working so that you can turn to your own business next.

In the United States, most automobile advertising is done by two very different types of businesses: major international auto manufacturers and local auto dealerships. Creative — and expensive — brand-building ads come from the manufacturers. Campy, unprofessional ads lacking creativity come from the dealerships, which always focus on getting warm bodies into their showrooms. Switch things up by trying to generate creative and fun (but not overly expensive) ads for local dealerships. By changing the style, you may be able to attract attention to the local dealership and break it out of the pack.

If you come up empty-handed at first (that is, you have no creative ideas for local-auto-dealership advertising), try working from a visual stimulus. Sometimes, that's a big help. Take a look at the fanciful photographic composition in Figure 4-2, and see whether you can write an appropriate caption for it. (The caption can be humorous, if you like.)

Figure 4-2:
Write a caption to make this image into an ad for a car dealership.

Using a visual image to stimulate your imagination is a good general technique for marketing and advertising, and you can easily adapt it to any creative campaign. Just select several interesting images that initially don't seem to be directly relevant to your product or purpose; then force yourself to write explanations or captions that make the images relevant. Your imagination will bridge the gap, and in the process, you may get a good creative idea that you can develop more fully later.

What did you come up with for Figure 4-2? Did you write a good caption to relate the image to a local auto dealership so that it could be used in the dealership's advertising? Good work! Here are a few ideas I came up with:

- Landing soon at a dealership near you . . .
- NASA reports the arrival of indisputable proof that there is advanced intelligence on other planets . . .
- The car of your dreams . . .

Each idea could be combined with the image in Figure 4-2 to create a print ad in a local newspaper. Or you could take one idea as a starting point for a creative process and build a full campaign around it. You could design a "Car of Your Dreams" campaign in which television spot ads, radio ads, and a longer YouTube video explore variations on the theme of how customers dream about their new cars — and, of course, how the local dealership makes those dreams come to life! To reinforce the message, the dealership could give out luxurious down pillows along with the new cars.

The overall title of the campaign could be "Coming soon to a dream near you!" Of course, dreams aren't "near" you the way that movie theaters (the originators of that phrase) are; they're *in* you. But in bending the old saying by substituting dreams for movies, you remind people that a local event is happening — the car of their dreams is appearing — and that they can come into the showroom to see it. The creative concept for this ad campaign fits the goals of an auto dealership's advertising, and it's also clever and different enough to attract curiosity and attention.

Narrowing Your Focus to Find Sources of Creative Advantage

It's a lot easier to generate useful, creative ideas when you have a narrow, specific focus. In marketing, a great way to drill down to specific areas is to work within the *Five Ps* framework:

- **Product:** Innovate to offer a better product through design, technology, packaging, or other product-related innovations. If you can't afford to invent the next hot product, be on the lookout for it, and become a reseller or licenser as soon as it appears — or, even better, try to think of new applications for your existing product that customers might find appealing.
- **Pricing:** Find ways to drive your costs down and offer a lower price, or explore creative ways to take some of the sting out of buying, such as by offering loyalty programs, layaway, innovative warranties, or other price-based incentives.

✔ **Placement:** Distribute your product in helpful new ways (via the Internet, for example), and make it easier for people to get what they want when they want it. Consider placing your product in stores or catalogs where it hasn't traditionally been sold. Distribution is the easiest way to score a creative home run.

✔ **Promotion:** Find clever, attention-grabbing ways to communicate with potential buyers and build the luster of your brand. Use unusual media or message formats. If everyone else is running serious ads, hire a comedian as your spokesperson, but if competitors try to entertain, switch it up with hard-hitting factual ads or exposés showing what's wrong with their products.

✔ **People:** Engage free help through social networking by getting people talking about your brand, or create a fresh sales and service model to make your company stand out. You may even decide to buck the trend and be the only company in your market that offers easily accessible sales and service people to help customers.

By making the rounds of the Five Ps, you make sure that you've considered a wide range of options for creative marketing. Don't let your marketing program stand still! You need forward momentum to make a business or brand a success, and creativity provides the energy for building that vital momentum.

Figure 4-3 shows the way that creativity works to surprise and please customers with unexpected benefits.

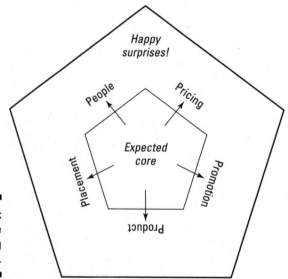

Figure 4-3:
The creative marketing pentagon.

Your core offering is (I hope!) roughly on par with all your competitors' offerings and is what's expected of you. You have a good product that you distribute, promote, price, and support in much the way that others do. You're in the game. Good! But that's not good enough; doing what's expected may keep you in the game but will never win it. To gain share and boost profits, you have to do something new, something that's a happy surprise for your customers — or maybe for your *competitors'* customers, who will defect and come over to your side!

Chapter 5

Being an Innovative Strategist

In This Chapter

▶ Imagining bold new strategies for your business

▶ Alternating between focusing on efficiency and innovation

▶ Selecting and investing in a portfolio of winning products

▶ Building strategic partnerships to expand the scope of your success

▶ Guiding people through the changes innovation requires

*A*strategist is someone who thinks strategically, and in business, that usually means doing some strategic planning. A *strategic plan* (yes, I do need to get my terms clear) is an intelligent, high-level description of how you intend for your business to do better in the future.

Typically, strategic plans set the stage with broad-brush approaches that reach out several years into the future. Then *business plans* clarify exactly how this year's operations will be budgeted and run so as to move in the intended strategic direction. That said, I can simplify what it means to be a strategist by saying that a strategist looks ahead and thinks about how to win big in the future. Usually, seeing a big win in the future requires some strategic vision, which arises from a combination of your knowledge and your creativity.

Winning strategies don't just fall in your lap. They require thoughtful analysis of the current situation, including your strengths and weaknesses and an analysis of your competitors, industry, technologies, and trends in your marketplace. As a strategist, you start by getting to know the playing field really well.

Next, you cast about for big-picture ideas that can lead to success in the future. Where do those ideas for future success come from? Sometimes, purely from your imagination; at other times, from observing a successful strategy in another industry and adapting it to yours. Sometimes, success comes from forming a partnership (or *strategic alliance)* with the right company so as to be able to do something exciting and new that neither company could do before.

There are lots of ways to make a splash as an innovative strategist. This chapter shows you how to leverage your strategic thinking into future success.

Thinking Big by Planning to Re-create Your Business

Some strategists don't take an innovative approach. They tend to project the future from what happened in the past. That's boring unless you happen to be the undisputed leader in a monopolistic, protected market. I don't think you can make that claim, so in this chapter, I assume that you need to innovate to achieve a significant jump in performance and success.

The basic strategic question you should ask, whether you own the business or just work in it, is "What's the best way to transform this business into something new, exciting, and better?" Think about how you can re-create the business, not just run it or work in it. The change in perspective that this question creates is powerful and often leads to helpful strategic insights.

Shifting from more of the same to creative planning

Do you do budgeting and planning? Most organizations do. However, the plans are usually based on last year, with minor modifications made to reflect obvious changes. That's not the way to come up with a breakthrough. Before you plan, stop to imagine ways to innovate in your basic approach, such as these:

- Expanding into new geographic areas
- Pursuing new types of customers
- Improving or adding to your product line
- Introducing a new technology or invention
- Partnering with one or more other organizations to do something you can't do by yourself
- Dramatically reducing your costs or turnaround times by innovating how you source or produce your products or services
- Distributing in new ways to save money, increase market coverage, or provide greater ease and availability of purchase
- Updating or replacing your brand name with something more dynamic

Without strategies such as these, your organization won't grow significantly, and it probably will start to atrophy as things degenerate into a lifeless routine and the business slowly becomes out-of-date.

Including a mix of traditional and creative elements in your planning

Most organizations write a budget every year, and many of them also write up a business plan specifying who's going to work on what. Major lines of business get their own sections, with a situation analysis (including strengths, weaknesses, threats, and opportunities) and plans about what to do next.

People who do a lot of planning do so because they like to work from plans. They're logical, careful people, and their plans make them feel more confident and provide the reassurance of a logical, well-organized approach. But keep in mind that the world isn't all that predictable, and successful innovations certainly aren't. So planning needs to include some creative elements along with the traditional organized and logical parts.

Include some brainstorming about possible future strategies and ideas. Take time to look at what the newest upstarts are doing, not only in your own industry, but also in other industries. Scan the advances in technology to see whether new materials, equipment, or processes may be coming into your industry soon.

When should you do your creative research and thinking? Early in your planning process. As early as possible. Otherwise, you'll get caught in the details of updating last year's budget and won't consider big-picture possibilities and fresh new ideas.

I recommend bringing a diverse group of between 7 and 14 people together for a half day or more of brainstorming about your business and its future strategy. Call it *blue-sky brainstorming,* or better yet, *blue-water.* Blue-water strategy is based on the idea that most businesses and brands compete head-to-head in crowded strategic waters that are red from the blood of their struggles against one another. However, research shows that the most successful businesses avoid direct competition and pick an unusual strategy that moves them out into a relatively competition-free area of so-called blue water. They innovate rather than imitate. Their success is determined by their degree of uniqueness. (A 2005 article in *Harvard Business Review* by W. Kim and R. Mauborgne explored this concept, using the term *blue ocean strategy* to describe it, and I recommend it as good background reading.)

The proven advantage of blue-water strategies is the reason you need to include plenty of creative thinking in your planning. If you don't, you're guaranteed to continue doing the predictable, and you'll face growing competition as the pack does the same. I'd much rather be the first company to have introduced a good memory-foam mattress, for example, than one of the remaining companies fighting to sell traditional mattresses. Wouldn't you?

Ensuring a Healthy Strategic Cycle

Businesses, and in fact all organizations, ought to cycle between two distinct strategic phases:

- **Efficient production phase:** You scale up and get good at doing the same thing consistently.

- **Creative searching phase:** You experiment and search for the next big thing to scale up.

Figure 5-1 shows how this innovation cycle works and is helpful in understanding where success comes from. Assuming that you're in a for-profit business, your main measure of success is profits. That's the solid line that curves across the top part of the figure. What drives profits? The most important determinant of profits in the long run is having something fresh and appealing to sell to your customers. That requires innovation. This is why the strategic phase has to shift from efficient product to creative searching *before* you max out the old innovations and start losing money. The dotted line in Figure 5-1 shows how you need to shift your attention (as an executive or planner and also throughout the organization).

At any one point in time, most of the organization should be doing just one of three things: producing efficiently, searching for the next big innovation, or transitioning quickly between these two phases.

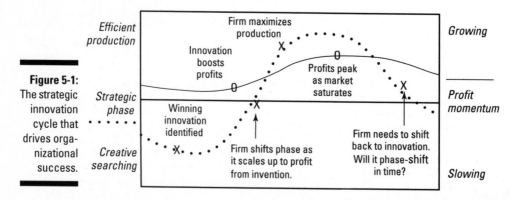

Figure 5-1: The strategic innovation cycle that drives organizational success.

Phase-shifting in strategic time

There's a big difference between efficient production and creative searching. Behaviors and attitudes are just about opposites. That's why the transitions between these phases are important. You need to recognize when the time has come to start seeking the next big strategic move and get creative. That's a strategic decision. It involves recognizing that you need to innovate and then committing time, energy, and perhaps people and money to the quest.

How do you shift from efficient production to creativity? You have to look up and around for fresh ideas and opportunities, and you have to look within for imaginative ideas. If you run a small business, much of the responsibility for expanding your imaginative horizons falls on your shoulders. If you have a larger group, responsibility can be shared more easily. Here are three good ways to get an entire group or organization to shift between strategic phases:

✔ **Use a strategic planning session to signal the beginning of a creative searching phase and take a needed break from nose-to-the-grindstone production.** Invite as many people into your planning discussions as you can. Run brainstorming sessions (see Chapter 6), which are open-minded and free in their form and style compared with normal staff meetings.

✔ **Use a suggestion box or e-mail a request for ideas.** Solicit ideas about anything and everything. Open the conversation with your staff by posing big-picture questions like "What do we want to be when we grow up?" to get people thinking creatively about the future.

✔ **Use yourself as an example, if you're the leader, to show people what's expected of them: efficient production or creative searching for new strategies.** Be clear on which one should be the priority so you can role-model the appropriate behavior. When necessary, transition as promptly and decisively as you can so it's obvious to all watching you that the phase has shifted again.

Influencing strategy from the bottom up

What if you're not in charge of the organization? Can you still help make sure that you're in the right strategic phase? Maybe. Start by talking with your managers about strategic phases and the need for periodic new directions. Ask whether your leadership is open to the idea and wants help coming up with new strategies. If so, ask for some time and permission to brainstorm freely with a small group about what new directions the organization could take.

If you volunteer to do some good strategic imagining and then report your findings to management, you may find that your initiative and vision end up driving future strategy. You don't have to be in charge to lead. You just have to have creative vision!

Investing in a Family of Innovations

A *portfolio* is a carefully selected group of assets you hold on to because you hope that they (or at least some of them) will benefit you in the future. You can have a portfolio of stocks and bonds in your investment account. With wise selection and appropriate diversity, the portfolio will grow in value and enrich you in the future. You can and should have a portfolio of products you sell (see the section "Managing Your Product Portfolio," later in the chapter, for details). But first of all, you need a portfolio of innovative ideas and projects, from which will spring tomorrow's winning products, processes, strategies, and so forth.

Your business needs a portfolio of innovations to enrich it in the future. Why? Sadly, you can't be certain of the future success of any idea or invention. Innovations have a risk of failure and a chance of success. They also have a life span. What was new and hot (and profitable) a few years ago is not today. A portfolio of innovations ensures a regular flow of new ones, some of which are going to be successful.

Figure 5-2 shows how the proportions of new products, projects, or other innovations usually fall out, assuming that you're right about the success of any innovation only half the time (it's like flipping a coin). At any one time, you've got a batch of new ideas and projects you're developing, shown in the figure as the first third of the pie.

If you assume that half of all innovations succeed, a third of the pie chart in Figure 5-2 represents your new crop of innovations, and a third represents the successful and profitable ones from your last crop. The final third is made up of the unsuccessful ones from previous rounds of innovation. It's not always obvious that they're failures, so they tend to linger in the budget and in your lineup for a while, parasitically slurping up a third of your resources. Keep reading to find out how to avoid this mistake.

Being tough on underperforming projects and products

One of the key insights of strategists is that resources are limited and should be shifted promptly to where a winning strategy is emerging. When you're first working on a new project (a new product, brand, market, or whatever), you need to be open-minded and give it a chance to succeed. But when it begins to look like the project won't cut it . . . cut it! Eliminate unpromising projects and products to make room for fresh ones with more promise.

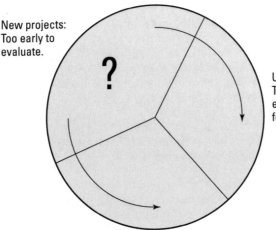

New projects:
Too early to
evaluate.

?

Unpromising projects:
Time to apply a critical
eye and pull the plug
for many of them.

Figure 5-2:
A pie chart
representing
your port-
folio of
innovations.

Successful projects:
Positive evaluation.

If you doubt your ability to imagine new options and invent or acquire new products, you may feel overly committed to the old ones. It's a sad truth of corporate strategy that management teams almost always hold on to under-performing business units, products, or projects for too long. They don't want to admit defeat, so they keep trying to turn the failure around. To avoid the trap of overcommitment to an unsuccessful project, strategy, or product, keep in mind that *it's easier to achieve success by starting fresh than by staying on board a sinking ship.* Or maybe a sports analogy is more useful. Imagine that your business strategy is like a season, and each project is just one game in that season. If you lose a game, you move on and try to win the next game. Don't insist on staying out there on the playing field long after the sun has already set, trying to win that one game you've already lost. Move on!

Making your next strategic move

It's important to pursue some exciting strategy that holds the promise of a rosy future. You can't rest on your laurels. That's another fundamental rule of strategic planning, but one that most people forget as soon as they achieve some success.

Companies don't stay on top forever. Dozens of supposedly top companies have fallen from grace over the past few years. What matters is not your reputation or current size, but your recent strategic moves. If your last big move was, for example, to make short-term profits by selling overly risky home mortgages, you're heading for disaster, as many lenders have learned in the past few years. But if you made a good strategic move, you're headed for success.

Banks that decided to grow rapidly by signing poor-quality, risky home mortgages, for example, didn't have a good strategy, but those that focused on lending to qualified borrowers proved to have more lasting success. A strategy based on a greedy appetite for easy sales that seem too good to be true is not going to be successful in the long run. Strategies based on real points of difference that give you some kind of advantage in the eyes of good customers are more likely to succeed.

What makes for a successful strategic move? For starters, it has to be big enough to make a difference in your overall performance. A little idea may not be enough; you have to think fairly big.

Also, a strategic move has to be creative to be successful. You need to do something that shifts the market. The term I like to use for innovative strategies is *reframing*, which means changing the way people think about and see something. A strong strategic move reframes the way customers, competitors, and industry expert commentators think and talk about your industry. The right strategic move has to be innovative enough to make your top competitors seem out-of-date. This needs to be your goal when you initiate a strategic planning process. Otherwise, there's really no point.

The third quality a strategic move needs is to be embraced by customers, who see it as offering them something substantially helpful or valuable. Otherwise, it won't be a lasting strategy. Lots of companies have used the strategy of reducing the contents of a package as a way to save money. A big package holds a small candy bar, for example. This strategy fools people for a little while, but eventually, you lose out to competitors who are less stingy than you. (See "Including customer value in your strategy," coming up in this chapter, for details.)

Deciding how big a strategy to pursue

A corporate strategy says what business you want to be in. A business strategy says how you want to run a particular business. A marketing strategy says how you will build the strength of a brand and boost its sales. The strategy of a project team within the marketing area might focus on developing a new, more compact version of the best-selling product. These strategies are nested, like a set of traditional Russian dolls. The more specific, narrow strategies fit into the broader corporate strategy.

Which level should you focus on right now? It depends on how well things are going. If you're getting great results down at the operating level and have one or more best-selling products that clearly have good momentum, focus on refining your already-winning lower-level strategies. But if things aren't as rosy as you'd like, move up from specific to more general, sweeping strategic questions until you find a way to turn your performance around. The worst-case scenario is that you have to go all the way to the biggest question of all — what business should we be in? — and change your fundamental strategic focus before you can capture the success you want. When that happens, you need a lengthy stay in the creative search phase of the strategic cycle (refer to Figure 5-1).

Including customer value in your strategy

It's not easy to guarantee what strategies will work for you, but it's pretty easy to tell you which ones won't. Basically, any and all ideas that don't add value from the customer's perspective are going to fail — at least in the long term. Find a way to make your customers' lives easier, save them money, amaze or entertain them, and so forth. Do something they like, something they tell other customers about because it's so great.

Mattress wars give sleepers what they want

A dozen or so years ago, investment bankers bought up the two leading mattress manufacturers in the United States: Simmons and Sealy. Being finance guys, the new owners set to work looking for innovations that would improve their profits. The big breakthrough came with the introduction of one-sided mattresses; the top is finished with soft quilted material for sleeping on, but the underside is bare. Traditionally, mattresses had two finished sides so that you could turn them periodically, ensuring the mattress a decades-long life. A single-sided mattress can't be flipped and tends to wear out much more quickly, but still, the strategists at Simmons and Sealy thought they were on to something. It costs so much less to make a one-sided mattress that they were able to lower their prices by a modest amount and still make a much bigger profit per sale.

The problem was that consumers weren't as impressed by the one-sided mattress as the accountants were. Simmons and Sealy began to lose market share to rivals. Furthermore, the excessively financial focus at these companies kept them from doing any real innovation in the product category. Upstarts like Tempur-Pedic pioneered memory foam as a mattress material, while Sealy and Simmons slowly sank. In recent surveys of the owners of various brands, about 60 percent of Simmons and Sealy owners rated their mattresses as comfortable. Compare this figure with 80 percent–plus ratings for top memory-foam brands like Tempur-Pedic and Spa Sensations, and the top rating of all, 87 percent, for another innovation: the airbed by Comfortaire (survey stats from Sleep Like the Dead, www.sleeplikethedead.com).

Memory-foam, latex-foam, and even some air mattresses can be more comfortable than innerspring mattresses such as those that Sealy and Simmons traditionally made. Why didn't these two market leaders invent these new, more comfortable options? They were overconfident and too focused on making a quick buck by reducing the cost — and value — of what they sold instead of trying to make their products better. So I come to the most fundamental rule of creative strategy: Try to make things better for your customers! That's what Tempur-Pedic was thinking about — and why it became an industry leader in a few exciting and highly profitable years.

Managing Your Product Portfolio

Most businesses succeed or fail on the strength of their products. To select and maintain a winning group of products, you need to recognize that all products have lives, rather like animals do. I guess you could think of them as your pets — except they ought to be hardworking pets, not pampered pets that cost you too much money!

Riding a best-selling product to the top

As you think about which products to sell, keep in mind that business success comes from having a best seller. Well, having two or three best sellers is even better, but you definitely need at least one, and that means a product that is popular and has growing sales. With a product like that, you get flooded with orders and have the happy problem of having to scale up to meet the demand. If you don't have a best seller now, promise me that you'll keep working on it. Invent, license, or buy at wholesale some new alternatives, and try them out.

Keep experimenting until you find at least one product whose sales create strong momentum for your business. Then brand it carefully with a clear, recognizable, consistent identity made up of a unique name and logo presented in a strong graphic style. The product's success builds the strength of your brand (which could be your company name or a unique name you give the product itself). It's good to have a recognized, trusted brand name. You can use it to introduce related products and create a *product line,* or selection of related products, based on your initial best seller.

That, in essence, is the product-based approach to strategic success. It's a good strategy, but it does have one limitation: Eventually, the product category will become outdated because someone will invent something to replace it. If that someone isn't you, you're probably in big trouble.

Understanding the life cycle of each product category

Even if you have a best seller, eventually its category will become outdated, and you'll need to upgrade or replace your offering. If you have a best-selling vacuum cleaner, and someone invents a new and better electric motor, you'll need to either redesign your product using the new motor or face declining sales and eventually have to withdraw the product from the market.

The product category — the general form or type of products that your product competes against — goes through a life cycle, as shown in Figure 5-3.

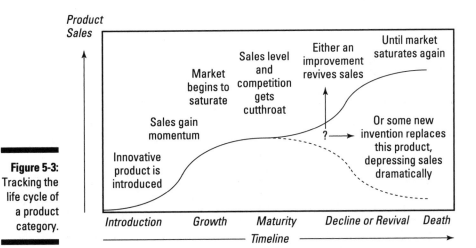

Product Sales

Until market saturates again

Either an improvement revives sales

Sales level and competition gets cutthroat

Market begins to saturate

Sales gain momentum

Innovative product is introduced

?———→ Or some new invention replaces this product, depressing sales dramatically

Introduction   *Growth*   *Maturity*   *Decline or Revival*   *Death*

———— *Timeline* ————→

Figure 5-3: Tracking the life cycle of a product category.

If the product category is fairly new — the result of a recent innovation — most of the potential consumers haven't tried it yet. This is called the *introduction stage,* and in it, there's lots of opportunity to grow your sales by educating the market about the new product and its benefits.

As word spreads, sales accelerate into the *growth stage.* In the growth stage, sales grow faster than the economy as a whole, and the companies that promote their brands strongly are able to gain leadership positions and ride their best sellers to profitable success. You've seen this happen in your lifetime over and over: CDs replaced tapes, and now digital forms of music are replacing CDs, for example. Make sure that you have one or more products that are in the growth stage, because being there is fun and profitable. (Promise me that if you don't have a product in a fast-growing stage right now, you won't rest until you've found one, okay?)

The growth stage is great, but it doesn't last forever. First, you begin to run into the ceiling imposed by market saturation, which is when almost everyone who might use a product like yours already has one. Then you have to compete to sell consumers their next replacement, which is slower going and marks the *maturity stage.* You can expect competitive advertising and lots of pressure on your pricing, so your profits may go down. Then something even worse happens: The product starts becoming outdated, and people stop using it in favor of something hot and new. This is the *decline stage.*

Even if *you* don't, *someone* will innovate, outdating your product category in the process. You might find yourself a leader in making and selling typewriters, for example. Not much profit in that, is there?

Figure 5-3 shows this life cycle and what happens as it nears its end. Either you (or a competitor) revive the product by updating it, or some outsider comes up with a completely new replacement and drives you and your conventional competitors out of business. By then, however, I hope you've got some new best seller in a more lively product category!

Keep in mind that every one of your products lives within a product category — and that its category has a life cycle. Growth-stage products are the most profitable, and you need to make sure that you have some at all times.

Mapping your product portfolio

A strategic approach to products helps ensure that you have a good new crop coming along, as well as a good selection of mature products that produce strong profits. In other words, you need a healthy portfolio of products. What does that look like? See Figure 5-4 for the way I like to look at any firm's selection of products to gain strategic insight into them.

As Figure 5-4 shows, it's very helpful to rate each of your products on two dimensions: *profitability* and *uniqueness.*

- **Profitability** can be measured by the product's *profit margin,* or the percentage of its sales price that you get to keep after paying all expenses related to producing and selling it. Profitability tends to be higher when there's less competition and when you have a larger share of the market than your competitors. In mature markets, profits are thin unless you have a dominant share of sales. Innovation may help you achieve stronger sales, allowing you to have better profits for longer.

- **Uniqueness** can be measured by comparing each product with its closest competitors. If it's similar to them, it gets a low uniqueness score. If it stands out as being unusual or different, it gets a high uniqueness score. If I do this analysis for a big company, I ask customers to provide the ratings of uniqueness, but that means budgeting for surveys or focus groups, which can be quite expensive. You may simply want to make your best guess and do the ratings yourself. Often, you can guess what your customers would say with pretty good accuracy.

As Figure 5-4 shows, innovative products are high on uniqueness, but if they're new and untested in the market, they're not likely to be all that profitable. They're represented in the figure by a graduation cap, and the goal is to develop them with the hope that they will graduate to market success and begin to produce profits. If so, your goal is to work on maximizing their profits and growing their market share.

After a while, the innovative products get old, and lots of competitors spring up. Then you know that time is limited (which is why they're represented in Figure 5-4 by an hourglass). Update them by giving them more unique qualities, or they'll fall into the bottom-right quadrant of the figure, where both uniqueness and profitability are low. These products need to be cut from your catalog at once to allow you to put your resources behind the products on the left side of the grid.

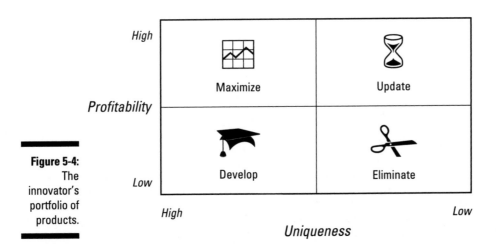

Figure 5-4:
The
innovator's
portfolio of
products.

A great exercise is to draw a big product portfolio grid on a large sheet of paper and plot each of your products on it, as shown in Figure 5-5. The portfolio shown in the figure has ten products in it. Three of them (E, F, and H) are old, and their profitability and uniqueness are low. They should be phased out. Two (I and G) are new and promising, and merit investment. They may develop into successful products that produce high profits. The dotted line shows the trajectory for products over their life cycles. They start in the bottom-left quadrant of the figure and ideally rise to high profitability before gradually becoming ordinary and ultimately outdated. (Refer to Figure 5-4 for explanations of the four quadrants of the strategic grid used in Figure 5-5.)

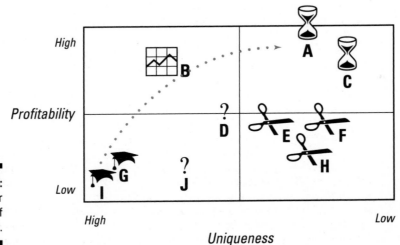

Figure 5-5:
Plotting your
portfolio of
products.

Planting enough seeds to make sure something grows

How many successful products do you need? A few would be great, but really, even one blockbuster would be just fine, right? So the question is this: What are the odds of a best seller? The answer depends on your particular business and industry, and on how you go about adding products to your line:

- ✔ **If you're a reseller:** You can go to trade shows, examine hundreds of products, and try to select some hot new products that you think will be popular in the coming year. You have the advantage of seeing finished products and picking the most promising, so you may be able to guess with reasonable accuracy. Perhaps one of every five or ten new products you sell will prove to be best sellers.

- ✔ **If you design and produce your own products:** You have to look farther ahead and exercise more imagination and guesswork. Perhaps only 1 in 20 or 50 of your initial ideas and designs will turn into a best seller.

Although I can't tell you exactly what your odds of having a best seller are, I *can* tell you that you won't guess right every time. You need to plant at least a handful of seeds to harvest even one best-selling product, so make sure that you look at plenty of options and test a few new ones every year.

Seeking Strategic Partnerships

Complementary strategies reinforce each other. Sometimes rather than an either–or choice, you actually have a complementary pair of options that are best chosen together. The make-versus-buy decision is a great example of complementarity. In innovation, *make* means inventing things yourself, whereas *buy* means adopting others' inventions (by purchasing and reselling or by licensing the rights to make them, for example). Exciting new research shows that high-tech firms with both active invention and licensing (make and buy) strategies do better than those that do mostly one or the other. I find that the same rule applies in other firms too.

I spent a week working with a team of lawyers and scientists at S.C. Johnson and Sons, helping them develop negotiating skills for when they go out and shop for inventions. A surprising number of the company's successful consumer products aren't invented in S.C. Johnson's own labs but actually are licensed from other inventors elsewhere. What I saw in that company applies to yours too: The expertise, imagination, and momentum of invention flows back and forth between your company and outside inventors, enriching your options.

If you need a basic essential for your business, either buy it or make it, depending on what's most economical. But when it comes to innovation strategies, try to both make and buy. Always put some effort into working on your own inventions, but also keep an eye open outside your walls for good ideas you could bring in.

In many cases, it's simplest to join forces with another company that has the capabilities or technologies you want. These long-term partnerships, called *strategic alliances,* are defined as cooperative agreements between two or more organizations that share complementary expertise or other resources to accomplish something they can't do on their own. Strategic alliances can include

- ✔ Working together to bring a product to market by taking advantage of each other's products, distribution, and sales

- ✔ Cooperating to develop or produce an innovative product

- ✔ Licensing a technology or invention to apply it in a specific industry

- ✔ Combining technical expertise to develop or produce an innovative product

- ✔ Cooperating to bring one firm's invention or product to market in the other firm's country or region

These are the most common forms of strategic alliances, but the possibilities are limited only by your imagination. A firm with strong retail distribution might cooperate with an industrial-chemicals company to sell consumer versions of its industrial cleaning products. The alliance combines consumer-products expertise with industrial chemistry — a promising combination that might lead to powerful household cleaning products.

Is there some business you could form an alliance with? Definitely! But you may not have identified it yet, so look around for a partner. Think of creative combinations of your strengths and other firms' strengths. (In strategic planning, strengths are often called *core competencies,* so if you hear that term, that's what it means.)

A good way to look for potential strategic alliance partners is to make a list of your major strengths and weaknesses; then look around for other businesses whose strengths and weaknesses mirror yours. If your company is great at sales but not so good at manufacturing, look for a manufacturer that usually works under contract and lacks a direct sales force of its own. Combined, your two sets of strengths make new strategies possible. When you identify a potential partner, see whether its executives will sit down with you and brainstorm ways of cashing in on your combined strengths.

Mastering the Art of Change Management

Change management is the artful leadership of a transition in your business. Innovation requires transitions. If you develop or switch to a new product, you have to update all your marketing materials, liquidate old inventory, and make sure that everyone knows how to sell and support the new product. If you expand to a new area, you may have to open new facilities, train new staff, and find out how to operate according to new customs. If you adopt a new technology, you have to master it yourself and make sure that everyone else gets up to speed on it too. While adjusting to the new technology, you may encounter unexpected problems that irritate people and make them resist the change.

Enlisting the eager believers and excluding the hopeless cases

Some people love change, but the majority resist it, at least at first. People who are naturally very creative and open to new experiences get bored when things don't change, so they welcome transitions and the challenges they bring. Such people are your allies when you're trying to bring about a change, and you should get them involved right away. Try to get them in leadership positions if at all possible.

The majority of people resist change at first and see it as an inconvenience. They may also feel nervous or concerned about possible negative effects. Help this nervous majority by explaining as clearly as possible what will happen to them during the change. Tell them early on about any effects that they'll experience personally. Then they'll be clearer about what's going to happen, enabling them to stop worrying and start focusing on their assigned roles.

Another group of people — fortunately, a minority — resists change very strongly, and you can't bring these people around simply by explaining how the change will affect them. They may be nervous and excitable or very rigid about wanting to have everything done a certain way. For them, change is threatening, and they'll probably refuse to help out. Only at the very end, when it becomes clear that the change is permanent, will they adjust their own behavior.

Protect your innovations from these strong resisters by

    ✔ Never allowing a change-resister to play a leadership role during a transition

- ✔ Keeping them out of planning sessions and away from the work of making the change as much as possible

- ✔ Avoiding hiring people like them, who are threatened by even a small change in the routine

Make being flexible and innovative a part of every job description when you hire in the future. It's important to keep people who hate change away from your workplace if you possibly can. Change management is much easier when you avoid the most difficult, highly resistant types of people in the first place.

When you know and work with people, it's obvious who's open to new experiences and changes and who's highly resistant to them. But what about people you don't know? One way to predict who'll be an ally during change is to ask people to voluntarily complete a Big Five personality assessment. Those who score high on openness (one of the five main dimensions of personality) are allies in change; those who score low on openness and low on calmness are resistant and shouldn't be part of the core team during a transition. You can obtain Big Five self-assessment forms inexpensively at www.tspectrum.com, or go to www.supportforinnovation.com for more information about assessing personality and selecting those who are natural innovators.

Making the destination visible to all

It's natural to want to talk about the plans and steps involved in any change, but people really need to hear about two other things first: the effect on them and the ultimate destination (where the journey is going to end). Painting a clear, attractive picture of the destination is particularly important.

Start with a real sales presentation of the goal and why you're so excited to be pursuing it; then keep reminding everyone of the goal and benefits. Each time you talk about what people need to do — the specific plan of action — remember to evoke that appealing image of the ultimate destination.

Branding your goal with a catchy or memorable name and image, just as though you were selling a product, is often helpful. Make your change tangible and appealing so that everyone keeps the goal in sight as they work.

Keep in mind as you "sell" the destination that there's no need to overpromise. Explain honestly and accurately what you expect the future to be. Don't exaggerate the benefits, because if you overpromise, you'll pay for it in terms of lost credibility and disloyalty later on.

Managing resistance during the change process

If you could wave a magic wand and bring about all the changes of your new strategy immediately, you'd encounter very little resistance. People might be shocked at first, but if everything were neatly in place in some new configuration, they'd adapt quickly. That's why speed is a good goal during the change process. Don't let people's anxieties and objections slow you down. Keep a fast pace, and push through the initial skepticism and resistance as firmly and promptly as you possibly can.

Figure 5-6 shows how the emotional state in a workplace is affected by a major change such as a new strategy or the adoption of a major innovation. People enter the panic stage shortly after the news of a change hits. Panic is especially high if people fear that they will be personally injured; they may worry about layoffs or increases in their workloads, for example.

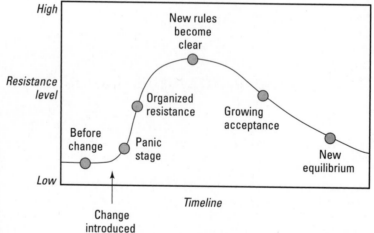

Figure 5-6:
The transition process.

As Figure 5-6 shows, people initially fear most changes, and their resistance climbs quite quickly as they hear and amplify negative rumors about what's going to happen. People resist uncertainty more than anything else, so focus your efforts on countering this effect with lots of clear, detailed communication about the change. Also push to implement the change as quickly as possible. As soon as the new rules of the game become clear, anxiety and resistance will start to fall.

Eventually, resistance will drop, and a new equilibrium will be reached in which most people accept the change and settle into their new routine.

Watching out for snap-back

Acceptance of change can be deceptive. Residual memory of the old way remains, and given half a chance, people will snap back into old patterns and ways of doing things. Therefore, you need to police the new stability and jump on any reversion to old patterns quickly and firmly. Don't let anyone get away with snap-back behavior, or soon you'll find that others are following suit and retreating to their old habits again.

Part II

Stimulating Your Creative Side: Thinking in New and Different Ways

The 5th Wave   By Rich Tennant

In this part . . .

*T*here's always another way, and there's a limitless supply of ideas. Creativity is the key to inventions, improvements, solutions, breakthroughs, and brilliant suggestions, but when you really need a better idea, it's often hard to produce one. This part arms you with an incredible number of tools and techniques to generate great new ideas.

Brainstorming a list of possibilities is as simple as recognizing the need for ideas and committing a little time and scrap paper to the job. You can produce good ideas all by yourself or with a group or team. Or you can look around for good ideas that you can adapt to your needs, exciting new products you can purchase, or patents you can license. The world is full of great new ideas and inventions, so you don't necessarily have to invent something completely new.

Whether you invent your own or take advantage of someone else's great new ideas, it's important to recognize the power of a good idea. Companies and careers are built on the strength of good ideas. This part helps you generate some of your own!

Chapter 6

Getting Juices Flowing in Brainstorming Sessions

....

In This Chapter

▶ Tapping into the creative energy of groups

▶ Selecting the creative thinking team

▶ Getting ready to facilitate a creative retreat

▶ Leading or participating in a brainstorming session

....

Groups *can* be smarter than individuals, but unfortunately, they usually aren't. The typical group of people — on a subway platform, at a sports stadium, or in a meeting — has a herd mentality. Most people don't step up and contribute at all, and the few who do tend to be loud-mouthed and narrow-minded. You can't expect groups of people to solve challenging problems or generate clever insights. They often get into arguments, come up with foolish ideas, or make serious mistakes. Unsupervised groups aren't much use to the innovator.

However, groups offer two potential advantages to you in your quest for a breakthrough idea. First, they allow you to tap into a diversity of knowledge and experience. Second, they make it possible to take advantage of healthy *group dynamics* (the ways people interact socially in small groups). If you get people thinking and talking in an open, creative manner, they often surprise themselves and you with the breadth and depth of their creative thinking. A group of a half dozen to a dozen people can, if well managed, produce 100 plausible new product concepts in a two-day retreat, allowing you to select the strongest ideas from their list for further development and testing.

I like to push groups to produce at least 100 concepts. It seems impossible to them at the beginning of the session, but with the right group processes, ideas begin to flow and build on one another until everyone is surprised and excited by their creative productivity. The trick is to facilitate a productive group process. *Creative facilitation* is optimizing the creative output of a small, select group of people by managing the group's dynamics. This chapter shows you how to be an effective facilitator of creative sessions — a skill you can use in dozens of ways as you put group creativity to use.

Identifying Opportunities for Group Creativity

One experience with a poorly run creative session may have turned people off to the idea of group creativity, so you may bump into initial resistance. If so, don't let the naysayers get you down! Group creativity is a powerful force, and it can make fast work of problems like the following:

- ✔ Low staff morale
- ✔ A conflict needing resolution
- ✔ Losses or lack of profitability
- ✔ A need for new products
- ✔ A need for a fresh new ad campaign
- ✔ A need for a new or updated brand identity
- ✔ Inefficiencies or repeated errors in a work process
- ✔ A challenge filling a staff position
- ✔ A tough engineering or design problem
- ✔ A need to do more with less in the budget

This list of opportunities for group creativity may seem long, but if you were to ask a well-facilitated group to brainstorm more opportunities for group creativity, I'm sure they could. In fact, that's a great exercise. At your next meeting, why not give your staff the challenge of generating 50 topics that could benefit from a group creativity session? I'm quite confident that they will produce a strong list. When they do, ask them to come up with a way to prioritize the list. Then see what the top five priorities are. You may find this exercise alone is enough to kick-start momentum for innovation in your workplace. This section looks at a variety of additional ways to get group creativity going.

Calling for help with a problem

Problems focus attention. When a hospital has trouble filling its nursing positions, everyone worries about it. They ask questions such as "Will we have to raise salaries for nurses, and if so, how can we afford to do that?" A problem is a great opportunity to initiate group creativity. However, be warned! Problems produce closed-minded thinking, so if you want to take a creative approach, you have to reframe the problem. *Reframing* is changing the fundamental way people think about something.

In the example of a hospital that's having trouble filling its nursing positions, the common responses are framed negatively. People worry that the hospital will go over budget or that healthcare will deteriorate. They use words like *impossible* and *crisis,* which get everyone thinking pessimistically. To shift the frame toward a more optimistic, open approach to problem-solving, you need to follow a three-step process:

1. **Make the case for exploring fresh options.**

   Be positively assertive, not critical and negative. Say, "We're stuck with unpleasant options and don't see a good way to resolve the problem. I want to pull together a team that will try to generate some fresh thinking about what to do." Be careful to disassociate your proposal from anything else going on. Make it clear that you're not taking sides, and also emphasize that you don't want or need problem-solving authority. Your results will simply be food for thought. Let people know that while you hope to come up with a good solution, you aren't asking for an advance commitment to implement whatever you suggest.

2. **Get permission to convene a creative group.**

   If you're a manager or executive, you can simply invite people to a brainstorming session. If not, you need to get someone with authority to back your proposal. Pick someone you have a decent working relationship with (someone who trusts you to be productive and focused as the group's facilitator). Choose someone high enough in the organization to allow you to tap into multiple departments or functions to achieve a diverse group with a breadth of knowledge and perspectives. You may also use your network to reach out and draw in people from outside your workplace who can bring fresh ideas or unique knowledge. Ask them when and for how long you can get them to commit; then line your insiders up for an event that fits the outsiders' schedules. (If your group will discuss any confidential information, ask participants, especially outsiders, to sign nondisclosure agreements.)

3. **Pick people who will bring positive thinking to the problem.**

   Screening for attitude is important! As I discuss in Chapter 1, underlying attitude makes a world of difference. Exclude naysayers who obviously have a negative attitude or a bone to pick. They'll only work against you as you try to facilitate an open brainstorming session. Find whatever excuses you must, but be firm: Nobody with a negative attitude is allowed to attend! (The later section, "In or Out?: Issuing Invites to the Brainstorming Session," gives you more advice on making thoughtful selections.)

If you use this simple three-step process to call for creative help with a knotty problem, you'll get a group that's eager and able to explore the problem from fresh perspectives. Positive problem-solving groups are very powerful forces; they often produce fresh new ideas and options, and may generate the next big innovation for your organization.

Inviting questions for consideration

A great way to identify creative options is to ask people to pose questions in a brainstorming session and see what you get. If asking for questions doesn't give you good results, pose questions of your own to stimulate engagement. A question such as "What's the most important problem for us to work on right now?" can generate a variety of answers, but often, you find that a third or more of the answers address the same issue. When you've identified an issue that's on many people's minds, you can brainstorm for solutions.

 You can also use open-ended, thought-provoking questions to get the group's creative juices flowing. Ask for input in the form of wish-we-had and wish-we-could ideas. Challenge everyone to share five "I wish we had . . ." and five "I wish we could . . ." sentences of their choice. Then pull together a group to sift through the resulting submissions, and select one from each category to work on in a brainstorming session.

Building on suggestions

A suggestion system can be used as input for creative groups. Start with suggestions offered by employees, either anonymously in a suggestion box or openly in response to a request for proposals. Instead of having management read the suggestions and pick the ones they like, assemble a group to brainstorm the suggestions. Try pulling suggestions at random (rather than filtering them based on merit), and challenge the group to find a way to make each suggestion work. Sometimes, the most naïve or impractical suggestions produce the greatest innovations when the group gets to work on them. Even a wildly impractical idea or suggestion can lead to ideas that may prove more practical.

In or Out?: Issuing Invites to the Brainstorming Session

Rounding up a good set of participants is one of the simplest and best ways to ensure an easy-to-facilitate creative group. Like a party, a creative group needs a good guest list. Put some thought into who might add fresh information or ideas, and look for ways to mix up the group with diverse people — including those who don't normally work together. You want to generate some *creative chemistry,* which arises when people with differing experiences, styles, and perspectives work intensely together.

This section helps you sort out your ideal group size and provides some additional criteria for deciding who should be in the group and who's best left on the sidelines.

Deciding how big to make the group

Your group should be no smaller than 5 (4 participants plus a facilitator) and probably no larger than 15. As you approach 20 people, facilitating the participatory process becomes more difficult, and your group will be characterized by more *social loafing* (lack of participation and mental laziness on the part of some members).

If you're a beginning facilitator, aim for a group of between six and eight, which gives you enough people to ensure a lively session but avoids the complexities of larger groups. Groups of ten or more require more active and skilled facilitation.

If you feel that your topic requires a larger group to include all the needed perspectives and experts, consider dividing the group in two and bringing in a second facilitator. Reserve adjoining rooms, and brief and debrief the group as a whole, but divide it for the actual brainstorming activities to ensure full participation by all members.

Excluding people who squash the creative spirit

Some people rain on every creative parade — people who often say things like "We already tried that," "That's impossible," or "We could never afford that," making it hard for others to be open-minded. Exclude closed-minded or negative thinkers. Also consider excluding anyone who, by virtue of high status or rank, might make others uncomfortable and unwilling to contribute. Finally, exclude people who've been around so long that they think they know it all. What they know is how things used to be, not how they could be in the future. You don't need negative baggage.

Be tough about excluding people who might ruin your event. It's far harder to shut them up when they're in your session and saying the wrong things than to exclude them from the get-go, so bite the bullet, and don't let them talk their way in. Be firm, impersonal, and polite — but mostly firm — in telling people who is and is *not* invited. It's your party: You're the facilitator, so you're in charge of the guest list. If others don't like it, too bad. They can facilitate their own sessions! (But they won't. The people you want to keep out are people who don't really believe in creative, open-minded discussion, so they'll never initiate a brainstorming session.)

Including people who contribute needed knowledge

Ignorance is bliss, as the old saying goes, and unfortunately, this saying often applies to brainstorming. A group that lacks in-depth understanding of a topic will come up with simplistic, impractical ideas that sound good only to people who don't know any better. Your group ought to include outsiders, not only for their fresh perspectives, but also for the reservoir of technical knowledge and experience they can give the group to draw upon. Just make sure to screen the experts for openness to new ideas so that you don't get experts who squash every suggestion.

Adding people who bring unique perspectives and styles

Group diversity is an essential part of good creative facilitation. Reach out as far as you can to draw a diverse group, including people from other organizations, cultures, and places. Also give thought to personality and style. Can you create a mix of artistic, free-thinking people with organized, logical ones? If so, creative sparks may fly when they start talking about their ideas. Group diversity can lead to *creative friction,* the inspirational tension that arises when people have competing perspectives. As the facilitator, your positive view toward diversity and the differing perspectives it offers will rub off on your group and help them achieve insight from creative friction.

Planning the Creative Process

The *creative process* consists of the specific activities you plan for your creative group. A very simple (but effective) group process is to assemble a group for a morning, challenge them with a problem or other creative goal, and have them work through a series of brainstorming activities. Collect the group's output by taking notes on large chart pads; then summarize it afterward in a neat report that you can e-mail or hand-deliver to the participants. Give them an opportunity to comment on or add more ideas to your draft report before you finalize it and distribute it beyond your group.

Many creative challenges can be overcome with a simple, one-session creative process. However, complex or especially difficult projects may require multiple meetings, often with team members conducting research between sessions. This section focuses on getting the timing right — figuring out how much time you need to allow to successfully work through the creative process.

Deciding how much creative distance you want to travel

Sometimes, you can't tell whether or not one meeting will do the trick until you see how far the group gets in its first session. However, you can often guess which projects are going to need multiple meetings based on the scope of the question, problem, or project. A project involving major obstacles or multistage design and problem-solving may require the group to cover more *creative distance* (the amount of invention required to accomplish the goal).

If you want a group to come up with a breakthrough design for a new electronic product, you can anticipate a need for multiple sessions (probably five or more). If you think you have a lot of work to do, schedule several sessions, either on consecutive days or, if that's not possible, once a week.

When I facilitate sessions for complex products involving electronic or other engineering challenges, I usually suggest an intense initial retreat of one and a half to two days, followed by research on the resulting ideas and then several more one-day sessions in which the initial ideas are explored and developed. However, when I work on projects with fewer technical issues or constraints, I often plan just one or two creative sessions. A group can generate dozens of interesting new product concepts for snack foods in a single day, for example.

Budgeting sufficient time

Creativity can happen in an instant, so in theory, a group ought to be able to achieve a breakthrough in a session of an hour or less. Sometimes, a half hour of brainstorming is enough, but rarely! Plan for a minimum of several hours of focused creative effort to ensure both quantity and quality of ideas. I try to get a group to commit to a full-day session, with a generous lunch break in the middle to allow them to recharge.

If you can possibly do it, break your creative sessions into two days of work with a good night's sleep between them. An afternoon session followed by dinner and relaxed social interaction sets a group up for a highly productive full-day session the next day. This approach takes advantage of the power of *incubation,* the unconscious creative processing that occurs between periods of intense focus on a problem or challenge. To trigger incubation, you need to get the group deeply involved in and focused on a tough problem before letting them go. Then bring them back for another session before they forget their earlier experience. Think of incubation as keeping a soup broth simmering on the back burners of their minds. It shouldn't be the main focus, but it shouldn't be forgotten and allowed to cool, either.

Multiday sessions work well because they allow for overnight incubation. Letting the group "sleep on it" is an effective facilitation technique. Also try to block in several possible meeting times reaching out into future weeks. If your group solves the problem brilliantly in the first session, you can always cancel subsequent meetings, but if it doesn't, you'll be glad you reserved additional times.

Deciding how many sessions to run

The simplest rule for deciding how many sessions you'll need is to double the number of sessions you think you'll need. If you think a simple one-day session should be enough, plan a two-day session! In my experience, groups either achieve a startling breakthrough very quickly (quite rare) or take much longer than you expect to produce something useful. So plan for a lengthy process, and you won't be disappointed.

If you have to map a process (an important first step when working on quality problems, for example), expect to spend the entire first session just diagramming the process. This means that you need to schedule at least two more sessions to work on redesigning the process, plus a final one to work on an implementation plan.

If you're brainstorming for new product or design ideas (for example, naming or branding a new line of business), you may be able to produce a lot of interesting ideas in just one or two sessions. However, if you also need to pick the best idea and develop it into something refined enough to actually implement, you need to book at least five times as much time for implementation planning as it took to come up with the concept in the first place.

Implementation teams need a *lot* of time. Schedule as many meetings as you can fit into the group's calendar before the drop-dead implementation date. You can always cancel sessions if the group manages to complete its work early.

Preparing for Your Role as Facilitator

As a facilitator, your primary goal is to encourage creativity and participation by the entire group. Your secondary goal is to channel and focus that creativity and participation in productive directions. In this section, I help you prepare for your role by rehearsing the skills you need to get people thinking and voicing their thoughts.

Practicing your questioning and listening skills

In general conversation, people mostly use *closed-ended questions,* which are questions that ask for only a narrow range of responses. A yes-or-no question permits only two answers, so it's obviously closed-ended. A question such as "What are the best approaches to the shortage of raw materials?" is closed-ended too, although in a less obvious way. It limits responses in two ways: by asking for solutions to a specific problem (the shortage of raw materials) and by asking for the *best* approaches. The use of a qualifying adjective such as *best, good, appropriate, affordable,* or *sensible* signals that you want only cautious, well-considered responses.

Because creativity requires open-minded thinking, closed-ended questions need to be weeded out of your facilitation vocabulary. Practice using open-ended questions — questions that challenge listeners to expand their thinking. Instead of asking, "Do you think we should switch to recycled materials for our packaging?" (a yes-or-no, closed-ended question), you could ask, "How many ways can you think of to use recycled materials?" That's an open-ended question with the potential to produce exciting new ideas and possibilities.

In addition to asking open-ended, creative questions, you need to be a good listener. People commonly listen with a critical attitude, which discourages open conversation. Facilitation involves listening with an open mind and making people feel good about their contributions. As you listen to ideas, suggestions, and answers, try to be positive and encouraging. Nod and smile as people talk. Thank them for their ideas or comments. Point out something interesting or useful about each contribution. These affirmative reactions will make the group feel good about contributing and will stimulate more contributions.

Also practice taking clear notes about what people say. Often, the facilitator needs to summarize the ideas the group generates, which may come rapidly. Jot down these ideas on a chart pad in big print. You want participants to springboard off earlier ideas, so make your notes legible. If you're not used to recording a group's ideas on a large pad or board, practice this skill with one or more assistants who can shout out ideas or phrases for you to write down.

Guiding the group away from negative dynamics

Most of the brainstorming exercises you're likely to use will have one rule in common: no criticizing other people's ideas. If someone says, "We could use organic materials for all our packaging!", encourage the group to build on this suggestion. Someone might add, "Maybe they make organic paper products now. Could we use organic cardboard boxes?" At this point, someone might say something pragmatic like "It doesn't make any sense to use organic packaging because people only care about organic products when it's something they eat. Besides, I don't think there is any certification for organic papers, so we probably couldn't even purchase such a thing in the first place."

Although this criticism might have some validity, as a facilitator you must prohibit such comments. Politely point out that you want the group to suspend judgment to allow the ideas to flow, no matter how impractical they may seem. Also point out that in many cases, the idea that seems wildest or silliest is the one that leads to a creative breakthrough.

Groups often respond well to facilitator guidance and stop critiquing ideas; however, sometimes the habit of criticizing is deeply ingrained, and the group continues to find fault with ideas. If this happens, ask the group to try a challenging exercise: Have them suggest *only* fantasy ideas that seem unrealistic and impractical. After generating wild and crazy ideas for 15 minutes or so, they'll probably be cured of their desire to impose practical constraints on their own thinking.

Other negative dynamics may also plague your group, such as the tendency for one person or a few people to dominate. If you see that participation is uneven, point out the imbalance, and ask the dominant contributors to take a break and let others speak. If the others continue to be hesitant, you may actually have to divide the group into smaller groups. People who are quiet in larger settings may become talkative in groups of three or four. Other remedies include calling on specific individuals or imposing a rotational rule requiring each person to speak in turn.

Both individuals and groups tend to fall into common thinking traps, called mental biases and group biases by psychologists. The worst one for innovators is the *rush to judgment,* in which everyone is quick to agree with the first plausible suggestion or solution. Early agreement may indicate that the group has failed to explore all the options. Challenge the group to consider more ideas before reaching a conclusion. Chapter 21 addresses additional thinking errors and group biases that you need to be prepared to remedy.

Controlling your nonverbal signals

The best facilitators do relatively little talking and let their bodies do much of the work. A relaxed, open posture, along with an encouraging, interested demeanor, works wonders in opening up a group and generating creative contributions. Nodding and smiling in an encouraging manner let people know that you like their ideas.

Also use your body language to energize the group. At first, ideas will come slowly. As soon as people begin to voice their ideas, move eagerly to the flip chart and begin to write the ideas down. Work neatly but rapidly, as if excited to capture a brilliant thought. As you write, keep looking back toward the speakers and nodding, so they know you're eager to hear more. As soon as you've captured a thought, turn and face the group fully to listen attentively to the next idea.

Watch out for habitual gestures, expressions, postures, stances, and movements. You need a different set of nonverbal behavior for facilitating creative groups because your habits are based on workplace norms, where free, open creativity is out of place. People look tight and controlled at work. Creativity needs to be loose and uncontrolled. You may want to practice in front of a mirror (a full-size mirror is best) so that you can work on a more relaxed, open, playful nonverbal presentation.

See Chapter 20 for more details on how to avoid noncreative body language and how to use creative body language to good effect as a facilitator.

Becoming familiar with the challenge at hand

As a facilitator, you need to bang your head against the creative challenge wall in advance and come up with at least a handful of creative ideas of your own. Research the topic to make sure that you have a good general understanding of its scope and are in command of the relevant facts. Check out comparable cases so you'll know how other organizations have approached the problem or challenge. Then spend some time brainstorming on your own. Put enough time into the problem to feel like something of an expert, with your own creative insights.

When you facilitate the creative group, do *not* begin by telling them what you think, even though your ideas may be more developed than theirs. Keep your knowledge and ideas in reserve. The purpose of preparing is to be better able to guide the group's thinking, not to dominate it.

As you facilitate, dip into your knowledge and ideas if there seems to be a gap in the group's knowledge or thinking. Offer your insights in the form of questions so the group feels like it owns the answers. For example, it's better to say, "What do you think about the example of XYZ Company?" than "I studied the XYZ Company's solution, and I think it could be applied to us."

Mastering the Core Brainstorming Methods

The term *brainstorming* is somewhat like a brand name that people tend to use in a more general sense (*Kleenex* rather than *tissue,* for example). Brainstorming was first coined to describe a specific method of generating ideas but has since become a handy, generic term for any and all guided group creativity techniques where the goal is to produce lots of ideas.

Almost all so-called brainstorming sessions begin with an introduction to the purpose and process, followed by a short warm-up to engage and loosen up the group and then a focused effort to express and capture any and all ideas that occur. The main goal is to be open and enthusiastic about all ideas and options, and this means suspending critical thinking.

Critical thinking is the enemy of creative thinking. There is a time for critical thinking, but it's not now. Make sure the group understands that the goal is to generate lots and lots of ideas first and then to sift through them with a critical eye later.

Warming up the group

Open the group's first session with an initial briefing in which you introduce yourself, the topic, and the process you have planned for the group to follow. Your initial briefing to the group has two objectives:

- ✔ **To orient the group:** Explain what the problem or opportunity is and what you hope the group will produce. Then summarize the process by explaining what they'll be doing and giving them a rough timeline for the activities. If you plan follow-up meetings, homework between meetings, or other activities that stretch into the future, summarize these as well. People like to know what's expected of them — especially the time commitments they're expected to make.

- ✔ **To set the tone:** Demonstrate an open, inquisitive, noncritical style. Make sure that you introduce your plans for the meeting with the need for openness in mind. If you come across as overly strict or narrow-minded, no one will feel good about being creative in your session.

You may also run the group through one or several *warm-up exercises,* which are brief, engaging activities that demonstrate the kinds of creative thinking you want the group to do. Following are four warm-ups to open the group up to creative expression. If your session is only an hour in length, run just one of these, but for half- to full-day sessions, take the time to run all four. Give the group no more than five minutes for each. Do them in quick succession from first to last (because they build increasingly difficult skills: fantasy idea generation, practical idea generation, process-oriented planning, and problem identification — which is a particularly challenging kind of brainstorming). Ask the group to

1. **Think of ten ways for human beings to fly, aside from the obvious ones involving airplanes or helicopters.**

   This exercise requires the group to think imaginatively and gets them in touch with their sense of fun and fantasy.

2. **Come up with ten ways to open a jar of jam on which the lid is stuck.**

   This exercise brings the group's imagination into the practical realm and demonstrates their ability to come up with useful insights.

3. **Design three options for "drops" whereby one spy could hand off secret papers to another in a public place without any possibility of being seen or caught.**

   This exercise engages the group in process brainstorming, which can be more difficult than product brainstorming.

4. **Invent a completely new kind of footwear that solves some major problem.**

   This exercise requires people to brainstorm problems as well as solutions, which orients them toward finding opportunity.

If you need to warm up the same group again on a succeeding day, visit www.supportforinnovation.com for my library of warm-ups you can use. It's best to run warm-ups each time you work with the group, and it's good to have new warm-ups each time.

Using Osborn's brainstorming rules

Alex Osborn is credited with the invention of formal brainstorming. His technique is a good one, and facilitators often utilize it. Here are the instructions you need to give the group in order to get them started:

✔ Don't judge or criticize the ideas.

✔ Offer wild and outlandish ideas along with practical ones.

✔ Aim for quantity, and don't worry about quality.

✔ Build on each other's ideas.

It's important to enforce these rules — politely and without blame or criticism, but with a firm hand. You may occasionally need to remind participants that wild and crazy ideas are welcome and that no criticism of ideas is permitted. Also, encourage participants to build on or add to each other's ideas. Most of the breakthroughs groups produce come from people springboarding off each other's suggestions.

Introducing variations to improve results

Sometimes a brainstorming group is hesitant and holds back, leaving you standing at the flip chart without ideas to write down. When this happens, try running the group through another warm-up exercise or two. Try warm-ups involving fantastic or humorous assignments, such as brainstorming ways to avoid taxes. If the group still holds back, try allowing individuals to express themselves anonymously. The following sections show you ways to do that and more.

Brainwriting

Make sure that each member of the group has a sheet of paper, a pen, and a comfortable place to write. Then ask them to write down five or more ideas as fast as they can, working in silence. After a few minutes, collect the papers and exchange them, so that each person gets someone else's list. Ask them to read the ideas they've been given and add more ideas of their own. Repeat the process once more if you like, asking participants to read the lists of ideas aloud this time. Capture each unique idea on your flip chart, and transition to traditional brainstorming by encouraging group members to add more ideas verbally.

Pass-along brainstorming methods

In *pass-along brainstorming,* you trade your flip chart for a single sheet of paper that you send around the room, asking people to take turns writing on it. Write the focus (a problem, opportunity, or other mental challenge) on the top. Then pass it to the first person to your left and ask them to write down one idea. That person then passes it to the next person, who adds one idea, and so on around the room. Keep it going rapidly, through several cycles, to generate a long list. Then read or post the list for all to see and discuss.

A variation on pass-along brainstorming I tried recently and really liked is to turn the flip chart away from the center of the room and have participants walk past it, one at a time, adding their ideas to the hidden list. They can pass the marker among them as if it's a relay race, and you can encourage a fun sense of urgency by timing how long it takes to generate 20 ideas. Getting them out of their seats seems to help them get in touch with their creativity.

For more pass-along methods (including the stuffy but well-known nominal group technique), see Chapter 7.

Fishbone brainstorming

Fishbone brainstorming uses a cause-effect diagram in the form of a fishbone to stimulate ideas about root causes of some outcome, usually a problem you want to solve. To use the technique, draw a large fish-skeleton diagram on a whiteboard or flip chart, with the front end for the effect and the rib bones for causes to be entered during the brainstorming. For example, the effect could be "Teeth don't stay white" (a problem for consumers of whitening services and products). Ask the group to think of possible causes, and write each cause that isn't directly related to another at the end of a separate fork of the effect diagram. Your fishbone diagram should look like the one in Figure 6-1.

For example, you might add labels such as "foods that stain," "other sources of stains," "inconsistent brushing," "soft/porous enamel," "incorrect use of treatments," and "ineffective treatments." The existence of multiple forking lines pushes the group to think of multiple causes. After you've labeled most or all of the main forks, you can drill down and explore each fork by adding smaller lines along it. For example, the label "foods that stain" might be given these sublabels: blueberries, coffee, tea, red wine, and colas. Figure 6-1 illustrates the value of the fishbone for exploring this problem.

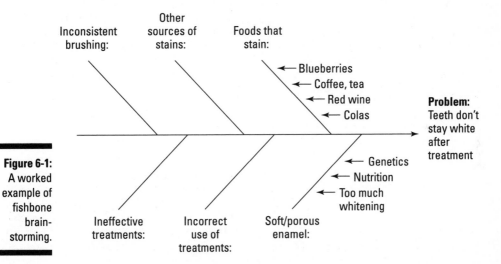

Figure 6-1: A worked example of fishbone brain-storming.

Often, the goal of fishbone brainstorming is to explore the causes of a problem to invent a good solution to the problem, so push the group to keep exploring causes until they gain insights that might lead to solutions. Then switch to brainstorming-style lists of ways to implement possible solutions.

For example, the group addressing ways of keeping teeth white might come up with the idea of *preventing foods and drinks from staining,* which might then lead to ideas such as color-free versions of foods and drinks or products that protect the teeth while eating and drinking.

Mapping the ideas

The terms *mind mapping* and *brain drawing* are often used to describe loosely organized visual lists in which related ideas are clustered together, and their relationships to each other and the main idea are shown with straight or curving lines. The fishbone diagram is a way to map causal relationships, but a simple idea map uses a looser structure based on any and all associations or relationships between ideas.

You can use idea mapping to help the group expand its thinking. Start by drawing a large oval in the middle of the blank paper or board, and write the problem or challenge there. Then add — or allow each group member to add with his own marker or pen — any and all ideas that come up. Cluster similar ideas, separate unique ones, and use lines to symbolize the interrelationships. Keep the visual symbols very simple so the map is easy to understand later on.

Loose relationships may be shown with dotted lines, while causal or directional relationships may be shown with arrows. Many software packages allow you to mind map on a computer (such as Microsoft's Visio, Edraw's Mindmap, and Mindjet's Mindmanager), but they're usually used to organize information rather than to generate creative ideas. I recommend using several large flip charts side by side or a large chalkboard or whiteboard so that the map can expand with ease. When the group runs out of steam, go over the map you've drawn at once, and convert the more interesting or useful ideas to an organized list. You may not be able to decipher the map in hindsight, because it's likely to get complex or messy.

Random word technique

The idea behind this technique is to engage creative thinking by challenging people to find associations between apparently unrelated words and the problem or project they're working on. For example, a group working on ways of improving customer service at an insurance company might be given the following random words and phrases: *steering wheel, mailbox, cupcake, massage, garden,* and *iceberg.* The facilitator would ask the group to try to relate one or more of these words to the problem. The group might come up with ideas such as

- ✔ Unhappy customers need to be "massaged" with lots of attention and special care until they feel relaxed and happy again.
- ✔ Customers should be celebrated and given special gifts (symbolized by cupcakes), so they know we care.

> ✔ Customers need to feel in control of their business relationship with their insurance company, so we should give them a virtual steering wheel in the form of a control panel on their computers that gives them the ability to manage all their insurance policies with ease.

It's amazing how readily groups can come up with good insights based on seemingly unrelated, random words. Try it yourself. Can you turn the terms *garden* and *iceberg* into insights about customer service? I bet you can!

Considering additional creative processes

As you facilitate a creative group session, keep an eye on the group's productivity. If they're eager, engaged, and highly creative, all you need to do is keep them focused on the topic and record their ideas. You don't need to provide a lot of structure.

Other groups need continuous encouragement to produce creative results. If your group is struggling to generate ideas, you'll need to be more active in your facilitation. I've worked with groups who needed me to structure every moment and offer starter ideas of my own to show them what to do in each activity. Just keep using creative activities and have faith in the creative process. Even the most hesitant, quiet groups can and do produce useful insights if the facilitator is sufficiently encouraging and persistent!

Sometimes you need to switch from the intellectual and verbal to more physical and emotional creative activities. Brainstorming and its kin ask people to generate ideas and words. If the group seems unable to do so with ease, consider activities such as stretching, dancing to music, or drawing. I'm an artist as well as an author and consultant, so it's natural for me to bring art into my facilitation.

Often, I ask a group to offer visual images that remind them of the problem or challenge at hand, and I draw these images for them on the board or on sticky chart sheets (3M makes giant Post-its that are great for this). I also invite members of the group to come up and draw their own images. Then we post them around the room and start adding lists of ideas that the images suggest to us. Art can be a wide-open back door to creative insights.

Wrapping it up

When the group has produced a wide range of ideas, wrap up the creative session by capturing the ideas clearly in writing. Then either transition to idea review and development or end the session (leaving it for another group or time to do the review and development work). You'll almost always find a few nuggets that can be turned into valuable innovations in the coming weeks or months.

Being a Brilliant Participant

Participants make the brainstorming session — or break it if they don't participate appropriately. When you step into a group meeting and pull up a chair at the table, you can either wait and see whether the other people open up and start to offer ideas freely, or you can take the lead and start offering ideas right away. It's helpful to be a creativity leader and start offering ideas and suggestions as soon as possible. In fact, by being one of the first to offer ideas, you may set the mood and make others feel comfortable offering their own ideas. It really takes just one or two brave participants to get a brainstorming session rolling.

Contributing great ideas

So you want to take the lead by offering a bunch of ideas and showing the rest of the group how it's done? Good! However, you may find that your idea well dries up just when you go to it with a desire to fill your mental bucket. There's something fairly intimidating about the expectations that come along with being a participant in a brainstorming session. Often, people find that creative ideas just won't bubble up the way they want them to.

If you feel that your creativity may fail you just when you want it the most, try these tricks to revitalize your innovative instincts:

- **Close your eyes and withdraw for a minute, allowing yourself to relax and stop thinking.** Concentrate on your breathing, if it helps you clear your mind. When you open your eyes, you may find fresh ideas welling up.

- **Scribble some private notes on your own pad of paper to stimulate your imagination.** A good exercise is to associate related or suggested words. Start by writing three to five words that are obviously related to the topic or problem. Then list three more words for each. As you write more words, allow yourself to make simple word associations based on rhymes or other qualities of the words themselves. For example, *savings* might suggest *shavings, cravings,* and *paving.* This exercise often frees the imagination.

- **Ask questions.** When you don't have answers, asking questions is the natural thing to do. If the room is quiet and people are having trouble coming up with ideas, start asking open-ended questions that may help you or others see the problem from a fresh perspective.

- **Ask the facilitator for examples.** Sometimes all it takes are a few starting ideas to get the brainstorming up and running.

Don't sit at the table silently if your creativity is feeling blocked. Try to free it through one or more personal actions. If you can't get your ideas flowing, raise your hand and tell the facilitator. It's the facilitator's responsibility to provide warm-ups and idea-generation processes that work for you.

Being an informal leader and cheerleader

You may contribute through two main activities during a group brainstorming session: suggesting ideas and encouraging others to suggest ideas. Sometimes the second role is more helpful than the first because it's common for half or more of the group to be nervous about participating.

Use positive, open facial expressions such as smiles, nods, and interested expressions, along with short verbal encouragement (along the lines of "Great idea" and "Good thinking"), to let other participants feel that their contributions are helpful. Positive reinforcement from other participants may be more powerful than encouragement from the facilitator, especially when the facilitator is an outside consultant. As a peer, you may boost the comfort level in a brainstorming session simply by showing that you're comfortable and eager to see the group produce.

Overcoming your own creative timidity

Some people express their creativity constantly in their day-to-day activities, but most people don't. If you don't use your creativity routinely, stepping into a brainstorming session may feel a little like standing up to perform in a crowded room. Stage fright may kick in, inhibiting your flow of ideas or making you hesitant to express them out loud. Here are some ways to over-come your creative stage fright:

- ✔ **Practice in advance or during the first break.** Try to fill a page with creative ideas on any topic. Try one of these if you don't have one of your own: how to save the earth from global warming, what the next big handheld device will be, or what to do about a lack of parking spaces downtown. Rehearsing the act of producing freely associated ideas will help you get ready to perform for the facilitator and in front of the group.

- ✔ **Write ideas down on a piece of paper instead of saying them out loud.** If the facilitator challenges or questions you about what you're doing, explain that your ideas don't seem to be flowing very well and you're finding it hard to speak them out loud. Ask if the facilitator or another group member can review your list and share any good ideas from it with the rest of the group.

✔ **Ask for clarification of the instructions.** Make sure that the facilitator is asking for any and all ideas, including "bad," "silly," or "wild" ideas. Say that you don't have any good ideas yet but that you can offer bad ones if the facilitator thinks it might be helpful for moving the group ahead.

If the facilitator confirms that your ideas don't have to be polished or refined, you'll feel more comfortable with expressing whatever comes to mind, and so will those around you. Misery loves company, after all. Think about the metaphor of having to perform in public. It's much easier when others are performing too, and the same holds true for voicing creative associations.

Chapter 7

Mastering Advanced Brainstorming

● ●

In This Chapter

▶ Persisting long enough to produce an excellent innovation

▶ Shifting your focus to see the challenge in new and better ways

▶ Using visual techniques to stimulate your thinking

▶ Maximizing the effectiveness of group thinking

● ●

C hapter 6 shows you how to work with a group to generate creative ideas or options. It's great to get a group together, close the door, and start brainstorming. But sometimes, you still come up short and need to try some more tricks. It's important to keep going until you have at least one really great idea.

A group (or even individual) brainstorming session is often just the beginning of a creative thought process. You may want to challenge the group with additional creative activities. You may also want to go back to your desk (or somewhere more stimulating to the imagination) and try your hand at generating more ideas of your own.

Fortunately, the supply of creative processes and techniques is limitless. (One recent study documented more than 150 brainstorming techniques!) And if necessary, you can always invent more. You're an innovator, after all.

This chapter shows you how to help yourself and others produce more and better ideas by using powerful tools and tricks that stimulate the imagination and tap into fresh new veins of thought. From creative ways to focus (or refocus) your brainstorming to visualization exercises, this chapter guides you in getting the most out of your group sessions.

Going the Distance to Cash In on Creativity

Usually, brainstorming starts with the simple question "Does anyone have any ideas about X?" Sure, people have ideas, and you can probably fill a large piece of chart paper, a whiteboard, or an electronic message board with these ideas — provided that you make sure everyone contributes; builds on others' ideas; and remembers not to criticize any contributions, no matter how seemingly stupid or silly. Following is a typical starting list of brainstormed ideas; in this case, it's ways to publicize a new shampoo brand.

How can we attract more attention to our new hair-care brand?

Get a celebrity to use it.

Give it to the ten most famous celebrities.

Give out trial-size bottles at top salons.

Raffle off a lifetime supply.

Give away a giant bottle.

Hide a coupon worth $1 million in one of a million bottles.

Make a movie about it called *Sharleen in the Shampoo Factory.*

When a group brainstorms, one idea leads to another and another, as the associative process takes hold and the group generates ideas freely. However, the list you produce may not be exactly what you need, just as the preceding list certainly isn't the final word on how to market that new shampoo product. Usually, the first list of ideas is rough and preliminary. It may even be naïve. If you give up after the first round, you'll probably convince everyone who participated that brainstorming is a waste of time. But it's not. It gets the creative process started. Like most things of any great value, creativity takes time and effort. Persistence pays off. Impatience doesn't. Don't give up after one or two preliminary efforts to generate ideas. Plan to go through multiple rounds of idea generation, examination, and regeneration.

Critiquing the results of your brainstorming

It's important to cycle between creative and critical thinking. That cycle is at the core of advanced idea-generation and design processes because it helps both to expand your creative thinking and to refine your ideas, solutions, and designs.

Often, it helps to take a critical look at the first round of creative ideas. A very simple and easy method is to ask everyone at the brainstorming session to cast anonymous votes for their favorite ideas. I've used the little-round-sticker method many times for this purpose. Give each person six stickers. (I like to use the inexpensive kind you'd use to price garage-sale items, but you can use others if you have them on hand.) Let the participants allocate their six sticker-dots however they want — across six top ideas, or concentrated on one or a few favorites. Then create a table or bar chart of the ideas and the number of votes each received. Save the top ones (usually, 6 to 12) for further research and development.

You may also want to research the options and evaluate them by using a more thoughtful, scientific approach. If there are technical issues, test or study them from a technical perspective and decide which ones are most practical. You might even make prototypes for advanced testing. If what matters most is whether prospective customers will like a design, survey customers to ask them what they think, using a well-executed picture of the proposed design.

Figure 7-1 shows the results of a customer survey in which 100 shampoo users were asked what they thought of a variety of possible designs for shampoo bottles. Each bottle was illustrated and described, and the respondents were asked to rank how much they liked each one. (See Chapter 8 for more ways of collecting customer input.) Clearly, the feedback from customers helps narrow down the list of possible package designs and helps the developers decide what approach to take to their new shampoo packaging.

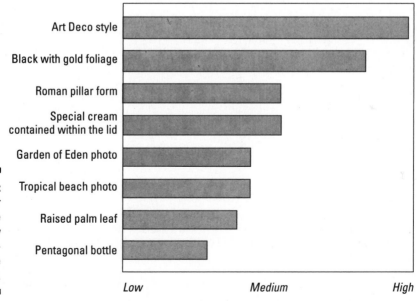

Consumer Appeal Scores for Shampoo Container Designs

Figure 7-1: Consumer preference for new shampoo-package designs.

To the surprise of the design team, an Art Deco approach to the shampoo bottle design was the most popular concept with customers, and Art Deco colors came in second place. The team had been favoring a tropical palm tree look, but customers pointed them in a different direction.

The shampoo development team decided to do some research by collecting old-fashioned photographs from the 1920s to find out more about Art Deco and see how to base a new brand on a Deco aesthetic. They began to look closely at vintage waves and bobs, and they formulated a shampoo and conditioner designed to help recreate those Art Deco looks. They also came up with the idea of packaging elegant Art Deco hair clips with trial packages of their shampoo and conditioner. The bottles were given a look akin to classic Art Deco buildings, and the label included a woman with bobbed hair and an elegant Art Deco dress in front of a Nash Ambassador Slipstream sedan. The name of the shampoo brand? Art Deco, of course!

Doing more research based on first-round questions

When I help companies generate ideas, I often find that my clients expect a full-blown solution or design to emerge from the first idea-generation session. Sorry, but it doesn't usually work that way. Even if the first day of brainstorming does produce a really great concept, it's still just a concept. It needs to be developed and refined, and there may be problems that need creative solutions along the development path.

Many brainstorming sessions raise more questions than they answer. If you emerge from a brainstorming session with a handful of new questions that help clarify and focus your thinking, you're doing pretty well!

I suggest that you keep a piece of chart paper taped up on the side of the room while leading a brainstorming session, with "Interesting questions to study" written across the top of it. As the brainstorming session goes on, periodically a question will come up that's important to the thought process but hard to answer. Write it on that list of important questions.

At the end of the day, review the list of questions, edit or add to it as the group sees fit, and then assign the questions to volunteers from the group. Their job is to research their questions and report what they find out to the rest of the group. It's amazing how often this research process produces the insight the group couldn't quite reach during the brainstorming session.

Start your next session with the same list of questions, and have the team discuss the research findings. Then see whether a better design or solution to your problem comes to mind. Often, it does.

Being persistent

Quantity ensures quality, at least when it comes to ideas. There's always debate about which (or whose) brainstorming techniques work best, but the one thing that's crystal clear is that highly successful innovators are more persistent than other people. They generate more ideas by spending more time working on their design goals or problems. They have *creative stamina,* or the persistence born of the knowledge that innovative results are a factor of focused effort, not talent or intelligence.

A great way to ensure persistence and productivity in idea generation is to plan for multiple brainstorming sessions, using a variety of techniques. The more the better. And a great way to start is to use techniques that focus your imagination, such as a specific question or problem statement.

Focusing Your Brainstorming in Creative Ways

It's difficult to see more and better options from just one viewpoint. Focusing and refocusing your view of the problem gives you fresh perspectives and fresh ideas. You can use a shift or narrowing of focus to generate more and different ideas. In fact, you ought to shift focus several times at least before you finish a brainstorming process. Otherwise, you may fall prey to the problem of fixation on one approach and fail to consider other possibilities.

Stimulating a shift in how people think about the topic

Shifting focus is a powerful way to get fresh ideas and insights. If you're not sure how to shift the focus, start by brainstorming about that. Use one of the following as your problem statement for a brainstormed list of ideas:

- Define or approach this problem in some new ways.
- Come up with analogies for the problem or goal.
- Think of similar situations or challenges others have already conquered.

Imagine a business that has an old, deteriorating building that needs expensive repairs. A group has been asked to come up with recommendations for how to approach the repairs: which to do in what order, which projects have synergy, which can be deferred with the least risk, and so forth.

The facilitator of the meeting poses a focus-shift question: "Is there another way to look at the problem of an aging building we can't really afford to keep up?" The group begins to brainstorm ideas, some of them silly and some potentially useful, such as

- ✔ Trade with some company that has a newer building and doesn't realize ours is in bad shape.
- ✔ Burn it down for insurance.
- ✔ Move to a new location.
- ✔ Tear it down and replace it with a modern, more efficient building.

As the group discusses options, it comes to the realization that it's inefficient and overly costly to keep patching up the old building and that, in fact, a replacement building might be a really good idea. It then shifts from the original task of writing a long-term maintenance plan to a new task: running the numbers to see whether moving to a better building might actually save money in the long run.

As in this example, prodding a group into considering a shift of focus is often immensely valuable. The mental thought process you go through when you find a new way to look at a topic is called *reframing,* and it has tremendous creative power because it opens up new lines of thought and action. Asking for new ways to look at a problem often produces a reframing of the original topic, which then leads to insights about how to approach it.

Fighting design fixation

Refocusing is especially important when the group (or individual) is guilty of *design fixation* — overly narrow assumptions about the nature of the answer or solution. Design fixation is very common, and it unintentionally narrows the focus of the group to just one family or style of possible answers.

For example, a group working on ways of designing more energy-efficient cars might be fixated on the idea that they have to design vehicles with two axles and four wheels: carlike designs. That could keep them from considering alternative forms, such as three-wheeled vehicles, vehicles with many extra wheels that act as flywheels to store energy, and hovercraft-type vehicles that have no wheels or that lift off their wheels at freeway speed, just to name a few of the alternatives that could be considered. Perhaps the single most energy-efficient transportation vehicle ever invented is the raft that runs on a canal between two major cities. Because rafts float, they require remarkably little energy to move. A freight-carrying raft on a canal may very well be the most "green" vehicle possible, but of course that old concept is not likely to be revived if everyone is fixated on carlike designs. (And what if you add a sail? Wind's free and extremely planet-friendly!)

Design fixation is everywhere — and usually hidden within the story of a company whose fortunes have declined. The U.S. automakers were fixated on large, heavy vehicle designs back when the Japanese automakers first gained a significant share of the U.S. market with their light, energy-efficient designs. Detroit could have designed similar cars, but they didn't because they just never gave the idea serious thought.

The best way to ensure that you aren't overly fixated on one approach is to include a design-fixation check somewhere in the fairly early stages of your creative process. Pose the following challenge to the group (or to yourself, if you're working alone):

> *Is there a* radically *different way to approach this problem?*

Then brainstorm as many fundamentally different alternative approaches as you can. For example, instead of making an energy-efficient car for commuters, you might consider canal-borne rafts, mini-dirigibles, moving roadways like giant conveyor belts, car trains for small electric vehicles to ride on for longer legs of their journeys, wind tunnels, and so forth. Maybe in the end you'll come back to an efficient hybrid electric-gas automobile, but at least by then you'll be sure that you couldn't have done it better by shifting to another family of possible solutions.

Sharpening the view with narrower problem definitions

Another powerful focusing technique involves drilling down to increasingly specific descriptions of what the problem or objective is. But how do you come up with these more specific strategies or approaches? Advance research helps — you can look for information about how others have tackled similar projects or problems. Also, you can always ask the group to help you brainstorm a list of general strategies and then conduct a second round in which you ask the group to develop specific ideas or designs for each strategy.

For example, you may start out with a broad goal such as "How can we boost revenue by at least 10 percent next year?" That sounds like an important objective for brainstorming, and it will certainly produce some suggestions. However, a broad question such as that tends to tap into fairly obvious answers and may fail to produce any fresh insights. Dig deeper for good ideas by narrowing the focus with more specific brainstorming topics, such as

✔ Can we turn one of our lesser-known products into a best-seller?

✔ Are there ways to upsell existing customers and get them to buy a lot more from us?

✔ What would we have to add to our products or services to justify a 10 percent or higher price increase?

These more specific questions are based on possible strategies for accomplishing the overarching goal of increased revenue. There are lots of possible ways to increase revenue. If you focus the question by naming a specific strategy, you're likely to get more ideas based on that strategy than you would get with the general statement of the goal.

Breaking the problem into smaller problems

Complex tasks are usually easy to break down into steps or stages. For example, the overall task of writing next year's business plan can be divided into researching the market, collecting financial data, doing projections, and so forth. A team may list a dozen chores associated with business planning, divide the list among themselves, and then get together to integrate their separate contributions into one master document.

The same approach can be used for creative problem-solving and design. A great way to divide and conquer is to start with a broad question and then brainstorm narrower, more specific questions that nest beneath the starting question.

For example, if you want to introduce a new vacuum cleaner that doesn't need to be plugged in, is good for the environment, has a very powerful motor, and not only cleans the floor but also filters the air, well, you might be as stuck for ideas as I am right now. Hmm. So break the problem down! You could start with a focus on motors. Are there any new motors that combine high power and small size with a very low use of energy to run? Maybe. If you find one, you can probably design a breakthrough product around it, so it's a great question to focus your brainstorming. Finding a better motor is a nicely focused project that might be fairly easy to research — for instance, you could get in touch with industry experts and associations like the Small Motor and Motion Association.

As you break complex, open-ended problems or goals down, eventually you get to a level where the questions are so specific that they require less creative effort and are more easily solved through standard research techniques. Then as you combine the specific findings from multiple, narrowly defined questions, you're able to build up to a high level of creative design again, this time with a clearer idea of how you'll accomplish the specifics.

Visualizing for Creative Success

A picture's worth a thousand words, but most people brainstorm in words, not pictures. Try to work at least one or two visual techniques into every creative session to tap into more aspects of your creativity. You don't have to be an artist to think visually. Here are some helpful ways to engage your visual thinking skills.

Introducing visual reference material

One great way to bring your visual thinking to bear on your challenge is to use visual images to stimulate your own and others' thinking. Gather photographs, diagrams, or actual physical examples of ways others have approached similar problems. Sometimes, gathering great solutions to dissimilar problems is also helpful, just because it's inspirational to see brilliant work in any field.

Spread the examples around your workspace or brainstorming room where your team can see them. Post pictures, plans, diagrams, and press clippings. React to these examples informally, just by seeing whether they suggest any ideas. If an informal approach fails to produce the results you want, pose formal questions about the examples, such as

- ✔ How many different ways have people tackled the solution of this problem?
- ✔ Could we combine the best from two or more of these examples to produce an even better option?
- ✔ Can we improve on the best of these designs?
- ✔ Can we adapt a clever solution to a different design problem and make it work for us?

These questions force the group to look at the images around them and process them for creative inspiration. Often, the result is an avalanche of creative ideas.

Using imagery to stimulate the mind's eye

Visual thinking can be done within the mind because we all have the capacity to visualize things, even if they aren't right there in front of us. Analogies and metaphors are helpful in stimulating visual thinking.

Challenge the group to paint brief verbal pictures that represent the problem. For example, they might think of a budgeting problem as being like "trying to carry too much weight on a small boat." Their effort to think visually may help them see new approaches and alternatives, because visual thinking often helps boost creativity.

Sketching ideas rather than describing them

Imagine you can't use words. How will you communicate an idea to others? You might draw a map or floor plan, a diagram or flowchart of a process, or a picture of a design for a new product or tool. Prehistoric cave drawings communicate to us today, showing us how hunters surrounded large animals and brought them down with multiple spears — an important innovation in its day. People have been sketching their ideas for a long time. It's a powerful way to communicate ideas, as well as to think of them in the first place.

Sketch pads and boxes of fine-tipped colored markers belong in every brain-storming session and ought to be used for at least one round of no-words-allowed brainstorming. Ask people to generate a sketch of an idea and then have them take turns explaining their ideas to the rest of the group. Figure 7-2 shows a good format for sketching rough ideas on chart pads, in which the sketch is accompanied by brief explanatory text. Very often, a round of idea drawing produces fresh insights that you can develop into useful designs or plans.

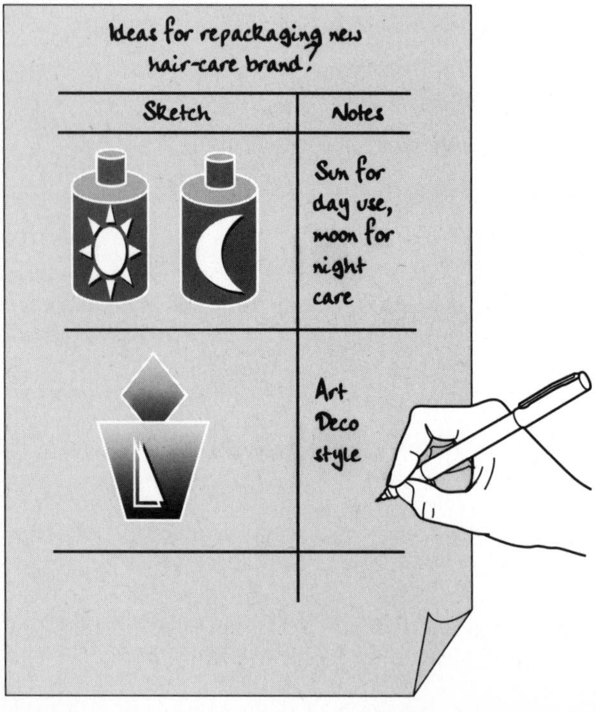

Ideas for repackaging new hair-care brand!

Sketch	Notes
	Sun for day use, moon for night care
	Art Deco style

Figure 7-2:
A helpful format for sketching design concepts.

Building solutions from standard geometric shapes

I sometimes draw a series of neat geometric shapes on the board or chart pad and challenge pairs of participants to design solutions to the problem, using only these shapes plus their imagination. Don't force the group to be too literal, because the goal is to stimulate fresh, imaginative thinking.

Some design elements you can offer include small and large circles, squares, wedges, rectangles, rods, cones, boards, and belts and elastic bands of various sizes. You can offer a simple list of shapes or draw the shapes on the board or chart pad. Instruct teams of two to four to imagine that they're going to build something that solves the problem at hand. They can give the shapes specific properties to meet their design needs. A circle can be a tire, steering wheel, timing wheel, gear, or anything else they need it to be that's circular. They may also use as many repetitions of each shape as they want.

A simple but potentially profitable design concept came out of a shape-brainstorming session with the goal of inventing new products for office or household use. The concept this team came up with was a set of mugs, each of which has a unique geometric shape so that people don't get confused about which one is theirs.

The results of shape brainstorming are almost always highly imaginative. After you run a shape-brainstorming session, have each group show its drawing and explain how it works. Then ask them to identify elements from the imaginative design drawings that they would like the real design or solution to have. From this list, begin to develop a real-world design.

Storyboarding an idea

A *storyboard* is a piece of poster paper that has a cartoon-style series of drawings and captions or speech bubbles. The format is often used in the advertising industry to show an idea for a television ad. It's also great for showing how you think customers might use a new product you're considering or how a newly designed service function might interact with customers.

Whenever you're working on a process that has people doing things, a storyboard can be used to tell the story of how the interaction might go.

For a fun and potentially helpful alternative, draw simple comic-book-style pages showing people working with or consuming a new invention or product. Then share the story with associates or a group you've assembled to brainstorm with you, and get their reactions. Showing has much more impact than telling and often generates rich feedback and suggestions.

Making small-scale models

Nothing is quite as helpful as a model of a new design that you and others can see, pick up, and handle. Architects often build balsa wood models of proposed buildings for their clients to examine and critique. Sometimes, the client realizes he doesn't like an element of the design when he sees it in three dimensions rather than just on the blueprints. Depending on what you're designing, you might use balsa wood, glue, paper, tape, flexible plastic sheets, or heavier materials requiring a wood or metal shop to help you.

If you need to impress someone, a sophisticated model is needed. But if you simply want to get reactions to a design concept, a simple, inexpensive, rough model will do.

Using sticky notes and a wall for your brainstorming

You can morph verbal brainstorming into a visual medium by using sticky notes.

To show you how sticky notes can help a group visualize solutions, imagine the case of a seaside hotel that does very well in summer but loses money in winter. The manager wants to generate ideas for drawing off-season guests and increasing utilization in the winter. Figure 7-3 shows a sticky-note brainstorming session. First, the facilitator posts a sticky note with an objective. Next, he chooses a list of random words out of a dictionary (see "Generating ideas from random words" later in this chapter) and writes them on sticky notes that he puts up on a wall in an "inventory" area.

Then the facilitator forms his group into creative pairs whose instructions are to select one random word and brainstorm ideas from it. Group members are told to associate possible strategies — no matter how wild or crazy the idea — and write them on sticky notes. Then they place their notes next to the random words that stimulated each idea.

As the members of the group post their idea notes, they or others may associate new ideas with the posted ones. If so, they're told to post their new ideas next to the ones that gave them the ideas. That way, the sticky notes grow along the associative pathways of the group's creative thinking. (See the next section for other ways to map ideas based on their relationships.)

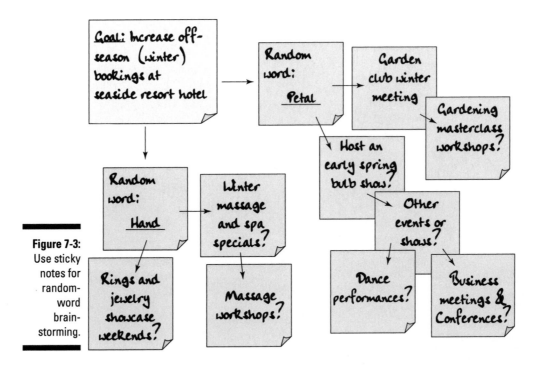

Figure 7-3:
Use sticky notes for random-word brain-storming.

Drawing a mind map

Mind maps can be used by individuals or groups to brainstorm new ideas. A *mind map* is a visual approach to taking notes in which you use lines or arrows to show the connections between concepts, facts, questions, and ideas. When you use mind maps to organize notes (a practice proven to improve student recall when studying), the arrows should reflect a logical structure for the content. However, when you use mind maps to brainstorm new ideas, the arrows indicate the associative pathways your thinking takes.

Figure 7-4 shows how a group uses a mind map to think about new product concepts for the coffee industry. It shows how you can use *big questions,* or questions that suggest important avenues of thought (they're shown in italic in the figure), as well as a variety of smaller questions and ideas organized in natural thought clusters.

As your mind map grows, it may be necessary to expand it by adding more sheets of paper. I recommend using very large sticky pads. A few sheets of them can turn a wall into a mind-mapping center, allowing multiple people to work simultaneously. However, when I mind map by myself (a practice I often use when I want to find new approaches to a subject), I use large drawing pads or, if I don't have one at hand, 11-x-17-inch sheets of paper on a conference table, taping sheets together if my map gets too big for the first one. I've sometimes used as many as six or eight sheets as I expand my thinking.

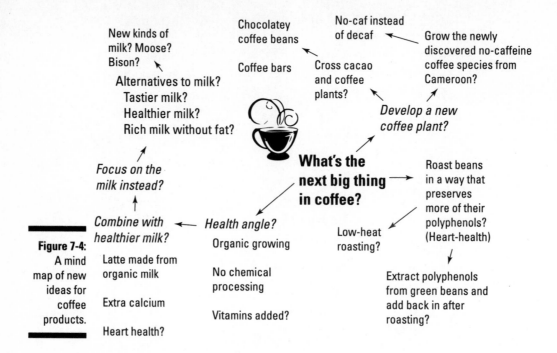

Figure 7-4:
A mind map of new ideas for coffee products.

Combining research with mind mapping

Mind mapping raises as many questions as it does ideas and proposals. Having a research tool at hand to answer those questions is very helpful. If your inquiry is general in nature, Wikipedia (www.wikipedia.org) or some form of encyclopedia may be useful. Also, you can invite experts such as chemists, engineers, or doctors to your mind-mapping session so as to have ready access to special expertise that can be integrated into the mind map. That way, your mind map is smarter than any of the individuals in the room and combines both their knowledge and their ideas.

In Figure 7-4, you can see how certain facts about coffee work their way into the mind map. Someone looked up alternative sources of milk, and someone else discovered a new species of coffee that raises the possibility of producing naturally uncaffeinated coffee with all the flavor of regular coffee.

You can use research to provide the structure for brainstorming solutions to a problem. Study the topic to learn what the principal approaches are. These become the general categories that you brainstorm within.

The example in Figure 7-5 concerns a workplace in which the management team wants to try to prevent the seasonal flu from spreading widely and infecting so many people that productivity is hurt. Their initial research suggests that three main categories of strategies might be productive: education, prevention, and containment. They then brainstorm possible ways to use each of these strategies in their own workplace. Their approach involves the use of sticky notes arranged in columns under the three main categories.

Using mind-mapping software

Concept development is a fairly simple challenge for mind mapping — all you really need is a lot of paper and markers to do it. But when you have a good concept, if you want to do another mind map to help you design it, you'll find yourself getting into a lot of specifics that can be hard to organize and keep track of. Enter mind-mapping software.

The size of a virtual page is unlimited, and software programs can keep track of all the ideas and information, including much more detailed information than you'd want to write out by hand. The latest software programs allow you to integrate electronic documents and Web links into your mind maps, making them extremely rich and detailed.

Some of the mind-mapping software programs allow shared use, so you can have a virtual team working on a mind map from distant locations. The facilitation can be a bit tricky, but it's interesting to see what you can generate as you cooperate with far-flung participants.

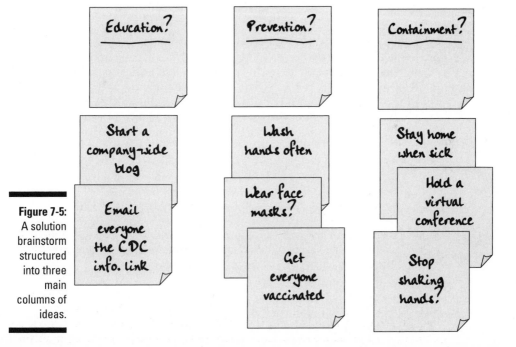

Figure 7-5:
A solution brainstorm structured into three main columns of ideas.

The Compendium Institute offers shareware for download from its Web site, `compendium.open.ac.uk`. FreeMind is another popular open-platform program. It's available for download at `freemind.sourceforge.net/wiki/index.php/Main_Page`. Commercial products include iMindMap (`www.imindmap.com`), Mindjet's MindManager (`www.mindjet.com`), and NovaMind's Mind Mapping Software (`www.novamind.com/mind-mapping`).

Clustering ideas and suggestions

A variant of mind mapping involves the initial generation or collection of lots of ideas, suggestions, and other helpful thoughts and bits of information, followed by an effort to cluster them into groups based on their relatedness. You can use a formal outline structure for organizing the ideas, but it's so linear that it doesn't lend itself to innovative thinking very well. That's where the mapping comes in. Cluster the ideas visually instead of putting them in an outline or table, and see what insights the effort produces.

I like to use index cards for the first step of a cluster-brainstorming session. Hand out a small stack of index cards to each participant. Then ask the participants to generate ideas, questions, or related facts — one per card. Let them work individually (a variation on the nominal group technique; see "Using index cards and the nominal group technique" later in this chapter), or have them work in breakout groups of two to four. You can even run a general brainstorming session, but have the facilitator write each suggestion on a card rather than on a board or chart pad.

When you have 30 or more index cards filled with ideas, gather the group around a large table and begin to seek order. What are the natural clusters of cards? Lay them out as best you can, trying to find group consensus as you go. What you're doing is actually an intuitive version of a statistical technique called *cluster analysis,* in which variables that correlate with one another are grouped to reveal underlying relationships and patterns. Your cluster map may reveal interesting groups or connections, too. It most certainly will stimulate more ideas, which you can add to the map, just as you would when doing a regular mind map (refer to the earlier section "Drawing a mind map").

Producing insights and proposals from your mind map

The mind map itself is not the end product. After the mind-mapping or cluster-brainstorming session is over, sit down on your own or with one or two associates to mine the map. Examine it for interesting ideas, fresh insights, or new ways to focus your research and development. Make a list of the promising outcomes. Decide who will follow up on each one, how, and when.

In fact, the journalist's classic set of questions may be applied: who, what, when, where, why, and how? If you answer each of these questions, you'll always have a clear idea about who's doing follow-up, when, where, and so forth. Create a summary action plan to e-mail participants with their who-what-where-when-why-how assignments.

The "why" is especially important as it defines the imagined benefits and helps clarify the potential importance of the work. I like to create a blank table with room to write the question or proposal at the top and with empty columns for each of the journalist's six questions. Fill in one of these tables for each promising finding from your brain-mapping exercise (or from any brainstorming activity), give the tables to appropriate individuals for follow-up, and gather again for a debriefing on their findings in a week or so.

 Follow-up is key when it comes to preliminary, free-minded brainstorming activities like mind mapping. Without it, all you've done is exercise your imagination, which isn't a bad thing to do, but it's better to harness the energy of that work to produce an actual, innovative outcome.

Maximizing the Power of Team Thinking

Creative teams are organized groups of people focusing on generating ideas, designs, or solutions for a common problem or goal; they bring together the diverse experiences, knowledge, and ideas of many people. Most people believe that a group will easily produce more and better ideas than an individual, which is why we form groups when we have creative challenges.

The whole idea of brainstorming is that a group should be more productive than an individual. However, that common belief is as much myth as fact. Quite a few studies have shown that individuals brainstorming on their own are more productive on average than groups. The psychologists who study this stuff even have a term for this misplaced faith in the group: *illusion of group productivity.* Groups don't usually produce as many creative ideas as they think they will, nor are those ideas as good as they anticipate. Most of their participants fail to generate a high number of ideas. What can you do to make sure that your groups *are* highly productive? The following sections outline some of the many good ways to get a real, live group to produce at a high level.

Using index cards and the nominal group technique

The *nominal group technique* (NGT) involves the individuals of a group writing their ideas on slips of paper, which are then gathered and shared with the group for voting, discussion, or other purposes. Traditionally, NGT has been used effectively for group decision-making.

Creative chitchat

One simple but effective way to make people produce more in group sessions is to have them participate in an electronic chat room, where they all post their ideas as fast as they can type, and every idea is visible to all who are invited to the chat. Research shows that electronic groups are often more productive than actual live ones. Probably the social influences of others' presence are lessened, reducing *production blocking* or the self-censorship of creative thought and expression. To make a chat room brainstorm effective, invite an appropriate group, brief them in advance, and stay in the chat room yourself to facilitate. You may need to ask a participant to avoid criticism of others' ideas, for example. Chat rooms are great places to generate input and ideas, but be careful not to discuss proprietary information online.

Here's how to take a vote by using NGT:

1. **Have each individual write down his first choice plus a supporting argument for it.**
2. **Have each member privately rank all the proposed solutions.**
3. **Tally the rankings.**

   The winning proposal emerges.

You can also use an NGT approach to generate ideas and share them with the group:

1. **Pose a question or challenge, just as if you were initiating a brainstorming session.**
2. **Pass out index cards or sheets of paper.**
3. **Have everyone write their ideas down in silence.**

   This differs from the brainstorming session in which you call on people to voice their ideas.

4. **Gather the first crop of ideas, and transcribe them (minus duplicates) onto a chart pad at the front of the room.**
5. **Hand out more cards and gather another round of ideas.**

   These ideas will be richer because group members will be inspired by each others' thinking.

6. **Repeat the gathering and summarizing of information.**
7. **Transition to yet another round of index card notes or to a traditional brainstorming session or discussion.**

When you think you have a good crop of ideas based on quantity (at least 30) and quality (a wide range of approaches including many unexpected ones), transition to a critical evaluation of the ideas. This can be done in one of two ways:

- ✔ **Unstructured:** Simply ask the group to discuss the ideas and try to reach a consensus regarding their favorites.

- ✔ **Structured:** Hand out index cards once again, this time with the instruction to identify and rank the top three ideas. As you hand out the cards, tell group members to give three points to their first-place choice, two to their second, and one to their third. That way, the top choice gets the most points, not the least.

Gather the rankings, tally them, and see which ideas got the most and highest votes. To compute the winners, add the numbers assigned by each member to each idea (three for a first-place ranking, plus two for a second-place ranking, and so forth). The idea with the highest total points is the group's top choice.

The NGT produces more and richer contributions from group members when there are pressures that might keep members from participating fully in a regular brainstorming session, such as the following:

- ✔ Some group members tend to dominate the discussion.
- ✔ Some group members are introverted and think better in silence.
- ✔ People are new to your team and uncomfortable with freely sharing their ideas.
- ✔ A supervisor's presence inhibits verbal sharing of ideas.
- ✔ Controversy or politics is likely to get in the way of open conversation.

Even if these factors don't seem to be present, I still recommend doing a round or two of NGT just to increase the productivity of your group. Mix it up with traditional brainstorming to maximize creative production.

Using pass-along brainstorming

Another great way to alter the creative dynamics and shake free a few more good ideas is to pass a piece of paper around the room, allowing each group member to add her own thought to the bottom of a growing list.

I don't recommend this as your primary brainstorming method, because it sidelines most of the group while one person writes, but as a quick way to change the dynamics, it can be quite useful.

Pass a tough question around the room

Write a thoughtful question at the top of the top sheet of paper on a lined pad. A question requiring creative thinking, not a technical or logical response, works best. Then pass it around the room, allowing each person to contribute his thoughts in turn. At the end, read the entire list and then open the floor for discussion. Sometimes, ideas will build up as each person takes turns writing, and a fresh approach will arise. If this happens, switch to a verbal discussion or begin to sketch or diagram at the front of the room to see whether the idea can be implemented to meet your needs.

Tell stories about strategic success

Sometimes, writers experiment by using pass-along brainstorming to write a short plot synopsis or story. They take turns contributing a sentence, a paragraph, or even a whole chapter. How will the story develop? None of them knows, but somehow, the story does develop, climax, and resolve, and interesting characters develop. The group-writing process can produce creative twists and turns that surprise the contributors.

I've adapted pass-along storytelling to the strategic planning process by having participants in a planning retreat take turns contributing to a story about a successful new innovator in their industry. The ideas that may surface when you engage people's imagination in this way can be amazing. Sometimes, one of the fictional, winning strategies works its way into the strategic plan, showing how imaginative exercises can bring to the surface fresh ideas that produce innovations.

Pass along a brainstormed list by e-mail

I sometimes use an e-mail version of pass-along brainstorming in advance of a creative session. It avoids the problem you have in a group of most people doing nothing while one person writes.

When you circulate a question by e-mail, you're really just adapting the old-fashioned chain letter to modern electronic brainstorming. Provide a circulation list at the bottom of the e-mail, with instructions for each person in the chain to add her ideas and then pass the e-mail on to the person whose name follows hers.

Put your own name at the bottom of the list (assuming you're the facilitator) so the accumulated ideas make their way back to you. Then clean up the list and print copies of it as a handout or blow it up as a poster to share when your group assembles in person. Or if you're not assembling the group in person, e-mail the master list back to all participants with a thank-you note that includes a brief description of how you're using their input.

Ask your pass-along e-mail participants to offer suggestions for creative or analytical questions that might help clarify the right approach to the project. If you use the pass-along method to develop a list of insightful questions, you can then do some research and gather information of relevance to each question. Bring the information to the brainstorming session, along with the master list of the questions, to provide the group with a research base that helps them with their thinking.

Generating ideas from random words

The *random-word technique* uses randomly selected words from a source such as a dictionary to stimulate fresh thinking. The idea behind this technique is to engage creative thinking by challenging people to find associations between apparently unrelated words and the problem or project they're working on. Figure 7-3 illustrates a random-word brainstorm, using sticky notes to mind map the associations.

Working individually, too!

Sometimes, I find that people are hesitant to innovate the old-fashioned way: by holing up somewhere with lots of research (such as background information, technical requirements, and examples of failed approaches) and persisting until they finally come up with a breakthrough. The fact is, sometimes you can run brainstorming sessions, ask for e-mail input, and consider dozens of employee suggestions and still not have a really great idea. That's when it's time to put on your own thinking cap and close and lock your office door (or studio — see Chapter 1 for ideas on how to create your perfect creative space).

Cycle between private and group work

Don't be afraid to turn away from group processes, ignore others who want to be helpful but don't seem to be moving things ahead, and just plain think about the problem. Persistence is certainly the single most powerful creative technique, and anybody can use it if they are, well, persistent enough. If you go off and think really hard about a problem and then come back with fresh ideas or insights, you may be able to refocus the group in a new, more productive direction and get better input from them.

In my experience, the leader of a creative process or the facilitator of a creative group needs to do some hard thinking of her own. Don't leave it to the group to come up with a breakthrough.

Contribute extra ideas after you've left the session

Individual work parallel to the group is valuable even if you're not leading the group but are just one of many participants. Take the project or problem home with you; incubate it overnight; and try your hand at a list of ideas, a design sketch, or another form of solution the next morning. It's amazing how often the really good idea waits until the brainstorming session is over to pop into your head. Try to send in at least one high-quality idea within several days after a brainstorming event.

If you plan on following up with additional ideas, you'll probably keep thinking about the topic, at least subconsciously, and a great idea is likely to suddenly leap to the forefront of your mind.

I spent three days brainstorming new breakfast-cereal concepts for Kellogg's and was very proud of the lengthy list of ideas our group produced for them. However, in the years after that session, I've actually come up with a number of even better ideas. The intense immersion in the topic primed me to think about it, and I guess I've been incubating it ever since. For example, my 5-year-old daughter loves cereal with milk and maple syrup, and so do I. It occurred to me this morning at breakfast that a Maple Krispies product could include small pieces of maple-sugar candy shaped like maple leaves that melt into the milk. Yum!

I checked Kellogg's Web site (`www.kelloggs.com`) and found that they have an open-innovation system called Great Ideas (click Great Ideas on their home page or go to `www2.kelloggs.com/GreatIdeas/default.aspx`). So I entered my product proposal on their Web site, and now I'm going to keep an eye on the grocery store shelf to see whether it pops up. I'm no longer under contract so I won't profit from the idea, but I'll still feel great if it gets adopted. See Chapter 8 for ways of enlisting volunteers like me through crowdsourcing. People love to share their ideas!

Chapter 8

Going Beyond Brainstorming

In This Chapter

▶ Asking customers to help you develop your ideas

▶ Mapping and redesigning processes

▶ Holding creative conversations by e-mail and in chat rooms

▶ Opening the creative process through crowdsourcing

▶ Tapping into your intuition for creative guidance

*A*n old expression whose origins I can't guess at says, "There's more than one way to skin a cat." I don't want to skin any cats, but I do recall that saying whenever I feel stuck and unable to come up with the breakthrough idea I need for my own business or for one of my clients. Brainstorming (see Chapter 6) and its variants (such as the nominal group technique and concept sketching; see Chapter 7) are powerful ways of stimulating the imagination and focusing it on useful innovations. You can use alternative approaches, however — lots of them! This chapter helps you find new ways to bump up your own imagination, as well as the creativity of a group.

Using Customer Input for Inspiration

Many innovations have to do with product development, service improvement, or other matters with a marketing or sales orientation. If you're interested in improving what you sell or inventing something new to sell, try asking your customers for ideas, suggestions, or — even better — complaints. Why? Customer complaints give you insight into things that seem like problems to your customers, and problems for your customers are opportunities for you!

Collect and save all customer complaints so that you can dip into the file to see what's bugging your customers. If a lot of complaints have to do with lost or late shipments, you can conclude that you need to innovate the way that you ship products to your customers. If the complaints are more about the products and what they do (or don't do), you see that product innovation is in order.

Organizing a focus group

Sometimes, you need to stimulate customers to give you more specific or deeper input than you can get from casual complaints. After all, customers usually don't put much thought into ways to make your business more successful, so if you want their ideas, you have to ask them.

A common — and highly effective — way to get customer assistance is to gather a group of customers in a conference room (usually, you have to offer them some cash and/or free products as an incentive), show them a series of new product concepts, and ask them for their reactions.

You can gather customers yourself or hire a market research firm to do it, in which case you'll be shopping for what the research industry calls a *focus group*. The research firm will help you decide what kinds of customers you want in the room and will not only get them there, but also provide a professional moderator and a recording, plus a written summary of the findings.

These formal focus groups are often useful for evaluating product concepts that are already fairly well developed. If you want input and suggestions for new products, however, a less formal (and cheaper) do-it-yourself group may be for you.

To run an informal focus group, invite customers you know already, because they're likely to be easy to assemble and eager to help. Offer a half dozen to a dozen of your good customers breakfast or lunch, and ask them to commit to two hours of conversation about your products and services. If you don't have a good meeting facility in your offices, rent a conference room at a nearby hotel, and arrange for the hotel to cater the meal.

When the group is assembled, thank everyone for coming, and explain that you'll be asking them to share their ideas, suggestions, and criticisms to help you design a new product, improve customer service, or meet some other worthy goal that customers would find beneficial. Go to a whiteboard or chart pad on an easel, and write the topic at the top. Then go directly into facilitating a brainstorming session.

Capture any and all comments and suggestions, and use enthusiastic, positive body language and verbal praise so your customers feel that their input is valuable — whether you think it is or not! It's essential to produce a positive customer experience, because these people, after all, are your good customers. Praise and feed them well, and send them thank-you notes afterward. Also, if any ideas from the session get implemented, let the people who came up with them know; they'll be thrilled to learn that their input was useful.

Asking customers to fantasize about their ultimate product

Ask your customers about their fantasies for your products. It's a great way to come up with fascinating new ideas and possibilities for product development. You can ask individual customers one on one when the opportunity arises, or you can send e-mail requests to your whole customer list. You might even hold a contest on your Web site (sending a press release to the media to announce it) in which you solicit the most imaginative fantasy product in your product category.

Suppose that you could have the ultimate watch — one that could easily do anything and everything you might want it to do. What would it be like? Hmm. Let's see. Well, just telling the time isn't really that exciting in this day and age, because your cellphone, laptop, car, and microwave all tell the time quite accurately. But the watch of your dreams might do more exciting and useful things. Perhaps it would include a mini-GPS (Global Positioning System) chip that would keep you from getting lost, remind you if you're about to miss an important appointment, and prompt you to pick up flowers to take home for your wife on your anniversary. In other words, your fantasy watch would keep you oriented in many ways besides time.

Nobody's asked me to describe my own ultimate watch so far, but if a watchmaker were to do so, she might come up with interesting ideas for new product development.

Inviting customer input, both critical and creative

Invite customers to give you feedback or review a new design, either via one-on-one e-mail communication or in an informal focus group (refer to "Organizing a focus group" earlier in this chapter). What customers should you ask to evaluate design options or new product concepts? You might want to ask just a representative sample of typical customers. Those people are the ones you want to sell to, after all. Asking the average customer is great if you simply want to see whether people like and think they'd buy a new design.

When you survey typical customers about their reactions to a new product design, have them rate the appeal of the design (as I discuss in Chapter 7) and also ask them to make choices. If they had to choose, would they buy your new design or one of the leading products already on the market? By asking members of your sample group to make choices, you simulate a shopping experience and may get more accurate information about how customers will react to your new design.

Another approach is to talk to *lead users* — sophisticated customers who can offer unusual insights on customer needs and wants. In business to business (B2B) sales, your sales force or sales reps can tell you who the lead users are because they stand out as being more sophisticated and successful than most. If you don't have personal contact with your customers, you may need to talk with a mailing-list broker about strategies for finding the most sophisticated users and contacting them to see whether any are willing to help.

Talk to the smartest, best customers when you want design ideas, not just simple reactions to completed designs. Lead users often suggest new designs or products that you can refine and introduce to the market with great success, as 3M has done. In B2B marketing, lead users are top companies that are innovators themselves; these companies can offer interesting ideas and suggestions to their suppliers.

Redesigning Processes

Process design is easiest when you work visually, which means process mapping or flowcharting. This method is great if you're working on a problem or challenge that involves a system, such as how to improve the quality of customer service in a hotel. The Ritz-Carlton Hotel Co., in fact, has used process flowcharting to great effect in improving the quality and reducing the cost of customer service.

To map and then redesign your own processes, follow these steps:

1. **Create a diagram that uses standardized symbols.**

   These symbols could include ovals for the start and end of the process, arrows for directional movement between steps in the process, rectangles for each step, and diamonds for choices or decisions (with two or more arrows going out of them to represent the options).

Figure 8-1 shows a simple flowchart for a call to the front desk from a hotel guest. This flowchart might be the initial one that you'd draw after asking a group to explain how a call from a guest to the front desk is handled.

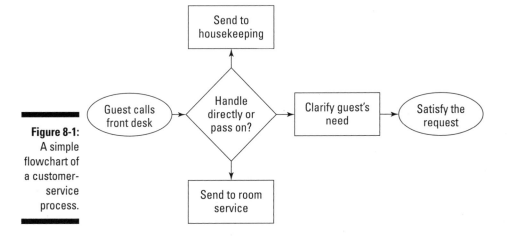

Figure 8-1:
A simple
flowchart of
a customer-
service
process.

2. **Ask the group to discuss the initial drawing and decide whether it leaves anything out.**

   Often, the first drawing proves to be overly simplistic. Figure 8-1, for example, doesn't explain what happens if the guest needs a hotel engineer to perform a repair or if the front desk can't handle the request. Nor does it show when the desk staff should pass on a difficult caller to a manager. More steps and options must be added to make the diagram complete.

3. **Continue to expand and correct the drawing until you have what appears to be a complete flowchart of the way things are done now.**

   When the current process has been fully flowcharted, it will be much easier for the group to study and improve it.

   If necessary, create secondary flowcharts showing how hand-off processes work. To continue the example shown in Figure 8-1, what does housekeeping do when the front desk passes a call to it?

4. **Point to any step in the flowchart, and ask the group about ways to improve it.**

   You could ask questions such as these:

   - What could go wrong here?
   - Could someone else handle this task better?
   - Why is this step done this way?
   - Could we take any steps out of this process to simplify it?

• Where do things go wrong in this process most often?

• Are there better ways to perform any of the steps?

Encourage group members to ask their own critical and creative questions too.

5. **Based on the group's feedback, use the flowchart symbols to diagram possible alternative designs.**

   In the hotel example shown in Figure 8-1, it may make sense to reduce the number of times that the front desk hands off customer calls. Hand-offs frustrate customers and introduce the possibility of problems such as dropped calls or busy signals.

The visual quality of the flowchart diagrams will help your group (or you, if you're working individually) to see many possibilities that are hard to imagine in the abstract.

Taking Advantage of E-Mail

Of the millions of e-mails sent and received every day, very few ask for creative input. How many times have you received an e-mail saying, "What do you think about X? Can you please send me some ideas?"

Why don't we use e-mail to generate ideas? That simply isn't part of the convention for the medium. E-mail is used as a vehicle for telling or asking people to do things, catching up with people, complaining about what people have done, or sharing general information efficiently. It usually isn't used for brainstorming. E-mail is a really, really good medium for generating ideas, however, because e-mail makes it so easy to contact people wherever they are and ask for their input.

Including a provocative question or situation

"What if…?" e-mails are good for generating fresh ideas. To create such an e-mail, you could use "Request for creative suggestions" as your Subject line; introduce the e-mail by explaining that you're asking for help on brainstorming initial ideas, including impractical or fanciful ideas; and then offer a scenario (a short what-if story) about your topic that imposes some kind of limitation and asks, "What would you do if you couldn't . . . ?" or something like that.

The limitation is a form of *provocation* — a mental challenge that stimulates fresh thinking. If you don't provoke creative thinking somehow, your e-mail replies will simply be the same old thoughts that people usually have.

The Commonwealth Fund, a charitable foundation in New York City that focuses on ways to improve the healthcare system, sent e-mails to pediatricians asking them how they would provide well-child care if a disease (such as a bad flu strain) closed down the outpatient medical offices that they normally used to see their patients. Doctors came up with lots of ideas for delivering routine healthcare to children without using their offices, such as providing services in schools, through TV broadcasts and Web sites, and via parent training. Although the actual scenario is unlikely to happen, many of the ideas were of general interest because they could supplement the current system of patient care.

The main point of interest for the purposes of this discussion is this: Hundreds of health professionals answered The Commonwealth Fund's e-mail. The foundation collected numerous suggestions without having to gather a group of people and run a time-consuming, potentially costly brainstorming session. You can take advantage of the economy and ease of e-mail brainstorming too.

Designing your e-mail for thoughtful consideration

Make sure that your e-mail has clear signals that mark it as an open-minded request for creative input so that it isn't handled like a normal e-mail. Normally, people spend fewer than 30 seconds replying to each e-mail, so to generate useful ideas from the recipients of your e-mail, you have to slow them down and get them to think about your question for at least a minute.

Here are a few ways to get recipients' thoughtful attention:

- **Make the case that it's important to get the recipient's help.** Include a brief (one to three sentences) description of the situation, explaining why you need creative ideas now and what you'll do with those ideas to solve a problem or improve a situation.

- **Use a provocation, such as an unusual scenario or examples of creative ideas that the recipient can use as a springboard.** For more information on provocation, see the preceding section.

- **Specifically ask for at least a minute of undivided attention and thought.**

- **Give the recipient a short time frame for replying (such as within the day or the week).**

> ✔ **Include five to ten times as many people in the e-mail list as you'd invite to an actual brainstorming session.** When you solicit ideas by e-mail rather than in person, you'll get fewer ideas, because e-mail recipients won't put very much time into answering your request. A few dozen people is a good minimum for your list.

When you use these five elements, your brainstorming e-mail ought to produce interesting responses. Follow up with a thank-you e-mail and a list of all the ideas offered (minus redundant ones). Ask your recipients to reply with any additional ideas that they may have had in the interim. The combination of the passage of time (which permits incubation to occur) and the list of other people's ideas often stimulates another crop of interesting replies.

When you complete your project, e-mail your contributors one final time, summarizing what you ended up doing and thanking them again for their help with the brainstorming stage of the project. They'll feel good about their participation and will be eager to help again.

Holding an e-mail contest for best idea

A contest can produce a flood of interesting e-mails. You can announce that you're holding a contest for something like a new name or logo, new product concepts, or the best way to solve a problem. Recognition generally is the best prize: The winner gets the honor of seeing his idea turned into reality. Make sure that you provide a ceremony, a naming opportunity, or some such form of recognition for the winner. Also consider providing a tangible reward, such as a generous gift certificate, cash prize, or trip. Creating excitement about a contest is a surefire way to generate participation.

Competition is a controversial topic in creativity research. Some scholars find that competition reduces the creativity of suggestions and designs, but others have found it to be helpful because it produces persistent effort.

Your contest may produce a fabulous idea, or it may not, so be sure to use other forms of brainstorming. Using diverse approaches is the best way to ensure that you get diverse ideas.

Engaging in creative e-mail conversations

You can also engage in e-mail discussions of a problem or design. Think of these discussions as creative conversations. It takes at least two interested parties to hold a conversation, of course, so you'll need to identify colleagues who are as interested as you are in solving your problem or improving your design. That selection process will limit your list — usually, to fewer than a dozen people.

Send each of your highly interested colleagues an organized summary of your thinking so far, and identify the problems or puzzles you're concerned about. Ask each person to reply with any suggestions or ideas that could move you ahead. Then reply to each response individually and thoughtfully, asking questions and probing to clarify or deepen your colleagues' thoughts.

In essence, what you're doing is conducting one-on-one brainstorming sessions via e-mail. This kind of creative conversation can go many rounds, leading to the exchange of dozens of e-mails if the topic is challenging.

Often, it's easier to have a lengthy conversation with someone via e-mail than in person, because both of you can work your answers into your busy schedules instead of having to block out a day to meet and talk. Also, by engaging in multiple e-mail conversations, you can *cross-fertilize* ideas from one person to another. Bring an idea from one person into your conversation with another person to ask for her reactions or see whether it stimulates a fresh idea from her.

Crowdsourcing for New Ideas

Smart mobs are groups of people whom you've focused in a productive direction, often by asking them for their ideas or suggestions, and sometimes by asking them to vote on the best of a set of ideas, designs, or options. An old-fashioned way to create a smart mob is to hold an election — the premise of democracy. A more modern way is to use *crowdsourcing,* which is the planned use of viral-media platforms to solicit ideas and reactions. Crowdsourcing can tap into the latent intelligence of large groups of people, turning them into smart mobs to help you innovate.

You can tap into any professional network to get expert input, or you can go to the general public for a wider range of possibly naïve — but also possibly more creative — ideas and suggestions.

If you're looking for a new brand name, consider posting a challenge to customers on social-networking sites such as Facebook and MySpace. (I assume that you already have pages for your business on these sites; if not, see my book *Marketing For Dummies* [Wiley] for tips on how to use these Web platforms.) You can offer a prize for the winning submission if you think that doing so will boost participation — which it often does. Also, send out a press release announcing the contest, and encourage both traditional reporters and bloggers to pass the word along. A contest to name a new product can create significant buzz and attract a lot of attention, potentially attracting thousands of participants to brainstorm with you.

Getting more help with your crowdsourcing

If you need help running the process of crowdsourcing ideas, look up the topic in a Web search engine, and you'll come across several companies offering solutions, including the following:

✔ **InnoCentive** offers a Web-based idea marketplace (at www.innocentive.com) where Seekers post requests and Solvers (more than 100,000 of them) offer suggestions. If a suggestion is adopted by a Seeker — some company or charity in need of help — the Solver wins a financial reward. You can sign up in both Seeker and Solver categories and begin to experience open innovation firsthand.

As you'll see if you join, InnoCentive keeps the identities of both Seekers and Solvers confidential and handles all aspects of their contractual relationships (such as licensing of intellectual property; see Chapter 17). The protection of identities is an interesting aspect of InnoCentive's approach to crowdsourcing that makes large companies more comfortable with the process by reducing their fears of being sued by the authors of unsuccessful inventions.

✔ **Mom Invented** (www.mominventors. com) sources its products from thoughtful mothers who come up with labor-saving, clever devices and don't know how to market them. The mother of a finicky eater, for example, designed a plastic cutter that trimmed the crust off a sandwich and sliced it in half with a single motion. Mom Invented now markets a line of Mini Bites Sandwich Cutters based on that idea and pays the inventor a 5 percent royalty. Everybody's happy! The business model is based on the concept that thousands of mothers are out there thinking of good ideas and will send them to the firm that publicizes its interest in crowdsourcing. The concept seems to be working pretty well.

Mom Invented has a unique set of products that I doubt anybody in a laboratory would have come up with. Take a look at the Web site to see what I mean. Then see whether you can tap into the creative ideas of a group of people whose experiences might make them good inventors for your product line!

✔ I'm particularly impressed by the offering from Cambrian House: **Chaordix**, a systematic method and platform that makes it easy to crowdsource on a large scale. See www.chaordix.com for details.

✔ Also visit **IdeaConnection** (www.idea connection.com) for another example of an idea intermediary that connects people based on their ideas and idea needs.

Keep in mind that any vendor is going to charge you for help with your project, so you may want to see what you can do on your own first, going to expert vendors only after you've exhausted your own capabilities.

An old-fashioned suggestion system simply involves putting a box with a slot on top in a prominent part of the workplace and asking employees to drop their ideas into it. You can do the same thing today by using a picture of a suggestion box on your Web site. Have participants enter their ideas (for a new product, for example) on a form that looks like a scrap of paper. When a user clicks the Done button, his idea slides into the slot on the top of the box — virtually, of course. Once a week, empty the box, post the ideas, and announce a weekly winner. At the end of the month or season, select the

overall winner, and hold a press event to present the winner an Innovator of
the Year award or something of that sort.

Even companies as large as Procter & Gamble (which has more scientists on
staff than Harvard, Stanford, and the Massachusetts Institute of Technology
combined) sometimes go outside for ideas. P&G queried thousands of scientists around the world for their suggestions on how to control wrinkles in
fabric, and it ended up signing contracts with several of those scientists to do
product development based on their ideas.

Going Deep for Intuitive Insight

Intuition is variously defined as looking within for insight, tapping into
tacit knowledge (what you don't know that you know), using preconscious
thought (ideas that pop into your head right away without apparent effort),
or using the subconscious (thoughts and feelings you're not aware of).

Intuition is probably central to the creative process, but researchers fail to
agree on this point — or on virtually any other. What everyone *does* agree
on is that creative thinking may draw on logic and analysis, but in the end
involves a leap of understanding that's very different from logical, step-by-
step problem-solving. Some people call this creative leap *intuition;* others call
it *creativity;* and still others call it *insight, imagination, instinct,* or *gut feeling.*

When you talk about intuition, you get into some interesting related ideas,
because some people feel that intuition taps into the spiritual or magical
aspects of the world.

Do you believe in intuition? It's an interesting question, because it gets you
thinking about how you make decisions. Do you rely on logic, or are you comfortable with an answer that feels right but that you can't explain logically?

If you're among those who see something magical or spiritual in the operation
of intuition, saying that you believe in relying on your intuition could imply
that you accept a spiritual or religious influence or that you believe in fate.
But for the topic of this discussion — innovating in business — it's not
necessary to sort out exactly how intuition works or whether any deeper
force is at work behind it. You can just take advantage of the fact that
intuitive approaches complement more-systematic ones and really do help
produce creative insights.

At its worst, intuition is associated with New Age approaches involving the
use of crystals, chants, and candles. At its best, it's associated with experienced executives who size up a situation and instantly know what to do,
or with experienced inventors or entrepreneurs who take one glance at
something and instantly know how to make it a whole lot better — possibly
making some serious money as they do so.

Using naturalistic decision-making

Intuition is beginning to get some serious attention among researchers who study decision-making for the U.S. Army and Air Force, where formal, logical methods don't seem to work as well in action as more naturalistic methods do. A field called *naturalistic decision-making* (NMD) has emerged, and researchers are increasingly appreciating an expert's ability to size up a situation, draw a rapid (and apparently intuitive) conclusion, try a course of action, and adjust again quickly if the feedback isn't what he expected.

So intuition definitely has a role in the workplace. How can you tap into your intuition in helpful ways as you try to make your mark as an innovator? For starters, use incubation (sleeping on a question of challenge overnight) to allow your own intuition to offer up possibilities. Also make a practice of asking experts for their ideas in casual, face-to-face conversations. Sometimes, an off-the-cuff remark by someone will reveal an intuitive insight that you can develop into a great new approach or option.

Going back to nature

Imagine someone who's struggling to figure out the direction in which she wants to take her career. She might do well to take a weekend trip to the countryside, visit a waterfall, take a long walk, and generally get in touch with nature. What will happen to the problem she's incubating as she takes this trip? It will probably begin to clarify into a new conviction about what's really important to her and what she wants to do with her life. It's very hard to come back from a trip to the countryside without some sort of clarity that you didn't have before. Intuition bubbles up with ease when you get out of your normal high-pressure environment.

I know some innovators who bring nature into their workplace to help them think clearly and creatively. They use fountains or small water-bubblers, lush potted palm trees, Zen rock gardens, or bonsai trees to help them get in touch with their intuition.

Other people swear by a relaxing yoga program or a long swim in the nearest lap pool. I've tried the latter technique and (especially if I take a swim break at lunch) have been pleasantly surprised by the ideas that pop into my head.

Asking a wise elder

Do you know anyone who fits the description of a wise elder? Someone who's seen and done a lot and now is good at listening to the troubles of younger people and asking penetrating questions to clarify their thoughts? Admittedly, many people are just as stupid in their old age as they were when they were younger, but some people seem to actually grow wise. Take advantage of their wisdom! Ask them for guidance.

Using soothsaying techniques

If you aren't skilled in *soothsaying* — the magical foretelling of events — don't worry; there's a book called *Soothsaying For Dummies*. That's the good news. The bad news is that this book is imaginary, existing only in the electronic game World of Warcraft. I guess that the publisher of the *For Dummies* series doesn't think that anyone in the real world will seriously need a reference to soothsaying, but in fact, some of the methods that fall under that heading can be useful ways of stimulating the intuition. In this section, I discuss two popular soothsaying methods: Tarot cards and the I Ching.

Runes, ancient bones, and any other soothsaying methods that you may want to try don't so much tell you what to do as help you unlock or clarify your own insights. They're tools for tapping into intuition. If you don't know exactly how they work, so much the better, because the very definition of intuition involves a certain amount of mystery — intuitive thoughts being those that you find hard to explain or justify to others.

Tarot cards

Do you have a deck of Tarot cards on hand? If so, try drawing a card while holding your challenge in mind in the form of a question. Then interpret the card you draw and see whether it helps you understand your question.

You could ask the deck, "What should we do about the rising competition and loss of profit margins in our main product line?" Suppose that you draw the Fool — a card showing a jester walking near a cliff, with his belongings in a bag tied to a stick across his shoulder and a little dog trotting along beside him. Now you just have to interpret this card in a way that helps you answer your strategic question:

- As any guide to Tarot-card meanings will tell you, the Fool symbolizes the beginning of a journey, which suggests that you'd better be prepared for a major project. This character is happy-go-lucky and not very mindful of the nearby cliff that he might fall over. Clearly, your main product line is in danger!

- On the bright side, the Fool may have what he needs to solve any problem, packed in that sack he carries. He just has to stop and unpack it. With this thought in mind, you might take a careful look around your company for some good ideas for inventions that could revitalize your product line, making it more competitive and less subject to profit erosion.

I'm a little embarrassed to admit it here in print, but I sometimes do Tarot-card readings for clients. Why? Because they can provide real insight. I think that the cards tap into intuition by providing interesting and unusual images, challenging people to apply those images meaningfully to their own situations.

Tarot cards are used in some parts of the world for games, and I believe that in those places, the cards aren't considered to be useful for soothsaying. (Too familiar, I suppose.) But if you don't know the games that the cards are used for, they become mysterious and otherworldly, helping you tap into deep-rooted intuitions.

You can go online and find any number of Web sites where you can do a virtual Tarot reading and get help interpreting the cards. I don't know whether these sites are as accurate as a traditional Tarot deck — and maybe it doesn't really matter — but they do save you the cost of the cards and an interpretive booklet. If you decide to buy your own deck, you may as well start with the Rider-Waite deck illustrated by Pamela Colman Smith, which is considered to be the most authoritative of the many designs now on the market. You may also want to consult *Tarot For Dummies,* by Amber Jayanti (Wiley), to find out more about the practice.

I Ching

The I Ching, an ancient set of Chinese divination symbols, can also be useful for exploring a tough problem or working on a business strategy. If you want to try it, pick up a book, or find one of the many Web sites where you can "throw the bones" for free and see what you get. Use the I Ching as you would a Tarot deck, posing a tough question about how to solve a problem or what to do in the future, and see what ideas you get from the reading.

Being inventive

The lone inventor is a person of almost mythical proportions who, through a mix of hard work and brilliant insight, is able to see things others can't. It may be that people with dozens of patents or scientific prizes to their names are brighter than most, but on average, inventors are rather ordinary in most ways; they simply behave differently from other people.

Thomas Edison, for example, didn't choose to spend his time campaigning for votes; he preferred to tinker in the laboratory. He didn't think of himself as being particularly intelligent. He focused on persistence and often told stories about the number of failures he experienced before coming up with a winning design. I think that his particular brilliance was in knowing that there ought to be some way to make an electric light bulb work. That much, his intuition assured him of. But what was the correct material for a filament that wouldn't burn out? Edison wasn't sure, so he kept trying different materials until finally he hit on one that worked — which confirms his adage that genius is 1 percent inspiration and 99 percent perspiration!

Being an inventor means following up on those hunches or intuitive thoughts with hard work. If you put in enough effort, you usually can figure out how to make something that you imagine into something that really works. Edison's formula is probably correct, though: You can expect intuition to get you 1 percent of the way, and you'll have to sweat out the rest the hard way.

Chapter 9

Turning Problems into Opportunities for Innovation

. . . .

In This Chapter

▶ Approaching problems with an innovative spirit

▶ Using analytical problem-solving methods with an innovative twist

▶ Being a restless creative thinker looking for breakthrough solutions

. . . .

*O*ften, a problem — especially a problem of crisis proportions — does more to focus attention than any innovative idea can. Executive decision-making comes to the fore when problems arise. We talk about having to make hard choices when a profit shortfall occurs, an employee's performance is poor, or a new product or technology isn't panning out as expected. A hard choice or tough decision really means that you have to choose among unpleasant options, and you don't have an attractive choice in the menu of obvious possibilities.

Whenever you think that you have a tough choice to make, step back and see whether you can improve your options through creativity and persistent innovation. This chapter shows you how to turn problems into innovations by reframing them as opportunities to rethink things and push positive changes through in a hurry.

Seeing Problems with a Fresh Eye

A fresh eye means seeing things from different perspectives and gaining insight that other people lack. You desperately need a fresh eye to help you see the possibilities in a problem.

Framing problems as creative opportunities

Reframing means changing the mental view. When you reframe a problem, you take a different perspective, often by changing your definition of the problem. Instead of seeing a cash-flow crisis as the result of overspending, for example, you might redefine the problem as a failure to manage cash flow tightly. Reframing a problem helps you see alternative solutions to it.

Tackling a survival exercise

Here's a simple scenario to exercise your innovative problem-solving. Imagine that you've been shipwrecked on a deserted, sandy island with no natural source of water, and you must survive until you're found — perhaps for a week or two. The island has some coconut trees. You find a few cases of water in old-fashioned glass bottles with non-twist-off lids, left behind years ago by someone who built a simple thatch-roofed shelter on the beach. A big old bucket is positioned at the lowest corner of the hut's roof to catch rain-water, but it's bone dry now, and there's not a cloud in the sky.

It's hot, you're thirsty, and you desperately need a drink, but you don't have a bottle opener. How are you going to remove those rusty, stiff metal caps from those fragile glass bottles without breaking the bottles and spilling their contents? You decide to go for a walk along the beach to look for some natural tools.

When I challenge people in a workshop to solve this problem, they often ask me questions to help them think it through. Asking probing questions (doing your creative research) is always a good idea! So if you have questions, I can tell you that yes, the hut was made with local materials plus stuff from wrecked ships, such as rope and nails. Also, there are rocks, shells, and sticks of all sorts on the beach. But no, there's no hidden toolbox on the island.

The first thing you need to do when you face a problem such as this one is decide to generate as many ideas as possible. That decision is a very important one to make when you're facing any problem, fictional or real. Students train in school to solve closed-ended problems, which have just one correct answer and usually one correct process for finding that answer. (If $x = 2$ and $xy = 6$, what does y equal? 3, right?) But most real-world problems are open-ended, meaning that you have more than one possible way to approach and solve them. In business, the most important problems never have a formulaic solution, so if you stop with just one answer, you'll miss other possibilities that might prove to be more advantageous.

Solving the survival problem

Okay, back to the problem of how to get a drink when you're stuck on a sandy island without a bottle opener. How many ways did you think of? Here are some ideas that I came up with when I first thought about this problem, in the order in which I generated them:

- ✔ Break the top off a bottle with a rock, hoping that I can save at least half the water and not contaminate it with glass shards.

- ✔ Look for a shell that could work as a natural bottle opener.

- ✔ Find a strong clamshell and a sharp rock. Use the rock to shape a notch in the shell that would snag the underside of a bottle top and lever it up, the way a bottle opener would.

- ✔ Clean out the old bucket, break all the bottles in it, and let the glass settle to the bottom. Then ladle out the water at the top of the bucket, using a scoop made from a shell or a coconut.

- ✔ Split open some coconuts, and drink the water inside them instead of worrying about those old bottles.

Which answer is the correct one? Hmm. Beyond the obvious fact that my first idea was pretty bad, it's not easy to say which is best. I *do* know that one of these ideas might be easier and more effective than any of the others in actual practice and that if I began to experiment with ideas such as these, I'd certainly find a way to keep myself hydrated until help arrived.

A classic creativity test asks people to think of as many uses as they can for a brick. Sounds dumb, I know, but try it sometime; it's not as easy as you may think. Practiced innovators generate many more ideas than other people do. Can you break ten?

Postponing the decision to allow time for creative thought

Innovators tend to take longer to generate ideas and options than ordinary people do, because they see problems as opportunities to exercise their creativity. They eagerly jump at problems, even contrived exercises such as how to open bottles without an opener or what to do with a brick, because creative problem-solving improves with practice. If you think of yourself as creative and look for opportunities to test your creativity, you'll continually improve your problem-solving skills.

Using creativity prompts

Use external reminders of the value of creativity to boost creative output. You can use simple influences such as a favorite quote about creativity, an inspiring picture or melody, or a clever ad or product as props to stimulate your imagination.

Here's an odd fact: When researchers administered the think-of-uses-for-a-brick test to a group of subjects, the subjects who had just been exposed to the Apple, Inc., logo came up with more creative ideas than those who saw the IBM logo just before doing the exercise. Why? Apple's brand identity reminds people to be creative, whereas the IBM brand evokes more logical, closed-ended problem-solving. A corporate logo is a small external influence, but even so, it proved to be enough to increase innovative problem-solving.

Approaching problems with optimism and hopefulness

It's easy to be thrown off balance by a problem, especially if it's unexpected. You can slip into a pessimistic viewpoint without even realizing it. When something bad happens, or a problem or challenge arises, be careful to avoid the pessimism path by following this advice:

- ✔ **Don't blame yourself unduly.** You're not stupid, and you aren't doomed to fail at everything you try! Self-talk needs to be positive and encouraging. We're our own worst enemies when it comes to the things we thoughtlessly say in the face or an error or problem. Take control of your self-talk!

- ✔ **Blame the process, not people.** One of the principles of quality improvement is to blame the process, not the person — that is, you should look for problems in the way you do business (such as lax controls), rather than assume that someone else is at fault. When other people try to blame you for a problem, turn the situation around by asking them to help you think of ways to make the problem less likely to recur. Redirect the focus to the external causes, and talk about innovations that would prevent such problems or solve them effectively in the future.

- ✔ **Look for openings created by the problem.** A small problem opens the way for small changes, and a big problem or a crisis opens the way for major changes. Every problem creates momentum for change, and as an innovator, you can use that momentum to good effect by introducing new ideas, practices, or products that people might have ignored or resisted if a problem hadn't come along to get their attention.

These three strategies help you overcome a reactive approach to problems, which I call *circling the wagons:* People get worried and try to fall back on traditional or conservative approaches instead of innovating. Usually, problems are at least partially due to traditional approaches, so trying to return to traditions in the face of a problem is a pretty useless form of denial. If you avoid playing blame games, seek understanding of the root causes of the problem, and look for openings to introduce change, you'll innovate your way out of most problems with ease.

See Chapter 3 for more information on how to maintain and spread an optimistic attitude so as to stimulate creative thinking and maximize the chances of successful innovation.

Applying Analytical Problem-Solving

You're taking a creative approach to problems, which is great! Don't forget, however, that analytical approaches can be powerful complements to creative thinking. In fact, unless you happen to think of a brilliant solution right away, you should do your homework and analyze the problem before proposing an innovative response. The analytical process enriches your creative thinking by helping you understand the problem more fully.

Using Dewey's problem-solving process

The modern, rigorous approach to problem-solving was best described by John Dewey (the man who also invented the Dewey Decimal System for inventorying library books) back in 1933, in a groundbreaking book called *How We Think.* Dewey provided a deceptively simple but powerful three-step process:

1. **Define the problem.**
2. **Identify alternatives.**
3. **Select the best alternative.**

Included in these three steps are all the key activities required to analyze a problem and come up with an innovative solution. If only more people would adopt Dewey's method, there'd be a lot more progress and a lot fewer problems!

Defining problems with creative insight

When you start with a careful effort to define the problem, you almost always discover that the problem isn't what it seemed to be at first or what other people told you it was. As a consultant, I'm very used to being called in to deal with a problem that proves to be poorly defined, as most business problems are. Problems get misdiagnosed in business for the simple reason that people notice symptoms of the underlying problem and leap to a diagnosis based on the initial symptoms. As in medical illnesses, business symptoms may have many root causes, and it takes a careful analysis to figure out what's really going on.

Use the problem-definition stage to reframe the problem and gain insight into it. Often, the greatest creative insight comes during this first stage, in the form of a new and better way to define the problem.

Brainstorming real alternatives that expand the solution set

The second step in Dewey's problem-solving method is thinking of a bunch of possible solutions, or a *solution set.* Usually, people make do with a fairly narrow solution set that lacks in both quantity and variety or originality of options.

Who or what is *really* to blame?

A new client recently told me, "Our managers need leadership training. They aren't very good leaders. We need you to train them." I asked, "Why do you have bad leaders? Didn't you seek out managers with leadership credentials in your hiring?" The client replied, "Leadership was part of the job description, but they don't seem to be doing it now."

Persisting in my effort to define the client's problem, I asked, "How do you know the managers are bad leaders? What's the evidence?" "There's a lot of complaints from employees," my client explained. "And employee performance is poor." I still didn't understand the problem, so I asked, "Have you considered any other possible causes for employee complaints and poor performance?" He replied, "No. What else could it be?"

Then our conversation went into a fact-finding phase that helped clarify the actual problem. We ended up scrapping the idea of a leadership workshop and instead looked into the ways that employees' work was being structured and

supervised. We found three urgent problems that needed fixing:

- A lack of time for managers to supervise employees and review their performance

- Inconsistencies between what employees were asked to do and what their performance review system recognized and rewarded

- Uncertainty about the organization's strategic direction and future stability

These three problems produced the symptom of dissatisfied employees who weren't working as efficiently and effectively as they could. By asking probing questions, I discovered that the client had defined the problem incorrectly and was about to spend time and money on a quick fix that wouldn't actually improve anything.

You should assume that any problem you encounter needs to be redefined, just as this one did.

Consider more than one basic approach, and develop at least three — preferably six or more — viable options. Your outcome is strongly affected by the size of your solution set.

Coming up with a healthy variety of possible solutions to a problem is fairly easy if you have experience with brainstorming, both alone and in groups. Use as many of the idea-generation techniques from Chapters 6, 7, and 8 as you can. Don't stop brainstorming until you have several options that have significant merit. Refuse to be forced to choose among a few narrow options that don't give you good outcomes, because there's always another way.

Selecting a solution wisely and well

When you're sure that you've defined the problem clearly and with insight, and you're sure that you've generated more than the normal selection of options, you're ready to choose the best solution. But which solution is best? In my experience, businesses very often look at fresh, new ideas but then revert to a traditional solution that fits old habits of thought and doesn't necessitate change on the part of the people who'll be asked to implement it.

In other words, the most popular solution to business problems is the most *familiar* of the various options. As you no doubt know, familiarity doesn't guarantee quality when it comes to solving a problem. In fact, a less comfortable and more innovative solution usually would be far better than the familiar one, but uncertainty and fear hold people back from opting for the innovative approach. Therefore, my first and most important piece of advice to you as you consider possible solutions for any business problem is this: Watch out for the bias toward the familiar! This bias blinds many organizations and managers to better options.

Here are some better ways to choose an option from your list of possible solutions to a problem:

- ✔ **Use comparative analysis.** List the specific features of each choice (such as cost, benefits, and time frame) in a comparative table so that you can compare the options on an equal footing.

- ✔ **Brainstorm lists of pros and cons for each option; then choose the one with the most going for it and the fewest problems.**

- ✔ **Build a future scenario — a fictional account of what your business will be like — for each of the possible solutions.** Go into detail, asking for input from the people who know the most about the affected areas and operations. Then compare the future scenarios, and pick the most appealing one.

Notice that none of these methods of choosing a solution involves a popular vote. I'm skeptical about putting complex choices up for a vote. With a vote, you're liable to fall prey to the appeal of the most familiar option rather than get the best one. I recommend voting only if you have a select group of experts who were all involved in the research and who thought about the options; otherwise, your efforts to be democratic may backfire. (The exception to this rule is a *collective* or staff-run organization. In a collective, the entire staff is involved in strategic decision-making and usually can tackle tough decisions in a sophisticated fashion.)

Performing a payoff analysis

Another way to select the preferred solution from your list of candidates is to perform a rigorous payoff analysis. This method — a staple of MBA programs — needs to be modified slightly to produce innovative results, but it can be quite helpful.

Suppose that you have a variety of options and don't know which is best. That situation is common in business, after all. You may have a chance to invest in a new product or startup company, a choice of several strategies, or uncertainty about which of several possible cost cuts to make. Which is the best path?

A logical way to compare several choices is to calculate the payoffs (often defined as *profits* or *returns on investment)* for each option and then pick the one that pays the most. But what if you don't really know how well each option will pay off? It's hard to forecast the future with certainty. If you're unsure, make low, medium, and high forecasts for each of your options. Ideally, that way you're bracketing what will really happen, and you'll be prepared, no matter how well or poorly things go.

Creating a payoff table

Use a *payoff table* to compare options and possible outcomes. A typical table contains three options and three projected outcomes for each option. Some payoff tables include a column for probability next to each outcome to let you multiply the payoff by the probability before summing to calculate the overall average payout. Other tables are used to aim for the highest possible payoff, and still others are used to identify the option that involves the lowest possible loss.

Payoff tables can help you achieve your goal, whether it's conservative or aggressive. It's up to you to decide how to set up and read the tables based on your priorities and the quality of your information.

Figure 9-1 shows a payoff table for three levels of investment in a new venture: a 5 percent stake, a 25 percent stake, and a 50 percent stake. Which level of investment makes the most sense?

	Invest:	Earn % of Profit:	Payoff after 2 years at 3 levels of profit:			Average:
			−$50,000	$150,000	$300,000	
Option 1	$10,000	5% ROI:	−$2,500 −25%	$7,500 75%	$15,000 150%	$6,667 67%
Option 2	$45,000	25% ROI:	−$12,500 −28%	$37,500 83%	$75,000 167%	$33,333 74%
Option 3	$80,000	50% ROI:	−$25,000 −31%	$75,000 94%	$150,000 188%	$66,667 83%

Figure 9-1: Comparing options with a payoff table.

If the venture in Figure 9-1 does well — meaning that it reaches the high profit projection of $300,000 — clearly, you'd like to have the highest possible stake in it. A 50 percent ownership investment costs $80,000 and, in the best-case scenario, would produce a $150,000 profit, for a return on investment (ROI) of 188 percent. (ROI equals profit divided by investment.) But what if the worst case happens, and the venture produces a loss of $50,000? In that case, you'd lose $25,000 by investing $80,000 — the least desirable outcome. A more conservative approach might be better.

The payoff table in Figure 9-1 averages the three levels of payoff to calculate an overall return for each of the three levels of investment. The third option — investing $80,000 — gives the highest return on average, so it may be the best option in spite of the higher potential for loss.

It makes sense to average the possibilities if you think that they're about equally probable. Otherwise — if, for example, you think that the first scenario is twice as likely as either of the others — you can refine your calculation by weighting the most probable option more heavily (such as by doubling it).

Boosting your payoff with creativity

The payoff table in Figure 9-1 is a classic business-school tool that can help you compare options and make more intelligent choices, which often helps you choose among options you've developed in a creative strategy session. It's a good tool, but it's not very innovative. What if you bump up payoff analysis by making it more creative? Here are some steps that can improve your payoff:

1. **Brainstorm more options.**

   There always seem to be just a few options in those payoff tables. Why? If you push ahead to come up with three more options (six total), you may hit on one that pays off at higher rates than any other. If you're comparing options that have been laid out to you by other people, do some creative negotiating to see whether you can shake more and better options out of them to sweeten the deal.

2. **Maximize the profits.**

   A payoff table usually uses low, medium, and high projections in an effort to bracket the likely range of outcomes. That's fine, but what if you could increase the payoff by innovating in the implementation stage? A really stellar creative effort could help you achieve a "very high" outcome. If you're willing to put your effort and imagination into the implementation, it's plausible to add a fourth column to your payoff table to project an exceeds-expectations or very-high outcome along with the low, medium, and high ones.

3. **Minimize the losses.**

   It's possible to find creative ways to buffer yourself against losses if the worst-case scenario occurs. Spend some time brainstorming ways to reduce risk and minimize the negatives. Can you cut a creative deal that protects you from some of the possible risks, for example? Could an insurance company provide a policy?

4. **Improve the quality of the projections.**

   Better forecasts reduce the chance of guessing wrong, and a creative problem-solving effort aimed at making better forecasts can help narrow the range between your high and low guesses. Take some time to look for more and better examples to compare your situation to. Collect alternative forecasting tools and try them out. (Have you conducted a survey or a focus group, for example, or looked at trends in competitors' sales?)

The creative problem-solver takes an innovative approach to business choices and isn't limited by the initial set of options in his payoff table. Treat this table as a starting point for your analysis, planning, and imagining, and you'll make better decisions than most people do!

Engaging Your Creative Dissatisfaction

Executive decision-making often takes the form of making informed choices. Forecasts and payoff tables help make your choice more informed, but they don't improve your options — just help you choose among them. The innovative executive doesn't just want to choose among options; she also wants to improve them. Executive decision-making ought to involve innovation, not just selection. If you don't see a great option, stop and think. Maybe you can improve the options before making your choice.

Recognizing the opportunity to be creative

How do you improve your options before deciding? Simple: Be dissatisfied. As I say repeatedly in this book, the first and most important step in innovation is deciding that you want and need to be creative. The next time the world dishes up a choice of options, reject the "Which one?" framing, and restate the problem as "Why be limited to these options?"

I use the term *creative dissatisfaction* to describe the way that innovative decision-makers work. It's amazing how often you can — and will — find a better choice after you engage your creative dissatisfaction. Be assertive about demanding more time, thought, and information. Incubate the problem overnight. Ask others what they think. In short, engage all the creative-thinking tools you know about (see Chapters 6, 7, and 8), and turn the process of decision-making into an opportunity for creative thinking, not just for choosing among existing options.

Figure 9-2 shows what happened when a company that made industrial cutting equipment was examining options for three new product designs. After testing prototypes and showing them to core customers, the sales force projected low, medium, and high sales for the three designs.

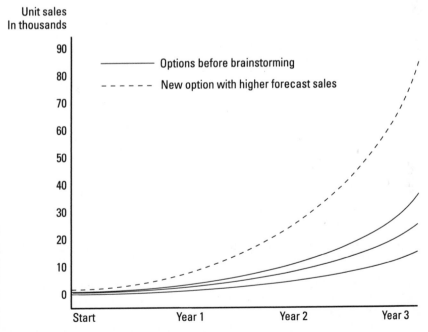

Figure 9-2: Improving the payoff by adding options.

Although the design with the highest sales projections was somewhat more costly to make than the other two, the executive team was eager to capture the most possible sales and was about to choose that option. Then one of the executives asked for some extra time to examine the three prototypes and think about the question. A week later, he presented a fourth design that combined good ideas from the other three but was made from off-the-shelf parts, which allowed for much lower production costs and pricing. The sales force was very excited and projected unit sales for this newest design at more than twice the level of the other three. Without a creative rethinking of the options, the company would have invested in a mediocre product that didn't sell nearly as well as the one it finally selected.

Considering the opportunity costs of not innovating

Neat payoff spreadsheets, graphs, and tables make your choices look fixed and discourage you from doing more creative thinking. Watch out for this effect! No matter how neatly a decision is presented in a payoff table or other businesslike format, it's still possible to come up with even better choices. The official term for failure to see and pursue a better option is *opportunity cost*. You don't pay opportunity cost now; you pay it in the future, when some competitor comes out with a better design and your own sales fall, making you wish that you'd taken more time to improve your own design.

In Figure 9-2, the opportunity cost is represented by the distance between the highest solid line and the dashed one. Without innovation, the best-case scenario is significantly worse.

Applying intuition along with logic

How do the great inventors and entrepreneurs come up with their breakthrough ideas? Not by constructing payoff tables and lists of pros and cons. Those and many other analytical activities — such as reading about the field and talking to experts — simply set the stage for a breakthrough. The real creative "aha!" moment comes from stewing about the problem for a long time until a fresh approach wells up from deep in your imagination.

Give yourself permission to imagine, dream, and create. Go for a long walk. Visit a museum. Play a musical instrument. Dance. Get out of your normal business context and see if a really great idea occurs to you. People who have great ideas are people who believe in great ideas and give themselves a chance to think deeply about the problems facing them. Give yourself permission to be a breakthrough thinker, and you'll find that the number and originality of your ideas increase dramatically.

Chapter 10

Going Shopping for Innovations

In This Chapter

▶ Searching for interesting new approaches that you can adapt and use

▶ Seeking knowledge from the leaders in your industry

▶ Working with innovative, forward-thinking suppliers

▶ Keeping in touch with the experts who know what the best innovations are

*I*f you work in a Fortune 500 corporation, you probably have a research-and-development (R&D) department made up of scientists, engineers, designers, and so forth, and your company probably develops the majority of its own innovations. But 90 percent of the world doesn't have the resources to develop most of the innovations it needs, so it does what every good consumer does: goes shopping!

Whether you're a retailer, wholesaler, or some other form of businessperson, you definitely need to broaden your view of innovation to include good ideas, inventions, and designs from beyond your own four walls. This chapter covers a variety of ways to tap into other people's great ideas in legitimate ways that benefit both you and the inventor.

Exploring Your Industry's Trade Shows

Trade shows are conventions for members of a particular industry. The show operators rent booth space to a wide range of wholesalers and suppliers. If you're a retailer, you'll find wholesalers at your industry's trade show. A medical convention, on the other hand, features producers of medical services and products who are looking for medical practices to supply, and a wood-products convention cues up suppliers who want to sell to lumber-yards, furniture manufacturers, and any other business that works with wood. There's certainly a national trade show for your industry, and there may be regional ones too.

Finding industry trade shows

How do you find a trade show for your industry? Here are some places to look on the Web:

- The Trade Show News Network: www.tsnn.com
- All-Biz.info's international directory of trade shows: expo.all-biz.info/

Exhibition/lang/en/year/2010/ (or substitute the current year)

- Bvents: www.bvents.com
- EventsEye: www.eventseye.com

Finding an innovative new product can be as easy as going to a leading trade show and looking for something fresh and exciting that you can purchase wholesale or license the rights to.

If, for example, you're involved in construction or building maintenance, you probably want to go to CONEXPO-CON/AGG, the biggest U.S. convention for the construction and agriculture industries (see www.conexpoconagg.com for the time and location of the next annual event). You might find new practices, products, suppliers, or business partners to work with. You might also find inspiration and go back to work with a fresh idea to try.

Assuming that you're in the construction industry, you may also want to attend shows that offer different perspectives, such as the Greenbuild International Expo (see www.greenbuildexpo.org for the next event). This show was started in 2002 and has grown rapidly because it features innovative sustainable building designs and materials; green building design and management; intelligent, energy-efficient lighting and air conditioning; less-wasteful plumbing fixtures; and so much more. You might come back from the expo with an exciting plan to introduce a new line of green building products to your market area, such as superinsulated windows and window shades; energy-efficient lighting, air conditioning, and plumbing systems; and recycled building materials.

BuildingGreen (www.buildinggreen.com) is another source of innovative ideas. It conducted a Webinar on energy-efficient lighting that opened my eyes to the possibility of a regional business focusing specifically on lighting audits and plans for larger commercial, educational, and government buildings. A specialist who could go into a facility and identify ways to cut energy costs by 10–20 percent just by redesigning the lighting systems probably would have a nice little niche business, don't you think?

Green building is a relatively new and fast-growing segment of the construction industry, and there's certainly an opportunity for one to three companies in your area to become local or regional leaders in green building. Why not be a leader?

Crossing Boundaries for Good Ideas

You're probably already aware that lots of fresh, new ideas exist beyond your doors. Some have been turned into successes already; others are waiting for some brave soul to develop them. Whatever the type and size of your business, you can be sure of finding more innovations outside it than within it, because most of the world lies outside your doors.

Your industry is a much bigger place than your individual workplace or business. If you work in advertising, you tend to look to other advertisers for new ideas. If you work in manufacturing, other manufacturers are your benchmarks, especially ones that make the same sorts of things your company does. If you work in government, you tend to look to other government offices or agencies for new ideas. As big as your industry or sector may be, however, it's still far, far smaller than the entire universe of possible ideas. It's important to look not only beyond your own company's doors, but also beyond your industry's doors, for fresh ideas and useful innovations. Many of the best ideas come from beyond the visible horizon of your industry's boundaries.

Toymakers such as Mattel, Inc., for example, get the majority of their breakthrough ideas from other industries, including electronics, plastics (injection molding and manufacturing), and entertainment. This fact seems obvious after you read it, right? A new Barbie doll, after all, has to be produced by using plastics technology from the wider world of industry, not from traditional toymaking. Mattel isn't expert in plastics and resins; it's expert in marketing toys. Also, a Barbie product may draw on the consumer appeal of a character from a teen movie such as Bella from the *Twilight* series — a successful product for the Barbie line. Mattel relied on the innovative work of a book author and a movie producer to create the Bella and Edward characters and then licensed the right to make Barbie dolls of them. If a leading company like Mattel looks beyond its industry for help with its innovation agenda, you should too.

Visiting the wrong trade shows

The most exciting innovations often come from visits to trade shows that are far removed from your industry. A bookstore owner, for example, might do well to attend a consumer-electronics trade show, because books are having to share attention with electronic media. What ideas might you get as a bookstore manager when you look to the consumer-electronics industry for inspiration? Here are a few that I came up with:

- ✔ For each best-selling print book purchased in the store, offer an MP3 file of the audiobook for free.
- ✔ Link large-screen computer terminals to online book previews so that shoppers can look at books even if they aren't in the store and then special-order them for pickup the following day.

- Offer titles in e-book format as an option to traditional bound books, and rent or lend an electronic book reader with each purchase of an e-book.

- Stock movies based on books alongside the books.

- Conduct frequent interactive online author chats with authors from around the world instead of bringing authors into the store only when they happen to be on a book tour (and perhaps install a giant surround-sound video theater in the store for these video chats).

These initial ideas illustrate the point that a bookstore ought not to exist in isolation from the world of electronics. Instead, it could be cross-fertilizing to offer innovations in the way it does business and the way its customers interact with books and authors. A few days at a major electronics or entertainment-industry trade show would stimulate the imagination of any bookstore manager and produce dozens of these sorts of ideas.

Use the directory links in the earlier sidebar, "Finding industry trade shows," to find major trade shows in complementary industries, and start to visit them. Make a practice of peeking into other fields and industries to see what innovations you can bring to yours.

Talking to outsiders

You may tend to focus on tangible things — actual physical inventions or new products in exciting styles and forms — when you go to trade shows or otherwise shop around for something new. It's also important, however, to keep your ear to the ground for exciting ideas that you can apply in your business.

How do you tap into fresh thinking from outside the boundaries of your business? One good way is to make a habit of talking to people who are outside your normal line of work. What's new in brain surgery, landscaping, recreational boat sales, and library management? I have no idea, but I do know that new ideas crop up in each of those fields, and those ideas just might translate to my business. To find out, I could do the following:

- Talk to people who work in completely different fields from mine about the latest trends and challenges in their fields.

- Read trade magazines, professional journals, and blogs from other people's fields and industries.

- Check the business news for reports of innovative behaviors in other fields.

The vast majority of people live and work beyond your neighborhood, profession, and industry. By focusing outward and asking questions, you open yourself to a broad flow of creative thinking.

Seeking out cross-training opportunities

A characteristic of successful entrepreneurs is that they often have experience in more than one field or profession. Take someone who started out selling insurance, then got a degree in nursing and worked in a medical center, and now runs an innovative consulting company specializing in helping companies find less-expensive healthcare plans for their employees. This person's mixed work background made her especially well suited to being an innovator in that field.

Likewise, a finance person who gets a chance to work on a marketing team for a new financial product launch might be exposed to marketing and sales for the first time. Through that experience, he would gain insight into how consumers view their personal finances, which might lead him to propose a successful new line of investment products.

Whether you're exploring a different area of your company or a different field or profession, look for opportunities to get some experience or training outside your profession.

Benchmarking Industry Innovators

It's easy to feel daunted by the challenge of finding an industry leader and then trying to discover what that company does that makes it so successful. Usually, a top competitor's winning strategies aren't posted on a Web site for you to imitate. Fortunately, that's not what I mean by *benchmarking* industry innovators. I'm simply talking about the little things you notice some company doing that you could do in your own business.

Millions of businesses operate around the world. Some of them are doing smart things that you might want to try yourself, so shop around for good ideas that you could adapt to your business. (See Chapter 17 for guidelines on what can be freely copied and what might have legal protection and should be left alone.)

Studying upstarts and startups

The dynamic new businesses in any industry are where much of the innovation takes place. Usually, these businesses are ignored for a few years or more, until some of them gain enough market share to scare the established firms and command attention. You can and should study upstarts before they become widely known, however — and even before they become successful, because some of the best innovations come from these fresh, new businesses. These companies represent the future of your industry. What does the future look like?

Highlighting bestsellers and new products

Any wholesale supply business has to do what science-classroom supplier Sargent-Welch does: offer a broad range of staples. It's important to keep bestsellers in your catalog and on your Web site along with dozens to hundreds of specialty items that a customer might need to order. If you don't have the depth of inventory to meet customers' needs, they'll take their searches — and their orders — elsewhere.

Sargent-Welch lists more than 1,000 products on its Web site (`sargentwelch.com`), but that's not what strikes me as being innovative. What impresses me is how clearly the site flags new products. A navigation bar on the left side of the home page includes New Products as a clickable option, and when you select it, the bar expands to show how many new products are available in a dozen specific areas. (When I last checked the site, it was offering 2 new microscopes, 27 new earth-sciences products, and 92 new physics products.) A science teacher wondering what to do with next year's physics class will be unable to resist browsing those new products for fresh teaching ideas and interesting new labs to offer. I'm inspired to check my own businesses' Web sites to see whether they do as good a job of pointing regular customers toward new products that they might find interesting.

Here are a couple of examples that illustrate the sort of businesses you should watch for:

✔ If you're in the news business, you may have noticed that a self-styled virtual publisher called Crowd Fusion, Inc., (`www.crowdfusion.com`) raised several million in funding in 2009 — a year marked by losses among conventional newspaper and magazine publishers and the failures of some of them. Crowd Fusion uses a better (read: much cheaper) way to publish news about a topic: It integrates and organizes content from the Web so that it seems like you're reading dozens of well-researched articles by professional journalists. Check out, for example, Super Eco (`www.supereco.com`), a virtual magazine rich with articles about everything green. It pops to life on the Web page because of the clever software provided by Crowd Fusion, and no doubt it draws readers from more traditional publications on the same topic.

Can you pick up something from Crowd Fusion? Here's a thought that the example suggests: You shouldn't hire journalists to research and write articles in the traditional way; so much content is posted on the Web every day that you can build almost any news-oriented product from what's already there (but a trained journalist is still going to do a better job of aggregating and editing material than someone without experience). You can compile source material manually if your ambitions are modest — a company newsletter or informative blog, for example. Or you could license Crowd Fusion–type software and use it to build fancy info-communities of your own.

✔ Another startup that catches my eye is Redux (`redux.com`), whose big idea is to provide *friendsourced* entertainment — in other words, you get to view video clips that your friends have recommended or are watching. Other content is cued up based on what your friends like. The company explains its unique benefit as offering videos, photos, music, and Web sites recommended by people who love the same stuff that you do. It's akin to other social-media Web sites but is more content-rich. I don't know whether this particular Web site will be the next big thing, but its idea may be. The content is unique for each viewer and is compiled based on that viewer's particular community of friends and their shared interests.

Could a business Web site morph into something unique for each visitor? Perhaps a supplier of cleaning products could have a Web site that looks one way to a homeowner, another way to a purchasing manager for a big corporation, and yet another way to a manager of custodial services for a school. Why not?

Interviewing innovative job candidates

You'll find that most people have interesting ideas if you just think to ask them for their opinions! Every job interview should include this question: "Can you think of something we could be doing better or smarter than we are?" In other words, while a candidate is trying to impress you and convince you that he's a great job candidate, he could suggest some ways that you could improve your business. If you ask, you'll certainly get some interesting answers. Further, if you really like an idea, you just might decide to hire the candidate who offered it — and assign him the task of helping to implement his suggestion.

Another tip for hiring is to look for evidence of innovative contributions in past jobs. Résumés usually don't feature creativity, because candidates make the (false) assumption that future employers are conservative and more interested in credentials than imagination. But really, why hire someone who doesn't have any ideas to contribute?

The easiest way for a company to become an innovative industry leader is to staff it with innovative people. Make sure that every new hire has a proven history of contributing valuable ideas and also has demonstrated an ability to think on his or her feet during the interview process. Describe a current problem or challenge during the interview, and ask for suggestions. You'll soon know whether you're talking to an original thinker and good problem-solver.

Please don't hire a résumé. No matter how good it looks, the person who can't answer your tough questions is the one who'll be coming to work for you — not her résumé.

Seeing what businesses are boasting about

Businesses that introduce a new product, reorganize to improve efficiencies, or open a new line of business tend to publicize what they've done. Browse business press releases to find out what innovations companies are boasting about, and see whether any of their accomplishments give you good ideas that you could implement in your own workplace. Here are some good places to check for interesting announcements:

- ✔ ThomasNet News posts dozens of interesting innovations from all industries (agriculture, construction, mining, electronics, manufacturing, and so on). See the New Product News feature at news.thomasnet.com.

- ✔ PR Newswire, which most U.S. businesses use, posts dozens of new releases every day. Go to www.prnewswire.com and select Browse News Releases or drill down into news specific to a category that interests you, such as Consumer Products and Retail or the Environment.

- ✔ PRZOOM offers free distribution of business press releases, making it a favorite for businesses around the world. Visit www.przoom.com to see whether the stories spark your imagination.

- ✔ Business Wire is another widely used platform for press releases. Although I find that it tends to have fewer stories about interesting innovations and more stories about economic trends and executive promotions, you might find the seed of a good idea in one of its daily press releases. Visit www.businesswire.com for inspiration.

You can find something interesting in the latest crop of business announcements; I'm sure of it. The trick is to skim this vast body of announcements looking for ones that trigger your innovative imagination.

Taking a positive approach to evaluating possibilities

As you look at innovative ideas from a wide range of sources, bear in mind that it takes open-minded imagination to find a way to apply them in your business. Ideas don't come ready-made for implementation; they're just starting points for your innovative thinking. Therefore, don't approach them with a critical eye.

Look at the pros and cons of every idea. Notice that the phrase *pros and cons* starts with *pros* — the benefits or good points of an idea — and considers the *cons* — the negatives — after noting the positives. You could quickly dismiss every idea that you come across, because all ideas have some issues or barriers that you'd need to overcome to make them work in your business. But if the benefits are substantial, it may be worth the time and trouble to adapt an idea to your own purposes.

Checking for alignment with your competencies

I can imagine a lot of great new business opportunities, because I do so much brainstorming with clients that it's just second nature to come up with ideas for innovations. I pass right by most of those ideas, however, because my own business portfolio doesn't include the right competencies. I don't do any large-scale manufacturing, for example, so a manufactured product probably isn't a good match for my business. Nor do I do anything involving electronics. Also, although my companies are competent in distribution and sales, they don't sell directly to consumers — only business to business. If I get an idea for a cool, new consumer product that somebody should manufacture and sell, I pass the idea on to an appropriate client. I know my limitations.

Even with a rich imagination and a copy of *Business Innovation For Dummies,* you'll find that plenty of ideas aren't a good fit for your business. As you evaluate ideas, check them for *viability* — meaning that the pros outweigh the cons, so the ideas ought to be successful — and then do a second level of checking to see whether the idea matches your capabilities. If not, keep looking. Ideas are free. You can throw away lots of them and keep looking until you find one that's a good fit.

Sourcing from Innovative Suppliers

Your business, like all others, sources a lot of materials, products, and services from other businesses. I estimate that about 90 percent of suppliers are relatively conservative, but 10 percent of them are quite innovative. A very simple way to be innovative yourself is to source from innovative suppliers. Let them do the hard work of developing a new approach and offering it to you as a turnkey innovation.

Evaluating suppliers based on their creative momentum

Companies usually select suppliers based on a mix of service and pricing. That's fine in the here and now, but success requires forward thinking. Add a third criterion — innovativeness — to the mix, and you'll select suppliers who can help you succeed both now and in the future.

Shopping for a bright future

An entrepreneur in Los Angeles decided that there was a need for a really innovative, fashion-forward home-lighting store offering products that weren't sold at Home Depot or any of the large lighting suppliers. Clearly, though, she wasn't going to manufacture all her own products to start with. Her business plan called for opening a boutique based entirely on products purchased at wholesale and then gradually building relationships with the best suppliers she could find; they would begin to make custom designs on an exclusive basis as she added more stores in other locations over a several-year period.

To find her initial product line, she visited the International Contemporary Furniture Fair in New York's Jacob K. Javits Convention Center. She also traveled to Asia to attend the Hong Kong Houseware Fair and to Germany to attend the Heim+Handwerk convention, which features advances in home construction and interior furnishing, with an emphasis on sustainability as well as arts and crafts. She assembled a list of several dozen unique vendors whose designs had never appeared in Los Angeles.

Her store opened a year later to positive reviews and was quickly regarded as being the leading innovator in home lighting, even though she had yet to design a single lamp herself.

It's easy to compare suppliers' prices, and service quality also is fairly easy to compare when you have a track record to go on. How do you know, however, which suppliers are innovating and which ones aren't? Here are a few key indicators to look for in a supplier:

- ✔ The overall look and feel of the business (including the people, printed materials, facilities, and Web sites) are modern and energetic. The business doesn't look old-fashioned or set in its ways.

- ✔ The people talk about new products and services frequently and make a point of sharing their latest thinking. They don't rest on the laurels of a static product line and past success.

- ✔ The business embraces new technologies in its own processes and operations. You find ample evidence of enthusiasm for progress and willingness to change.

- ✔ The people ask questions about your business; they seem to be eager to learn and to share their own learning. Avoid arm's-length suppliers who are interested only in writing your order.

Suppliers who meet all of the above criteria are innovative, and they're likely to help you stay on the leading edge of your own industry.

Asking your suppliers for free consulting

When you've shifted over to suppliers that are innovative, price-competitive, and good at servicing your orders, you're ready to invite them to help you improve your business. This strategy is very powerful, and I don't need much room in this book to describe how to apply it. Basically, you want to get into constructive discussions with your suppliers by asking them what they think you could be doing to improve your business.

The suggestions that suppliers come up with often involve using their products or services, of course, so you need to keep in mind their natural bias to make a sale. Often, however, their ideas have merit, and there's nothing wrong with, say, switching to a different product if that switch benefits your business and your customers. Be open to ideas and proposals from innovative suppliers, and you'll have a virtual R&D department that's eager to help you innovate.

Bringing your suppliers together to brainstorm

It's rare, but remarkably effective, to bring multiple suppliers together and pick their brains for improvements and innovations. The reason it's good to get two or more of your suppliers in your office at the same time is that they may come up with a really clever way to combine their ideas, products, or services. Bringing them together forces them to think outside their normal boxes and helps you form creative new approaches to sourcing.

Call in your suppliers at least once a year to brainstorm ways to improve your business. Gathering half a dozen suppliers, each from a different industry, will ensure a rich mix of perspectives and possible cross-fertilization of ideas.

Going to the Experts for Help

In many industries and professions, associations or other organizations publish standards and research on best practices. These organizations can be sources of innovations that help improve the quality of your services or product.

The Sunnyside Child Care Center at Smith, located in Northampton, Massachusetts, is a small organization without a major budget for research and development. It taps into the expertise of the National Association for the Education of Young Children by maintaining accreditation with that organization, which means that its staff and practices are subject to expert review and especially high standards of practice. It also purchases an advanced report-writing system from Pearson Education, Inc., which provides rich feedback about each child's development to the teachers and parents. Parents feel confident that their children are getting a great start because of the advanced methods and tools used. Not all day-care centers have the resources to do their own research on early childhood development, of course, but if a center shops around for expertise and brings in leading practices, it can gain a reputation for being innovative and expert — and so can yours!

In any field or profession, fewer than 10 percent of people stay up-to-date with leading-edge thinking and practices. By staying in touch with your industry's experts, you can be on the leading edge with those who implement new practices and approaches. Make sure that you belong to — and participate in — your industry's trade associations and your profession's membership societies. Attend workshops led by innovators, read experts' blogs, and make a point of knowing what the new ideas and practices are.

Chapter 11

Coming Up with Creative Combinations

In This Chapter

▶ Studying successful combinations for inspiration

▶ Finding fresh combinations of your own that produce winning innovations

▶ Mixing and matching problems and solutions to see what you can invent

▶ Trying creative ways to brainstorm unimagined combinations

▶ Combining a conventional need with unconventional information or ideas

▶ Delivering the benefits of a product in some new, unexpected form

his chapter shares a secret of successful innovators: You're far more likely to invent a winning design by combining two existing ideas or designs than by creating something entirely new. More likely, you will succeed by doing what most innovators do: combining earlier ideas, processes, or products into something that has new utility and that can be packaged and sold as your own.

In this chapter, I show you how to create innovative new products by using your existing products as building blocks. I also cover ways of building new designs and strategies out of fresh pairings of existing designs and ideas. Whether you're creating a new ad campaign, a new product design, or a whole new business, there's usually a way to shortcut the innovation process by standing on the shoulders of the many innovators who've come before you.

Finding Inspiration in Successful Creative Combinations

Genetic recombination is the root of biological creativity, producing offspring with a mix of genes from their two parents. The power of combination is the key to individuality in nature and to innovation in business. For every completely new-to-the-world invention, there are a hundred successful innovations that combine existing ideas or things in fresh and useful ways.

A map plus satellite triangulation equals the Global Positioning System (GPS), invented in 1993 by the U.S. Department of Defense and now finding everyday use in boats and cars for navigation. Fast-forward 25 years for the combination of GPS plus camera, which produced the Eye-Fi Geo card. This card records the location in which each digital photo is taken, so that years later, when you've forgotten where you took that snapshot, the GPS coordinates will be available. (The data storage card is intended to be integrated into cameras, because Eye-Fi doesn't make cameras itself.)

Combine GPS with hook-and-eye tape to get a motion detector for the elderly who are living alone. Strapped to an arm or leg, the device sends an alert to a remote relative when it detects prolonged lack of motion. ARKNAV International, Inc., introduced a product based on this combo concept. Clever, huh?

Now combine a GPS with a simple digital recording device to get a *back-tracker* — a GPS unit that you can consult when you realize that you're lost so you can retrace your steps. The combo is being marketed to hikers and backpackers by Qstarz under the brand name GPS BackTrack. (Can someone adapt it to help me find my car when I lose it in mall and airport parking lots? I bet! But where did I put my backtracker . . . ?)

All these combinations involve the idea of orientation or navigation combined with something else to give it special value. Can you invent something new and useful that involves a GPS device and [fill in the blank by brainstorming 20 useful objects]?

Here are some more combinations that created helpful innovations:

- ✔ Emergency whistle + mini-compass = Essential gear for hikers and boaters to clip to their zippers or life-jacket rings. (Update it with a mini-GPS?)

- ✔ Unbreakable water bottle + carabineer (D-ring) clip attached to screw-on lid = Clip-on water bottle for students and hikers to attach to a backpack.

- ✔ Cellphone + music player, Web browser, and other applications = Great new do-everything phones.

- ✔ Yogurt + fruit + keep-dry packet of granola = Update of a great combo concept that's gaining market share now.

- ✔ Photo + video = A combination of recording options that's becoming standard on digital cameras. (Finally, still and moving pictures in a single camera!)

- ✔ TV + Internet + telephone = A combination of services now offered by many cable companies to take advantage of their high-capacity lines.

- Clothing + appliances + groceries = A combination of product categories that everybody else thought didn't belong in the same store until Wal-Mart did it.

- Book + computer = The Amazon Kindle and other book readers that display the text on lit screens rather than on pages. Goodbye, printing presses?

- Couch + bed = The classic sleeper-sofa and the fold-out futon, both of which were major furniture innovations in their day.

- Footstool + wireless speakers = A simple furniture item that has a wireless speaker built into it to make surround sound easy in any room.

- Whitener + mouthwash = Listerine's Whitening Rinse product, which is catching on by taking market share from toothpaste-whitener combos.

- Computer keys + touch-sensitive screen = A touch-sensitive screen with dimples so that you can feel the keys in the dark.

These examples aren't just for fun. I put them in this chapter because reviewing dozens of combination innovations is the best way to power up your imagination and invent good combinations of your own. Pharmaceutical companies do the same thing. Have you noticed that commonly used combinations of drugs are now being melded into one product to simplify life for patients (and increase profits for the drug companies)?

Finding Innovative Combinations of Your Own

It's inspiring to realize how many successful innovations are really combinations of two (or sometimes three) existing designs. Now that you know the best-kept secret of innovation, you're ready to try your hand at almost-instant inventing by finding fresh combinations that you can call your own. I've given a lot of thought to how to come up with good combinations, and this section lays out several methods that you can try.

Revisiting classic combinations for quick wins

When you look at historically successful combinations, keep in mind that they're good for more than just inspiration; a surprisingly large number of new products actually revisit old creative combinations. Some combinations are just so natural that they can support product after product. How many ways are there to combine chocolate and nuts, for example? I guarantee that a candy company will introduce a new product based on this perennial combination sometime in the next year. The product might be almond-butter cups rather than peanut-butter cups, so it will seem exciting and new, but really, it's just a minor change to an old combination.

Take a close look at classic combinations to see whether you can find a way to revise them and make them your own. It's a fair bet that a combination others have succeeded with more than once in the past will support at least one more success in the future!

Brainstorming combinations with one of your core products

Brainstorming is a simple exercise that can produce profitable new lines of business, but for reasons that escape me, most businesses never do it. All you have to do is set one of your own products in the middle of your conference table, assemble a creative group (see Chapter 6) to sit around the table, and ask the group to come up with 50 ideas for combinations with that product. The goal of 50 ideas is important because it gets the group to use a freewheeling, rapid-fire approach in a hurry.

If, after 23 ideas or so, the group hits on a brilliant one and wants to switch over to developing it, okay. If not, keep pushing ahead to 50 ideas; then pull the best 20 and brainstorm ways of refining or bettering them until you finally come up with the winner that you want to develop and introduce.

Suppose that your company sells kitchenware, and one of its perennially popular products is a line of bright-colored enamel colanders. A colander is simply a bowl with holes in it to let water drain out, used to wash fruit and vegetables or to strain cooking water off pasta. What could you possibly combine with a colander to create a fresh innovation? Hmm. I have no idea either. It's a tough example, actually. But I've brainstormed ten ideas to get you started:

- ✔ Combine the product with fresh grapes, peaches, and other delicate fruits to make a gift colander that replaces the conventional gift basket and provides a more useful leftover product than a basket.

- ✔ Redesign the product as a decorative ball or cylinder that holds a candle. Its light would shine out of dozens of holes in the attractive red, blue, black, or white enamel of the Candle Colander.

- ✔ Offer miniature colanders full of chocolates. (Why? I'm not sure, but the idea seems like fun. Maybe the chocolates could be shaped and flavored like fresh strawberries, raspberries, and blueberries.)

- ✔ Make a disposable paper colander.

- ✔ Make a cloth colander that's a joke hat.

✔ Make miniature colanders that screw onto bases and serve as salt and pepper shakers.

✔ Make miniature colanders that screw together to form elegant, enameled metal tea and spice infuser balls.

✔ Combine a teapot with a colander that sits inside the lid to form an infuser that's more elegant than the normal wire-mesh version.

✔ Combine the colander with a flat sheet-metal pan to create a Colander Pan. (What's it for? That's a good question for a second round of brainstorming. Maybe it sits inside a regular pan to create a better roasting pan.)

✔ Make light covers and shades from colander-style metal with holes in it.

Okay, those ten ideas are a start, but if I were trying to come up with combination innovations for that kitchenware company, I'd push the group to generate four more sets of ten ideas before assessing what we had. Often, the third or fourth set produces the biggest winner — not the first set.

Maybe a colander combined with a saucepan could form a new and better way to steam vegetables in the same colander you used to wash them. Why not add a third item to the combo: a plastic storage container that also fits the colander so that the vegetables never have to leave their colander? You'd have the new Hiam Vegetable System, soon to be sold in stores everywhere!

The point is, a virtually limitless number of combinations is out there, and all you have to do is keep thinking of ideas until you hit on the one that fits your business and turns customers on. What if you don't? That's okay, because you can come up with inspired combinations in other ways.

Recombining fundamental innovations

There are innovations, and then there are the great innovations that all others build on. Take the wheel. It took 3,000 years for humanity to perfect the hub-and-spoke wheel. Now you can take this design and combine it with countless other things to make . . . oh, perhaps a million other products. So many inventions use the wheel in one way or another, odds are that you can come up with yet another one.

Another fundamental innovation is the ball. Yes, the round sphere. It took a long time for people to recognize that the world is round. Before that, no one was very interested in making or using ball-shaped objects. Since then, however, people have come up with lots of uses for spheres: ball bearings, ball joints, baseballs, gumballs, and ballpoint pens, to name a few.

Figure 11-1 shows a clever invention by James Dyson, the famous British inventor who created the Ballbarrow — a combination of a large rotating ball underneath a plastic wheelbarrow. The advantage is that the big ball doesn't get stuck in the mud like a traditional wheel does. Dyson went on to combine a ball with a vacuum cleaner, producing the breakthrough design shown in the figure.

Hinges, levers, ramps, steps, ratchets, and gears are all examples of fundamental innovations that find their way, through combination, into thousands of other inventions every year. The container is another fundamental invention, re-created in different materials and forms millions of times, depending on the application. Can you build on one of these fundamental innovations to create something more specific that meets a modern-day need? Or how about starting with a more recent fundamental innovation, such as the computer chip, electric motor, radio, or robot?

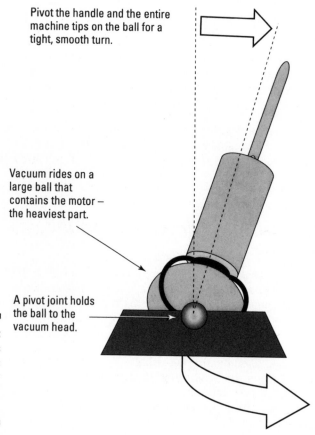

Pivot the handle and the entire machine tips on the ball for a tight, smooth turn.

Vacuum rides on a large ball that contains the motor — the heaviest part.

A pivot joint holds the ball to the vacuum head.

Figure 11-1:
James
Dyson's
improved
vacuum
design.

It's snowing pretty hard outside my office window as I write this chapter, which makes me want to combine a radio (for remote control), a computer chip (for intelligent navigation), a motor and wheels (for mobility), and a small-scale snowplow or blower to make myself a SnowBot. The machine would be busy clearing my front walk and driveway while I write, so I wouldn't have to wait for the expensive crew with snowplows and snowblowers to show up hours after the end of the storm, when a foot or more of snow has accumulated and clearing it is a big problem.

The SnowBot would be an engineering challenge but certainly not an impossible one, because fundamental innovations would provide building blocks for the project. NASA sends rovers around the surface of Mars, so surely it's not hard to make a little rover that clears snow. If you're good at this kind of thing, please get working on it. I'll buy one!

Combining Problems with Solutions

The idea behind this method is to start with a problem (as in Chapter 9) and then look for solutions to other problems that might be adaptable to your problem. In other words, use combinatorial creativity as a shortcut to inspiration as you develop alternatives.

Finding problems similar to your own

Often, problems have similarities. Your problem may have something in common with another one that's already been solved. The security camera, for example, is a solution to the need for continuous monitoring of high-security areas, such as the cash registers of all-night convenience stores. You may have a different security need, but the basic concept of using a camera to meet that need could still apply.

When I heard on the news a few nights ago that nine houses had been burned down in my area, it got me thinking that fire alarms and extinguishers could be combined with other readily available products — such as lights, prerecorded voice instructions, and digital video recorders — to improve home security. Many commonplace items and designs can be used in specific ways to solve specific problems, and the result is often a valuable innovation. Sometimes, even though you're working with readily available components, the combination of them is nonobvious and actually qualifies for patent protection. (Turn to Chapter 17 for advice on when and how to protect your intellectual property.)

Here are some ideas that combine existing solutions with the new problem of how to be prepared for a fast-moving nighttime house fire caused by a fire bomb or Molotov cocktail:

✔ More people would escape nighttime fires if each door had an emergency light — perhaps a wireless LED light mounted above the door that would go off only when the heat, smoke, or carbon-monoxide detectors were activated.

✔ If the house alarms were integrated into a central system, as many are these days, there could also be a speaker at each exit door and window, and one of them could be activated to indicate the safest evacuation route based on where the heat and smoke were detected in the house.

✔ If a fire is localized and has not progressed beyond control yet, a quick application of a fire extinguisher may control it and save the house — but finding your fire extinguisher in the dark is often a challenge. Why don't fire extinguishers have wireless emergency lights on them, too?

✔ There's no reason not to integrate a fire extinguisher into a central alarm system. A simple on-off switch in the cradle would indicate whether the extinguisher was in place or had been removed for service or use.

✔ A further combination occurred to me when I thought about the modus operandi of the arsonist (or arsonists) whose activities made my local news: tossing a flaming bottle of gas onto a porch or through a window and then running away. Nobody's seen the arsonist(s), because the fires strike in quiet residential neighborhoods at night. It would be handy to have a simple digital video recorder mounted in an inconspicuous weatherproof box on a pole or otherwise placed out of reach, with the camera aimed at the front of the house. This device could be tied to the house's heat and smoke alarms, and it could be set to transmit its past hour of memory to a central station as soon as an alarm is tripped so as to provide insight into the origins of the fire.

The digital camera mounted outside the house could also stream a live image for the alarm-station operator to view, which would help the operator decide whether the alarm was real and make any call to the fire department more prompt and informed.

These ideas aren't difficult to imagine, really; I don't think that any of them would win an inventor's award. They flowed quite naturally, however, from a focus on a specific problem.

Looking for problem themes

What makes your problem like others that may already have good solutions? The answer is *problem themes* — general, abstract statements of what's wrong. After you generalize your problem, look around for other problems that fit the general category. Maybe one of their solutions can be adapted to your needs. I have a problem with squirrels getting into my office and studio, for example. They climb onto the roof, gnaw holes in the trim, and slip into the interior of the walls, from whence they sneak around the building and cause no end of trouble.

I called an expert, who examined the building and announced that because the crawl spaces were inaccessible (to him — obviously, not to the squirrels!), he'd have to trap the squirrels outside. He warned me, however, that he was liable to trap lots of the wrong squirrels — ones that weren't actually living in the building. He further warned me that his bait might actually draw more squirrels to the roof of the building, where he wanted to place his traps.

That solution didn't sound perfect. I wondered whether I could come up with a better one.

To use problem themes as the starting point for finding a better way to keep squirrels out of my office building, I needed to brainstorm some very abstract statements of the problem, such as these:

- ✔ How to keep something or someone out
- ✔ How to make sure that someone or something isn't inside when you plug a hole
- ✔ How to catch the right animals, rather than others that happen along

As I looked at the last item in this list, I thought about flapper valves, which allow water to go one way but not the other. These valves are used in simple pumps all the time. Instead of hammering wire over the holes in the trim, I could make a flapper door out of plywood and stiff rubber — or, better yet, out of sheet metal and a strong spring hinge. This door would permit an animal to push its way out of the hole but not go back in. And wouldn't the same design solve the other problems on my list too? Abstracting the problem led me to think of a way to combine my squirrel problem with another problem — how to allow water to flow only one way — and come up with a more effective solution than the exterminator's approach of spreading kill traps all over my building's roof and yard.

I'll make up some one-way squirrel doors and install them over the holes the creatures made in my roof trim. If these doors do the trick, maybe I'll commercialize the design. CheckOut might be a good brand name for a new line of pest-control products based on this design. Maybe I'll trademark the name as well as apply for a patent. (For details on how to do both things, see Chapter 17.)

Getting Resourceful in Your Search for Combinations

Remember that the big-picture idea is to innovate. If you're stuck for a really great design or idea, and combinatorial innovation isn't producing what you need, explore some really creative approaches to finding unique combinations.

Pairing things that nobody thinks should go together

Oxymoron inventions are what I call those improbable combinations that, when done in a clever way, so often produce breakthroughs.

Here's an example of an oxymoron: fuel-efficient jets. Airplanes gulp immense amounts of jet fuel, so if you want to travel without a big carbon footprint, stay on the ground. But wait — as I write this chapter, Boeing is working on a new fuel-efficient mid-size plane in an effort to overcome this problem.

Playing with words to find unexpected combinations

Word-play inventions use components or ingredients inspired by word combinations. Sometimes, words are similar because they come from the same root word. Recognizing a familial relationship between words may help you see relationships between the things the words represent, too.

Tablet and *table,* for example, come from the same root: the Latin word *tabula,* which means *board* or *plank.* Planks of wood or slate were used for many purposes in ancient Rome. People ate on tables made of tabula and wrote letters and records on smaller planks, which is why a table can be a grid of information as well as something to serve dinner on.

You don't have to find logical connections between words to play with them and produce creative insights. There's no particular rhyme or reason to why certain words rhyme, but still, a list of words that rhyme is a good starting point if you're looking for possible combinations. Take this list, for example: *rhyme, dime, time, grime, crime, thyme, prime,* and *climb.* Can you think of a new product, using a pairing from this list? How about Time Climb, a game in which you start in the Middle Ages and have to climb your way to the present by finding all the key inventions along the way. No? Well, how about a cheap disposable clock called a Time Dime? I visualize it as a miniature pocket watch and timer the size of a dime, made from a simple computer chip and LED display, priced at — you guessed it — 10¢.

Cereal maker Kellogg Co. often runs brainstorming sessions. During one of the sessions, someone asked a creative question: "How can we help people eat smarter?" A literal answer to the question wasn't requested, but one answer proved to be insightful: "Why not include something that literally makes people smarter?" The result was Live-Bright brain-health bars, now in early testing. The bars include DHA, an omega-3 fatty acid that is thought to boost brain activity.

Imitating without violating intellectual-property rights

Copycat products borrow shamelessly from someone else's successful product concept, even if the concept doesn't appear to fit another brand or product line. Why not give it a try if you have distribution and the other company has a good product concept? All you have to do is find a way to combine the other company's concept with some element of your approach or brand to make it your own.

McDonald's, the hamburger chain, envied Starbucks' success, so it introduced its own line of supposedly gourmet coffee drinks under the pseudo-French name McCafé, using a massive television ad campaign to train customers to think of McDonald's as a legitimate source of lattes.

The trick, of course, is to borrow only a good *idea* — not a patented, trademarked, or copyrighted design or expression. See Chapter 17 for information on avoiding legal trouble, and check with your lawyer if you have any doubt.

Combining a customer want with a solution you can sell

Need-driven inventions are products or services designed to address a need or want expressed by consumers and explored through extensive surveys and discussion groups.

Procter & Gamble's surveys about laundry detergents revealed that people hate it when their clothes age and deteriorate after repeated washings. To address this need, P&G identified chemicals designed to preserve fabrics and added them to laundry detergent. The result was Tide Total Care, introduced in 2009.

Seeking Unusual Information

Combining things is great, but what about combining ideas and information? The principle of innovating through combining also applies to intangibles, not just tangible things, and you can find your way to a breakthrough design by combining ideas and information in fresh ways.

Barack Obama's 2008 presidential campaign, for example, combined the candidate's name and image with the concept of change.

Casting a broad net

It's hard to find information that leads to fresh combinations of ideas. The problem is that you don't know what to look for. A solution wouldn't be original or innovative if it were obvious, right? This problem has an official name: the *relevance paradox*, defined as the difficulty of finding information when you don't already know that it might be helpful or relevant.

In other words, you look for the information that you already know is related to your question or goal, but you don't look for information that you don't know about. So how do you overcome the relevance paradox and find information that could help, even though you don't know about it in advance?

Sometimes, if you gather information at random, you get lucky and hit on a surprisingly relevant fact or idea. The trick is to hold your puzzle, problem, or objective in your mind as you scan many sources quickly, waiting for something to pop out of the flood of information and come to your attention.

 A more guided way to look for information that you didn't know would help you is to use analogy to guide yourself toward imagined information or solutions. If a business facing bankruptcy is like a sinking ship, what would be the equivalent of a radio call to the Coast Guard, or a toolkit containing everything needed to patch a hole, or a way to offload the valuable cargo to another ship before yours sinks? These three strategies are fairly obvious for sinking ships, but could they also be applied to sinking businesses? Well, let's see. You could try the following:

   ✔ Search for turnaround consultants, who, like the Coast Guard, rush in to help when a business is about to go down.

   ✔ Look for a short-term patch in the form of emergency financing or a way to sell or close the worst-performing line of business.

   ✔ Seek a buyer who will cooperate with a bankruptcy process by acquiring your most valuable assets and continuing to service your customers.

Seeking weak signals

You can also look for *weak signals* — opinions and facts that contradict the prevailing wisdom and are outshouted by the mainstream — to find alternative viewpoints. Usually, you can find people who have contrary opinions or different approaches from the mainstream, and if you seek out these contrarians, you may find that they have a point. If you operate in an industrial setting, for example, find out how small-scale tinkerers in home workshops are tackling the same things that you do in factories.

I bet that someone out there has a fresh approach to generating power. One farmer, for example, built a cylindrical turbine with its feet in the water of a stream, its arms spread to catch the wind, and a round solar panel on top. Depending on the weather, the three components contribute differentially, but the turbine almost always produces at least a trickle of electricity. I don't know whether the design is worth scaling up, but it might be inspirational to someone at a power company.

Trying Unusual Forms

The form that something takes is partly due to necessity. A coffee mug, for example, needs to hold liquid, sit flat on a table, and be easy to pick up and to sip from. But form is also due to design traditions that can blind us to other possibilities.

Combining a function with an unfamiliar form can produce breakthrough innovations. I saw a fun example of this principle back when the popular singer Taylor Swift hosted *Saturday Night Live*. As hosts are expected to do, she opened the show with a humorous monologue. Her opening, however, didn't follow the conventional form of a spoken monologue with pauses for (ideally) audience laughter. Instead, she picked up a guitar and proceeded to sing a composition titled "My Musical Monologue." The sketch was clever and got a lot of laughs, and the idea of setting it to music worked well for her, because she's a good singer and songwriter but (presumably) an inexperienced monologuer.

What combinations of form and function can *you* come up with to amaze your audience or win customers? Can you offer the same benefit while changing the form of your best-selling product?

To help you see how to match new forms to old benefits, think about the benefits of a cup of coffee. Can you give someone the same benefits in solid form rather than liquid? Sure! I bet that you've already come up with coffee ice cream packaged in coffee cups and sold alongside hot coffee as a new option, right? Or maybe you were thinking about coffee-flavored gum with caffeine in it. What — you weren't? Okay, had you thought of a coffee patch — like a nicotine patch, but infused with the caffeine and other xanthenes that give coffee its energy- and mood-boosting effects? Or do you have yet another possibility in mind?

You can find lots of ways to combine new forms with existing product benefits and create breakthrough products. Give it a try!

Clever combinations for designer display boards

No doubt you've used a chalkboard, whiteboard, or bulletin board. But have you ever seen a combination whiteboard and bulletin board? How about a corkboard inside a locking cupboard to keep your postings neat and controlled in a public or semipublic place such as a hotel lobby?

These simple combinations, with nice frames added, make up a product line with hundreds of options for the company Art Concepts (www.artconceptsstore.com). Its wallboard superstore features dozens of categories made up of combinations. Combination boards are just one example, alongside fabric-covered corkboards and fabric-wrapped wallboards. Three-way combinations also enrich the company's catalog. The French board, for example, is made of cork wrapped in fabric, with a crisscross of diagonal ribbons tacked to it for holding small pieces of paper or photographs.

Imagine the best combination for organizing your bulletin board or planning wall, and you can have it made in the company's custom board center. Art Concepts shows that simple materials, combined in creative ways, are more than enough to make a unique and appealing line of business.

Part III

Applying Creativity and Innovation to Daily Challenges

The 5th Wave   By Rich Tennant

"But rather than me just sitting here talking, why don't we watch this video of me sitting here talking?"

In this part . . .

As an innovator, you need not approach daily tasks the way others do. Your imagination gives you the power to bring new perspectives to everything you do, from tackling budgets and cost cuts to resolving disagreements.

This part helps you decide how to apply your innovative ideas to some of the daily routines of the workplace — making an impact when communicating with others, turning conflicts into opportunities to innovate, and improving your organization in the process of seeking ways to save money.

Chapter 12

Delivering Fresh Presentations and Proposals

· ·

In This Chapter

▶ Assessing the audience to decide how much creativity is appropriate

▶ Developing a compelling, original point of view

▶ Writing a presentation that convinces others of your point of view

▶ Communicating creatively through your words, visuals, and other elements

▶ Designing slides with creative restraint

▶ Branding your presentation

· ·

A good presentation is unobtrusively creative. In business and professional spheres, audiences are rarely looking for wild, crazy, and creative; they're looking for smart, helpful, and insightful. They want you to be professional and an expert on your topic. Also, of course, they don't want to be bored. But you're not an entertainer — you're a presenter. Big difference. The entertainer pumps up the laughs, action, or artistic elements to combat boredom. The presenter relies on creative insights delivered in a credible style.

If you harness creativity in the right ways, your audiences won't even realize you're being creative. They *will* notice that you're interesting and insightful. They'll think you're smart and well spoken. They'll be impressed. People will come up to you afterward to shake your hand and ask you for advice.

The credibility you need to be a high-impact presenter comes from gaining a creative insight on your topic so that you have something fresh and important to say and then presenting it in a clean, impressive, and moderately creative manner. This chapter walks you through both phases of this process of becoming a credible presenter of fresh proposals.

Building the Credibility You Need to Be Creative

Credibility is the impression of knowing what you're talking about and having a strong, convincing message. It's the secret ingredient behind winning proposals and popular public speakers. Some executive coaches work specifically on credibility — that's how important it is for top corporate leaders. And, of course, politicians who lose credibility don't get reelected. But what about the rest of us? Do you need to be credible too?

If you don't establish a high degree of credibility right away, your proposals, presentations, and sales pitches will be unsuccessful, and your ideas, no matter how innovative, will fail for lack of adequate championship. Your first goal in planning any business or professional presentation is to figure out how to establish your credibility.

If you want to present any fresh, innovative thinking, credibility is especially important because it helps you make the case for your ideas. That's what innovators do — successful ones, anyway. Using your credibility to make your case means understanding your audience and what they're likely to expect, as well as thinking about how you'll present yourself and your credentials as an innovative thought leader.

Sizing up your audience and context

If you look up "creative presentation ideas" in any Web search engine, you'll be inundated with results. Hundreds of articles and blogs tell you to do things like leave the titles off your slides, deliver your presentation blindfolded, sprinkle homemade cartoons through your slides, add a theme song, make everyone get up and dance, or dress like a clown and do tricks. Caution! Every one of these ideas is going to get you into trouble with the majority of business audiences, because most business and workplace audiences are conservative in their views of what a presentation ought to be.

A business audience usually expects you, as a presenter, to

- ✔ Conduct yourself professionally, as appropriate to your position and the place and time of the presentation.

- ✔ Summarize the conventional wisdom and current thinking on the topic, even if you go on to disagree with it.

- ✔ Be organized and clear, which means telling the members of the audience what you're going to tell them and not wasting their time on things they consider to be irrelevant.

Most business audiences want you to be traditional in your conduct and approach. If you have a good new idea to propose, they'll listen — provided that you establish yourself as a highly credible source.

Providing enough structure to reassure the audience

It's important to project a competent, successful persona when you speak to any professional audience, which means dressing somewhat more formally than the audience members do and comporting yourself in a calm, professional manner all (or most) of the time. (Assume business casual dress for a conference audience and formal suits for anything in the executive suite.) If you're a good performer, you can slip out of your professional role briefly to deliver a punch line or warm up the crowd, as long as you're able to move comfortably back to your professional persona to move the presentation along to the next chunk of hard content.

Most audiences prefer a competent, professional, credible presenter who seems to be organized and conscientious. Most people, however, are a bit disorganized, especially when rattled by stage fright. The conventional prescription for stage fright is to know your presentation well. Practice delivering it until you know each talking point by heart and don't have to worry about losing your place.

To overcome stage fright, it's important to know your content, but even more important is knowing your venue or the context in which you'll be presenting. No amount of practice in front of a friend can prepare you to speak in front of 200 strangers. Seek out speaking experiences that build up your audience-hardiness by exposing you to larger groups and to people you don't know. Volunteer to give presentations at work whenever possible to gain experience and build your comfort level. Also consider joining a Toastmasters group (www.toastmasters.org), where professionals gather to practice their speaking skills.

To appear to be conscientious — namely, organized, structured, and full of clear plans and solutions — create numbered lists of steps and options, as well as an overall outline for your presentation that breaks it into three to five main topic areas along with an introduction and conclusion. These structured elements give the audience the reassurance that it instinctively needs, and you appear to be organized and on top of things, which is essential to your professional demeanor and your ability to command the audience's respect.

When you provide enough structure and order to your presentation through outlines; numbered lists; and clear, helpful diagrams or charts, you win audience members' respect and trust. They view you as being credible, which gives you permission to be creative. Without credibility, any efforts you make to be creative will fall flat, and your audience will be skeptical of your ideas — and of you.

Engaging the audience

Most business presentations are boring. That's too bad, because boring presentations fail to hold interest and don't make a strong impression. Whatever your purpose and medium, don't be boring! Standing on your head or adding colorful icons to your slides, however, won't rescue a boring presentation. You should use creativity for other purposes, such as to drive home a key point in an interesting way or to generate new options or solutions.

Don't try to fluff up a presentation with bad jokes just to avoid being boring. Superficial uses of creativity undermine your credibility as a presenter. Instead, make sure that the core content of your presentation is significant and brief so that it's inherently interesting to the professionals in your audience.

To avoid boring your audience, follow these rules as you plan and write your presentation:

- **Speak for the minimum acceptable period — not the maximum.** Less is more! If you're brief, what you say is more likely to be remembered.

- **Deliver the expected.** It's important to reassure audience members by showing them that you're on topic and delivering what they came for. If you get too creative, you may fail to deliver the expected, so keep in mind that the expected is the foundation of your presentation.

- **Add pleasant surprises on top of the expected.** This area is where your creativity can do the most good. Build something exciting on top of a solid foundation so that you both meet and exceed expectations.

- **Avoid employing overly informal, zany, or superficially creative techniques and tricks.** Conduct yourself with gravity.

The best way to engage an audience is to have something to say. What's your point? If it's a compelling one, simply make it, support it, and explain how to implement it. Your audience will appreciate the clarity of your thoughts and the efficient way in which you present them.

Finding Your Unique Insight

You need to formulate a point of view before you can write a good presentation. Your particular perspective on the topic ought to be fresh and useful, and you can develop a unique point of view by giving your innovative instincts free rein.

The following steps help you ensure that your presentation has a unique perspective that adds insight to the topic. If you fail to schedule enough time for all four of the preparatory phases, you'll flub the actual presentation by simply reciting what you've read without adding any insight of your own.

1. **Perform background research by**
    - Gathering relevant sources
    - Reviewing the facts
    - Making a list of the main problems, concerns, or goals
    - Finding out what other people have proposed

2. **Let the information incubate by**
    - Setting the project aside
    - Sleeping on it
    - Toying with ideas as you work on other tasks

3. **Find your insight by**
    - Developing theories
    - Refining your best ideas
    - Adopting a unique point of view

4. **Prepare your presentation by**
    - Organizing facts and thoughts around your unique point of view
    - Writing your presentation
    - Editing to make it briefer and more focused

Starting with research

Imagine that you've been asked to speak about the economy and how it may affect your industry's future sales. You might prepare by reading articles on the topic; examining the effect of past economic cycles on your industry; and gathering expert opinions, quotes, and forecasts. If you do all that research, however, you still won't be prepared to write a good presentation, because you won't have your own point of view. In school, students are initially expected simply to summarize what adults have to say on a topic. As students reach higher levels, they're expected to develop their own theses and to present them with supporting arguments and facts. So are you, because you're an adult, not an elementary-school student!

Ask yourself this question as you study your research: "What is my unique point of view on the topic?" If you've read multiple sources and compiled a good fact base on your topic, you have the raw materials that you need to come up with your own thesis.

Incubating the facts until a fresh perspective pops out

Converting the raw inputs of information and other people's opinions into your own unique perspective is a creative process. You must allow your creative mind to churn and consider the research you've done (see the preceding section). If you've immersed yourself intently in researching the topic and gathering source material, you'll continue to think about the topic during your rest period, which is how you tap into the power of incubation. Incubation happens when you sit on a topic or question after you've hatched an "egg" of information about it.

Often, it takes a distant viewpoint to see things clearly. Back up by generalizing the problem or goal, and see whether a more general statement will help you gain insight. Rather than struggle to find an innovative way to reorganize your company's sales force to boost sales (assuming that's what your assignment is), you could ask yourself general questions such as these:

- ✔ How do experts organize routes and territories to minimize drive time and maximize efficiency?

- ✔ What conditions produce the highest performances for salespeople?

- ✔ Which territories or types of customers are going to experience the greatest future growth?

These are good general questions that anyone might ask in any company. If you answer them for your specific business, you'll almost certainly gain insight into how to reorganize your sales force for maximum future sales. Incubating insightful questions is a great way to move toward your unique point of view.

Sometimes, your incubation of the problem produces questions that need more research. For example, if you think it's important to find out which territories or types of customers are going to experience the greatest future growth, you may do some additional research. And from that second round of research, you may find that a great thesis pops right out, ready to become the organizing theme of your presentation. For example, you may find that the traditionally strong territories are going to be eclipsed by smaller ones that experience faster growth. In that case, your recommendation would be to concentrate your top salespeople on the emerging territories so as to gain a dominant share of their business before your competitors realize how valuable these territories are going to be.

Brainstorming for insight

What if the steps covered in the section "Finding Your Unique Insight" don't work for you? Sometimes, you incubate a topic by sleeping on it (see the preceding section), and when you wake up, you still have no clear insight.

You can *make* yourself come up with insight on your topic. Any number of creative-thinking techniques can help. Brainstorming, in all its variants, is generally the first thing to try (see Chapters 6, 7, and 8), and it's fine to brainstorm on your own, even though people usually think of the technique as a group activity. Discipline yourself to generate at least a page or flip chart of wild ideas. Then back up (literally — step away from the paper) and see whether anything pops. Usually, one item in the list proves to be particularly helpful, and you may develop and refine it into the point of view you need.

Here's an example of brainstorming a unique point of view for a presentation — in this case, a presentation on the economy's effect on your industry:

1. **Research your topic.**

   Your research tells you that sales lag the economy, so this year's economic growth, or lack thereof, is a good predictor of your industry's future growth. This information isn't very exciting, however, because most people already know it. Your challenge is to address the topic from a unique point of view.

2. **Brainstorm a list of observations about the topic.**

   Your list includes these items:

   - Everybody knows that you can predict industry growth based on recent economic trends, but people usually don't bother to do so.

   - In the last recession, the leading companies were hurt the most because they were too aggressive and had to cut way back when sales dropped.

   - In the last growth period, a few smaller companies grew to be industry leaders by innovating, but most stayed small.

   - Most people don't think that they can do anything about economic cycles, so they don't pay much attention to those cycles.

3. **Examine your list to see what catches your eye.**

   As you look at the list, you keep coming back to the observation that most people don't think that they can do anything about economic cycles and therefore don't pay much attention to them. You realize that this observation means that many people in your audience won't think your topic is important. You wonder whether this point is actually much more important than people realize. Is it a hidden driver of success?

4. **Develop your chosen thought into a unique point of view in the form of a *thesis statement*, which is a clear, single-sentence answer to a question your presentation explores.**

   Often, your thesis statement is the explanation of an important problem or puzzle that concerns the bottom-line performance of a business — whether yours or a customer's or client's. Your thesis statement should be important and nonobvious to your audience so that they feel they gain insight by listening to you discuss it.

For example, as you pose the question "Is the economy a hidden driver of success in our industry?", you sense that you're finally closing in on a unique and interesting point of view. You hypothesize that the major changes in market position occur during important shifts in the economic cycle and that it would be possible to take advantage of this effect.

5. **Develop your unique point of view by refining the question.**

   You might do this as follows: "Economic shifts always shake up our industry, and if you prepare, you can take advantage of this effect." Wow! This observation is interesting and valuable. You've got yourself a great point of view in the form of a thesis statement that addresses the perennially popular question of how to be successful in business.

When you write your presentation, start by making the statement you come up with in Step 5; then support and explore it. I guarantee that your audience will be spellbound.

Sometimes, you'll think you've got the perfect point of view to organize your presentation around, but when you start to write the script, you see holes in your thinking. Don't be so wedded to your point of view that you insist on sticking with it even if it proves to be hard to support.

Most people fail to add fundamental value as speakers because they don't go the extra creative mile by finding their unique point of view. Don't make that mistake. Be the standout speaker who really has a fresh, valuable point of view to offer.

Avoiding fixating on the first big idea

If you find yourself worrying about the thesis that you thought you were going to use, go back to the beginning (Step 1 in "Finding Your Unique Insight") and start all over again. Yes, this may mean trashing your draft, but if it's no good, it belongs in the trash bin, not at the podium. You aren't done until your big idea holds up under the challenge of turning it into a well-reasoned, well-organized presentation. Sometimes, getting the insight that you need takes several tries.

Outlining a strong framework for your presentation

When you have a unique point of view for your presentation, you may design a presentation that presents the content in a straightforward, clear, simple manner. Think of this first stage of writing as framing the "house" that will eventually be your finished presentation. The initial draft is a framework of clear, strong sentences that lay out the main points and subpoints of your presentation.

You may find it easiest to write this first draft in outline format than in fully fleshed-out paragraphs.

With a good, clear, clean, outline-oriented draft in hand, you're ready to think about how to pump up your communications. It's time to get creative again. Consult the next section for ways to give your communication the power of subtle, professional creativity.

Making Your Point with the Five Tools of Creative Presentation

Your most important contribution to your presentation or proposal is your creative insight on the topic. You're a professional making a presentation, so don't feel like you need to add bells and whistles. You convince your audience of your thesis by being credible and well prepared, not by being entertaining.

When you have your content blocked out, you're ready to think of creative ways to make your main points. Confine yourself to five main ways of using creativity to make your point more compelling and clear:

1. **Cite or quote authoritative sources.**

2. **Present relevant and useful facts to prove your point.**

3. **Provide visuals to illustrate your point.**

4. **Offer analogies to help make your point clear and memorable.**

5. **Tell relevant stories about people or businesses.**

Use these five techniques gently. Don't overuse them. One fairly lengthy story is enough, for example. Also, if you have three tables of impressive statistics, avoid the temptation to add ten more tables. Each technique grows old quickly. Audiences like variety.

Figure 12-1 illustrates how to bring creative persuasion into your presentation in professional, appropriate ways.

When it comes to how you'll make your main points, keep in mind that a good presentation is unobtrusively creative. The techniques in the preceding list are unobtrusive ways to add some creative power to your presentation, so long as you don't overuse any of them.

Never use creativity to fluff up a presentation or cover up a lack of substance. Avoid using the gimmicks that many presentation coaches suggest. Don't feel that you have to work humor into your presentation, for example, unless you're naturally funny, your humor is clearly relevant to the topic, and your humor couldn't possibly offend anyone. Those constraints are big ones, though, so usually, humor is inappropriate. Also avoid using theatrical tricks. You aren't a trained actor. Most of the gimmicks that you find in books on spicing up presentations are going to fall flat and make you look like you're trying too hard to entertain.

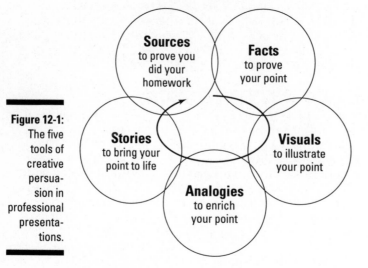

Figure 12-1:
The five tools of creative persuasion in professional presentations.

Incorporating sources and facts

Every high school and college student knows that sources and facts are the bedrock of a good paper, so why do people forget to use them as soon as they graduate and go to work? I think that adults have a natural instinct to suppress our paper-writing experiences, but it's helpful to keep in mind the core lesson: Build up a solid base of sources and facts in support of your thesis statement.

Even if you think that you've done enough homework, think again. By the time you incubate your original research and come up with the thesis that will form your unique point of view, your fact base may be out of step with your evolving argument.

Make a list of three essential facts that would lend the greatest support and credibility to your thesis. Then, if you don't already have them at hand, go and find those facts stated by authoritative sources. If you plan to say that children younger than 16 create most of the new fashion trends these days, for example, you could bolster that thesis with

✔ A quote from a designer saying that she gets great ideas from her children

✔ Statistics on how many of the last ten hot fads started with children

✔ Statistics showing that the spending power of children is increasing

When you present three good facts from authoritative sources, you convince most audience members of your point. If you want to provide additional support and proof, do so cautiously to avoid overwhelming the audience. If you go on and list ten more facts, most audience members will forget the first three. Don't overwhelm them with a list of facts that drives the three strongest proofs out of their minds.

Engaging the mind's eye with good visuals

Exactly how many words is a picture worth? Wrong question. Pictures don't substitute for words; they *illustrate* the words. Don't try to substitute a picture for any of the words in your presentation. Add pictures (including graphs, photographs, and videos) only if they work as powerful illustrations of important points.

Knowing when and how to use graphs

Use graphs when you need to make statistics clearer. Here's how:

✔ **Line graphs:** Trends should be illustrated with traditional line graphs showing time moving to the right and quantity moving vertically. Use an X mark for each data point, and connect the points with a line to help the eye see the trend or direction of movement.

✔ **Bar charts:** Use bar charts to compare statistics, such as sales by region. Avoid cramming more than six bars onto a single graph.

✔ **Pie charts:** Use pie charts to show how something is divided. You can illustrate what percentage of your sales comes from what products, for example, by showing each product as a slice of pie.

That's about it. I don't recommend using more-complex types of graphs. Keep it simple when it comes to graphs, because many people have difficulty reading them.

Incorporating photographs and videos

Show as you tell by providing a good, clear picture of your subject. As you talk about teens and their fashion trends, show several pictures of teenagers wearing current fashions. As you talk about your products and which are selling best, show photos of the products. You get the idea. The basic rule of illustrating a presentation is the old saw "Keep it simple, stupid!" (KISS).

Illustrate anything that's best seen rather than heard. If a video would illustrate the use of your product better than a still photograph would, use the video.

Don't go beyond that simple goal, however. As with everything in your presentation, less is more when it comes to visuals. If you have only a few graphs and photographs, you can allow the audience to look at them longer, which means people may actually remember what you show and tell them.

Don't include video unless it really adds value. Video takes up presentation time and competes for the spotlight with you, the presenter.

Here's a good rule: Show, but don't show off. Restraint is the key to effective illustration in any professional presentation. Too often, presenters include a flashy video, a series of impressive photos, or a deck of complex graphs just because they hope that the audience will be impressed. Business audiences aren't impressed by excess, though; they're impressed by restraint.

An analogy is like a newly cleaned window

Analogies offer fresh new viewpoints on the subject. They engage the right side of the brain, which is where creative thought and intuition are based. When you use an analogy, you get your audience to engage creatively as well as logically. That's a good thing! People find presenters more interesting and presentations more persuasive when they have engaged both sides of their brains in the process of listening and watching. Analogies are great for engaging the whole brain by stimulating a little subconscious creative thought on the part of your audience.

To show you how an analogy stimulates the audience to think creatively, I want you to reread the header at the top of this section: "An analogy is like a newly cleaned window." To get this analogy, your brain has to visualize a newly cleaned window and then figure out how it relates to the point.

How *does* it relate? Well, a newly cleaned window is easy to see through. It entices. It draws the eye over to it and makes you want to look out (or in?) to see what's there. An analogy does the same thing in a more abstract way: It gets the audience to look at your point from a fresh perspective. The analogy attracts attention because it's a new way to see the subject.

How analogies engage the audience's imagination

After your audience members have digested your analogy and figured out what the connection is, they may not know it, but they're significantly more engaged in your presentation. You've just gotten them to do an activity for you. This activity went on in the right frontal lobes of their brains, so nobody noticed but you.

Even though processing an analogy is an invisible activity, it's a very powerful one. It builds engagement with your presentation and strengthens agreement with your point.

A surefire way to create great analogies

To come up with your own analogies, ask yourself this question: "What is [fill in your subject] like?" If I'm preparing to talk to a group of inventors about how to market their new ideas, I might ask myself, "What is a new invention like?" To answer my question, I may write it at the top of a chart pad or dry-erase board and then force myself to brainstorm a list of possible answers. A new invention is like

- A mongrel puppy, because it's cute and appealing, but you don't know what it will look like when it grows up

- A new baby that needs lots of care and feeding before it's ready to walk on its own two feet

- A sand castle on a beach — and you don't know whether the tide's going away from it or about to wash over it

- A steaming-hot plate of food just out of the oven, which is best served while it's hot and shouldn't be neglected until it gathers flies

Think about each analogy until you can see the point it supports; then pick the analogy that buttresses the point you most want to make. If I want to argue that inventors shouldn't sit on their ideas, but rush out and seek support for them right away, I might use the analogy that an invention is a hot plate of food just out of the oven that ought to be served quickly. I actually find, however, that most inventors take their ideas into the world prematurely. Therefore, I probably would use the analogy that an invention is like a new baby that has to be supported for several years before it gets its balance and even begins to walk on its own feet.

Telling tales

I intentionally put storytelling at the end of my list of creative presentation techniques because I want you to try the other four techniques first (see the preceding sections for details on using sources, facts, visuals, and analogies). The first four techniques are easier to hang on your outline than stories are, because stories take time and attention away from the main story: your presentation.

Stories have tremendous power when they're used right, but use them cautiously because of their tendency to hog the spotlight.

Weaving a story into the threads of your presentation

A wonderful way to use a story is to find a case history (an actual example or a fictional one) that you can weave throughout your presentation. Introduce the main character of your story and his or her goal or dilemma in your introduction; then return to the story briefly at the end of each section of your talk to show how the main point of that section applies to the story. As you work through your topic outline, you also work through the chapters of your story, so that both the story and your presentation keep pace and climax at the end. When you do things this way, the story never hogs the spotlight; it has to share the spotlight as you alternate between storytelling and presenting the gist of your content.

Another good way to use a story is to set up the problem you're going to solve. Early in your presentation, introduce a brief case history or example of a person or organization that ran into trouble; then explain that you're going to show the audience how to avoid the pitfall that so-and-so fell into. The story helps the audience get personally engaged in your topic.

Condensing your story into appealing sound bites

Stories need to be brief and clear. Avoid using more than three characters — the people or organization that the story is about.

Suppose that I decide to share a story about Barbara, an inventor who ran into all sorts of problems as she struggled to bring her new product to market. I know that this inventor's story involves a whole cast of characters: her consultant (me), her graphic designer, her patent attorney, her product engineering team, her bankers, and so on. To make the story compelling and clear for the sake of a presentation, I must narrow it down and simplify it. Audience members don't need to find out everything about this inventor; they just need to know the most compelling and relevant aspects of Barbara's lengthy story. Good storytelling keeps the plot and characters simple.

When you tell your main story, dim your slides and approach the audience to create a different context for the story. The audience will focus on you more fully and pay close attention to your story, and they'll appreciate the chance of pace.

Avoiding being upstaged by the story

A great test of any story is whether you can tell it in one minute or less. If not, go back to the drawing board and find ways to shorten the telling.

If you have personal stories that illustrate your central point, include one or two — but no more than that. Even if you're a celebrity, the audience will lose interest in your personal life history surprisingly quickly. I'm sorry to be the bearer of bad news, but it's not actually all about you. Your presentation is the star; you're simply supporting it. Don't let your own stories hog the spotlight, but let the spotlight shine on your main point. That way, everyone will leave the room knowing what you think, and most of them will agree with you.

Branding Your Message with an Appropriate Look and Style

When you've drafted your presentation or proposal and gathered appropriate sources, facts, visuals, analogies, and stories to support it, you're ready to package it in a clean, consistent, appealing style. The following sections break down the primary elements that contribute to the style of your presentation.

Matching tone and style

Your tone and style may range from animated and informal to contained, professional, and formal, depending on your content, context, and audience. If you're giving a formal talk on a serious topic to a high-level professional audience in a formal lecture hall, for example, choose a formal, self-contained style, and look, speak, act, and dress accordingly.

Creating a visual signature

Your *visual signature* is the look or style of all slides, handouts, backdrops, charts, videos, and other visual elements, including your outfit. Choose a visual signature that fits the tone and style of your presentation. A serious, professional topic needs a visual style that emphasizes a clean, professional look through conservative colors, traditional font choices, and formal-looking graphs or charts.

Choosing colors for your slides and handouts

Select a color scheme that's modestly creative and fits the tone and style of your presentation. For a formal presentation, for example, choose your colors from a palette of blue, black, and white, with an occasional very small splash of red or gold worked in for contrast. Sorry, that's it! Green, purple, orange, and other colors belong only in informal presentations.

You may think that limiting your color palette to blue, black, and white will cripple your creativity when it comes to graphic design of your slides and handouts. Not so! Some of the greatest works of art were done in black and white. In fact, it's easier to create an elegant, clean, appealing look when you limit your palette. You can use a gentle gradient of light blues in the background, for example, with the headline in dark blue and the bullet points below it in black. If you combine this color scheme with a nice contrast between a headline font of 44-point Arial or Helvetica and 32-point text in the same font, you'll have a very clean, appealing graphic look.

Also, to add more graphic interest to a slide or handout with an Arial header, switch the body copy to a contrasting font, such as Times New Roman. If you do, check readability by backing away from your computer screen a few yards. Is the new font still readable? If not, go back to Arial, which is highly readable from a distance.

One exception to the rule of limiting your main palette to blue, black, and white comes into play when the topic of your presentation has its own color scheme. You may want to use that scheme instead. For example, a sales representative for a drug company may design a presentation about a new drug by using the colors from the drug's orange-and-green logo. However, to keep those orange- and green-themed slides or handouts professional and easy to read, most of the text should remain black. Stay as close to the core professional palette as you can, and use brand colors for accents rather than for your main text or headers.

Creating an effective design

Here are other design elements that you can use to add creative appeal to a slide in subtle, professional ways:

- Alternate among one-column text, two-column text, and graphs to vary the format.

- Introduce a single straight line between the header and the text, reproducing that line in the same position on every slide. Yes, I know that this line is a very simple and conservative design element, but keep in mind that good presentations are *unobtrusively* creative.

- If you want to get really radical, place a border (perhaps in a contrasting color) around the text, or use a small logo or photo in the bottom-right corner of every slide. The border or logo unifies the varied slide formats, making it clear that graphs, bulleted lists, and multicolumn bulleted lists all belong to the same presentation.

Adding a logo

The visual logo should relate directly to the topic. Use a large version of the logo on the title slide and a smaller version at the bottom of all other slides.

You can get creative with your visual logo as long as you keep the design simple, small, and relevant. See Chapter 4 for tips on how to design creative brand identities, including logos and titles that you can use for your presentations.

I'm helping update a one-week course on leadership and management for the U.S. Coast Guard, and the slides in the new deck have a deep-blue background color, white text, and a small photograph of a Coast Guard cutter racing through the water. The boat is in the bottom-right corner of the slide, and it's white with the Coast Guard's distinctive red stripe across its bow. This boat isn't an official U.S. Coast Guard logo but an image selected specifically for these slides; it gives the entire set an appealing and consistent image.

Knowing the difference between good and bad design

Figure 12-2 shows good and bad uses of creative graphic design for professional presentations. As the figure demonstrates, gratuitous use of design elements can be confusing, overwhelming the content and the presenter.

Figure 12-2:
Bad (a) and
good (b)
slide
layouts.

a
b

The bad example mixes many fonts, each of them fun and interesting but none of them appropriate for a professional presentation. It also uses too many visual elements. The sticky-note theme with a faint star in the middle doesn't relate to the topic or add any value; it's simply distracting. The artist's palette from the clip-art menu also fails to add value, and it increases the visual business of a slide that's already too busy.

The good example in Figure 12-2 sticks to one font, Arial, using a large, bold version of it for the headline. It also uses much more *white space* (open space around and between the design elements). The lines are farther apart, and the slide has a calmer, cleaner, more open style, which makes it much more readable and pleasant to look at.

The only artistic design elements in the good example are the two lines that define the area for the text and an old-fashioned key at the bottom of the slide. This key is the logo for the presentation, which I plan to call "The Key to Effective Presentations." Placing the key at the bottom of every slide reminds audience members of the title of my presentation, thereby effectively branding it in their minds.

Repeating your auditory signature

Your *auditory signature* consists of one or a few phrases or keywords that you weave into your presentation often enough to embed them in the memory of the audience members.

Avoiding slide-design pitfalls

It's easy to get creative in designing your slides. Most presenters use Microsoft PowerPoint to make their slides, which is fine, because the program is easy to use and hardly ever crashes during a presentation. PowerPoint, however, offers many negative temptations. Here are some things to avoid doing when you design slides for your presentation:

- ✔ **Don't use WordArt.** WordArt is a selection of comic-book-style fonts, using curvy, colorful 3-D characters. It can make a word look really fancy. But you aren't selling words; you're selling your argument. Treat it with dignity by using traditional fonts.

- ✔ **Don't use free clip art unless it really, truly is a good illustration of a point.** PowerPoint users have access to lots of clip art, but very little of it helps you hammer home a key point.

- ✔ **Don't use too many slides.** People almost always create too many slides when they first draft their slide decks. More may seem to be better, especially if you're

anxious about what you'll say, but if you have dozens of slides, you'll be reduced to reading them out loud with your back to the room, and no one will remember a word you said.

Try to give yourself at least a minute per slide. If your presentation involves rich slides that contain graphs or multiple bullet points, give yourself three to five minutes per slide. Based on that formula, a 20-minute presentation doesn't need more than 10 to 15 slides.

- ✔ **Don't use backgrounds that include recognizable objects** (such as balloons, bridges, chalkboards, clipboards, flags, paper currency, or clouds). These objects are cute for the first few slides but grow tiresome and distracting long before your presentation is done.

- ✔ **Don't use unconventional, hard-to-read fonts,** either alone or in combination. Good graphic design is subtle, not presumptuous.

Your signature should relate to your main point. For example, if your thesis is that sales territories should be realigned to focus effort on fast-growing regions, you may want to keep reminding your audience that it's important to "organize for the future," and you may use that phrase as the title of your presentation, too.

Controlling your body language

After choosing your style, visual signature, and auditory signature, ask yourself how your body language can best support these other elements. If you're presenting in an exciting, informal style to a youthful audience, your body language probably ought to be informal and relaxed. You may see yourself sitting on the edge of the stage, taking questions and offering unscripted answers.

If you chose a formal tone and style, your body language should be more controlled and formal to match your tone and to go with your formal clothing and demeanor. Keep your hand gestures fairly modest and controlled, and stay on your feet, with your jacket on the whole time. Don't let your nonverbal behavior clash with the rest of your presentation.

Whether your style is informal and relaxed or formal and upright, smile at your audience from time to time. Work a smile in when you're introduced and when you're thanking the host for the opportunity to speak. Also smile when you're listening to a question or comment from the audience. It's natural to frown when you're listening intently, but overcoming this natural tendency makes a huge difference in how the audience sees and remembers you. Audiences tend to rate smiling presenters as being smarter and more creative than others, and they tend to agree with presenters who smile. Practice smiling while you listen.

Chapter 13

Negotiating Creative Win–Wins

In This Chapter

▶ Exploring options for innovative resolution

▶ Encouraging parties to shift to a collaborative approach

▶ Focusing on the underlying problem and how to solve it

▶ Working the most promising ideas and suggestions into a final solution

*L*ife is full of conflicts. Why should business be any different? There are conflicts with co-workers, employees, managers, customers, and suppliers. Then there are occasionally really nasty conflicts — often about the disputed terms of a business contract — involving legal action or the threat of it.

The average small business has a dozen conflicts a year, by my estimate, not counting minor disputes that don't have much effect on the bottom line. A big business or a large government entity such as an agency or city, on the other hand, may have hundreds of conflicts that need care and attention in the course of a year.

Before responding to a conflict, stop and consider creative options and what you may be able to propose that could change the conflict for the better. This chapter shows you how to take a creative approach and how to innovate solutions that improve the outcome over what it initially looked like you would be stuck with as a result of a conflict. Redefine conflicts as opportunities to cooperate in innovative problem-solving, and you'll soon find yourself looking forward to conflicts rather than worrying about them.

Turning Conflicts into Creative Opportunities

Each business conflict is an opportunity to transform what initially seems like a simple tug-of-war or power struggle into a creative solution that gives something of benefit to all parties involved. Good things can come from conflicts. Put on your innovator's hat whenever you see tempers flaring or legal claims rising, and see whether you can create a new and better outcome than those initially on the table. It's amazing how often you can transform a conflict into an opportunity to better the situation if you simply reframe the struggle by opening your creativity toolbox instead of reaching for the nearest verbal weapons.

Identifying conflicts with rich potential for innovation

What makes a conflict a great candidate for an innovative approach? First, the outcome must matter. The outcome is what's at stake — what the parties to the conflict are hoping or striving for.

It's amazing how many conflicts are really quite trivial. People get caught up in the heat of the moment and invest a lot of emotional energy in something that really doesn't matter. Jockeying for position when cars are merging on a road, for example, is foolish because when the cars get in line and up to speed again, a difference of 30 feet one way or the other is going to amount to only a second or two of travel time. But that fact doesn't stop drivers from getting quite agitated and angry about whose turn it ought to be.

When you look at the conflicts in your workplace, select only those with potentially significant outcomes for innovative problem-solving.

Imagine that you're in a dispute with a printer. The printing company had said it could print your next catalog for the same price as the previous one, but now it claims that too much time has passed and costs have gone up, so it has to bill you 20 percent more. Ouch! Finding a way to reduce or eliminate that cost increase would make a definite difference in your bottom line, which makes your dispute with the printer a good candidate for a creative approach to conflict.

Next, assess the potential complexity of the conflict. In many aspects of life, complexity seems to be undesirable, but in conflict, complexity is good because it suggests many alternative approaches. A simple argument about whether your waste hauler will come into your parking lot to make a pickup or whether you'll have to carry your trash out to the street isn't going to offer a lot of opportunity for creative redefinition. If the company's driver really won't drive his truck up to your loading dock to make the pickup, fire that company and hire a competitor that's more eager for the work.

A series of meetings with the union representing nurses in your hospital, on the other hand, is potentially complex, because there are many possible terms and conditions to be considered and because the work itself is complex and varied. Therefore, a union negotiation is a wonderful candidate for innovation. Such negotiations usually aren't done in a creative manner, however, so the opportunity for breakthroughs is passed by. Make sure that you take an innovative approach whenever the conflict is complex and has a significant outcome.

Reframing the disagreement to introduce creative problem-solving

Reframing means offering a new perspective or way of seeing the conflict. It's a high-level skill that takes some practice and self-possession but is well worth mastering. The most effective and experienced negotiators use reframing, and you can benefit from their example. Here's a three-step method for reframing that works quite well:

1. **Listen to the general way that the other party is thinking about the conflict, not to specific claims or complaints.**

    Ask yourself this clarifying question: "What do they think this conflict is fundamentally all about?"

    A business partner who complains that you're not holding up your end of an agreement might really be focusing on the fact that his company isn't making as much profit as expected. Instead of saying that, though — because contracts usually don't guarantee profits — he's attacking you for lots of minor issues as a way to blame you for the problem.

2. **Think about the best way to view the conflict — an approach that could open more possibilities for successful discussion and cooperative problem-solving.**

    Your goal is to redefine the problem in a way that helps generate more and better possible solutions. You may decide that an angry business partner's complaints are best viewed as symptoms of a changing marketplace, because that could lead to innovative approaches to improving sales for both of you.

3. **Explain that you don't see the conflict the same way that the other party does.**

    Say, "What I think this is really about is . . . " Fill in the blank with a clear, well-considered statement of an underlying problem that could form a productive focus for creative problem-solving.

    If the other party ignores your statement and continues to argue from her viewpoint, reiterate your statement and let her know, politely but firmly, that right now you're interested in discussing the matter you've raised — not other matters. Explain that you're making this request because you're sure that it will help both of you move forward.

Your reframing needs to be based on a clear understanding of the underlying issues. Your superior insight gives your argument strength and ensures that the other side will consider your viewpoint.

Usually, reframing a conflict needs to evoke a sense of shared concerns. Say "we" rather than "you" to signal that the new viewpoint is a shared one. You might tell an angry business partner that instead of bickering about who gets what part of a dwindling profit margin, "We need to look together at ways of improving the profit margin so that the original agreement will once again be profitable for us both."

By framing the discussion around shared interests, you help the other party take a more cooperative problem-solving approach. Reframing is a way to try to get him to come around to your side of the table — metaphorically or literally, if you're meeting in a formal setting.

Signaling your good intentions to create buy-in

At first, the other side may not believe that you have good intentions. People tend to be suspicious in conflict situations, so they get defensive, which means that they assume they're under attack. Take care to signal your good intentions in every way you can (except by conceding any points — it's still early in the conflict, and you don't need to commit to anything yet!). Here are some ways to signal good intentions:

- Ask for more details about the other party's complaints or concerns.
- Listen respectfully to complaints or concerns, without interrupting or arguing. (A time for debate may come later, but not now.)
- Ask for examples or evidence of the problem to help you understand or diagnose it.
- Keep a calm, friendly demeanor as you continue to signal that you want to problem-solve. If the other party tries to start a fight or argument, return to your reframing of the conflict as a problem for both sides that needs to be improved through joint action. Be firm and clear that you want to problem-solve rather than argue.

Beginning the dialogue with easy win–wins

Don't make the mistake of diving into the thorniest issue first. The people on the other side may want to get you to do this, because that issue probably is the one they're most worried about. It's more productive, however, to pick the low-hanging fruit first — in other words, to tackle some easier problems and show that you can resolve them to everyone's satisfaction. That method builds confidence, trust, and momentum for the tougher issues.

Assessing Everyone's Conflict Styles

People are individuals, of course, which means that each of us tackles conflict in his or her own way. Fortunately, people follow some broad patterns of behavior in responding to conflict:

- **Engagers versus avoiders:** Some people naturally engage, wanting to assert their interests and get involved; others find conflict so unpleasant that they want to walk away. Those who engage naturally are able to collaborate or compete without feeling uncomfortable about conversing with someone who disagrees with them.

  Is the person you're dealing with a natural engager, or does he seem uncomfortable with the whole idea of conflict? If one of you is uncomfortable with disputes, you'll need to overcome that instinct to engage in collaborative problem-solving and find an innovative solution.

- **Competitors versus collaborators:** Some people naturally compete to stick up for their own interests; others are more agreeable and want to try to take care of everyone, not just themselves.

  Which type of person are you? Which type is your opponent? If one of you is competitive by nature, you'll need to overcome that instinct to work toward an innovative outcome.

When you define yourself or anyone else on both of these main dimensions of conflict behavior, you get five possible conflict-handling styles: collaboration, competition, compromise, avoidance, and accommodation. Of these styles, only the collaborative approach to conflict can produce a good innovative win–win outcome, so you may need to manage everyone's conflict behavior to make sure that everyone uses the correct style. This means recognizing what style or approach people are taking in a conflict and not being drawn into responding in kind. Instead, reassure competitors that it's okay to let down their guard and collaborate. With avoiders, you also need to reassure them — but in a different way, by showing them that it's safe and not stressful to problem-solve with you. Everyone *can* collaborate, even if it's not their first instinct to do so.

Identifying the natural collaborators

People who naturally like to collaborate (rather than compete, compromise, accommodate, or avoid) are people who

- Tend to be trusting and trustworthy
- Are naturally team-oriented and somewhat selfless
- Appreciate other people's perspectives and can see more than one side of an argument
- Are open-minded and probably of above-average intelligence

Collaborators make natural innovators because they like to explore ways of improving the outcomes for everyone. Their generous instinct to try to take care of both sides leads them to want to find better outcomes, and that desire to improve on the initial set of options is precisely what starts the creative problem-solving process.

Reassuring the competitive negotiators

A competitive approach is characterized by secretive behavior and a focus on what's in it for you, not the other side. Many people take a competitive approach in conflicts and negotiations. That approach is fine when you're trying not to be fleeced by a used-car salesman, but if you're trying to resolve disagreement in a project team or with a long-term supplier or distributor, it only makes things worse.

If people seem to be unwilling to discuss their concerns openly and won't share their information with you, you can assume that they're being competitive. Point out the advantages of a more open process, and reassure them that they won't give anything away by sharing information or ideas. To innovate a better solution to the conflict, you have to agree to consider options without commitment to them. You might explore the idea of giving something up in exchange for something else and then change your mind if the deal doesn't work out.

Competitors hold other people to their concessions and won't allow them to take those concessions back, which keeps people from feeling free to explore options. Make it clear to them that problem-solving isn't a formal, competitive negotiation and that you have every right to trial-balloon ideas without being forced to commit to them.

Making sure that your own style is consistent with your goals

What's *your* style? Are you competitive (or do you appear to be)? If you hesitate to share all your information with the other party, she may read you as being competitive and won't take your invitation to collaborate at face value.

The best way to generate open-minded, creative discussion of options and solutions is to set an example of this behavior yourself. Ignore (for the moment) the conflicting sides and positions, roll up your sleeves, and act as though everyone is working together to solve a big problem. Your example will do a great deal to get everyone in a problem-solving frame of mind. It's always more effective to show people what to do than it is to tell them.

Bridging the Gaps to Form an Ad Hoc Problem-Solving Team

When you reframe the conflict or negotiation as a creative problem-solving effort (see the preceding sections), and when you guide everyone toward a collaborative style, you make teamwork possible. As you work on the conflict, keep in mind what it feels like when you've been in freewheeling brainstorming sessions with a friendly group of people who are committed to finding a breakthrough innovation. That's the style and feel you want — not the normal take-sides atmosphere of conflicts.

Sharing your own interests and issues first

To set a good example of teamwork during a conflict, don't talk about your demands or positions, and definitely don't make threats or ultimatums. Instead, talk openly — and with faith that anything is possible — about your real needs or concerns.

The act of opening up to share your concerns and thoughts honestly and without competitiveness encourages others to do the same and sets the stage for innovative problem-solving instead of straight competition. Instead of opening with a tough demand, you may open with an explanation of your concerns, followed by an attempt to describe what you think the other side's concerns may be. Then ask them if you've gotten it right or if they would like to add to or modify your summary of their concerns.

Building a creative problem-solving team

Sometimes, you need to change or expand the number of people involved in the conflict before you can innovate your way through it. Ask yourself whether the people who are talking (or arguing) would make a good brainstorming group; then, assuming that they come up with a good solution, ask yourself whether they have the expertise and authority to implement an innovative solution (see Chapter 6). Often, the parties to a conflict or negotiation aren't capable of innovating, for reasons such as these:

- They lack the imagination or breadth of knowledge needed to generate fresh, innovative perspectives on the conflict.

- They lack the enthusiasm and authority to implement a solution, because innovative solutions to problems often involve changes in procedures and organizations.

Going farther with honesty and straightforwardness

A group of nurses once sat down with their union representative to renegotiate their contracts with a hospital. Management from the hospital sent the head of human resources and a lawyer, who sat on the other side of the table and initiated a very formal, somewhat antagonistic negotiation. Then one of the senior nurses said, "Look, most of us have other offers. There's a shortage of nurses in our area. And some of us are going to take those offers because we don't like the way we're treated. Some of the doctors are really rude and critical of us, often for no good reason."

The lawyer for the hospital interrupted with the objection that her complaint had nothing to do with the terms of the employment contract. The nurse replied, "Actually, our treatment has everything to do with our contract. See, if this continues to be an unpleasant place to work, we're going to demand more salary and benefits, and we're going to hold out for every little thing — more generous overtime, more vacation and sick days, better parking. You name it, we'll fight for it, because we don't think we're treated well or respected. Now, if you want to ignore the underlying problems with how nurses are treated, you can pay us enough more that we'll put up with the bad treatment, or you can get some of the doctors in here and start working on what we really care about: respect."

This nurse's honesty startled the other negotiators, but she was so senior and so well respected that they took her seriously. Along with a new contract, they initiated a series of meetings involving both doctors and nurses, in which a skilled mediator helped them identify their issues and discuss how to work better together. The nurses were pleased that many of the doctors improved their conduct, and turnover went down. Also, the contract negotiations went fairly smoothly as a result of this additional initiative to improve working conditions.

It's not surprising that people or groups in conflict aren't always perfect problem-solving teams. Before you proceed with the discussion, you need to recognize what the group lacks and expand your conflict group by supplementing it with people who can help you find and implement a breakthrough. Treat the conflict just as you would any other opportunity to innovate. Don't treat it the way that people normally treat conflicts, bringing to the table only people who have a direct interest in the conflict and strong opinions about it. Expand the number of people until you have a good group — one that's able to take an objective, creative perspective and consider fresh viewpoints and alternatives.

Transitioning to Solution Brainstorming

The most powerful thing you can say in any conflict or negotiation is "How would you complete that sentence?" It's an interesting question, because the answer reveals how people think about conflicts. Many people think that the most powerful thing you can say in any conflict or negotiation is "No," because it means that you're sticking up for your own interests and not being overly accommodating. Others argue that "Yes" is the most powerful word, because it suggests that you're getting to agreement. (In fact, a famous book about negotiation is *Getting to Yes,* by William L. Ury, Roger Fisher, and Bruce M. Patton [Houghton Mifflin Harcourt].)

I find that the most powerful thing you can say in any conflict or negotiation is this: "Let's look at multiple options before deciding."

If you offer this suggestion, and people ignore it or look at you like you're from Mars, repeat it with more specificity. You may need to say, "I won't agree to anything until we've looked at a minimum of five alternatives." What this assertion does is force the others to begin thinking about multiple options, which puts them at least one step down the creativity path. They may think that you're being difficult and may tell you so (perhaps in colorful language), but be firm in your insistence on examining multiple options before making *any* commitments. In the end, if they want to resolve the conflict with you, they have to give in to this demand for creative thinking about the conflict.

Making sure that everyone knows it's safe to share ideas

There are four main reasons why people don't share ideas freely during conflicts:

- They fear that what they say may be used against them.
- They want to use some of their knowledge against the other side.
- They don't have many ideas.
- They don't believe that the outcome will be better if they problem-solve rather than compete.

Of these four reasons, the first two are all about trust. If you think that the other side will exploit a weakness or leverage a need or constraint to pressure you to agree to a bad deal, you certainly won't be open with him. It's to your advantage to avoid showing the other party what you really want; that way, you can bargain away something less important in exchange for something that you really need.

Suspending judgment

The main thing you need to do — and persuade others to do — is postpone all decisions about what positions to take and who's right or wrong. This technique is called *suspending judgment,* and it means holding off from resolving the conflict (or fighting about it) long enough to do some good problem-solving and research and to engage your creative intelligence.

You can postpone resolving almost any conflict for another day or week to give yourself time to think. Deciding is all well and good, but thinking is even better and ought to be done first!

Facilitating brainstorming when participants are hostile

In Chapters 6 and 7, I review ways to facilitate brainstorming sessions. The same techniques and approaches work in any situation in which you want to generate alternatives, including conflicts. Sometimes, however, a conflict makes for more hostility and less buy-in than you have in a normal brainstorming session. To push forward and get some helpful creative thinking in spite of resistance, try these tips:

- ✔ **Offer creative ideas of your own — as many of them as you can.** You can't count on other people to participate as fully as you'd like them to, so come to the table with plenty of fresh ideas to get the creative process under way.

- ✔ **Be firm about the rules of brainstorming.** Don't permit criticism of ideas (see "Suspending judgment," earlier in this chapter, for ways to apply this rule to conflicts), and require everyone to build on ideas — even if those ideas were first suggested by the other side in the conflict.

- ✔ **Be optimistic!** Point out that there's always a chance of finding a clever new approach that benefits all parties, and if you fail to do so, you can simply go back to resolving the conflict the old-fashioned way by bargaining or compromising, so there's really nothing to lose by trying to find a creative new approach that offers more for everyone.

Identifying and Refining Win–Win Ideas

A win–win idea gives both sides of a conflict the feeling that they've won because they get more than they expected to.

A classic story about negotiating illustrates this point. Two sisters were arguing over the last orange in their kitchen. Their mother asked them what they wanted it for. One sister said she was going to bake a cake, and the recipe called for grated orange rind; the other said she wanted to eat the fruit. The mother laughed. The sisters didn't need to argue, because they wanted different parts of the orange. They simply needed to communicate more clearly.

Not all disputes have win–win solutions as simple as the one concerning the orange, but many do have possible win–win solutions. I know a woman who moved her popular retail store to a new and better location in the center of an old New England town. What she didn't realize before the move was that the town has tight specifications for store signs. The large sign she had used at her old location was rejected by the town hall, and she was unhappy about the prospect of having to use a much smaller, less conspicuous sign. I suggested that she up a meeting with the person responsible for the decision and approach the discussion in a collaborative way rather than as an opportunity to vent her anger. She met with the powers that be and asked for help in coming up with some alternatives that would meet her goal of making her store name visible while also meeting the town's regulations. They were able to come up with an alternative that was a win for both sides. Everyone was happy, and nobody had to call their lawyer!

Agreeing that some ideas hold significant promise

When you reframe a conflict as an opportunity to innovate so as to meet everyone's needs better, you can begin to generate ideas. The ideas may be sketchy or flawed at first, because that's the nature of ideas, but it's important to focus on the merits of the first batch of ideas. Talk about the things you like in each proposal or suggestion, and overlook (for now) the bad points. Encourage the other side to identify the strengths of specific ideas, too. This positive focus helps make people feel safe about proposing more ideas, and it also tells you what each side wants to build on as you try to refine or improve on the initial ideas.

Working the top three ideas until one emerges as best

When you've got a good number of ideas and suggestions — at least a dozen — ask the other side to identify the three strongest ones. See whether you can find enough positive things about those three items to make them your top three too. If not, put forward your own favorite suggestions, and start another round of brainstorming to find a way to combine the best elements of both sides' favorite proposals.

Generally, you'll find that with enough discussion and thinking, an obvious best option will emerge, and both sides can endorse it happily.

Chapter 14

Innovating to Save Costs

. . . .

In This Chapter

▶ Maintaining a spirit of innovation when times are tough and costs must be cut

▶ Identifying the biggest expenses and chipping away at them first

▶ Seeing what others have done to cut costs

▶ Implementing cost savings with care

. . . .

ost-cutting is a necessary evil that comes to the forefront periodically — either because of a down economy or because of some challenge that's more specific to your organization, such as the loss of a major customer or contract. It would be nice if every business grew at a predictable rate and spending never got ahead of income, but the reality is that every business has to go through the cost-cutting wringer now and then.

If you take a creative approach to saving costs, you can often minimize the damage and sometimes even turn things around with clever ideas that save costs and help revive your future prospects. The call for cost cuts should be a call for creative thinking, not just mindless hacking at the budget.

Avoiding the Creative Frost Effect

When times are good and the budget is growing, everybody thinks that innovation is a great idea. All it takes is a little bad news for people to circle the mental wagons and put a chill on the creative spirit. For a long time, I didn't understand the paradox of turning away from innovation in tough times, when creative thinking is needed most. Then I heard about the psychology of innovation, and it all made sense.

The psychological factor that drives innovation in workplaces is called *creative self-efficacy,* or employees' beliefs that they can be creative in their work roles. I prefer to call it *creative determination,* which is a clearer, easier-to-remember name.

In innovative organizations, employees' creative determination is always high. Unfortunately, the changes that come along with falling sales and tighter budgets tend to make people feel that their ideas aren't wanted. They begin to lose their feeling of creative determination. They get the message that it's not a good time to suggest new things because there's no time or money for new ideas. As a result, they stop thinking creatively and start feeling that there's nothing to be done about the bad times except hope that their jobs aren't cut before things turn around again.

Boosting creative determination

How can you avoid feeling that there's no point in trying to be creative in bad times? Here are some things you can do for yourself (and, if you're in a leadership position, for others) to combat the creative chill that comes with tight budgets and lean times:

- ✔ Find ways to say yes to some ideas instead of dismissing everything as being too expensive.
- ✔ Refocus creative thinking on ways of cutting costs, saving jobs, and reducing the effect of hard times.
- ✔ Encourage participation instead of closing down lines of communication with staff.
- ✔ Continue to plan for the future, even if you have to postpone many of the best plans until you have more funding for them.
- ✔ Talk about creative problem-solving, not just cost-cutting, so everybody knows that ideas are needed.

In tough times, it's very common for management to lock staff out of the discussion on what to do. Managers have a practical reason for this autocratic style: They fear that they may need to cut hours or jobs and believe that they shouldn't discuss those options with employees. That's not necessarily true. Often, it's better to lay the potential worst-case scenarios right out on the table and invite employees to help you try to come up with better approaches.

People feel better if they know the worst instead of wondering and guessing, and they like to feel that they have at least an outside chance of improving the situation by coming up with options and ideas. In workplaces in which employees are encouraged to brainstorm about ways to cut costs and respond to losses, morale is higher, and problem-solving is more creative and effective.

Avoiding pessimism about the future

One thing's certain: If times are bad now, there's a good chance that things will be better in the future. Good and bad times tend to alternate, so optimism is the most logical viewpoint when times are bad. Humans aren't logical beings all the time, of course, and our reactions to bad news are usually more emotional than rational. Still, it's a big help to remind yourself — and others — that it's reasonable to expect things to get better in the future.

A pessimistic attitude makes you feel that you can't do anything about the current problems. Nothing could be farther from the truth! A tough problem is a great opportunity for innovation (see Chapter 9 for details on problem-solving).

Before making any major cuts (such as cutting the payroll or closing facilities), take a day to assemble a team of your best and brightest employees or friends and associates, and ask them to brainstorm on this theme: Is there some way to solve our cash-flow problems by boosting revenue rather than making drastic cuts? Sometimes, you can find innovative ways of adding to the bottom line that make cost-cutting irrelevant.

An auto parts supplier was struggling with reduced wholesale business after a nearby dealership closed. In a brainstorming session, an employee who commuted from a distant town mentioned hearing that a supplier that served a neighboring region was closing. Upon further research, the rumor proved to be true, and the employees agreed to take turns making sales calls and working extra hours to expand into that neighboring territory. Within six months, the company had acquired several dozen additional customers — auto repair shops that ordered parts daily — and had a profitable new route for which it hired a new driver. No jobs were lost and one was gained through the use of a how-can-we-grow-revenue brainstorming session.

Trying a clean-slate approach

When it comes to saving money and cutting costs, it's easy to get reactive and feel that it's no time for highly creative thinking. Not so! If there's ever a time to consider radical alternatives, this is it. Often, it takes a really fresh approach to make a big dent in costs, because the obvious has probably already been done.

How do you overcome the natural conservatism that creeps in when times are tough and budgets are tight? A great exercise is to gather a brainstorming group (see Chapter 6) and pose this challenge: "Imagine that our [fill in your system, process, product, facility, or piece of equipment] was destroyed last night, and we have to create a new one. You can design it however you like. Come up with the most economical and efficient design." When group members begin to imagine what a completely fresh new approach to design would be, they question old assumptions, eliminate inefficiencies, and generally come up with much better ideas and approaches.

Imagining that something has been destroyed overnight and has to be redesigned is just a hypothetical exercise; you probably won't actually redesign from scratch. So why do the exercise? Often, it produces insights you can use right away for partial redesigns that produce significant savings.

Follow up on the first question by asking, "What ideas from this exercise can we apply to the actual process/product/facility?" It's a good bet that the group will come up with at least one transferable idea.

Focusing on the Biggest Cost Categories

When managers think about ways of cutting costs, they usually focus on payroll, which upsets employees. Employees tend to see lots of other ways to save money and think that job cuts should be a last resort. The problem, however, is that payroll is a huge piece of the spending pie for most organizations. Managers are correct to focus on this big expense category, because it's hard to save a lot of costs by cutting expenses for things that don't contribute much to the budget in the first place. There are more ways to take a bite out of costs than just announcing layoffs, however.

Identifying spending categories

A three-step process is helpful for identifying cost savings:

1. **Target the five largest categories of spending.**

2. **Identify the three biggest subcategories within each of those major categories.**

3. **Solicit employee suggestions, ask suppliers to help, and run brainstorming meetings for each of the subcategories.**

These steps ensure that your creative energy is sharply focused where it can do the most good. A 1 percent reduction in a minor expense will hardly make a dent in your budget, but a 1 percent reduction in a major expense will be significant on the bottom line.

Here are some typical major spending categories (which vary from business to business, of course):

- Energy
- Facilities
- Health insurance and other employee benefits
- Inventories
- Maintenance
- Parts purchases
- Salaries
- Shipping

✔ Telecommunications

✔ Travel

✔ Vehicles

✔ Water (a major expense for factories that use water in production)

It also helps to break down a broad category of costs by asking more specific questions about things that contribute to it.

A client of mine that designs and manufacturers fine furniture found that its energy costs were driven largely by three big expenses: air conditioning, lighting, and the drying room where products were sent after being painted. When a cost-savings team ran three separate brainstorming sessions focusing on each of these three areas of energy spending, it came up with significant innovations to cut costs in all three areas:

✔ Install sheer white cloth in south-facing windows to reduce passive solar heating, and set thermostats 2 degrees higher (savings of 3 percent).

✔ Turn off every other overhead light fixture, and use spot lighting at the few workstations where bright light was really needed (savings of 2 percent).

✔ Switch to a faster-drying spray paint to reduce drying time by 50 percent (savings of 6 percent).

The combined savings from these three brainstorming sessions resulted in an 11 percent cut in energy consumption at the facility — a major cost savings.

Take a look at your budget, rank your expense categories, and then ask pointed brainstorming questions about the biggest cost centers (see the next section). If you pose the question "How can we cut costs?" and ask employees to brainstorm answers, you'll get a lot of answers about very small expenses, such as cutting spending on staples and sticky notes. Those suggestions may be useful, but you'll get bigger savings if you start by analyzing your budget categories and then ask for ideas about how to save money in the three to five biggest categories first.

The furniture manufacturer that used a lot of energy for air conditioning, factory production, and lighting asked, "How can we cut our energy bill by 10 percent or more?" To give employees a personal incentive to think about the question, management added the following note: "A savings of 10 percent of our energy costs will allow us to retain 20 jobs that would otherwise have to be cut." A lot of good suggestions came in, and after those suggestions were implemented, the net savings was 11 percent. It pays to focus people's creative attention on the biggest costs, because those costs are where you'll realize the greatest savings in the shortest period.

Focusing on major sources of error or rework

Mistakes are costly. Any errors or problems that recur are great opportunities to save money. Here are two examples of repetitive service and quality problems in organizations:

- ✔ A hotel sometimes overbooked its least-expensive rooms, forcing the front desk to give customers suites at a single-room rate.

- ✔ An eBay shipper got complaints about damaged shipments from 1 percent to 2 percent of its customers, requiring it to offer refunds or replacement products.

In each case, the fact that the same problem occurred periodically meant that the organization had an opportunity to study the root causes and eliminate the most important ones. Any repeated error or mistake has many possible causes, but only a few of these causes will be responsible for the bulk of the problems. If you focus on eliminating one to three of the biggest causes of the error, you'll make a big dent in the number of errors you see.

Learning from Others

There's nothing new under the sun, as the old saying goes. That's not entirely true, of course. A brilliant innovation is a powerful asset specifically because it *is* "new under the sun" and can be patented and protected as it's commercialized. When it comes to cost savings, however, there probably is something old that you can try, which is why it's particularly important to look around for approaches that have worked elsewhere.

Sending out your scouts

As an advance assignment for a cost-cutting meeting or brainstorming session, ask everyone who'll be attending to gather at least ten examples of cost-cutting from other organizations. Then spend the first half hour or more of your meeting sharing the examples that everyone found. To facilitate this round of sharing, stand at a whiteboard or chart pad headed "Take-Away Ideas," and make note of anything that the group thinks might be useful in your organization.

At this point, keep the discussion fairly brief; just note the main idea and any simple added points about how or where to apply it. Later in the meeting, you can ask the group — or small breakout teams of three or four people, if the group is larger than a dozen — to brainstorm specific action plans based on the ideas you jotted down. If the group uses a reported idea as a springboard and comes up with a better or more appropriate idea of its own, that's great! You don't have to do exactly what others have done, but you certainly should try to use their approaches for inspiration.

Reviewing examples of cost-cutting measures elsewhere

How have other organizations cut costs and saved materials or energy? Here are some examples that I've seen in cost-cutting exercises:

- ✔ **Periodically send requests (via e-mail and craigslist) to businesses that are moving, asking whether they're discarding some of their furniture or equipment and would like for you to take it away.** This technique is a great way to get furniture, fixtures, and equipment for free!

- ✔ **Use college and business-school interns for lower-level work.** They need the résumé-building experience, and you need free (or almost-free) labor. It's a classic win–win situation.

- ✔ **Call or visit all your suppliers to ask what they can do to cut their prices.** It's surprising how often you can negotiate a better price or rate just by showing up and asking.

- ✔ **Try to reduce the number of suppliers you buy from in exchange for deeper discounts and more service from the remaining ones.** Shift business away from the suppliers that balk at offering deeper discounts and toward the ones that meet your pricing needs.

- ✔ **Consider purchasing basic supplies in bulk and storing a larger supply.** If you can bypass your regular supplier and go directly to a large manufacturer, you may achieve enough savings to make it worthwhile to hold inventory (but check with your regular supplier first to see if it will match the savings).

- ✔ **Form or join a buying cooperative in which smaller businesses pool their purchases, thereby gaining access to volume discounts and more negotiating power with suppliers.**

- ✔ **Share space with one or more other businesses.** Lease or sublet several of your offices to lawyers and accountants, for example, and double up in the remaining offices.

- ✔ **Ask your landlord for a rent reduction.** If the market is soft in your area, and you've been a good tenant, the landlord may be willing to reconsider the rent rather than lose you.

- ✔ **If your business has many local competitors, watch for ones that go out of business, and acquire their phone numbers from them.** You'll get some of their repeat business when customers call the old phone number to place an order. It's a remarkably inexpensive and effective way to find new customers!

✔ **Use telecommuters to do self-managed jobs such as Web design, engineering, and writing.** If you have people come in only half-time, you can reduce the number of offices you provide by half!

✔ **Outsource functions that are generic, including basic payroll, accounting, and data entry.** Consult *Outsourcing For Dummies,* by Ed Ashley (Wiley), for more on how to use this cost-saving strategy.

✔ **Check your rates for credit card transactions and online merchant banking, and shop around for better rates.**

✔ **Identify inventories that aren't turning over, and ask the suppliers to take back some of these supplies or products at cost.** Getting these materials off your books will put cash back into your account.

✔ **Cut your inventories by working with suppliers that can guarantee quick, reliable delivery so that you don't have to worry about running out.** Inventories are a major hidden cost center in many businesses.

✔ **Save ink and toner in your printers by being more concise and by using smaller fonts that use less ink.** Thin, unadorned fonts like Arial and Lucida use slightly less ink than traditional fonts do. New typefaces such as Ecofont use the least possible ink to make a clearly legible letter. My favorite, however, is Arial Narrow, which uses less ink and, by compressing the letters slightly, also saves paper.

✔ **Increase your scale.** Economies of scale are the savings you achieve when you produce and sell more, because some of your costs (such as rent and payroll) are fixed and don't go up when you do more business. Consider giving away more samples and offering to supply prospective customers for free for a month, just to get your volume up. You may be able to outgrow your cost constraints!

✔ **Limit telephone use.** Telephone conversations are important for customer service, sales, and problem-solving, but employees probably overuse the phones for other purposes. Switch to using e-mail as much as possible. It's faster and far cheaper than talking.

✔ **Turn the thermometer up and down.** If you relax the dress code enough that people can layer up or layer down for the weather, you can allow the office temperature to fluctuate more with the ambient temperature. Allowing a seasonal temperature range of 12 degrees Fahrenheit can save you 10 percent to 15 percent of your annual heating and air conditioning costs.

Do these cost-saving ideas get you thinking? I find that if I seed a cost-cutting session with some ideas from earlier brainstorms, the new group gets up to speed and produces helpful suggestions much more quickly and easily.

Asking around

It's amazing how happy people are to talk about their own accomplishments. To find out what other companies are doing to save costs, try asking people who work at other companies. If they've been involved in the cost-cutting effort, they'll be excited to share their results with you.

A great way to find people to ask for cost-saving techniques is to go to industry events, such as a chamber-of-commerce luncheon or a regional conference for your industry or profession. One doctor I know went to a two-day conference about medical diagnostics, and while she was there, she asked other doctors from primary-care practices what they were doing to cut their costs. She came back with dozens of ideas to try in her own medical practice.

Using Savings-Creation Methods from Idea to Implementation

Savings creation is what I call the special toolbox of cost-cutting-oriented brainstorming, idea review, and implementation of methods that individuals and groups can use to reduce the budget and make ends meet. This section contains some of my favorites.

Finding out where the losses really are

It's easy to see if your overall budget is in the red, but it's far harder to know exactly where those losses come from. *Cost accounting* involves the allocation of various costs to specific products or processes, and it's a tricky thing to do well. Sometimes, the allocation formulas used in your accounting system are inaccurate and don't tell you where you're really losing and making money. Take some time to examine your accounting, and research how costs are — and should be — allocated. You may find that a location, route, product, or process is less profitable in fact than it looks on paper, while another is more profitable. Your cost-accounting research will help you make the right cuts.

I worked with a freight transportation company to identify which of its hundreds of trucking routes were making and losing money. With the help of some expert accountants, I discovered that some of the company's figures were off and that certain routes were losing more money than anyone realized. When we improved the cost accounting, it became obvious that certain routes needed to be cut and others needed to be priced higher to make the overall operation more profitable.

Generating effective cost-cutting ideas

Set the tone for a cost-reduction brainstorm by emphasizing the shared benefits and encouraging people not to be defensive or protective of their own turf. Point out that it's better to cut costs in your own area or department than to have others do it, because you have more creative control by making the cuts yourself and can minimize the negative effects. Build buy-in by discussing the benefits of a participatory approach to cost-cutting versus a top-down one.

Focus the brainstorming on the biggest cost categories so as to generate ideas with the biggest possible effect (see "Identifying spending categories," earlier in this chapter, for details).

Encourage creativity! People get very serious and conservative when it comes to cost-cutting, and they overlook the more innovative approaches. Point out to the group that simple cost-cutting is a win–lose equation: All it does is save money by taking things away. By getting creative and making innovative changes in the way you do business, you can shift from win–lose (winning cost savings by losing something that you used to have) to a win–win approach, in which changing how you do things produces a cost savings without a corresponding loss.

All the innovative brainstorming methods that I cover in Part II are fully applicable to cost-cutting and can help you produce innovative ideas that turn the problem of a tight budget into an opportunity to find new and better ways to operate.

When you hold a cost-cutting brainstorm, I recommend starting with a review of really successful cost cuts (ones in which an innovation helped cut costs while improving the way that the business works). A few inspiring examples will help show the team what you mean by win–win innovations (see "Reviewing examples of cost-cutting measures elsewhere," earlier in this chapter).

When your group runs out of ideas (as it will after the first hour or so), start another round of ideas by challenging them to think about ways to

- ✔ Pool resources with others.
- ✔ Reduce steps in business processes.
- ✔ Switch to less-expensive alternatives.
- ✔ Be more flexible about time or place.
- ✔ Get rid of anything that isn't used frequently.
- ✔ Get rid of lines of business that don't make a profit.
- ✔ Outsource more services and functions.

These seven general strategies are extremely powerful and can produce substantial cost savings. If you can come up with even one idea worth implementing in each of these categories, you'll cut costs substantially — perhaps by as much as 25 percent to 30 percent.

Evaluating cost-cutting proposals

When you've got a good list of possible ways of cutting costs, evaluate each one by using three criteria:

- ✔ **How much will the cut save?** Assigning a financial value helps you decide which ones should be implemented first.

- ✔ **What problems will the cut create?** Some cost-saving ideas are relatively pain free, but others cause inconveniences or may even make other costs rise. Consider the effect before implementing any idea.

- ✔ **How will the cut affect quality?** Make sure that you're not undercutting your product or service quality with the cost reduction; otherwise, the cut will come back to haunt you in the form of falling sales.

These three criteria give you a quick initial screening. After that screening, you can further analyze the ideas or proposals that look best based on these questions:

- ✔ **How long will it take to implement the idea and see real savings from it?** If it takes too long, you may do better to focus on something that has a quicker payoff.

- ✔ **Do we have the expertise and time to implement the idea now?** Avoid proposals that require expensive extra effort or hired expertise.

- ✔ **Is the proposal focusing on a function, division, product, or location that loses so much money that we may simply want to shut it down?** There's no point in making minor cuts in something that's a candidate for elimination; you may as well make the big cut right away.

Implementing cost savings

Implementing cost savings is not very different from implementing any innovation, but some things about cost savings differ. Cost savings can easily feel like a loss, for example, producing pushback and resistance. Also, businesses are complex systems in which everything is interconnected, so it's not always easy to predict the effects of cost cuts (see "Observing the consequences," later in this chapter). Following are some tips to help you implement your creative cost savings.

Informing those who will be most affected

When someone imposes cost savings on you, it doesn't feel so good. The results may include irritation, resistance, and possible sabotage of the program. If you don't see any good way to make the design of the cost-saving project participative, impose it hard and fast, pushing through the resistance as quickly as possible and with such a firm hand that employees quickly accept it as the new reality. Fast implementation will hasten acceptance. Also make sure that you inform those affected by the cuts fully and clearly. Tell them exactly how they will be affected so they won't be left wondering and listening to rumors.

A brainstorming process is a good opportunity to include people who may be affected. Invite representatives to participate in the idea-generation process. Include everyone in your progress reports. Make the creative cost-saving effort more transparent to reduce resistance.

When you select a cost-saving idea, pull together a small, action-oriented design team to decide exactly how to implement it. This design team should include representatives from the main groups that will be affected. Participation really does help ease the transition.

As you choose people to include in the design team, make sure that you avoid including anyone who is negative and obviously will resist change. Some people don't think innovatively, and they aren't going to be helpful in your cost-saving process. Let them grumble from the sidelines — but don't let them have a turn at bat. Keep the project in the hands of people who have a reasonable amount of creative determination and believe that they can improve things through innovative behavior.

Observing the consequences

Often, it's not the quality of the cost-saving idea itself but the quality of the implementation that determines whether you succeed or fail.

The biggest problem that most cost-saving plans run into is unintended consequences — outcomes that weren't part of the original plan. Unintended consequences can be good or bad, actually, but the bad ones are the ones to watch out for. Here are the three main types of unintended consequences:

- **Positive unexpected benefits, such as greater savings than anticipated (also called windfalls):** Sometimes, the implementation goes more smoothly than expected and creates big, immediate cost savings as well as goodwill for future cost-saving efforts. I like to implement easy, positive cost savings before tackling harder ones in the hope of building positive moral and momentum — an intended unintended consequence.

- **Negative side effects, such as a drop in productivity as an unintended result of cuts in payroll:** Like medicines, cost cuts often have side effects. Try to anticipate them by brainstorming a list of possible side effects in advance and then building as many safeguards into your plan as possible. If you see significant side effects after implementation, track their financial effect, and subtract that sum from the gains to calculate the net cost savings. If the outcome isn't positive, scrap the plan and try something else.

✔ *Perverse effects,* **or opposite results from what was expected:** Historians speculate that the Treaty of Versailles, which was intended to create peace in Europe, might actually have caused World War II by imposing humiliating conditions on Germany. Oops. When human behavior is involved in a cost-saving plan, watch out for perverse effects. If you create a perceived shortage of something, people may hoard it.

I recall one company in which an effort to ration basic office supplies such as paper, tape, and sticky notes produced hoarding. Some people hid large quantities of office supplies in their desks and file cabinets, and one woman actually took home cases of supplies in a misguided effort to ensure that her department would not run out. The purchasing department was forced to purchase more to supply those who hadn't hoarded.

As you implement cost-saving plans, follow through with a checkup every week to see whether the effects are positive or at least that the positive effects outweigh any negative ones. Around one in five cost-saving plans has to be revised during implementation. "Learn as you go" is a good rule for cost savings.

Filing weekly progress reports

Cost-saving initiatives aren't part of the normal business routine; they're special efforts that tend to come in waves when the situation requires belt-tightening. Because cost-saving initiatives are outside the regular work of the business, they tend not to be tracked or accounted for very rigorously, which means that they may not be completed as thoroughly as they should be.

To ensure follow-through and successful completion, keep central records on each and every cost-saving initiative. Give each one a unique name or numerical code, note the start date, identify the people who are responsible for implementation, and log their progress reports. A paper-based system in a file cabinet is fine unless you use project management software, in which case you should take advantage of the central management capabilities of your program.

Have each cost-saving team report in every week to make sure that no projects fall though the cracks. Also, collect details on what's done and how much is saved.

Asking teams to document what they learned

At the end of each project, ask the implementation team to write a short lessons-learned memo to document any insights they gained, including insights about how to control costs (which might include further suggestions) and how to manage cost-control projects in the future.

Documentation allows you to learn from the experience and also to ensure accountability. If something seemed like a good idea upfront, you want a system that ensures that the idea actually gets implemented. Many cost-saving ideas require change and accommodation, so there will be some resistance to them. Centrally tracking and managing all cost-saving projects shows everyone that the projects matter and that management is watching their progress. That's your best way to ensure follow-through.

Part IV
Implementing a Major Innovation

The 5th Wave   By Rich Tennant

"Take it easy. It's a nice idea – not a fourth 'M.'"

In this part . . .

Your ideas deserve proper implementation because
without good implementation, they may not succeed.
Implementing something well means getting people
excited about your ideas and plans and helping them figure
out how to use your new methods or inventions. Most
good ideas fail to get implemented, so take this step
seriously and budget some time and effort to making
sure your ideas come to fruition.

In this part, you get help with building networks, teams,
and coalitions to move your projects forward. You also
address the challenges of protecting all your intellectual
property so that you can maximize the success of your
unique contributions. In addition, I show you how to take
the ball and run with it yourself as an innovative
entrepreneur.

Chapter 15

Managing the Development of an Innovative Idea

In This Chapter

▶ Managing innovation with a step-by-step plan

▶ Organizing and managing the development team

▶ Building a network of partners to help with development and implementation

▶ Introducing your innovation

My fifth child was born a week before I wrote this chapter — a healthy girl named Eisa — and as the family gathered to greet her, someone pointed out that her lips were chapped. "Blisters," my wife corrected. "From nursing." Indeed, new babies get blisters on their lips, and it seems like you ought to do something for them, but nobody sells a product for the purpose. My eldest son, Eliot, said, "Why doesn't somebody sell a product called Baby Balm?" Why not? My wife, Deedee, pointed out that natural lanolin might be a safe product to use. Within a few minutes, we had identified a need, coined a catchy brand name for a product, and decided what to make it of. Great!

But we still haven't marketed Baby Balm because manufacturing and selling it aren't as simple as imagining it, and I doubt that we ever will. I'm an author and consultant, not a manufacturer, so it's not a great match with my business. If it were, though, I'd need to formulate and test the product, obtain approval to sell it from any relevant regulatory authorities, select a contractor to manufacture it, design an appealing and functional package, line up retail distributors, and launch it with an effective marketing campaign. As with most innovations, there would be many steps involved in implementing our idea.

This chapter addresses the tough challenge of implementing an innovation, whether it's a new product, process, or any other design or idea. Studies show that more innovations fail because of poor implementation than because of bad ideas. Protect your good idea from failure by implementing it carefully and well!

Planning the Innovation Process

You need to understand a process to manage it, which means deciding on the likely length of your innovation process, the stages it will go through, and the results you expect at each stage. Create a simple plan of action containing steps, a timeline, and some measures of performance. Hand out copies, and post one of the copies prominently in your workspace. This document, simple as it is, will guide you through the innovation process and let you know when your team slips off track.

Some of the biggest and most successful innovative organizations use a general innovation process as a template to help them plan each project. (For a good example, see Procter & Gamble's innovation process in the section "Emphasizing planning, preparation, and refinement," later in this chapter.) If you do a Web search for "innovation process," you'll find dozens of results, some of them for processes with just a handful of steps, others more elaborate and complex. Which is correct? None, actually, because none was developed specifically for your organization and process.

You'll need to adapt a generic multiple-step innovation process for your particular project, adding or modifying the steps until they capture everything that you think you'll need to do to achieve success. As a starting point, use the generic innovation process shown in Figure 15-1, an all-around model that captures the main management stages of almost every innovation process. Don't stop there, though. Add detailed substeps within each of the four main stages to customize it to your specific project.

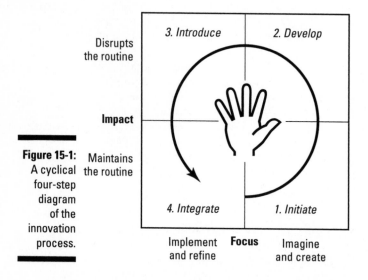

Figure 15-1: A cyclical four-step diagram of the innovation process.

Figure 15-1 shows Hiam's Innovation Cycle. Yup, this is the way I draw the innovation process for my students and clients. I symbolize innovation with an outline of the human hand, because human hands, with their opposable digits, give us the capacity to make tools and build things with them, thereby making us the innovators on our planet.

The figure also shows innovation as a cycle, not as a linear process. The idea is that the end of one process should lead to the beginning of another. Don't stop innovating just because you have a success. Use the momentum from that success to start another project.

In addition to planning the process stage by stage, you need to keep a close eye on progress, and be prepared to respond and adjust when things go wrong. What can go wrong will go wrong, as the old saying goes, so you need to anticipate possible problems and have contingency plans in place. Knowing the common hazards of implementation prepares you to navigate them. The following sections examine the six things you must do to control the most common sources of trouble.

Being flexible about the design

For starters, you may find that your idea, design, or invention doesn't work as well as — or in the way that — you expected. Design problems and unintended consequences are common, but they need not derail your project entirely. The trick is to assess and evaluate continually so that you can catch flaws in your design while there's still time to correct them.

Learning as you go is the secret to good implementation. Don't be pigheaded and insist on sticking to the original plan if it's not working as planned. Stop, rethink, and revise.

Clarifying the goal

Poor goal definition is a big cause of implementation disasters. Ask yourself exactly what you're trying to accomplish, by what date, and how you'll measure success and failure. Develop a detailed written statement of your objectives, along with measures or indicators of success. Break success into waypoints or check-ins along the way so that you'll know whether you're on track and won't have to wait until the very end to find out that you have a mess.

Clear goals add the discipline you need to make your implementation run smoothly; they keep you focused and moving in one clear direction. Without clear goals, nobody knows just what he should be doing, and often, people work against one another by trying to move the innovation in their own competing directions.

Communicating early, often, and widely

Make sure that you communicate regularly with everyone who may be important to the implementation, because poor communication derails a lot of innovations. Spread information about the innovation, including progress reports, expected effects, and what help you'll need at each stage.

Keep in close touch with anyone who controls information that you and your implementation team may need. A good rule of thumb is to talk every week to every person who might be important to the project.

Emphasizing long-term benefits

When people feel that they need to pursue their immediate interests, they often get in the way of implementation by resisting change. It's important to keep them talking and thinking about longer-term benefits. In the long run, every employee and department is part of the overall organization, and an innovation that's good for the organization can be good for every member of it. The big-picture idea is that a rising tide lifts all boats. Watch out for knee-jerk, defensive, short-term reactions, and try to keep the dialogue focused on the medium distance rather than the immediate.

Monitoring the results

Poor monitoring of results is a big factor in many failures. Make sure that you have regular progress reviews, either in person or through detailed written reports followed by phone conversations to review them (if it's not feasible to meet in person).

After you choose your criteria for evaluating success, stick with them! Often, people get so committed to the idea of succeeding that they let their standards slip, and they refuse to fail an innovation when it doesn't meet benchmark measures. It's great to be emotionally committed, because commitment means that you'll work hard and be a creative, persistent problem-solver, but try not to let your commitment cloud your judgment. Sometimes, you simply have to pull the plug and admit that the plan didn't work out as expected. Persisting beyond reasonable evidence of success is just plain foolish, and tight monitoring of results can prevent it.

Building strong implementation teams

Implementation almost always takes a group of people to make it happen. But as you probably know from your own (perhaps painful) experience, teams don't always work smoothly and well. Some teams have a real shortage of team-work because managers don't build teamwork simply by telling people that they belong to a team. You have to provide a sense of unity and shared purpose.

Teams need to be established and managed over the life cycle of the implementation process. See the next section for details on making your teams tick.

Innovating in Teams

The lone inventor may be a heroic figure in common folklore, but in fact, almost all innovations are developed by teams. Sometimes, an existing — and well-functioning — team already exists and can simply take the new idea and run with it. More often, you have to form an appropriate team and manage its development at the same time that you manage the development of your innovation.

Maintaining momentum through the four stages of the team's life

Here are the stages of team development:

1. **Charter the team.**

   Identify the need, obtain authorization, and invite members.

2. **Build the team.**

   Create momentum through purposeful goals. Your team members will be motivated by exciting goals and will feel eager and enthusiastic to achieve them.

3. **Structure the work.**

   Establish work assignments, plans, and milestones.

4. **Finish the work.**

   Iron out any problems, and make sure that the innovation is functioning properly at full scale.

Unfortunately, developing and managing a team is a separate duty from managing the development of an innovation. Teams are chartered and managed for many purposes, not just for innovating, and whenever you have a project team, you need to manage it through these four stages. To manage the team through all its stages, you need to form it with an eye to the diverse membership that will make it productive in every stage.

Tapping into diverse contributions by team members

Different people bring different strengths to a team. After all, that's the big idea behind teamwork, isn't it? As you charter your team, try to anticipate the various strengths and skills you may need, and seek team members who cover all your needs — including those with sufficient authority to access needed resources.

Round out your team with people who are dissimilar. Diversity adds initial complications as you work to unify your team and build strong morale, but as soon as you get the team up and running, that same diversity becomes a tremendous asset that gives the team a wide range of perspectives to tap into.

In addition to the normal range of human differences — experience, expertise, background, and so on — you need to have a range of creative styles. Different creative styles ensure that you have people who are good at the four main types of tasks that a project team has to perform:

- ✔ **Exploring:** Creative thinking, questioning, probing, and provoking
- ✔ **Energizing:** Motivating, engaging, encouraging, and supporting
- ✔ **Structuring:** Organizing, planning, tracking, and evaluating
- ✔ **Finishing:** Completing, checking, transitioning, and terminating

Human nature being what it is, most people are good at only one or two of these roles. The trick is making sure that your team has a range of people, each of them naturally good at one of the four roles. Including all four roles is the most important thing to think about in team building, aside from the inclusion of people who have appropriate expertise and authority.

The Team Roles Analysis assessment instrument (see www.tspectrum.com/team_roles.htm for ordering information or www.supportforinnovation.com for a summary) predicts team role behavior quite accurately, based on the simple insight that creativity and extraversion combine to determine how people behave on project teams. For example, someone who is open to creativity and also extroverted has the temperament of an Energizer. The following list shows how each role is based on these two dimensions of personality:

- ✔ **Social-creatives** are extraverted and creative, and perform the Energizer role with ease.
- ✔ **Individual-creatives** are introverted and creative, and make natural Explorers.
- ✔ **Social-logicals** are extraverted and analytical, so they find it easy to Organize the work of others.
- ✔ **Individual-logicals** are introverted and analytical, and make great Finishers because they stay on task and aren't happy until the goal is achieved.

As you form your team, think about what expertise you'll need, what authorities might be helpful, and how to cover all four of the team roles by including people who fit these four descriptions.

If you know the people in question and have worked with them before, it will be obvious who is creative or analytical and who is social or individual. (If not, give candidates a Team Roles Analysis assessment as part of their screening.) Look for all four combinations of these traits. If you're lacking a role on your team, recruit someone to fill it, even if that person lacks specific expertise in the project, because the project won't get finished unless you have all four roles represented on your team. (Don't say I didn't warn you.)

Finding your strongest team role

Are you a creative Explorer who's great at imagining things in the early stages of a project and can provide the vision and creativity to bring the team's work to life?

Are you an Organizer who excels at planning, coordinating, and tracking the work of team members?

Are you an Energizer who enjoys communicating with team members, and brings enthusiasm and excitement to the team and its mission?

Are you a Finisher who's focused on the ultimate goal and won't be happy until it's achieved?

A team needs all four of these roles. Sometimes, one person can cover more than one role, but often, it works best to let different people play different roles. Knowing your own strongest role (from experience or by taking the Team Roles Analysis questionnaire; refer to the preceding section) will help you see how to contribute to the interpersonal dynamics of the team. Whether you're the team leader or one of the team members, you ought to step to the forefront when your strongest role is needed.

Self-awareness of your strengths is important to good team contributions. Bring your technical expertise and your personal strengths to the team by understanding what you have to offer and then talking to the team about what you can contribute. Get the others to think and talk about their strongest contributions, too. A team is greater than the sum of its parts if — and only if — all members share their greatest strengths, not their greatest weaknesses!

Determining what the team leader needs to do

To succeed as team leader, you need to ask yourself a simple question each day: "What does my team need to succeed?" Then make sure that the team gets what it needs to the greatest extent possible. Whatever the team's needs are — tangible resources, technical help, or intangible things like encouragement and optimism — you're responsible for helping the team get those things so that it can keep working productively and well.

To assess your team's ongoing (and often changing) needs, ask yourself whether you need to do work for your team in any of the following seven areas, which come from my *Team Leadership Inventory* (published by Trainer's Spectrum at www.tspectrum.com):

- ✔ **Team formation and maintenance:** Establish and cultivate the team, such as by holding a morale-building celebration of progress.

- ✔ **Boundary management:** Manage the barriers to teamwork, such as by intervening with a team member's department head to get permission for her to attend more of the team meetings.

- ✔ **External communications:** Make sure that the team communicates fully throughout the organization and with innovation partners beyond your organization.

- ✔ **Internal communications:** Encourage the team members to communicate openly and freely with one another, such as by holding regular progress briefings.

- ✔ **Team vision:** Make sure that the team understands and stays focused on its main mission.

- ✔ **Performance management:** Keep team members on track through clear assignments and progress check-ins.

- ✔ **Member and leader development:** Seek new information, and build skills.

Use these seven team needs as a checklist for reviewing your team's status, and put effort into any of them that seem to be lacking. A deficit in internal communications, for example, can derail a project quickly. Many implementation efforts fail because the team doesn't function well, not because of any fundamental flaw in the innovation itself. Don't let team dysfunction ruin your innovation!

Considering a skunkworks to protect your team from interference

Sometimes, a development effort is so intense and difficult that a normal team can't do it, and you need to create a super team with a high degree of focus and intensity. If the level of difficulty and effort is much higher for your project than it is for regular work in your organization, you may need to isolate your team to maintain a level of exceptional performance. Set up a highly protected, innovative team in an isolated area for those really challenging projects that ordinary teams can't accomplish.

Skunkworks are development or implementation projects that are handled by a team with a secret agenda working in isolation from the rest of the organization.

The term is used generically by many people in business. The term Skunk Works, however, is actually protected as a trademark by the aerospace company Lockheed Martin Corp., where the term was first coined, so if you're a consultant who wants to offer services for setting up such teams, you'd better find your own name. Lockheed Martin's first Skunk Works team, established in 1943, developed the P-80 Shooting Star jet fighter in record time under the pressure of wartime needs. If you're working on a new jet fighter, you should follow all 14 of the official Lockheed Martin Skunk Works rules at www.lockheedmartin.com/aeronautics/ skunkworks/14rules.html.

For a less-intensive (and secretive) project for general business purposes, the spirit of the approach is pretty well captured by these guidelines:

✔ Give the team leader considerable control and autonomy.

✔ Give the team an ambitious goal and plenty of resources to pursue it.

✔ Define clear specifications for the outcome so that the team knows exactly what it's supposed to produce.

✔ Let the team work intensively and without interruption.

✔ Minimize outside communication to prevent criticism and negative thinking.

A highly autonomous, isolated team working in secrecy isn't a good idea for most innovation efforts, but it may be helpful if you have a self-sufficient group of experts who are highly motivated to do something that's so out of the ordinary that it would be difficult to do in the regular work environment.

As for keeping the work secret, unless you're working under security restrictions (as Lockheed Martin often does under military contract), the only practical contribution of secrecy is to reduce external criticism and prevent outsiders from holding you up by restricting your resources. If the team emerges from isolation with a well-developed invention that's ready to use, resistance may never be an issue, and the rest of the organization may embrace the work.

If the invention requires adaptation on the part of other people, however, it might be wise to give them detailed briefings early in the project, rather than spring the results on them later as an unpleasant surprise. Secrecy is a double-edged sword: It gives the project team a greater sense of safety and unity, but it also slows the recruitment of partners and the spread of information during implementation. Because of these negative consequences, skunkworks teams aren't advisable for most innovations, but they're great for innovating in an intensely creative, driven manner within a less-creative larger organization.

Building Development and Implementation Networks

A strong development team is a powerful thing, but it may not be sufficient to get your innovation all the way off the ground. Often, you need resources outside your team — resources that you can't really afford to bring inside your team by hiring more people or that simply can't be hired in. That's why a network is usually part of the implementation process.

Think of the inventor as being the core, with the development team arranged in a tight circle around him or her. The network of partners that you build forms a wider circle surrounding and supporting the development team. Beyond the network is the wide world in which you plan to implement the innovation. The network helps support the team's work and also builds a bridge to the people you need to adopt your innovation.

Networks vary from temporary to established. You may be able to tap into your existing personal, professional, or commercial networks for help with your innovation. Alternatively, you may choose to create a network specifically to aid your invention or development processes; start by examining all your existing networks to see whether any might be helpful to you. By tapping into existing networks, you may be able to ramp up to collaborative activity more quickly because the relationships already exist.

The people and organizations in your existing networks are motivated to help you because they may provide help to return a favor that you've done for them (or will do for them). You may run into resistance to innovation within existing networks, however, because their members often have a stake in how things are traditionally done and may resist your efforts to introduce change.

If you need to create a new network to help you develop or diffuse your innovation, start by identifying people, teams, organizations, and/or institutions that may see some benefit in collaborating with you. When you invite these people or groups to participate, make the potential benefits clear and specific. In other words, tell all the parties what's in it for them.

A partnership approach to cleanup

Like many other U.S. cities, Wichita, Kansas, faces a problem: cleaning up old industrial sites where groundwater is contaminated by tetrachloroethene (used to dry-clean clothes), trichloroethylene (used to clean metal parts), and other chemicals. To simplify the cleanup process and reduce its cost, city engineers were eager to try innovations such as the use of bioremediation and reactive walls rather than conventional pump-and-treat methods and hydraulic control rather than aquifer restoration. Any treatment that minimizes the amount of soil and water that a city has to move is good because it's cheaper, but deciding to try new treatment methods is one thing, and actually implementing them is quite another.

For starters, federal regulators have to be convinced that alternative approaches will work, so a careful technical analysis has to be performed to sell the concept. Then the work has to be funded. Wichita uses a tax increment district (TIF) to raise funds. Inside the TIF, property taxes are frozen, and as the cleanup work goes on and property values rise

because of it, the city taps into some of the increased land value to help it secure bonds used to raise funding for the work.

In addition, the city of Wichita offers liability releases for current property owners to get them on board with the program by removing their fear of costly lawsuits.

To pull off a major remediation project, Wichita typically builds an informal team that includes neighbors, property owners, and the engineering firm working on the project, as well as banks that provide help with financing. The success of such projects depends on the skill with which city officials build partnerships to sell, fund, and implement their innovative approach. The term that they use for all that coalition building and cooperative planning is *partnering*, and it's the most important element in a successful cleanup.

For more information on this case, see the Human Sciences Research Council's description at www.engg.ksu.edu/ HSRC/97abstracts/doc59.html.

Members of networks tend to collaborate because each member sees a benefit from collaboration, but it's important to recognize that each party may be pursuing slightly different benefits. You may need to balance these differing goals and protect your innovation from the potential for conflict and competition that these goals represent.

Launching the Innovation

The baby bird must eventually leave the nest. Will it be ready to fly? Only if you anticipate its needs and problems, and make sure that it's ready for the rough-and-tumble world beyond the protected boundaries of your development team.

Emphasizing planning, preparation, and refinement

Procter & Gamble's system for launching a new product is a pretty good one for just about any innovation. It consists of the following six steps:

1. **Discovery:** This step is the research stage, in which creative ideas are developed.

2. **Design:** Concepts are turned into prototypes, and detailed planning is done to refine the concept and prepare it for implementation.

3. **Qualify:** This step involves a thorough analysis of the market potential, risks, and potential rewards to make sure that the design is strong enough to be worth launching.

4. **Ready:** Designs that make it through the qualification step are prepared for launch.

5. **Launch:** This step is actual rollout of the innovation, which is often staged so that an initial test can be performed and the details of the launch plan refined before the innovation goes national.

6. **Leverage:** Successfully launched products are studied to see how they can be refined by improving their management and introducing efficiencies to cut costs.

The take-away lesson from P&G's innovation process is that half the steps — Steps 4 through 6 — are dedicated to getting the launch right. The idea of a specific step called Ready is great! I want you to incorporate a similar step in your management of innovations. Take time to assess the needs and barriers to implementation or launch, write a launch plan, and make sure that you know what resources you'll need.

With careful preparation and planning, the Launch step goes much more smoothly, but nasty surprises sometimes occur. Flaws are revealed in the design, unintended consequences are discovered when people start using it or you find more resistance and less understanding than you'd expected. That's okay. Just return to planning and adjust your approach based on the feedback.

I also love the idea of a Leverage step. This is a great term for the process of refining and maintaining the implementation. When your launch is over, it's easy to take your foot off the gas pedal and sit back, but avoid this temptation; it's not time to rest yet! A successful launch is just the beginning of a new process. It earns you the happy opportunity to refine your design and perfect your production and marketing or other specifics of the implementation. (See Chapter 16 for ways to maximize the spread of your innovation.)

Promoting the project

Whatever your innovation is — a new idea, such as getting nurses to use hand sanitizer before touching a patient, or a new consumer product, such as a P&G launch — you need to put careful attention into telling your target market about the innovation. Promotion is always integral to a good launch.

Promoting the project means building support within your organization and throughout the network of business partners you're going to need to implement the innovation. You've got a variety of ways to go about building support and participation for the implementation. Use all your options to influence others to help you, including communicating the details of the innovation, explaining how to use it, and providing support for those who are struggling to use it for the first time.

Communicate

Tell the story of your innovation simply and well, cutting through the complexities and getting to the benefits so that people understand right away. Communicate often, and communicate with everyone who has a stake in the innovation or in the old ways that have to be discarded to implement the innovation. Your role as a communicator is important. Don't forget to tell and retell the story of your innovation, pointing out why it's important and good.

Explain

Share expertise and information to fill in missing knowledge about how to implement the innovation. Often, innovations have a technical aspect, and people may resist implementation simply because they don't understand the technology. Help by teaching and by bringing in other teachers who have even deeper expertise than yours. Filling the knowledge gap is a key part of implementing any innovation.

Authorize

If you're in a position of authority, use your positional power to get your subordinates in line and working on the implementation. Redefine their roles and duties as needed to make sure that they're pulling the innovation forward. In addition, talk to others with authority, and get them on board too. Make sure that those in positions of power give out the needed assignments to move your implementation ahead.

Negotiate

Identify the people and groups inside your organization and beyond it who need to be part of the implementation process. Open friendly negotiations with those parties to get them to agree to do their parts. Pull any political strings you may have, and call in personal favors if need be, to align the right implementation partners for your plan.

Support

Offer encouragement and empathy as needed for anyone who's having trouble or experiencing uncertainty and doubt. Implementation can be a rocky road, and you may need to keep spirits up by using your relational skills. It's helpful for people to know that you care, not only about the innovation, but also about them!

Projecting the rate of adoption

Along with the timeline and budget for your development work, you need to make a projection of the spread of your innovation, because this timeline is important for your planning. If you develop a new, stronger, food-grade inner bag for use in boxed packages of cereals, cake mixes, and the like, your projection of the rate of adoption by makers of those food products will tell you how quickly to ramp up your production of the bags. You don't want to overproduce inventory or overinvest in manufacturing equipment, but neither do you want to come up short. Chapter 16 shows you how to project the *diffusion curve* (the rate of spread of your innovation).

Chapter 16

Spreading the Word to Diffuse Your Innovation

. . . .

In This Chapter

▶ Developing a sound strategy for spreading your innovation to all potential users

▶ Using appropriate media at each step of the diffusion process

▶ Using giveaways to speed the diffusion process

. . . .

*D*iffusion is the sometimes-difficult process by which a good new idea or invention takes hold and spreads throughout a social network, which could be your market, your industry or profession, or even an entire country. Understanding how ideas, inventions, and innovative products spread is essential to your success as an innovator. Often, it's not the best design that wins the day, but the best-promoted design. You need to know how to spread the good word and get everyone excited about using your innovation to ensure its ultimate success.

This chapter shows you how to maximize the chances of success for your new idea by taking advantage of the natural pattern of diffusion.

Strategizing to Spread Your Innovation

The term *diffusion* comes from chemistry, in which it refers to the movement of particles through liquids or gases. High school science classes demonstrate diffusion by releasing a drop of perfume in the front of the room and then seeing how long it takes for the scent to reach every desk and student. (Not long.) Most innovations, however, encounter far more resistance than perfume does as it passes through the air, so you must master innovation marketing to make sure that your innovation gets the recognition and success it deserves.

Brushing up on history

Did you brush your teeth this morning? I did. Everyone does, right? But brushing one's teeth is a relatively recent thing in human history. Toothbrushes were invented in the 1600s in China, from whence they spread slowly, carried by travelers to Europe and Japan. The early toothbrushes were expensive, handmade from bone handles, with natural boar bristles inserted into drilled holes in the handles and held in place by tiny wires. Before the early 1800s, people mostly used toothpicks rather than brushes, and their teeth decayed at an alarming rate.

Toothbrushes didn't catch on in America until the mid-1800s, when the first patent for a toothbrush design was issued in the United States. (It was awarded to H. N. Wadsworth in 1857.) The biggest moment in the history of the toothbrush, however, came in 1866, when Florence Manufacturing Co., in the town of Florence, just a few miles from Amherst, Massachusetts, where I'm sitting as I write this chapter, began to produce a mass-market

toothbrush under the brand name Pro-phy-lac-tic (and yes, it was actually spelled that way, with four hyphens — branding has gotten more savvy since then!). The mass-produced toothbrush caught on when the price became affordable and advertising spread the word about it, and the company did very well.

The toothbrush finally took off in the United States more than 200 years after its invention because the Florence Manufacturing Co. was already advertising its hairbrushes and was familiar with the emerging practice of advertising in newspapers. A mass advertising campaign helped diffuse the toothbrush innovation by making people aware of it.

This toothbrush example illustrates the need for widespread communication with target users to spread an invention broadly. You need a strategy to spread your innovation too — ideally, one that gets the word out in fewer than the 200 years it took for the toothbrush to become an everyday household item!

Identifying potential adopters

The people who will use your idea or buy and use your invention are the *adopters* of your innovation. Who are they? How numerous are they? What will it take to get them to try your invention? The more insight you can gain on your future adopters, the better, because you need to figure out how to hasten the rate at which they adopt your innovation. First, though, it's important to get a good idea of the scope of your potential market (the number of people who are likely to adopt your invention) by asking yourself these questions:

✔ Is it something that the average household or person could afford to buy and/or use?

✔ Is it something that a typical (as opposed to big) business could afford to buy and/or use?

✔ Does it compete with multiple alternatives, or does it stand alone as a unique invention?

The size of your potential market is reduced if your innovation is highly specialized — something that most people or businesses wouldn't ever need. Consider an example from my own experience.

Over the holidays one year, my daughter Sadie made a gingerbread house decorated with frosting and candy from a kit sold at the grocery store. It looked great, but it fell apart because the roof and wall pieces were plain rectangles that had to be held together with frosting, which isn't the most durable of construction adhesives. So I drew up a design for gingerbread pans that would interlock via dovetail joints and would be more structurally sound.

What's the potential market for this invention? Hmm. I could calculate it by counting households that

- Have young children
- Do arts-and-crafts activities at home
- Celebrate Christmas
- Can afford to spend money on specialty pans
- Like to cook

According to the U.S. Department of Commerce, there are about 115 million households in the United States. Wow, I'm going to be a millionaire! But wait — only 78 million households have children, and of those, about half don't have children younger than 18 living at home. I don't expect many teenagers to want to use my gingerbread-house pans, so I'm going to cut that number in half to target households with young children.

Now my target market has dropped to around 25 million households — still a good number but certainly less than I first thought. I have to cut it again when I consider that some households with young children don't go in for traditional Christmas activities like making gingerbread houses, and some of the ones that do aren't going to feel like spending money on specialty pans. Then I have to cut my estimate farther because some of the remaining households don't do much cooking.

I'm down to a market of about 10 million households now. Maybe I won't become a millionaire from this invention after all. In fact, I may not be able to sell it through mainstream grocery stores because the potential market is too small. Almost all households buy potato chips, for example, and they buy them year-round. My invention — a specialized set of pans for making better gingerbread houses — is used only once a year by at most 10 percent of households, so unlike potato chips, it probably isn't worth the shelf space from a grocery store's perspective. I'll have to market my specialized baking pans some other way, such as via a targeted direct-marketing campaign using e-mail and a Web store.

Working through the mental exercise of analyzing the potential market for an invention tells you a lot about who might use it and how widely it might eventually spread or diffuse, but you still don't know how fast it will diffuse. The pace of diffusion is also a key strategic consideration, and I discuss it in the following section.

Finding out how fast your innovation will spread

If your invention is a good one — and I assume that it is! — you can expect it to spread at some natural rate. That rate may be quite slow, however. It's amazing how gradual the early spread of a good idea or invention often is, as you see in Figure 16-1, which shows the typical diffusion curve for an innovation.

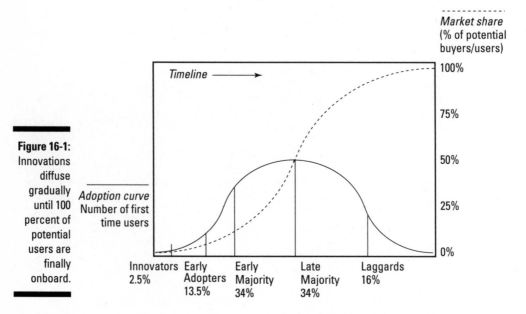

Figure 16-1: Innovations diffuse gradually until 100 percent of potential users are finally onboard.

As Figure 16-1 shows, on average, a small fraction of the potential user base for any innovation actually adopts it early on. Only 2.5 percent of potential users are innovators who embrace new ideas and products quickly and eagerly. Another 13.5 percent are so-called early adopters, who are fairly open to innovations and willing to try them after a few innovators have taken the first plunge. The third group to adopt an innovation — the early majority — is a bigger group, and when you reach those people, you're assured of establishing your innovation.

Diffusion usually follows an S-shaped curve, like the solid line in Figure 16-1. Without special help from you, that curve may be a very stretched-out S with a gradual slope that spreads out across years. The length of the diffusion is related to several factors that you can consider as you make your best guess about the speed of spread:

- ✔ **An innovation that depends on other innovations (such as a supporting technology) may have to wait until the related technology spreads.** If your invention is a fold-out portable keyboard that turns a phone into a fully functional word processor, your market will be limited by the speed at which cellphones with large, easy-to-read screens and powerful processors are embraced by people who do a lot of writing.

- ✔ **An innovation that requires a significant change of behavior will spread more slowly than one that fits into existing behaviors.** The treadmill, for example, allowed people to run in their homes or at fitness clubs. People who already ran outside found it easy to adapt to the new machine, and it spread quickly. The cross-country skiing machine spread much more slowly, however, even though it offers a better all-around workout than a treadmill does. The problem is that most people don't already ski cross-country, so the motion is unfamiliar to them.

- ✔ **An innovation that is costly to make will probably have a high price tag until economies of scale are reached.** High initial cost is a big barrier to adoption and slows the diffusion curve significantly.

- ✔ **An innovation that is costly to adopt is doomed to slower adoption than easy-to-use innovations.** It didn't cost very much for you to switch from music CDs to digital downloads, for example, because you could get free software and use your existing computer to download songs. You can't use your existing computer or television set, however, to watch movies in ultra-high-definition (UHD) — an emerging standard that's expected to become available in the next five years or so. Existing monitors will have to be replaced by models that produce resolutions four times higher than today's high-definition monitors, and the new monitors probably will be quite expensive at first. Expect a slow, forced march to UHD, with many consumers resisting because of the cost of switching over.

Setting the strategic parameters

When you've identified the likely first users and the ultimate user base, you can see the diffusion path fairly clearly. Add your analysis of any barriers to diffusion (such as high cost) to get a general idea of whether the innovation will spread slowly or rapidly.

To refine your timeline, look for comparisons with innovations that have had a similar effect in the past, such as an earlier-generation technology. Also look at contemporary innovations and how fast they're spreading to the same user base. This information gives you a clue about whether adoption curves are getting faster. Technology-based consumer innovations, for example, spread more quickly now than they used to because consumers are increasingly savvy about and interested in new technologies.

When you have a general sense of the timeline of spread and know who will be adopting the innovation when, you can draw your own diffusion curve showing specific estimates by year, based on the generic one shown in Figure 16-1 earlier in this chapter. Treat this curve as your base projection, assuming a natural rate of diffusion; then ask yourself what you can do to speed the pace of adoption above the natural rate.

I don't know about you, but I'm usually pretty impatient to get people to recognize and try something that I've created, and I'm also eager to get market share before someone else does, so I like steep diffusion curves and very rapid adoption rates.

Targeting those early adopters

It's best to hasten the diffusion curve by reaching out to enlist innovators and early adopters right away. (I explain early adopters in the section "Identifying potential adopters," earlier in this chapter.) To refine your strategy for spreading your innovation, ask yourself a couple more questions about the potential user base or market for your innovation:

- ✔ Who is most likely to want to try something new right away?

- ✔ How can I reach out to inform and excite these innovative users who like to be the first to try anything new and forward-thinking?

By aiming communications at innovators and early adopters, you can jump-start the diffusion process and make sure that it gets momentum fairly quickly. Often, you can use standard marketing methods too, but you'll be aiming at the most innovative and daring of your potential customers, so you need to choose your message and your media with them in mind. (See my book *Marketing For Dummies* [Wiley] for more information on designing a marketing program.)

Signing up beta testers

Beta testing is the initial trial use of an invention or process by a small group of sophisticated users. One good way to get early adopters to try your innovation is to give away samples (see "Priming the Pump with Freebies," later in this chapter) — but not just to anyone. Focus your trial offers on those people or organizations who have a proven track record of embracing the new and are suited to beta testing your innovation. It's okay to confine your beta tests to those on your short list and not to make the offer to the public.

Getting community leaders onboard

Back in the 1970s, government social workers in northern Finland were frustrated that people seemed to be unwilling to change their diet and lifestyles to reduce the risk of heart disease, which was a major cause of death in the area. Public information campaigns involving advertisements and educational brochures didn't seem to have any effect. People were set in their ways — which included a sedentary lifestyle and a diet including too much animal fat.

With the help of Everett M. Rogers, a professor at Stanford University and the world's leading expert on diffusion of innovations, a team of Finnish social scientists recruited 800 community leaders in North Karelia, a region of several hundred thousand people. The 800 lay leaders were invited to attend training sessions and were armed with in-depth knowledge of lifestyle changes that prevent heart disease. The group included people whom others

respected and looked up to as role models. Recent follow-up studies show dramatic effects. The innovative ideas about healthier living spread rapidly from the small core group, and the rate of heart disease in Northern Finland fell significantly over several decades — a fairly short period of time for a major improvement in public health.

Your goal may not be to prevent heart disease; it may be to persuade manufacturers to adopt your new technology or consumers to embrace your new product. The dissemination process is the same for both goals, however. Rather than spreading your advertising or publicity over thousands and thousands of people, try targeting only likely role models and leaders. Win a few hundred leaders, and you'll soon find that you have tens of thousands of followers onboard too.

When you start selling a product, you're required to be even-handed and consistent about pricing it, which means that special offers targeting only the privileged few won't fly legally. (To make sure that your pricing approach meets legal requirements, check with your corporate lawyer first.) But in the initial testing stage, before you're selling it to the market as a whole, you can usually be as selective as you want.

Your testing program can be more or less formal depending on how long and involved a test you need to perfect the product. Go for formality if you need sites where you can study users as they adopt a software program, for example, so that you can set up a way of recording bugs and observing user behavior. Be more informal if you simply want to get a bunch of people to try something new.

A Dutch bulb breeder contacted garden clubs in the northern United States with a request for volunteers to try a new, hardier variety of tulip bulbs. The feedback in the spring was very positive, with many gardeners asking for more, so the breeder introduced the bulbs into the region and launched a successful new product line.

Recruiting informal champions

Find people who act as informal leaders, or *champions,* and persuade them to be the early adopters. How? By giving them individual attention, free samples and support, or special education on using the innovation. This method works surprisingly well. You can recruit your champions face-to-face or (if you're good at Web marketing) by targeting bloggers who have lots of followers and Facebook members who have lots of friend requests.

Designing Your Media Mix for Maximum Diffusion

Your *media mix* is the selection of advertising and other marketing communications you use to inform potential users about your innovation and (hopefully) persuade them to buy and use it. You can't just do what you see marketers of established products doing, because their marketing mixes don't have to spread the word about something innovative. Your mix needs to be more informative that those of established products, and it also needs to narrow the message to those most likely to take an early interest: the innovative, early adopters who will be first to buy something exciting and new.

Aiming for intelligent, sophisticated buyers

As you expand beyond the first group of beta testers, look for innovators and early adopters who have a track record of embracing the new. If you sell other products through salespeople, then you probably can introduce your new product through your salespeople, too. If you don't sell directly, then you'll need to advertise. Either way, aim for people who are most likely to buy an innovative product — the sophisticated, innovative customers who have a track record of embracing new technologies and ideas.

Letting your sales force select the innovators

In a relatively small business to business market, you may already know who the early adopters are: the businesses that are leaders in their markets and have intelligent, sophisticated buyers. Your sales force or sales representatives can identify the top 15 percent of their customers based on how open-minded and innovative they are, and you can design a special informative sales presentation to tell them about the new product.

Using an indicator to pull innovators out of a larger list

What if you're targeting a larger, less-well-known market, and you don't know who the most open-minded customers are? This situation is a problem when you're launching a new consumer product, for example, because the United

States alone has millions of households, and it's pretty hard to find a list broker that identifies them based on how innovative they are as consumers. To get around the problem, identify a marker of innovative consumer behavior that you think fits your situation. Something relatively new that fewer than half of consumers or consumer households have bought will help you identify those whose past behavior indicates that they are open to something new.

The 25 percent of U.S. households who had high-definition television (HDTV) at the beginning of 2009, for example, are more likely to upgrade to 3-D TVs in 2010. Companies planning to launch 3-D TVs in 2010 can look to HD early adopters as their initial target market. With that clue, manufacturers can identify the best states and cities in which to test the market for 3-D TV. Using their own sales records or widely available consumer research by firms such as Nielsen, companies can identify the cities with the highest percentage of HDTV users and focus their initial promotion of 3-D TV there. Washington, D.C., for example, is an innovative market, and a third of households there had HDTV at the beginning of 2009. Compare that city with Detroit, where a fifth of households had HDTV at the start of 2009, and you can make a pretty good guess about where 3-D will diffuse more rapidly.

Emphasizing personal media in the early days

In addition to personal selling, educational workshops and press interviews are good ways to spread the word during the early stages of diffusion. They work well because they give you opportunities to speak directly with people who are interested in your innovation. Advertise an educational workshop — possibly a free one — about your innovation. Send out a press release or, if the innovation is really newsworthy, hold a press conference to let the media know about your innovation and the workshop you're holding.

Working with opinion leaders or lay leaders who in turn spread the word through their personal networks is also a great strategy. There's more of an educational element to the communication in the first stages of diffusion, so personal approaches to communicating make the most sense.

Using industry events to find early adopters

Go to conferences and trade shows (see Chapter 10) where you can present your innovation and talk to people who find it interesting. These events gather many of the most forward-thinking people in an industry — just the people you should be talking to and sharing samples, demos, and spec sheets with.

Using social media to generate electronic chatter about your innovation

Social media can be your best friends during the launch of an innovation. Blogs, professional online newsletters, technical and professional chat rooms, and broad-spectrum platforms such as Facebook (www.facebook.com) are all great places to generate a buzz about your innovation. If you're not already part of the online conversation in these places, find someone who's comfortable with them to help you begin to communicate about your innovation.

Blogging and being blogged about

Bloggers are an especially powerful force for spreading the word about an interesting innovation. Spend some time scanning for bloggers who might be interested in your innovation because it's a match with the kinds of topics they've covered in the past. From these potentially hundreds or thousands of bloggers, cull the ones who have only a few readers, and focus on those who have high readership (at least 100 followers). Get in touch with the leading bloggers to let them know about your innovation, and ask them whether they'd like to try it. If some of the most popular bloggers start talking about it, the news will rapidly spread among their readers.

Offering "show and tell" in streaming video

If your innovation is interesting to watch in action, get some early users on digital video, and post (or, better yet, have them post) one to three minutes' worth of footage on YouTube (www.youtube.com).

The *if* in this advice is important. If your video is dull, it won't get noticed, so this strategy isn't very interesting for, say, a new book. Who wants to watch video of someone reading a book? Video is great for promoting a new toy, however, and many toymakers have learned that an informal product review by a friendly customer (often, the son or daughter of an employee) will generate interest.

It's also helpful to post video of your product prototype and ask for input. Not long ago, I came across a video posted by the inventors of a tabletop device that uses hand-operated paddles to bounce a ball back and forth in the style of the old Pong computer game. I wouldn't have guessed that this design would attract much interest, but with 90,489 viewers (well, 90,488, if you don't count me!), it obviously is generating some enthusiasm. Comments posted on the site included helpful suggestions for making the design better, because it had a small problem: The ball sometimes got stuck in the middle, out of reach of the paddles. With that many viewers and lots of friendly advice, the designers of the tabletop game just might have a winner.

Figure 16-2, however, shows the curve of cumulative viewers of this tabletop game video plotted by day over the course of two weeks. You can see a healthy S-curve of growing interest in the first week, followed by a leveling-off of the curve. That tells you that the audience for this video is probably going to max out at around 100,000 viewers, which is good but not outstanding.

A video that *goes viral* — meaning that it diffuses broadly and rapidly in Web communities — shows a longer upward slope to its curve as it reaches millions of viewers. From the data in Figure 16-2, you can guess that the

tabletop game would have a dedicated but limited audience if it were introduced to the market. Keep in mind, however, that YouTube viewership is a
reflection of how entertaining the video is, which may or may not be directly
linked to how interesting the innovation shown in the video is. A second,
more entertaining video of the same game might succeed in going viral.

What if the inventor made a video called *War of the Pong Nerds,* in which two
players argue about who's winning and, halfway through the game, knock the
game off the table and start to fight about the score? The idea is silly but potentially the stuff of YouTube legend. And if you can become legendary on YouTube,
you can probably make it in the mass market out here in the real world, too!

Posting informative videos about technically intriguing products

Companies have discovered that a boring but informative video approximately two minutes long will win viewers on YouTube if it's about a new and
interesting product. As I write, microprojectors using light-emitting diodes
(LEDs) as their light source are entering the market, and 3M has a video
about one such microprojector that's had more than 100,000 views.

The video isn't good theater; it simply shows a salesman making a presentation
to a prospect, using a microprojector. Why have so many people watched it?
Forward-thinking consumers who are eager to try new technologies go looking
for product information, and YouTube is an accessible place to find it.

Figure 16-2:
An S-curve
indicating
how interest
in a
prototype
video on
YouTube
grew and
then leveled
off over a
two-week
period.

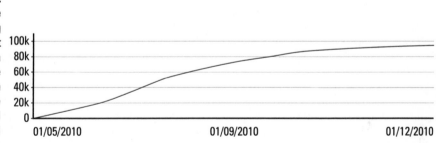

Adapting your marketing to the inflection point

At some point, your innovation reaches the *inflection point* in its diffusion
curve — the point where the line begins to slope upward at growing speed.
Innovative products don't sell at the same rate next year as last year. As

these products approach the early middle half of the market (where the most progressive of the average users or consumers adopt the innovation), sales should pick up. The inflection point comes none too soon for many innovators, who have been struggling to build the market and reach economies of scale in production and marketing.

Knowing where you are in your innovation's diffusion curve helps you project sales realistically. The curve also helps you decide what media to emphasize as you promote your innovation. As you reach the inflection point, where your sales begin to go up at an accelerating rate and you've penetrated more than 13 percent of your potential market (refer to Figure 16-1), switch gradually to less personal, more mass-oriented media to spread the good word about your innovation. Try the following techniques:

- ✔ Billboards and transit advertising, which are cheap and good places to start a mass-marketing campaign

- ✔ Advertising on local and cable television stations

- ✔ Banner advertising on mass Web sites such as Yahoo, Google, YouTube, and MySpace

- ✔ Mass mailings to purchased lists of potential customers (send postcards or catalogs, depending on the depth of your product line)

- ✔ Promotions in mainstream media such as newspapers, magazines, and radio talk shows

If one in ten consumers has tried an exciting innovation, you can be fairly sure that the other nine have heard about it and want to find out more. Publicity and advertising can combine to meet your need for information. As more people become familiar with the innovation, the news value goes down, and you'll get less editorial coverage, which forces you to buy more advertising to stay visible.

Priming the Pump with Freebies

Some innovations lend themselves well to free sampling. If you have a new product that isn't too expensive to make on a per-unit basis but has significant startup costs, consider doing a big initial run and giving most of it away. This strategy may speed the diffusion of your innovation and get you quickly to that inflection point, where sales start to grow at a rapid rate and profits are easier to come by.

Normally in business, you try to avoid giving your product away, but when you need to stimulate the diffusion of an innovation that nobody's heard about, the opposite advice may apply. Sometimes, the product is its own best advertisement, and your marketing money is best spent by giving away product.

One of my clients is an inventor who created and patented the SmoothClip, a clever molded-plastic device that clips onto the bottom of a tube. Different sizes fit different tubes, from lip gloss to body lotion, allowing you to push the product up the tube and out the end easily and smoothly, with little waste and mess. It's a great design. How do I know? My client has given away a lot of the devices, and everyone who has one loves it and tells all of his or her friends to get one, too. The clips aren't even available in stores yet, but they already have a following.

Suppose that the SmoothClip is your innovative product. My advice is to make the injection molds — the biggest upfront cost — and then do a run of several thousand items just for giving away. If you hand out the clips in a large, fashion-forward urban market (Los Angeles would be great), packaged so as to display the brand name and a Web site for ordering, you'll probably get lots of orders from that giveaway, and the diffusion process will have been started. You may have to sell through sampling, personal demos, and the Web site until the diffusion curve reaches its inflection point. By then, you'll have a good enough initial user base to attract the interest of major retailers.

If you're considering trying a major sampling effort or other ways of getting people to try your innovation for free, make sure that you really have a large potential market that's worth investing in upfront. If your research indicates that 60 percent of women and 5 percent of men frequently use cosmetics in tubes and are likely to want your new clip to help them control the application of these products, you can project a potential market of roughly 65 percent of the adult population. That's a nice fat market with plenty of potential to repay your initial investment in free samples. It's safe to say that you could give away 10,000 clips to stimulate the diffusion of your innovation, because you ought to be able to sell hundreds of thousands of units when the product catches on.

Chapter 17

Protecting Intellectual Property

· ·

In This Chapter

▶ Identifying, valuing, and tracking your intellectual property assets

▶ Protecting your work with copyrights and trademarks

▶ Patenting inventions and designs to limit your competition

▶ Keeping trade secrets

▶ Securing essential records and documents

· ·

*I*ntellectual property includes the innovations and other creative expressions of your ideas that you own — assuming that you manage and protect them appropriately so as not to lose control of them. You can — and often should — pursue legal protection of inventions such as process and product designs. You also should copyright your writings, videos, audios, and images, whether you're producing them for sale or using them for advertising or other nonsale purposes.

What about your business name and logo, and the names and visual identities of your products? It's essential to protect your claim to your own brands, too, especially if you plan to invest in marketing them and making them memorable to potential consumers.

Your intellectual property — whether it's a unique invention, a how-to booklet, or a brand identity — has economic value, and the reality is that someone else may try to take it. Unless you apply for patents, file for copyrights, and register for trademarks when and how you should, you may find that what you thought was yours isn't, and you have no legal recourse when someone else starts using it.

Understanding the ins and outs of intellectual-property law and practice is essential to the successful implementation of innovations, whether you're a lone inventor, an entrepreneur seeking funding, or an employee taking the lead in developing a new product, process, trademark, or any other expression of creative design. This chapter helps you get a start on identifying and managing your intellectual property, but you will probably need to get professional help from a lawyer who specializes in intellectual property, because it does get quite technical and I can't cover such a detailed and broad subject thoroughly enough in a single chapter. If you want to read more about the topic, turn to *Patents, Copyrights, & Trademarks For Dummies* by Henri J. A. Charmasson and John Buchaca (Wiley).

Determining and Keeping Track of Your Intellectual Property Assets

What do you have that might qualify as valuable intellectual property? Most businesses have a lot of intellectual property (sometimes referred to as IP) to protect, and sad to say, they usually don't take proper care of that property. Intellectual property could be even more valuable to your business than hard assets like trucks, equipment, and buildings. Intellectual property is a major asset, and so you may want to seek expert advice from an IP attorney as you assess your IP and decide what needs protecting.

Deciding what merits protection

Here's a checklist of some of the main kinds of intellectual property. If you, you business, or your employer has any of the following, you need to have a strategy to protect their value:

- ✔ Secret formulas, recipes, or processes that competitors may want to get their hands on
- ✔ Inventions, including designs for products and processes that you think may be original and of commercial value
- ✔ Ideas for inventions that haven't been fully designed yet but that you think may be worth developing further because they could be original and valuable
- ✔ Designs that you think are exceptional and recognizable and that you wouldn't want competitors to copy
- ✔ Written works, including fiction and nonfiction (such as this book), whether long or short, that you think are original and of value
- ✔ Works written for performance, such as musical, dramatic, or choreographic works
- ✔ Pictorial, graphic, or sculptural works of artistic value
- ✔ Motion pictures and other audiovisual works, including television and streaming video ads and short videos
- ✔ Brand names that are distinctive and associated with your business or products and that you wouldn't want competitors to use

✔ Logos or visual symbols that are distinctive and associated with your business or products and that you wouldn't want competitors to use

✔ New varieties of plants that you developed and want to sell without competitors or customers reproducing them on their own

✔ Business records and files, including records of past and present projects and products, that you'd be unhappy to lose to theft, fire, or other disaster

What would you pay for the Coca-Cola formula and name, for example? A lot. It's the most valuable brand in the world, and it pretty much *is* the company. Protecting this asset is key to the success of the company. Most business people wish they had intellectual-property problems as big as Coca-Cola's: how to keep someone from stealing the formula and how to police the trademarks associated with the brand. These problems are billion-dollar problems because of the value of the assets involved.

Assessing the value of your intellectual property

After you list your intellectual property, you need to think about the value of each item on that list. Three common ways to value IP are

✔ **Estimate what price you could get by selling the IP.** To estimate a sales price, look for similar intellectual property that's been sold recently and use any examples you find for comparison. IP is often sold; companies license or purchase patent rights to inventions as well as brand trademarks. If you have trouble finding good examples to help you value your IP, ask an intellectual property lawyer for help.

✔ **Estimate what you may earn by using the IP over the next five years.**

✔ **Calculate what you've invested in the IP.** If you have good records of what you spent to acquire or create the IP, valuing it on a cost basis should be easy.

An accountant may be able to help you value your intellectual property; the accountant's approach is usually based on cost — what you've invested in the intellectual property.

Which of the three methods is the right one for valuing your IP? It depends on who you talk to and what the value will be used for. If you're selling your IP, then fair market value is your guide, even if it's less than what you invested. For listing IP on a balance sheet, your accountant will usually use a cost basis. But for deciding which property to emphasize for protection and future investment, an earnings basis is best.

Calling the SWOT team

For especially valuable intellectual property, you may want to do a *SWOT* analysis, identifying *strengths, weaknesses, opportunities,* and *threats* to the asset. The SWOT analysis is a way to brainstorm and research specific factors that may affect the asset and your protection strategy for it. It looks at internal (within-company) factors and classifies them as either strengths or weaknesses. For example, if you produced a movie with a major star in it, that actor's market appeal is a strength for the movie. If, however, the movie got bad reviews because the plot is boring, then that's a weakness that may offset the strength.

A SWOT analysis also looks at external (marketplace, environmental, legal, and social) factors, and classifies them as either opportunities or threats. For a movie production company, for example, the sale of pirated DVD copies of a movie in Beijing is an external threat, whereas the ownership of a really great script for a sequel to a best-selling movie is an internal strength.

To conduct a SWOT analysis, start by listing strengths of the IP in question, such as that there are many years of patent protection remaining, or that the design is unique and increasingly popular. Next, list weaknesses, such as a concern that an earlier patent might be similar enough to encourage the owner to file suit against you. Then list opportunities, such as an offer to license your design or an idea for combining it with another invention to make something that may be easier to sell. Finally, list threats, such as the rumor that an industry leader is working on an invention that might antiquate yours.

Keeping track of the protective steps you've taken (or need to take)

After you've gone through the checklist in the earlier section "Deciding what merits protection" and gathered some expert advice from a qualified intellectual-property lawyer who's familiar with your industry, you should be able to create a detailed list of each piece of intellectual property that you (or your employers) own. Follow these steps to create a complete table of your IP:

1. **Create a blank table with six columns.**

   You can create this table electronically by using the Table command in Microsoft Word or by creating a worksheet in a spreadsheet program such as Microsoft Excel.

2. **Label the first (leftmost) column Our Intellectual Property, and use as many rows as necessary to enter its contents.**

   List each piece of potentially valuable intellectual property in this column.

3. **Label the second column Protection in Place, and use as many rows as necessary to enter its contents.**

Use this column to list any trademarks, copyrights, patents, secrecy practices and contracts, backups of data files, insurance policies, and any other forms of protection that are currently in place.

4. **Label the third column Up to Date and Complete?, and use as many rows as necessary to enter its contents.**

   Don't just put checks or yes/no entries in this column; specify what's been done recently to ensure complete protection of each IP asset in your list. Often, when an IP audit gets to this step, many or all of these cells are left blank, because in far too many businesses, the intellectual property isn't managed on a regular basis (such as quarterly).

5. **Label the fourth column Quality of Protection, and use as many rows as necessary to enter its contents.**

   Some of the IP assets won't have any protection, others will be under-protected, and still others will be well protected. In many cases, you won't be sure which label to enter for an IP asset because you won't be certain what can or should be done to protect it. That's okay. Just enter a question mark for that asset for now; then do your homework to find out what's appropriate and necessary to do next (see Step 6).

6. **Label the fifth column Necessary Actions, and use as many rows as necessary to enter its contents.**

   Summarize the next steps needed, if any, to secure full protection for the IP asset.

7. **Label the sixth column Value of Asset, and use as many rows as necessary to enter its contents.**

   For each asset, enter a dollar value (if you have a sense of what the market would pay), a loss value (if you have a sense of what losing the asset would cost you), or a general value assessment (such as low, medium, high, or very high). See the earlier section "Assessing the value of your intellectual property" for tips on how to set a price on each asset. Try to use a consistent method throughout your table to make it easy to compare the items based on their value.

Knowing the value of an asset helps you decide how much to invest in increasing your protection of it and also helps you prioritize your action plans. Most likely, you should focus on high-value, underprotected intellectual property first. Sometimes, however, a known threat to a specific IP asset exists, such as a copycat competitor, in which case you'll probably want to focus on that asset's protection first.

Copyrighting As Much As You Can

The easiest form of intellectual-property protection is the *copyright*, the exclusive legal right to reproduce, publish, sell, or distribute the matter and form of something (as a literary, musical, or artistic work). This book has a copyright in the author's name (mine), which I've assigned to the publisher in a contract that gives Wiley the right to publish my work in exchange for royalties (payments based on a percentage of sales). Authors, musicians, and other artists know that they need to protect their work with copyrights, and so should businesses — but they often don't.

Even though filing for copyrights is easy, you may still want to get legal advice about what to protect with copyrights and how. You may be able to protect certain wording that's of value to your sales and marketing, unique computer code that you don't want copied, photographs and videos used in a trade-show kiosk, and many other forms of authored content.

Adding copyright protection to your work

The first thing to do with any original authored work is to post a copyright notice on it that conforms to the legal requirements for such notices in your country. In the United States, notices usually take this form: the word "Copyright" and the symbol ©, followed by the first year of publication of the work and the name of the owner of the copyright. By posting a copyright notice, you declare your claim of ownership of the work.

Is your Web site protected? I bet not! To help prevent your competitors from using content on your Web site, post a copyright notice clearly on key pages.

By publishing original content with a copyright notice (in a printed brochure or catalog or on the Web, for example), you gain significant legal rights. If someone later publishes something that's very similar and apparently derived from or copied from your materials, you can take legal action to force that person to withdraw the material, and if the other person profited at your expense, you may also be able to regain some of your lost profit.

You can strengthen your proof of authorship and be better prepared to defend your copyright by filing with the U.S. Copyright Office of the Library of Congress. Go to www.copyright.gov, and click Forms. On the Forms page, you can take a tutorial before filing electronically (which costs $35 and is relatively simple and easy), or you can fill in Form CO on your computer and then print it and return it by mail (which costs $50). Fill in the form entirely online and print it without making any edits, because the information on the form gets incorporated into a bar code as you enter it. It only takes a few weeks at most to complete the copyright process in the United States.

If you want to copyright a group of publications at the same time, there's another form for that, and you can still use an old-fashioned paper form for filings if you prefer.

The Web site for the U.S. Copyright Office of the Library of Congress contains lots of helpful advice, forms, and information, such as how to incorporate property copyright notices into your published documents and how to make packaging and licensing agreements for software, music, videos, and other authored materials. (If your content or authored product is of potentially high value, however, don't do it yourself; hire a competent lawyer to spearhead the effort.)

Getting copyright protection when you're not the author

If you hire employees or freelancers to write or design materials for your company to use, you may find that you can't copyright those materials, because you're not the author. To get around this problem, specify in advance that you're employing these people to create works for hire, and that they're waiving any and all copyrights and recognizing you as the owner of all copyrights pertaining to the work in question. Software companies routinely ask programmers to sign such releases of rights, and so do many magazines, newspapers, and other publishers that work with multiple authors.

Protecting Your Brands through Trademark

All businesses should have proprietary brands that add value to what they sell. A *proprietary brand* is a business name or other unique identity (such as a product name) that you own and use for your own benefit. If you purchase a branded product wholesale and then sell it retail, its brand name isn't yours, but if you make the product, you may give it a proprietary brand name of your own. Even if you don't control the brands that you sell, you certainly should protect the brand name of your business, whether it's a store or other kind of business entity.

Managing your brands is partly a creative challenge and partly a legal one:

- ✔ On the creative side, brand management involves the development of creative brand identities that are attractive, memorable, and trustworthy. Putting good creative effort into brand development pays off, and most businesses could and should do more of it.

- ✔ On the legal side, brand management involves a host of activities, from standardizing and describing your brand identities to registering for trademark protection in your own country and other countries (see the later section "Applying for a trademark in the U.S. and elsewhere").

✔ If you're establishing a new business, you should also register your business name with appropriate state and federal regulatory bodies. Some U.S. states require new businesses to file with the Secretary of State, while others send you to the nearest courthouse or town hall to register your name if you're a small, unincorporated business, while still requiring incorporated businesses to file at the state level. You also need to set up your business identity with the Internal Revenue Service and obtain a tax identification number for it. For marketing purposes, you should also buy a URL that incorporates the name of your brand for use on the Web. There's plenty of homework to do if you're setting up a new business, so talk to your lawyer and accountant, and consult a detailed reference such as *Entrepreneurship For Dummies* by Kathleen Allen (Wiley).

You may think that you can take charge of trademark filings and do everything yourself because the databases — and the forms — are online and easily accessible. Not so! If your trademark is at all likely to be valuable to you or anyone else, you ought to use a competent lawyer to spearhead the effort. There's a lot I can't explain in this section because it's complex and technical, and there's still more that I can't explain because trademark law is a specialty . . . not my specialty. You wouldn't take out your own appendix if you had appendicitis, and I don't think you should handle your own trademark legalities either.

Ensuring that your brand is trademarkable

When you develop or improve a *brand identity* (a name, logo, and possibly a tag line or other elements, presented in a specific manner both verbally and visually), you give a clear, distinct personality to your brand. (For help with branding and naming, see my book *Marketing Kit For Dummies* as well as *Branding For Dummies* by Bill Chiaravalle and Barbara Findlay Schenck [Wiley].) Whether that brand is a business, product line, or specific product, there's considerable value in a good brand identity.

A brand is worthy of a trademark if it meets these criteria:

✔ **It's consistent:** A consistent presentation is part of the strategy for protecting the brand's value. The more consistent you are in the way you show your brand, the stronger the brand will be. If you don't already have one, create a *style sheet* — a set of instructions with examples showing exactly how the brand name or company name is to be displayed everywhere it appears. (Graphic designers who develop brand identities are familiar with the requirements for style sheets and can help you create specifications for your brand.)

✔ **It's unique:** A unique brand is one that people can't easily confuse with any other. For example, if you want to introduce an air-filled plastic wrapping material made of recycled plastic, you might choose to call it EarthBubbles®, which differentiates it uniquely from its leading competitor, Bubble Wrap® Brand Cushioning, a trademarked product owned by Sealed Air Corporation of Elmwood Park, New Jersey. You couldn't call your product Better Bubble Wrap or anything that uses the term "bubble wrap" because Sealed Air Corp. owns that trademark.

✔ **It's identifiable:** A brand name or logo design needs to be clearly, specifically defined, right down to the exact wording, the kind of lettering, the colors used, and other particulars, so that it's easily identifiable in every instance.

It's good to make sure that there is plenty of elbowroom for your trademark. Refine it with more specific language (such as a second term) if it's too hemmed in by existing marks.

Applying for a trademark in the U.S. and elsewhere

The U.S. Patent and Trademark Office in Washington, D.C., handles registration of trademarks in the United States. Go to its Web page at `www.uspto.gov/ trademarks` for information on trademarks, searches, and registrations.

It's a good idea to seek protection of your trademark in foreign countries as well. The Madrid System for the International Registration of Marks makes it possible to register in many countries at the same time through a single filing with the World Intellectual Property Organization in Geneva, Switzerland (`www.wipo.int`).

Trademarks are granted for specific uses. Suppose that you want to register the name Orion as a trademark for a new line of handheld navigation aids for hikers and sailors. You would apply for protection for these uses, not in other categories. Your trademark might be similar to one in another category (a registered trademark for Orion Capital already exists, for example), but your request might still be granted if the proposed use is unique to your category.

To strengthen an application to register a trademark, make it more specific and unique. The name Orion isn't as easy to protect for a handheld navigation device as Orion Navigator, for example. Adding the second word to the name makes it truly unique. I can't find any products with that name by searching commercial and Web databases; I also can't find any U.S. trademark registrations in that name (see "Searching for existing patents" later in this chapter).

Similarly, Navigator is a relatively weak name for a handheld navigation device because it's fairly obvious (possible a generic term), and also because it's been registered as a trademark for a Web browser, an automobile, and other products. Even though these registrations aren't in the same category as your product, they might impinge on the perception of uniqueness in consumers' minds. Distinct and unique trademarks are the strongest kind.

That recognizable red cross

The American Red Cross has such a well-known name that it was able to raise more than $6 million on one day — the day after the horrible earthquake in Haiti in January 2010. Online donations flooded in because many concerned people felt safe trusting the organization with the task of getting that relief to the victims of the quake. You could say, then, that the American Red Cross brand name is worth $6 million a day in donations. Wow.

The American Red Cross has a legal team working on the protection of its distinctive logo: the red cross from which the organization takes its name. The logo is sometimes licensed to companies for use in marketing, such as on Band-Aids, marketed by Johnson & Johnson.

The organization also engages in legal action to defend its control of its distinctive logo. Red Cross attorneys insisted that Lions Gate Entertainment, the producer of the movie *Saw III*, remove the red cross from the risqué uniforms worn by nurses in posters advertising a Halloween blood drive sponsored by Lions Gate. Even though the drive was a charitable effort to get donations to the Red Cross blood bank, The Red Cross determined that the association of the Red Cross logo with the nurses in the poster was inappropriate.

Increasing your chances for trademark approval

To prevent confusion and possible legal trouble (in the form of suits from companies that think you've infringed their trademarks), make sure that your brands and logos can't possibly be confused with existing ones. If there's even a chance of confusion, you could be forced to give up your mark. This is where your creativity comes in. Adjust or improve your logos and brand names until they truly stand apart from all others!

To check whether your name and logo are distinctive, search relevant databases, starting with the U.S. Patent and Trademark Office's Trademark Electronic Search System (TESS). Go to www.uspto.gov, and click Search Marks to find a basic TESS search option.

Establishing your rights by using your mark

If you've just designed a new logo and want to protect it before starting to use it, you need to file an Intent to Use form along with your application for a U.S. trademark, because trademark law (unlike patent law) requires use. You can't just sit on a brand name or logo; if you don't use it, you lose the rights to it. Begin to use your design as soon as is reasonably possible, and make sure that you file a Statement of Use within six months of being granted your U.S. trademark based on an Intent to Use filing.

If six months is too soon, you can file an extension request and gain another six months for a $150 fee. In fact, you can extend the deadline five times, but eventually, you must show proof (examples and samples) that you're actually using the trademark in commerce; otherwise, you lose your rights to it.

Unlike patents, trademarks can be applied for *after* initial use without forfeiting any rights — unless someone else happens to file for a similar trademark in the interim, in which case you'll wish that you'd been more prompt so as to prevent competitors from thinking that the trademark was available.

If you have a great logo in hand and want to begin using it, and if you're quite sure (based on searches of relevant trademark and business databases) that nobody else has a similar one in your class of business, go ahead and start using it. Print it on letterhead; stamp it on products; use it on packaging, labels, displays, Web sites, and advertisements. If you haven't been granted your U.S. trademark yet, show your intent to trademark your logo by including ™ after the brand name or symbol. After your trademark is granted, you should switch to ® directly following the trademark, to show that it's registered.

Pursuing Patent Protection

So you have an invention, such as a new product or process, that you think is unique and special, and you want to protect it from copycats and imitators. Great! Figure out whether it qualifies for patent protection by asking yourself these questions:

- ✔ Is it useful?
- ✔ Is it unique?
- ✔ Is it nonobvious?

If your initial answer to all three questions is yes, there's a good chance that your innovation is patentable. Your opinion isn't the one that matters, however. It's up to the U.S. Patent and Trademark Office to decide whether you'll receive 20 years of exclusive rights to your invention — or not. Often, applications are turned down, although a rejection may be due to a poorly written application or a lack of proper background research rather than anything fundamentally wrong with the invention itself.

Can you file for patent protection yourself? Sure. You can also do your own retirement planning, fill your own dental cavities, and replace the roof of your two-story house — if you don't mind running the risk of messing up your patent application, ruining your teeth, and falling off your roof. Okay, that's a bit harsh, because some amateurs do succeed at winning patent protection, but generally, it's wise to get good legal advice, and that means spending some money. Patents usually cost more to obtain than other forms of legal protection for your intellectual property, and take longer, too — as long as a year in many cases.

Searching for existing patents

All too often, entrepreneurs and inventors get well into the application process before discovering that someone has patented something similar already. Just because you haven't seen a similar invention for sale, don't assume there are no competing patents! Many patent applications are rejected because an existing patent covers some or all of the design or invention. No doubt the inventor who submitted the rejected application thought that she had done something completely original, but with millions of patents on file, it's easy to repeat something by accident. Professional patent lawyers examine all similar patents carefully and may suggest editing the application to differentiate your invention more clearly from past patents. You can improve your chances of success by doing your own preliminary search.

There are two U.S. patent databases: 1976 and before, and post-1976. It's important to search both. The earlier patents are most likely expired. Expired patents are still relevant, however, because your invention isn't unique unless no previous patents — expired or not — are substantially the same.

Take advantage of full-text search post-1976

Patents filed since 1976 are in easy-to-search digital form and are kept current to today's date, which is pretty impressive for a government resource! To do a quick search (the best way to scan for any patents that might overlap with yours), follow these steps:

1. **Identify a few terms that describe your invention very specifically.**

2. **Go to the Quick Search page at the U.S. Patent and Trademark Office Web site (`patft.uspto.gov/netahtml/PTO/search-bool.html`).**

3. **Enter your search terms in the Term 1 and Term 2 text boxes.**

   Use the most general terms that describe the utility or basic functionality of your invention, such as *squirrelproof* and *bird feeder*. Terms can be more than a single word long.

4. **Set the Field 1 and Field 2 drop-down menus to All Fields.**

5. **Click Search.**

   A screen displays all patents since 1976 that use your two search terms in their title or text, arranged from newest to oldest.

No matter how unique you think your invention is, you'll be surprised by the number of patents that pop up as matches for your search terms.

Study search results that match your invention

When you get your search results (see the preceding section), open the most recent patent (or the most recent one that seems to be at all similar, if the search returned too wide a mix of patents). Then read the abstract. Abstracts are usually very clear and simple, so you can get the big idea behind the invention right away.

Check to see whether your invention is similar to the one in the most recent application. If it is, you're probably going to run into trouble. Most likely, you'll need to redesign the invention to make it more unique, or think up another invention and give up on that one. Don't give up too soon, though. Multiple patents can address the same utility or function, but in different ways. Numerous patents have been granted for squirrelproof bird feeders, for example, because each feeder has a unique design. Maybe your design is unique and better than earlier attempts, and your application will be granted!

Continue through the list of search results, checking each one for similarities. As you review a result, read the full text of the abstract, and click the Images link at the bottom of the page to examine any designs that may be similar to yours. Check to see that nobody has used your design or a similar one.

Check references in recent patents for the numbers of earlier patents

Look at the References Cited section that appears just after the abstract. Most patent filings reference earlier patents that may be related (and point out important differences). The homework that these earlier inventors did to identify relevant patent documents is helpful as you do your own research; it can point you to additional patents that your search didn't turn up but that you ought to be aware of before you write your application.

What if someone patented something similar to your invention before 1976, when digital filings started? Then you have to go into the old-fashioned paper files, which used to mean going to Washington, D.C., and asking to review actual files. Now the pages of patent filings between 1790 and 1976 have been scanned and are online as TIFF images that you can search from this link: `patft.uspto.gov/netahtml/PTO/patimg.htm`. Unfortunately, you can't search by term. You have to enter a patent number, which means that you need to know that the patent exists and what its number is.

Budgeting the cost of filing a patent

Expect to spend a minimum of $20,000 to file for a U.S. patent application and possibly another $10,000 for foreign rights or any minor changes that might be required. Conventional advice is to budget $15,000 for your filing, but I think it's wise to double that amount.

Keep in mind that a budget of $30,000 for your legal work is quite modest compared with what a large firm might spend. Big companies tend to submit multiple applications in an effort to cover their inventions in multiple ways, such as a patent covering the basic design very broadly, along with several applications covering specific forms and applications of the design.

You don't pay just to file a patent; you also have to pay to maintain a patent. Other filings and fees may be required over the years, as well as costs associated with defending the patent from violators. It's hard to estimate such costs, because they vary significantly, but they can be anywhere from $5,000 to $100,000 per year, depending on the scale of the patent and the sales resulting from it.

Deciding whether a patent is worth the investment

Many entrepreneurs and inventors tell me that they've been told by experts not to bother with a patent application if they don't have plenty of additional money to spend on defending the patent. I think that's the wrong way to approach the decision of whether to file. If the innovation proves to be valuable — if you're making significant money by selling something based on your patent — plenty of funds should be available for legal work, and you'll want to defend your rights assertively. If you don't have significant sales, you won't need to defend the patent, so don't worry about future costs now; they tend to be self-funding. Focus on the initial investment and on whether it makes sense to spend money to file for a patent.

The following checklist can help you decide whether to invest in a patent application:

✔ **Is the invention or design likely to be profitable?**

If not, there's not much point in filing. If you see potential economic value to the invention or design, go on to the next question.

✔ **Is the invention or design likely to be eligible for protection?**

The answer depends on whether the item is novel, useful, and nonobvious. If you think that your item qualifies on all three counts, go on to the next question.

✔ **Can you make money from a patent covering your invention or design?**

Sometimes, people come up with concepts that seem to be clever and original but are so far from their general area of expertise that they may not be able to flesh out the idea fully or bring it successfully to market. This question gives you a reality check, making sure that you have a real business reason for proceeding. If you think that you can turn the idea into a practical design that can be patented and marketed (or licensed to someone who can market it), you probably should apply.

✔ **Can you raise the cash needed?**

If you answered "yes" to the first three questions, you're probably fairly sure that an investment in a patent application could provide a good return. If you can divert nonessential funds to the application cost, go ahead and fund it yourself. If you'd have to skip several mortgage payments to apply, you need to find a partner or investor who has deeper pockets than you do. Don't bet the farm on a patent application!

Saving money by filing patent forms yourself

Sometimes, inventors file their own patent applications, and some of these low-cost applications do get granted, so it's possible to beat the cost of a lawyer-driven patent application process. But it's likely that you'll make some mistakes and get weaker coverage than you would with proper legal representation, so I view self-filing to be the very last resort.

To download instructions and application materials for filing your own U.S. patent application, go to www.uspto.gov/patents/process/file/efs/index.jsp.

To file online in the United States, you'll use EFS-Web, which makes it quite simple to submit PDF pages for review by the U.S. Patent and Trademark Office. If you're a confirmed do-it-yourselfer, check the instructions on the EFS home page at the preceding link.

Writing a really compelling and well-designed patent application is a legal art, and I recommend hiring a patent attorney who's familiar with both the patent office and its technology.

Considering foreign patent protection

U.S. patents don't protect you in other countries. The United States has signed the major international treaties concerning patents, but these treaties simply give you the right to file for patent protection in other countries too. It's up to you — or your lawyer — to decide which countries to file in and to do the proper searches and filings according to those countries' regulations and deadlines.

If you decide to seek international protection by filing in other countries or regions (such as the European Union), keep in mind that foreign filings can interfere with your efforts to obtain a patent in the United States. You may need to obtain permission from the U.S. Commissioner of Patents and Trademarks before filing in foreign countries so as to avoid compromising your U.S. application.

Filing a provisional patent

A possible way to stake your claim to an invention without spending thousands of dollars on an official filing by an intellectual-property attorney is to file a provisional patent yourself. In the United States, go to the U.S. Patent and

Trademark Office Web site at `www.uspto.gov/patents/index.jsp`, and follow the instructions for provisional filing. Then get to work on your application. You don't want to leave it provisional any longer than you absolutely have to.

If you think that your invention is really valuable, but you can't file a patent application for financial reasons, you need to keep it secret (see "Protecting Trade Secrets" later in this chapter). If someone else finds out about your invention or sees your plans, he can copy you, and you won't be able to do much about it because you don't have a patent.

Even worse, if other people spread the word about your invention before you file, and the information becomes common knowledge, your application will probably be denied simply because other people are imitating your invention. Hey, I warned you. File now if you can possibly afford to do — or at least file a provisional application to show your intent and establish a timeline.

Assigning or licensing your patent rights

When your patent application is granted, you gain rights that you can assign or loan under licensing agreements. Scientists working for drug companies and electronics firms, for example, routinely assign their rights to their employers because their employment contracts require them to do so. Also, companies often license the right to use a patented invention to another business in exchange for a fee or royalty of some kind.

Such arrangements are best designed and managed with expert legal help.

Protecting Trade Secrets

You may think your application for a patent will be denied, or you may not want your control of a recipe or design to expire — which all patents eventually do — so you may decide to simply keep it a secret. Of course, this approach works best when nobody can tell what your recipe or design is just by looking at it. You may be able to keep secret a special formula for a soft drink or a manufacturing process hidden inside a locked building, so these are candidates for trade secrets.

For example, your recipe for Aunt Matilda's Magical Muffins may not be patentable, because no matter how wonderful the muffins taste, people have been baking all sorts of muffins for a long time, and you probably can't establish that your recipe is truly unique and nonobvious. Still, if your muffins taste better than the competition's, you really don't want other people to start using your recipe, so you'd better keep it secret.

If you have a new recipe or process that you think is a good candidate for trade secrecy (because it's not something others could figure out just by studying your product and it gives you an advantage over the competition), start by securing the information carefully. Limit the number of people who know the secret to the absolute minimum, and make sure that each of them signs a contract committing them to keeping it secret. Also keep all records of the secret under lock and key somewhere very secure, such as a bank vault. You have to take every reasonable precaution to keep your recipe or formula secret if you want the courts to treat it as a trade secret.

Unlike a patent, a trade secret has no legal time limits; the only limit is how long you can *keep* it secret, so you could maintain secrecy indefinitely. If your time horizon is very brief, you may also want to rely on secrecy instead of a patent, because winning patent protection can take a year or more.

Taking reasonable precautions

Here are some strategies for keeping a trade secret:

- Don't tell anyone!
- Break a process into multiple steps, and have different people do different steps so that nobody but you knows the entire process.
- Keep the recipe under lock and key in a safe-deposit box or in your lawyer's office.
- Warn your employees and anyone else working with you that the recipe is secret and that you expect them to respect your right to keep it secret.
- Require everyone who might be exposed to the secret to sign a nondisclosure agreement so that they can't tell other people what they find out.
- Minimize employee knowledge of the trade secret.
- Don't try to maintain a trade secret that overlaps with a patent, because the contents of your patent application will become public if and when a patent is granted. (If you want to keep something secret until you find out whether it's patented, however, that's fine, because patent applications are sealed until the patent is granted.)
- Maintain tight physical security to limit employee access to your secret and to prevent intruders from seeing it at all.
- Be very cautious about licensing trade secrets, because licensees may be more likely to reveal your secret accidentally than you would be.

You may also want to keep customer lists and certain business methods secret. Many companies consider their customer lists to be trade secrets.

If you've built up a valuable database of customers and don't want anyone else to use it to try to take your customers away, you'll need to maintain much tighter security over it than most companies do. For starters, don't let any salespeople have access to the master list. Give them only specific call lists generated from your master list. Salespeople may be tempted to take their call lists out of the office and use them at the next job.

Enforcing a trade secret

If you take all reasonable precautions to keep a business process secret, but a competitor manages to discover it by being exceptionally sneaky, you may be able to take that company to court and get an order preventing its use of the secret. In the United States, at any rate, courts generally take a dim view of corporate espionage and award damages to the company whose secret has been stolen.

In a well-known case, a competitor took aerial photographs of a DuPont plant being built in Beaumont, Texas. The pictures were taken before the plant's roof was completed, so from the photos, the competitor was able to figure out DuPont's secret method for making methanol. DuPont sued to prevent the company from using or disclosing the information, and the court ruled in favor of DuPont, stating that the company had taken reasonable precautions to protect its formula and should not be required to take exceptional steps to prevent all possible types of espionage.

Keeping Your Records, Writings, Plans, and Designs Secure

A business's intellectual property includes lots of information that may not qualify for any form of legal protection but that is still of high value, such as financial records, customer lists, blueprints and engineering specifications, research studies, and strategic plans.

In the past, most of this intellectual property consisted of paper documents, so companies protected their most critical documents and plans by storing them in fireproof cabinets and safes. That's still a decent idea for protecting your most important papers, but now, most important documents are stored on computers. In general, you should seek technical assistance from experts on electronic data management and protection. Following are some specific protective measures for electronic data:

✔ Limit access to electronic documents to a short list of essential people.

✔ Create password protection of the actual documents where the software program in which they were created permits. In addition, electronic documents may be stored on computers or discs that are password protected.

✔ Isolate key documents from your daily-use computers and networks.

If you're concerned about a trade secret's protection, consider keeping it on old-fashioned paper only to eliminate the risk of someone hacking into your computer network and releasing secret documents to the public.

When you audit your intellectual property, take a look at data and document security along with the more formal legal IP categories (copyrights, trademarks, patents, and trade secrets). Businesses tend to back up historical documents such as accounting and tax records, but I find that they often overlook records of creative and innovative thinking. Be sure that you include the following in your backup plans:

✔ Records of the design process for new products or processes

✔ Logs of any brainstorming or idea-generation sessions

✔ Records of creative processes that proved to be productive in the past

✔ Suggestions, proposals, and ideas that haven't been evaluated or acted on yet

✔ Market research, both quantitative (such as survey results) and qualitative (such as customer suggestions, complaints, and opinions)

✔ Innovation plans and records, such as records of research and development or new-product teams

✔ Prototypes and test results from product trials or experiments

✔ Records of failures (so that they don't have to be repeated)

Innovation-oriented intellectual property needs special protection because it's grist for the innovation mill in the future. Identify, organize, and catalog records of innovation, and make sure that the artifacts (documents, prototypes, and so on) are stored safely and, if feasible, backed up in a remote location.

Consider the businesses in New Orleans whose intellectual property was endangered by Hurricane Katrina and the subsequent flood. Some of these businesses had backed up everything on servers in other cities and were able to resume operations right away; others weren't so lucky.

Chapter 18

Building a Business Around Your Innovation

In This Chapter

▶ Evaluating your innovation to see whether it will support an entrepreneurial venture

▶ Preparing a winning business plan

▶ Finding the funding you need to move ahead

▶ Marketing your patents and inventions to licensees

I have an idea for a line of baby clothes inspired by the continual changes and wash-ups I've experienced as the father of five children. Any parent can tell you that baby stains on clothing don't come out in the wash, ruining all those lively pale pink, blue, and white infant outfits that one tends to be given as baby presents. Any parent can also tell you that those stains tend to be located in two strategic areas: on the front of an outfit and . . . well, in the diaper region. I'm thinking about establishing a brand of infant clothing called MustardSeed Nonstain Clothing for Fashion-Forward Babies. All the clothing will be mustard-colored in high-stain areas. The pretty blues and pinks can be used for trim, accent colors, and piping in low-risk areas of the garments.

If I'm serious about my idea, how do I go about building a successful business based around it? This chapter covers the basics of *entrepreneurship,* or the development of innovative new business ventures. This process of development breaks down into four key steps: doing your homework, writing your plan, funding your venture, and selling your invention.

Doing Your Development Homework

You may be ready to run with your great idea, but it's important to hold onto your enthusiasm for long enough to refine your design and figure out how to scale it up to the quantity or size needed for full implementation. You need to make sure that your innovation is ready to take to market, and the only way to determine that is by doing some homework.

Researching and refining your idea and market

If you have an idea that you think has the potential to be a good business, start by doing your internal and external homework:

✔ **Research your idea to refine it and turn it into a clear and specific thing — a prototype product or the plan for a specific business process or type of business.** This homework helps you make sure that you have more than just exciting ideas. You need to firm up those ideas and make them practical and specific.

✔ **Research your potential market — your customers and competition — to see whether your hunch is right that you'll have buyers for what you plan to offer.** No matter how well developed and clear your plans may be, it's up to prospective customers to decide whether your product is going to be popular or not. Check out existing options and pricing; explore attitudes and needs; and if possible, test the product or concept on actual customers to see what they say and do.

This research process is really just about the same as it would be for any commercial innovation. You start with what seems like a good idea and then firm it up through careful, persistent work. Do as much as you can to develop your concept into definite plans or designs first, and test your proposed offering on customers as well as you can. Build a solid case for why customers will think you have something new and special that they'll want or need.

Deciding whether to proceed with your innovation

After you've done your homework and refined your idea into a clear plan or prototype that tests well on prospective customers, you're ready to make a judgment: whether to go forward or not. This stage is an important moment of truth: You look critically at what you've developed and at what you've found out about possible market reaction to it, and then you decide whether you have a solid winner.

No matter how well you follow the standard advice on business planning and fund-raising for your new business (I cover both topics later in this chapter), you won't find entrepreneurship easy or rewarding unless you have an out-of-the-box great idea. Don't rush ahead with the first decent concept you think of. Keep thinking. Use the creativity methods in Chapters 6 through 11 to come up with a really astounding idea that powers your new business through the entrepreneurship process with ease. After you have your great idea, you can move on to business planning.

Protecting your intellectual property

Is anything about your new business concept proprietary and potentially protectable? If you have a product or process that you don't think others are on to yet, you should explore patenting it or see whether it would be best maintained as a trade secret (see Chapter 17). Similarly, a uniquely appealing design may qualify for a design patent.

If you anticipate relying on patent protection for an invention, focus on obtaining at least provisional protection before you show your invention to prospective customers or investors. In fact, don't show it to anyone except a patent attorney who's on retainer to you. When it comes to patents, be careful not to allow the details to slip out to the general public before you apply for coverage.

Next, you have trademarks to consider. Sometimes, the gist of a new business concept is a cleverly appealing brand name. If you have an idea for gathering large snail shells and packaging them in cute little house-shaped boxes under the brand name Pet Shells, you may want to try to obtain a trademark for that brand name to prevent others from using it should you actually manage to create a hot new consumer fad.

When you do your trademark and patent homework, you may find that someone else has filed a similar invention or mark already. There are two records in the U.S. trademark database for Pet Shell, one of which is dead — expired due to lack of use — and the other live. Apparently, others have tried to turn the idea into a hot consumer fad, probably without success. If you find that someone has gotten intellectual-property protection before you, you'll know that you need to go back to the drawing board and come up with another great idea. Don't write a business plan or recruit any investors for concepts that someone else already owns!

Writing a Winning Business Plan

Investors who read business plans are unimpressed by fancy spreadsheets and elaborately optimistic projections. They look for a solid concept, a great team to develop it, relatively low risk, and evidence that there are eager customers waiting to buy. Keep in mind the investor's perspective as you pull your team together and begin to write your business plan. (And consider getting your hands on a copy of William Sahlman's *How To Write a Great Business Plan* [Harvard Business Review]; visit hbr.org to purchase a copy.)

When I was just starting out in my career as an author and consultant, I sometimes had blocks of time where I didn't have any paying work lined up. I was living in Silicon Valley, home of thousands of high-tech startups, so I put out the word that I was available to entrepreneurs to ghostwrite their business plans. I was amazed by the flood of requests and worked on close to 100 plans in the several years it took for my own business to grow large enough to elbow out other work. In all that time I spent writing business plans, I found out a few things about the difference between the rare plans that raise capital easily and produce winning businesses and the many plans that don't:

- ✔ **Quality of the business concept:** The biggest difference between a winning business plan and an ordinary (meaning disappointing!) one is what happens before you start writing. It's easy to write a winning plan for a strong — really strong — concept that's well developed and researched before anyone tries to craft a business plan for it. Do your homework and make sure that you have a winning business concept before you bother with writing a formal plan. See the earlier section "Doing Your Development Homework" for how to make absolutely certain that your idea is ready to take to market.

- ✔ **Clarity of the concept:** The second major difference I saw between winning plans and unsuccessful ones was *the clarity of the concept*. Entrepreneurs who stumble over the question "Tell me about your business" aren't ready to write a good plan. Before you start outlining the plan, ask yourself this: What key fact or assertion do you want to express to readers? You need to decide on your plan's core message before you start writing because everything that you write needs to support that message.

  Suppose that you're thinking about starting a business that makes custom bikes for serious riders, especially people who want to ride in extreme conditions and need extreme off-road bikes. What's the core reason for starting this business? Your reason may be this: "Extreme riders put so many demands on a bike, and themselves, that no off-the-shelf product can meet all their needs for performance and safety." That's a good clear statement of your intended purpose. Details such as whether you'll make the frames of strong, ultralight Reynolds 953 stainless-steel tubing are secondary to the main statement of your concept.

- ✔ **Length of the concept:** It's difficult but essential to simplify your story to the point that you can make it sound compelling in a single sentence. When you can write a winning one-sentence version of your concept, you're ready to go ahead and write a full-length, formal business plan.

- ✔ **Strength of the team:** You need people who know how to build the business and are well respected and well connected in the industry. If you don't have your dream team already, hold off on writing that business plan and start recruiting partners instead. Savvy investors read the résumés before they read the plan, so make sure that you have a team that looks great on paper.

The following sections walk you through the elements that make up your business plan, with the elements listed in the order in which they appear in your plan.

Design the cover, title page, and table of contents

It's rarely necessary to bind a business plan in a fancy or flashy manner. The custom is to present it in a simple, conservative (dark-colored, for example) paper binder like the kind you can buy at any stationery store. Give it a neatly printed title, centered one third of the way down the front cover. The title should read *Business Plan for [Your Innovation]* in 16-point Times New Roman or a similar font. Center the date on the line below the title, using 12-point type in the same font as the first line. In other words, the cover should look very simple and traditional.

The title page should mimic the cover but add — two thirds of the way down, in centered 12-point matching type — an address with full contact information for the business.

On the next sheet of paper, provide a table of contents. Set the header in 16-point Times New Roman or a similar font, centered at the top of the page. Leave a couple of blank lines below the header and then list each main section, followed by a dotted line that leads to a page number in a column on the right side of the page.

At the bottom of all pages following the table of contents, center a page number in the same type style as the main text — 12-point Times New Roman or a similar font.

If you recall writing research reports or term papers for high school or college, the style I'm describing may seem familiar. It's a traditional, straightforward, professional way to present information without frills or decorations. It shows that you mean business and are serious about your proposal, instead of trying to dress it up and oversell it with fancy graphic design. Let your innovation shine in the uniqueness of your proposal itself, not in the way you present it on paper. Lenders and investors are conservative — and why shouldn't they be? They're risking their money. A flashy plan puts them off.

Write the executive summary

The Executive Summary section is the first thing that most investors and lenders read. Keep it remarkably clear, brief, and to the point. The first sentence of your summary should be the one-sentence description of your concept that I asked you to develop before you started writing (refer to "Writing a Winning Business Plan" earlier in this chapter). Complete the first paragraph by providing several sentences of general information to explain how you'll be able to do what you say you can.

Imagine that your first sentence is this: "Water Bicycles, Inc., will revolution-ize cardiovascular exercise by selling floating bikes that can be ridden for exercise and fun in pools or at beaches." This description sounds intriguing, but to show that you're serious and for real, add something such as this: "The company has applied for patents to protect its unique designs and has demonstrated their use and popularity through extensive consumer trials." A plan opening with these assertions is bound to intrigue most readers.

Next, write a paragraph starting with the words "This plan's purpose is to...." Complete the sentence by describing your fundraising or other needs, such as "obtain a bank credit line of $100,000 to fund initial production and marketing costs." Follow this sentence with a description of the benefits anticipated for the funder, such as this: "As this business plan explains, Water Bicycles, Inc., has a solid management team, a patented and appealing product, and a financial plan that should produce ample returns, allowing the business to pay down the proposed line of credit or refinance it through an equity offering within one year."

For the rest of the executive summary, touch very briefly on the main sec-tions of your plan. Devote no more than a few sentences to summarizing the main topics of the plan: operations and management, products, marketing, and financial projections. Mention the next year's budget and projected sales, but don't go into any detail. Ideally, the executive summary will be less than a page long.

Print this section (and all other sections) of your plan on one side of good-quality white paper.

Write your market analysis

The Market Analysis section of your plan needs to be thoughtful and detailed because it's where you prove there is demand for what you intend to sell. Describe the benefits of your product or process and the people who will most want to use it. Explain what the competition is offering and why your new offering will be more appealing to specific types of customers. Analyze the range of pricing in the market and show why your proposed pricing will be viewed as reasonable. If you've done any testing or market research, describe your results here too.

Make sure that you include a clear, specific description of how you'll market and sell the product, including what kind of advertising you'll do and what kind of sales force, distributors, or retailers you'll use to bring your product to market. Include marketing budgets, sales commissions, reseller markups, and other marketing costs here.

For help with sales-force design, advertising plans, pricing, and other mar-keting topics, see *Marketing For Dummies,* 3rd Edition, and *Marketing Kit For Dummies,* 3rd Edition (both from Wiley).

Prepare a company description

In the Company Description section, describe the form of organization your business is in or will take when you secure financing. (In the United States, a business can be organized as a sole proprietorship, partnership, or Subchapter S corporation.) Identify all owners and the terms of their ownership interests.

Explain your operations (what you'll produce and how) and your facilities (any offices, factories, or other places where you'll be performing work). Give any other details about the company and its operations and activities that might interest a potential investor or lender. Keep your account factual and specific, and avoid speculation and exaggeration.

Write a description of your innovation

In the Description of the Product section (or Description of the Process, depending on what sort of innovation it is), provide a clear, brief description of what you've invented; then go into sufficient detail about the specifics to convince the reader that your invention has merit and is likely to be successful.

As I say at the beginning of this chapter, you ought to have a valuable innovation of some kind. Don't start a business just to start a business. The United States has more than 100,000 gas stations, for example, and more than half of them have convenience stores, so starting a business that manages gas station/convenience stores isn't very innovative. You need to explain why yours will be better than competing stores and worth the risk of investment. In this section, explain your invention clearly and accurately, emphasizing technical information and avoiding anything that sounds like an excited sales pitch.

Provide one to three objective facts to justify your claim to innovativeness and value. You might say, "There are more than 100,000 gas stations in the United States, but ours will be the first to offer simultaneous fueling, cleaning, and computerized mechanical diagnostics, because we've invented a patent-pending service system that performs all these functions inexpensively and in the same length of time it takes to fuel a car at a traditional gas station."

Support your description of your innovation by providing information about the competition and showing why your concept is special. If you have (or are pursuing) intellectual-property protection, describe those activities here. Also, review the practicality and costs of scaling up to full commercial operation. If you haven't worked out how to scale up, admit it, and explain that you're seeking funding to work on your development of the invention.

Describe the organization and management of the business

In a section titled Organization and Management, start by introducing the management team, which should include people with the technical and business expertise to make the plan a success.

Describe the management team and employees, explaining what each of them do. Review the operations of the business in more detail here, explaining how each step will be managed and what the main concerns or risks might be. Give an overview of your staffing plans or practices, including a summary of the costs of salaries, benefit plans, and other details that will determine your overall payroll costs. Add information about your legal and accounting support; identify and give contact information for your corporate attorneys, auditors, and accountants.

Include a short section in which you discuss any major changes that you'll need to anticipate and plan for as the business grows. Will you need to move to a larger facility or hire more supervisors, for example? Describe your plans for handling such challenges.

Summarize marketing and sales

Use the Marketing and Sales section to describe the target market and the ways in which you'll inform and persuade prospective customers. Your purpose is to convince potential lenders and investors that you really can make your sales projections and produce significant and growing revenue. If you're not sure of that yourself, do some more research. Identify salespeople who will agree in writing to come to work for you when you have your funding in place, or sign contracts with distributors or sales representatives (firms that do your selling for you). Include these contracts in an appendix, and reference them in this section.

Provide an analysis of your target market — the people or businesses you think will purchase your product or service. Be specific about who you'll sell to, how many will buy per month and year, and how much they'll buy. These estimates will form the basis of your sales projections, so think them through carefully, and explain your thinking clearly enough that potential investors or lenders will be able to understand how you produced your sales forecasts.

Present your service or product line

Every product has competition. If your innovation is a big improvement over old products, that's great, but you still have to win customers, which means changing their habits and getting them to send their money your way rather than elsewhere. It's helpful to start your About the Product section with a table comparing your product's features with those of its closest competitors. Then describe the details of your product and how you plan to produce it. The main point of your description of producing the product is to show that you understand the costs involved and can realistically produce your product for less than half of what you'll be able to sell it for.

If you have any trade secrets, don't give them away, but do describe generally what advantage they give you.

If you have or expect to get patent protection (check out Chapter 17 for more on protecting your intellectual property), describe what you're applying for in general terms, but don't give your invention away unless you've already won all the patent protection you're applying for.

Reference any photographs, diagrams, specifications, or drawings of your product that appear in the appendix so that readers know to look for them there. If you think it's helpful, include one clear black-and-white photograph of the product as an exhibit in this section.

Explain your funding needs

This section is usually called Funding Needs, and it describes what the venture requires in the way of debt or equity investment. Make this section clear and simple, providing specifics about what financing you'll need and when. Your description of your financing needs should be based on the cash-flow projection in your financials. A *cash-flow projection* lists beginning cash, plus cash receipts for each month (such as investments and payments), then subtracts spending for the month to see whether you have enough cash to meet your spending needs.

Carry the net (whether negative or positive) from the first month over to the beginning of the second month in your cash-flow projection, because it's the beginning cash for that month. The second month's net becomes the third month's beginning cash position, and so forth, across the months of your cash-flow table. I recommend using a spreadsheet program such as Excel or iWork to build your cash-flow projection; they make it easy to edit and revise as you work out the details of your plans.

When you have a year or more of monthly cash flows projected in a spreadsheet, you'll be able to see your financing needs. Most new businesses have little to no sales in the first year, but lots of expenses, so the losses accumulate from month to month. Keep projecting cash flows for future months and years until you reach a point where the numbers finally shift to the positive. That's when your plan should begin producing a positive cash flow, giving you the ability to repay a loan or provide profits to investors.

When you have a detailed, careful cash-flow projection covering the entire development period until the time when cash flows turn positive, scan the monthly bottom-line numbers to identify the biggest loss — often a year or two into the venture. The amount of this loss is approximately the amount of financing you need to raise in order to fund your venture. You'll need to infuse that much cash in one or several stages during development in order to keep your business checkbook from actually going into the red.

Revise your cash-flow projection by showing sufficient investments or loans to prevent the balance from being negative. Then produce a summary of funding needs based on the timing and amounts of funds your cash-flow analysis indicates you'll need.

Be specific about how you'll use the funds — to purchase capital equipment, to cover short-term operating expenses until you reach sufficient volume to break even, or whatever else you need the funding for.

Prepare your financials

The Financials section should include three to five years' worth of historical financial statements, if you've been in business that long. Show yearly income statements, balance sheets, and cash-flow statements. If your business is a startup, of course you won't have historical statements, so you need to include only projected financials.

Your projected sales should be based on the sales projections in your Sales and Marketing section, and the costs should relate to the description of your business in the Organization and Management section.

If you don't know how to prepare income statements, balance sheets, and cash-flow statements, get an accountant to help you. To be as accurate as possible, develop a detailed list of expenses and budgets, brainstorming as many details as possible, so that you're able to build up overall expense projections from very specific guesses about component costs.

Many business plans include an analysis of the financial statements, with ratios and trends identified, much as a stock analyst might do in examining a major public corporation.

If you're planning to approach a bank for a Small Business Administration (SBA) loan, check its requirements for financial statements and exhibits. See the checklist of required papers at www.sba.gov/tools/Forms/small businessforms/fsforms/index.html, or contact the nearest SBA district office by phone for help. (For locations and contact information for all offices, see www.sba.gov/localresources/index.html).

Prepare an appendix of supporting documents

The appendix is an optional — but in my opinion *extremely* useful — part of a business plan. If you're using your plan primarily to raise funding (whether via loans, a line of credit, or equity investments), the appendix should include documents that support your funding request by showing that you're financially responsible and qualified to run a business and handle its finances. Exhibits for the appendix may include

- ✔ Credit histories for key members of the management team and for the business itself if it has been around long enough to have one

- ✔ Résumés and letters of reference for key members of the management team

- ✔ Documentation of relevant patents, trademarks, copyrights, licenses, building permits, operating permits, leases, or contracts

- ✔ Plans, diagrams, schematics, or photographs of facilities, processes, or products described within the plan

- ✔ Copies of supporting research documents, such as articles or studies

- ✔ Records such as photographs and testimonials showing the results of field tests or customer reactions

You can think of a good business plan as being a presentation of your business concept involving both "show" and "tell" elements. The main body of the plan tells your story in words and numbers, leaving the appendix to illustrate the story. Use the flexibility of the appendix to full advantage by including as many supporting and illustrative documents as you can. A business plan of 25 pages with a 30-page appendix is a potential winner because it's just long enough to provide detail without being unreadably long, and it has a convincing amount of supporting material in its appendix.

Funding Your Innovative Venture

The majority of business startups are financed informally by people who are directly involved in the business themselves or have relatives who are. The initial investments are usually modest, as are the businesses. New retail stores, home-based crafts producers or importers, and small firms specializing in equipment leasing are examples of the millions of small businesses that are started every year. How are they financed, and how well do they do?

You've probably heard that more than half of all new businesses fail in the first year. You may also have heard that successful new ventures have to apply to *venture-capital firms* — companies that raise large pools of private funding for entrepreneurial investments. Both beliefs are wrong.

The failure rate is better than people think, but not stellar. Only a quarter of new businesses fail in the first year. It takes four years for half of them to fail. After ten years, only a third remain standing, according to Scott Shane, a professor of entrepreneurship at Case Western Reserve University, who tracked a sample of startups over a ten-year period.

It's also untrue that venture capital funds most startups. Venture-capital firms provide larger investments than individual investors do, and they're often involved in the most newsworthy ventures, so they tend to seem more important than they really are. If you're starting a small, local business, you won't qualify for venture capital. However, if you're starting a business based on an innovation that has the potential for national or international success, it makes sense to ask venture capitalists to review your plan. You just might be a good match for one of them.

Pairing up with venture capitalists

Venture-capital firms generally seek to make investments of between $250,000 and $1.5 million, and they like to invest in businesses that aren't brand new, because a few years of demonstrated growth makes the investment far less risky for them. They look for entrepreneurs who have stellar résumés (high-level management or technical experience in the industry) and an innovation that promises to produce explosive growth in the next five to seven years. If your business doesn't fit this profile, don't bother trying to approach venture-capital firms.

You can locate venture-capital funds by asking a friendly stockbroker to find out what funds have been actively raising capital in recent months (indicating that they have new funding to invest). At the time of this writing, however, fund-raising by venture-capital firms is at an historic low, with only a few actively recruiting investors. As the economy regains strength, this number should rise back to a few dozen or more a year.

Plenty of venture-capital funds aren't actively raising money right now but may have money to invest. Locate them by attending regional events sponsored by an association of venture capitalists in your area. In the United States, contact the National Venture Capital Association (NVCA; www.nvca.org) for an up-to-date listing of regional organizations. Some of these groups hold occasional events in which entrepreneurs are invited to present brief summaries of their plans and get to meet potential investors.

Generally, the best way to locate lists of venture-capital firms is through published sources. Most fund-raisers have to resort to published directories in books such as *Directory of Venture Capital,* by Kate Lister and Tom Harnish (Wiley), or *The Directory of Venture Capital & Private Equity Firms* (Grey House Publishing) for master lists with contact information.

Lots of firms offer to help entrepreneurs find venture-capital financing. These intermediaries or middlemen usually live off the fees they charge entrepreneurs, and in my experience, they rarely provide much value for the money. A real venture-capital fund won't charge you to apply. It may treat you impolitely, keeping you at arm's length and not taking your anxious calls to see whether anyone has read your plan, because the firm probably reviews thousands of plans a year. As long as the firm doesn't charge you a large reading fee or other consulting fees, however, and simply agrees to add your plan to its pile for review, it probably is legitimate.

Avoid the many other firms that advertise or blog actively on the Web and are looking to make a quick buck from entrepreneurs instead of actually funding them. A good rule of thumb is to stay away if a firm wants you to pay upfront. Legitimate investors and their agents don't impose upfront fees for services.

Locating angel investors

Angel investors are wealthy people who make direct investments in startups and growing businesses. You can locate them through brokers or financial managers who provide high-end, customized wealth management services or through personal networking. Ask around; make everyone you know aware of your startup and any investment opportunities that it presents. Lawyers may also be a good source of referrals.

Some Web-based services say that they connect entrepreneurs with angel investors. I'm not sure how well this approach works, but as long as you're not spending money on the Web search, I suppose that it's worth trying. Check out businesses such as FundingPost (www.fundingpost.com) to get a feel for this option.

Compared with venture-capital firms, angel investors often look for smaller, earlier-stage investments. An investment of between $25,000 and $150,000 is about right for most angels. In exchange, they will want you to be incorporated or to establish a formal partnership with them, and they'll need legal papers giving them clear control of a portion of your firm. You'll have to negotiate with them to determine what valuation makes sense. If you're not making any money, no matter how exciting your innovation is, you're probably stuck with a low business valuation and may have to give up 10 percent to 50 percent of your equity in exchange for your first major infusion of funding (about the same percentage a venture-capital firm would take).

An experienced angel investor has probably worked with dozens of entrepreneurs and will bring a professional eye to your business plan, which is helpful. Look for an angel who can offer not only funding but also relevant management or board-level experience and who will be an asset to your board of directors.

Get a good lawyer to review your contract with an angel investor. Such an investor will have a good lawyer (if not, don't do business with him!), and you should, too.

Obtaining loans

The thing about debt is that it has to be serviced monthly and eventually repaid. If you currently have a positive cash flow for your venture and can afford to make the payments on a bank note or credit line, perhaps it's okay to apply for debt. Many entrepreneurial ventures, however, aren't far enough along to service debt reliably. Ideally, the lenders realize this situation and won't allow you to borrow enough money to get into trouble, but if they aren't wise enough to say no, you should be cautious yourself.

If you do have reliable and growing profits, you can apply to your bank or other banks in your community. Speak to a lending officer to see what products the bank has that might match your needs. If you're not quite established enough to get a bank loan, the SBA may be able to help you with a loan guarantee. Your banker should know about this option and how to apply.

Selling Your Inventions

Professional inventors generate good ideas at a faster rate than other people do. They're also good at refining ideas into viable inventions that they document clearly and well and at filing well-prepared patent applications that have a high success rate.

Sometimes, inventors build businesses based on their patents, but most inventors license their patents to established businesses. A license arrangement gives the licensee the right to use the licensor's patent in exchange for an upfront fee and a small share of profits. Licenses may be exclusive (no other licensees are allowed) or nonexclusive. Exclusivity makes sense when the licensee will have to invest in development and production before sales can commence.

If a product's patent is broadly applicable, the inventor may offer narrow exclusivity to a licensee for a specific application but reserve the right to sign up other licensees for other applications. The goal is to make sure that a well-qualified company is selling your invention in a market that it understands.

Part V
The Part of Tens

In this part . . .

Not all paths to innovation have to be complex or completely time-consuming. This part provides you with easy-to-use tips for innovating in all areas of your business and career. You'll find inspiration and practical advice on how to give your career a jolt, how to stimulate innovation in a meeting or team, how to generate more good ideas, and how to implement your ideas and plans with success.

Chapter 19

Ten Creative Ways to Boost Your Career

. . . .

In This Chapter

▶ Challenging yourself to try to make a difference through your work

▶ Taking an inquisitive approach that leads you into new areas and fresh ways of thinking

▶ Approaching work with a desire to stand out as a patiently persistent innovator

. . . .

Creativity is the secret ingredient in highly successful careers. A lot of famous people have used creativity to advance their careers more rapidly than others around them. Here are ten good ways to make your mark as an innovator and leader among your peers.

Look for Opportunities to Stand Out

Ordinary careers are made up of consistent performances, year after year. Consistency is a good way to keep your job, but it doesn't help you get ahead. Exceptional careers are made of breakthrough performances — memorable problems or situations in which you've played leading roles.

To stand out, look for a tough challenge, a difficult assignment, or a new program or invention that needs a champion to be implemented. Be the person who steps up and wrestles with the problem or opportunity of the month or year. Be a volunteer and a risk-taker. Tackle something that might really make a difference. A certain amount of boldness is necessary if you want to do anything that will be remembered.

Share Your Enthusiasm for Innovative Ideas

Many people assume that it's inappropriate to talk about new ideas and approaches in the workplace. After all, most people around you don't, so why should you? It might make you seem like a troublemaker or malcontent, right? Wrong. Many people secretly wish that things would improve in their workplaces and have private complaints and concerns about how things are done. They welcome someone who has fresh ideas and a positive attitude toward innovation. Just so long as their own necks aren't sticking out, they're happy to see someone else propose new ideas.

It's better to be the employee who suggests new approaches than any of the timid people who don't have the courage to propose an idea or point out the flaws in everyday procedures. Just make sure that you aren't too strident. Recognize that the majority of good ideas get shot down. Even ideas that get adopted have usually been shot down a few dozen times before they finally take hold, so be good humored about the process, and don't get mad if people are slow to recognize that you're right. A patient innovator is a successful and popular innovator. An impatient innovator is destined to work alone.

Look for Emerging Problems You Can Help Solve

It feels good to be part of a team that figures out how to resolve a major problem. Have the courage to dive headfirst into the most troubling area in your field, and be one of the leaders who innovates to improve it. The only caveat is that you need to pick your place of work carefully. Look for like-minded people in a situation where there's enthusiasm for change so that you don't feel hampered by traditional, narrow-minded thinkers.

Take, for example, the shortage of primary-care (general-practice) medical practitioners in the United States. This shortage is an artifact of the cost-saving pressures applied by the insurance industry, which have turned primary care into a race to see a new patient every 15 minutes and then to squeeze enough procedures into the visit to make it profitable for the medical practice. Many doctors and nurse practitioners are turned off by general practice and have gravitated toward specialties in which they make more money and have more control of the way they practice medicine.

It's smart to avoid a problematic area — or is it? Somewhere, some medical practice is going to solve the problems of primary care and create a new model that spreads across the country. The doctors who innovate to resolve the major issues of primary care will be seen as leaders in the field of medicine, and they'll have rewarding careers.

Look for Emerging Opportunities You Can Surf

Another way to be a winner is to jump on a wave that's gaining strength and looks like it will be one of the big ones that transforms society. You may find that you face a few years of uncertainty and slow growth by trying to position yourself in the vanguard of an emerging field. It's hard to know exactly when an industry will take off. Many people today have spent decades struggling to turn solar power into a major industry that replaces fossil fuel. I think that they're right, conceptually, but I'm not sure whether this will be their decade. My advice is to pick an emerging field that you're excited about and really believe in so that you'll have the satisfaction of doing meaningful work while you wait for your chance to become a billionaire.

My great-grandfather, Edwin S. Webster, and his business partner, Charles A. Stone, met at registration in the beginning of their freshman year at Massachusetts Institute of Technology. Both were intrigued by the emerging field of electrical engineering and decided to major in it. They were the first two graduates with degrees in this new major, back in 1888. The next year, because no firms were hiring electrical engineers at that time, they founded a testing laboratory and consulting firm in Boston called Stone and Webster. Their timing was impeccable. Within ten years, the firm was doing major projects all around the country, and it played a leading role as electrical plants, trolley systems, and streetlights were introduced in cities throughout the world. My great-grandfather was a smart guy who focused his career on an emerging field and put his considerable energy and enthusiasm into growing it.

Do Something You Really Enjoy

There's a strong link between creative thinking and doing, on one hand, and happiness on the other. Unhappy people don't do very much or very good creative work; they worry rather than imagine. Now apply this principle to your career. How are you going to do your best work and contribute innovative ideas to your workplace and profession? Certainly not by being unhappy and stressed in your work!

What interests you? What was your favorite summer job when you were a kid? What are your top hobbies? These sorts of questions help you zero in on the field or profession that you're most likely to make a mark in. It may seem to be less economically promising to focus on, say, knitting compared with accounting, but if you do accounting just to pay the bills and really love knitting, perhaps a shift of careers is overdue.

Start thinking about how to create a role for yourself in the world based on a genuine interest, and when you've figured out how to meet your minimum economic requirements in that field, make the switch! If you're midway into a dull career and have a bunch of dependents and a costly mortgage, it may take some years to figure out how to switch careers to something you really love, so you'll need a long-term plan with a lot of innovative thinking and entrepreneurship along the way. But even if it's for five or ten years, having a plan feels great. It took me ten years out of college to cement my plans to make a living as an author, but now I'm glad that I persisted in moving in that direction, because I love the work.

Consider Working on Commission

Careers that are based on sales commissions include real estate, investment banking, automobile sales, industrial-equipment leasing, commercial lending, insurance, and business to business sales. People who work in these careers are responsible for drumming up enough business to earn their own incomes, making them basically entrepreneurs who build personal business networks, often under the umbrella of some larger company. A real estate agent, for example, may do her own marketing and build her own roster of satisfied customers while working in a real estate company's office and competing against the other agents there.

Why work on commission? Most commission-based jobs leave you more freedom to pursue sales your own way so long as you produce. The autonomy of commission-based work is great for self-directed, motivated people who are eager to experiment with different approaches until they find a success formula that works for them. It's true that the average entry-level salesperson doesn't make much in the way of commissions and may give up after a year or two to take a "safer" job. But you're not average! The top-performing sales-people in many industries are able to build successful careers, first within the boundaries of a firm's sales force and later by going out on their own and creating their own real estate firm, sales-rep company, or other venture. (See Chapter 18 for tips on successful entrepreneurship.)

Build Two Careers at the Same Time

Some people have double majors in college, and some people have double careers. Having two careers means working two jobs, so it may not be appealing as a career strategy at first, but building two parallel career paths has many benefits:

✔ Two career tracks in different industries or fields expose you to many more opportunities than a single career path does.

✔ A *shadow career* (something that you do in your extra time, such as on weekends or in the evenings) often grows over time to become your primary activity, especially if it's the thing you most enjoy doing.

✔ By working in multiple fields or professions, you gain a breadth of experience and knowledge that allows you to see creative combinations and options that other people don't.

Study

Nothing educates the mind like education, to coin a redundant phrase. Before my own career took off fully, I used to have enough time to teach regularly in business schools in my area, and my favorite gig was teaching an evening or weekend MBA class, because my students were working adults who had decided to come back to school for an advanced degree. Adult learners are fun to teach because they're . . . well, adult! They have experience, motivation, and discipline that they probably lacked in their teen years. Many of my students from that period are now leaders in their fields, and a surprising number have made it as entrepreneurs.

But wait — why is that surprising? To be a successful entrepreneur, you need to be self-directed, motivated, and disciplined, and you need enough real-world experience to be able to imagine useful innovations. Add some new ways of thinking and a little mental training, and you've produced a recipe for innovators who will rise to the top.

I highly recommend going back to study something that you think will be useful or interesting. If you're already in school, take a course in a different department to add breadth to your studies. If you haven't been in a classroom for a while, sign up for a course at the nearest community college, or if you can't find a conveniently located classroom, take a course online. Your studies may not turn into a full-fledged degree program, but either way, taking classes will enrich your thinking and power up some parts of your brain that may not have had enough exercise lately.

Volunteer

Whether you're taking a tough work assignment that nobody else wants or helping a homeless shelter raise funds, volunteering can have a big effect on you and your career.

Volunteering is a great way to build confidence and get practice in problem-solving, leadership, and innovation. It often involves working with teams, so it strengthens your communication and facilitation skills. Also, when you offer your efforts for free, it's amazing how many doors open to you that might have stayed closed if you were looking for paid work. Volunteering is a great way to get some experience in a new field that interests you or that you think may someday be combined with your own field of work for a future innovation. Take a look around, and see what you can volunteer for right now that would enrich your own working life at the same time that it helps other people.

Champion Someone Else's Good Idea

To be a leading innovator, do you have to be the one who comes up with the next big idea? No, that's not true at all. Many people make their mark as leaders in their fields by embracing a great idea early, before other people realize its qualities, and championing its development.

There's a time window — often a really big one — between invention and rapid spread. During that period, an innovation may stagnate or spread very slowly, as early adopters try to get the kinks out and make it work. The idea of electronic medical records, for example, was around for several years before it began to gain traction in actual medical practices. During that time, a few innovators saw the potential for digitizing medical records and began to try to make it work. Some of their efforts failed, but others emerged as industry standards. I wish that I'd been involved in one of the successful companies supplying medical-records systems, because they've found a fast-growing market niche and can hardly supply the demand.

Take a look around your industry or workplace, or in one of the fields in which you volunteer or do part-time work. Does someone have a really good idea or invention that just hasn't caught on yet? Start studying it. Experiment with it in your own work. Blog about it. Go to industry conferences, and lead discussion groups about how to make it work. Being an early champion of someone else's breakthrough idea is a great role, and without such champions, many innovations would fail to catch on.

Chapter 20

Ten Tips for More Innovative Meetings

In This Chapter

▶ Turning ordinary meetings into extraordinary innovation sessions

▶ Finding time for creative problem-solving

▶ Getting everyone involved in the thought process

Do you like meetings? In surveys, almost all people say that they dislike the meetings they have to attend in their workplaces. As a consequence, meetings are shorter and fewer than they were in earlier decades. Besides, everyone's so busy that they have precious little time to talk. They need to stay at their desks, cranking out work that was due yesterday.

Fewer face-to-face meetings, however, mean that far fewer innovative ideas come up, because many of the best ideas arise in discussions at meetings. The best solution to the I-hate-meetings syndrome is to run better meetings rather than cut back on them. This chapter contains ten tips for making meetings count toward your monthly quota of brilliant breakthroughs.

Ask for Original Information and Ideas

Questions such as these help open a meeting to creative ideas and insights:

✔ "What else could we think about before deciding what to do?"

✔ "Are there any fresh ideas or suggestions?"

✔ "Does anyone know anything that we haven't discussed yet or have new information or a different viewpoint?"

Challenging the group to come up with fresh ideas or new sources of information almost guarantees increased creative thinking. You have a variety of human minds sitting around the table; use them fully by asking each person to make a unique contribution to your meeting. Nodding doesn't count.

Reorganize Your Meetings, Not Your Staff

How many times have you seen something like this in the business news?: "XYZ Co. announced that it is reorganizing its Z division and consolidating the A, B, and C departments into a new strategic business unit reporting directly to the chief executive officer." Behind every such announcement smacking of redrawn organizational charts is a performance problem that made the CEO think she needed to pay more attention to the A, B, and C departments (or wherever the problem happened to be). Reorganization only helps if disorganization is the root cause of the performance problem, however, and it rarely is.

The next time you or your boss starts talking about redrawing the organization chart to solve some problem, suggest holding a problem-solving meeting instead. Run it as a straight-ahead, no-politics session with freewheeling generation of any and all possible ideas and solutions. See what comes up. You'll probably get a better, less drastic solution than redrawing the organization chart.

Re-solve Old Problems

It's a great exercise to dredge up old problems and revisit them. One problem per staff meeting and a limit of ten minutes are good rules for keeping this exercise from overstepping its bounds. Hindsight often reveals a better way to solve a problem, and it's interesting to see what improvements you can make on the old solution. Sometimes, you end up discarding the previous solution and replacing it with a far better solution. Now, that's a productive use of meeting time! It also signals something essential to creative enthusiasm and the innovative spirit: Nothing's carved in stone, and a better idea is always welcome.

A software company in Palo Alto, California, faced a shortage of parking for visitors. It solved the problem by requiring lower-level staff members to park off-site (across the street at a commercial lot or in any spaces available at meters along the street). Also, all senior staff members were required to park in the back of the parking lot and leave the best spaces next to the door free for visitors. Problem solved. But was the solution the *best* solution?

Forcing lower-level staff members to pay to park on the street was a major sore point that hurt morale — an unintended negative consequence of the plan. A better idea came up in a staff meeting later: Rotate access to the limited spaces in the company lot among all staff members. Also, someone pointed out that the visitor spaces weren't needed most days and that the company rarely held a large enough gathering to require them all for visitors. It would be perfectly feasible to anticipate days when all the spaces were needed and days when only a few would have to be blocked off for drop-by visitors. Staff members whose turn it was to park on the street could use the open visitor spaces on a first-come basis. With these two changes, the parking situation seemed to be more under control, and morale went up.

Use a "Sideways Thoughts" Board

An old-fashioned military acronym, TBDL, used to mean *to be decided later.* I've attended some meetings in which a chart pad or section of a chalkboard was designated as the TBDL area, where people could write notes about questions or suggestions that didn't fit the agenda item being discussed. It's a good idea and should be done more often. The meeting needs to stay on topic to cover each agenda item, but discussions often raise other thoughts and questions that deserve discussion time too.

When I use this technique, I set up a chart pad with *Sideways Thoughts* written across the top of the page. Sideways thoughts — those ideas and questions that arise through association during discussion of a main agenda item — are well worth capturing and reviewing later for insights that could lead to future innovations. (I don't use TBDL because I don't like to limit the list to decisions. Usually, the most productive sideways thoughts are questions or suggestions, not formal decisions that need to be made.)

Pay Close Attention to Body Language

When you meet around a table in a conference room, as people so often do in workplaces, you have an opportunity to tune into body language, which expresses things that verbal and written communications don't. The most important messages embedded in body language are emotions — how you feel about yourself, other people, and the topics of conversation. Usually, people are unconscious of their nonverbal messages, but if you pay attention to posture, facial expression, and tone of voice, you can become a student of body language and then use it to draw more and better information and ideas from those who are attending the meeting with you.

Avoid making these all-too-common body-language errors at business meetings:

✔ **Withdrawal** is signaled by leaning back, facing away from the person who's talking, and by doing things like texting or reading while others are talking. It sends a strong message that you're not interested in the topic and also may be interpreted as saying that you don't like or respect the other people in the meeting. Withdrawal behavior shuts down creative discussion and prevents people from speaking their minds or sharing all their information.

✔ **Contraction** is signaled by looking down, bowing the head, drooping the shoulders, and slumping. It sends the signal that you're depressed or secretly defiant and makes people think that you're not onboard or part of the team.

✔ **Expansion** is signaled by expanding the chest, leaning back, holding the back straight and head up, and sometimes by raising the shoulders. It sends a strong message that you think you're superior to others and don't care what they think. It's associated with high status and arrogance.

When you've familiarized yourself with the three nonverbal postures that prevent innovation in meetings, it's time to master *approach* — the behavior that boosts innovative discussions and stimulates free and open sharing of information and ideas. Approach is signaled by leaning forward slightly, squaring up to face the person speaking, and making a fair amount of eye contact with the speaker. You can also nod or use encouraging short phrases such as "Okay," "Uh-huh," "Interesting," and "What else?" to keep the flow of discussion going.

Approach signals interest in the speaker and the topic. Without the subtle encouragement of approach behaviors, people don't speak freely in meetings. Whether you're in the boss's seat at the head of the table or holding down one of the other seats around it, you should use approach behaviors to encourage whoever is offering a contribution to the meeting. That way, people will *feel* encouraged to contribute their thoughts.

If you're interested in reading more about nonverbal behavior and communication, I recommend the classic book on the topic, Albert Mehrabian's *Nonverbal Communication* (Aldine Transaction).

Control Routine Topics Tightly

The problem with many meetings is that they wander off topic and waste time on trivialities. If you want to go over the week's progress, by all means do — but make sure that each person's progress report is brief and to the point. Limit individual reports to two minutes or less. (Handouts can be used if there's too much information for a brief review.) Keep questions relevant and brief, and don't let anyone grandstand by talking at length during the progress review.

Many of the topics on meeting agendas can be handled with discipline and focus. Most topics are best handled with a fairly high level of control so as to keep the meeting on track and prevent anyone from wasting others' time. A tightly run meeting gets through its agenda quickly, much to the relief of the attendees. Allow extra time for low-structure discussion of any interesting topics that may be on your mind or that have been posted to the Sideways Thoughts board (refer to the earlier section "Use a 'Sideways Thoughts' Board") during the structured part of the meeting.

Schedule 50-minute meetings with 30 minutes' worth of agenda items to allow for 20 minutes of creative thinking at the end. Use the time to brainstorm about a problem or opportunity, or simply open the floor for general discussion and see what interesting ideas or problems come up. By covering your agenda items promptly and with discipline, you leave plenty of time for creative discussion during the meeting. This facilitation method of tight followed by loose takes care of today's business and also allows innovative thinking about the future.

Control or Exclude Spoilers

Spoilers are those people who rain on your creative parade. They come in various flavors:

- ✔ Difficult people who complain and demand all the attention during a meeting

- ✔ Self-styled experts who always shoot down ideas and insist that they're the only ones who know what will work

- ✔ Contrarians who like to argue and debate and who leap to criticize new ideas before they've even been fully formed

- ✔ Pessimists who grumble and like to share their bad news

It takes only one spoiler to ruin a meeting and make most of the other people withdraw. It's really, really hard to generate good ideas or do creative problem-solving with a spoiler at the table. That's why you have to insist that the spoiler stop his spoiling behavior at once. If not, get the person out of the meeting as soon as possible, and don't invite him to the next one. (Yes, appropriate meeting behavior should be part of employee job descriptions so that incurable spoilers can eventually be fired.)

Brainstorm at Least Once a Month

How often should you stop and think about your work instead of just doing it? The answer depends on the level of innovation you need or want to achieve, but the range is somewhere between once a day and once a month. If you hold fewer than a dozen brainstorming sessions a year, you're really not making even the minimum commitment to innovation. It's all well and good to study innovation and know how to facilitate creative groups, but the point is that you actually have to *use* the techniques in this book, not just read about them.

I can't find any surveys showing how often the average business asks its employees to participate in a full-blown idea-generation or brainstorming session, but in my own experience of visiting hundreds of workplaces, I'm sorry to say that I don't think the average employee is asked for ideas more than once a year at best. Ramp it up, guys! If we don't ask ourselves and our co-workers and employees to imagine a better future, we won't create one.

Ask for Multiple Alternatives

Regardless of the topic of a meeting, there's almost always a decision to be discussed. Some bosses just announce their decisions, preferring an autocratic style. (But what style do employees like? A more participative one, of course.)

To get better input for decision-making, use meetings to generate three to five viable alternatives. Then examine the pros and cons of each alternative and make your selection. The result is bound to be better than the first option that sprang to mind, and by including the group in your thinking process, you've used the meeting to generate buy-in as well as better decisions.

Meet Somewhere New and Different

If the weather's good, take your group to the lawn in front of your building (if there is one) or to the nearest park for a brown-bag lunch and informal staff meeting. Or hold your meeting in the private dining room of a local restaurant and treat everyone to a company lunch. If a restaurant doesn't fit your needs or budget, look for a different location within your own company, such as a large conference room or one with a better table than where you usually meet.

The idea behind changing your venue is that the environment influences the mood of the group and may be used to loosen up people's thinking and encourage creative expression. A fun or attractive environment stimulates free thinking. A fancy, formal environment signals that the meeting is special and its subject is an important one. A meeting on the shop floor or in the warehouse signals that you want everyone to roll up their sleeves and work on the details of a production or other process. Adjust the environment to fit your agenda and signal the kind of participation you expect from those present.

Chapter 21

Ten Ways to Stimulate Your Creative Genius

In This Chapter

▶ Developing a habit of persistent problem-solving and invention

▶ Avoiding common beliefs and assumptions that blind you to fresh insights

▶ Beefing up your creative muscles by doing creative things and spending time with creative people

*H*ow do you come up with really brilliant ideas when and where they're needed? If you can do that, you can do anything. Doors open to those who have better ideas. And it feels good — no, great — to be the author of a breakthrough business strategy or the inventor of a great new product or process.

But how can you power up your creative genius and produce more and better big ideas? Here are ten tips that range from specific practices you can try to lifelong habits you may want to adopt.

Persist, Persist, Persist

Are geniuses born or made? Talent, we assume, appears early in life. Child prodigies are so remarkably brilliant that they receive special recognition from the beginning and grow up into leading thinkers, composers, or athletes, just as their proud parents and the rest of society expects them to. Wolfgang Amadeus Mozart began composing at the age of 5, history tells us. What were you doing at the age of 5?

We don't listen to or perform Mozart's early compositions, however; we know him for his mature work. It was the fact that he loved music from an early age that explains why he was an excellent performer in his teens and composed really great work in his 20s. He had, by virtue of his love of music and the support of his musical family, devoted more than a decade to practice and study by the time he was in his teens. What modern science tells us is that practice makes perfect, and talent is a relatively minor contributor to the success stories of leading scientists, musicians, athletes, artists, entrepreneurs, and inventors.

The trick is to focus, practice, and learn — persistently and for a fairly long time. It takes time to become a sudden success. Lots of time. Thomas Edison invented a light-bulb filament that wouldn't burn out right away through the simple but tedious process of testing every material he could think of. He performed hundreds of unsuccessful tests, more than anyone else, so he learned more about how different materials performed and eventually hit on the right one.

Have faith in your own potential for creative genius! By persisting where others give up, you can and probably will find a better solution to a problem, or a better design or invention. It's the persistent people whom history recalls as having been geniuses. Heck, if your ideas are important enough, people may even make up stories about your amazing early talent — whether you actually exhibited any or not.

Work on BIG Problems

Most people spend most of their time solving small problems and ticking items off endless to-do lists. A working life ruled by details is all well and good, but it doesn't add up to any breakthroughs. Take time — at *least* one day a week — to focus on something big. That's the biggest secret of successful innovators. They elbow aside the mundane and routine stuff and actually find time to focus on something major, such as

- A big question, like how to replace fossil fuels with renewable energy, how to prevent breast cancer, or how to modernize an old family business to give it growth potential for the new generation
- A big problem, like how to turn around a failing business or what to do with an empty old warehouse or factory on the edge of town
- A big opportunity, like how to contribute to the challenging goal of making airports and airplanes more secure from terrorist attacks

Major questions, problems, and opportunities are the stuff of creative genius for the simple reason that if you contribute solutions, you will be hailed as a hero, not just given your cost-of-living increase.

If you're not focusing on anything big, you're wasting your creative energy entirely on the little things of life. I agree that little things *do* matter; it's helpful to remember to buy dog food and diapers on the way home from work, or to pay your electric bill before the power company shuts the power off. But little things don't add up to anything big; they just add up to a long to-do list. Remember to take the time to focus on something big too.

I don't like shopping lists, because I view chores as getting in the way of more important thinking and work, but sometimes I have to sally forth with a shopping list. Here's something you can do to make grocery (or any) shopping more productive: At the bottom of every list, add a big question you want to think about, and then think about it as you walk through the aisles, filling your cart. I don't know how many trips to the grocery store it will take you to get a breakthrough idea, but I do know that, eventually, you'll come up with something good.

Rotate Among Three Knotty Problems

Challenge yourself with not one, not two, but three major puzzles or problems at the same time. See whether you can invent three better products, processes, or solutions. This advice may seem counterintuitive, because it's hard enough to crack just one tough innovation puzzle, but you increase your chances of having a breakthrough idea by working on several main problems simultaneously. Research and think about one topic until you feel stale or at a dead end; then set the folder aside and turn to the next one. When you get stuck on it, go to the third and then back to the first.

Being able to set a tough problem aside for a while helps you be persistent. Another benefit of rotating among three problems is that you increase the chances of having a breakthrough by a factor of three. If you solve even one of them, you'll have a good invention or solution in hand that you can work on implementing. The third benefit of this approach is that you often get cross-fertilization of ideas; your work on one problem can enrich your approach to another.

Pick problems or puzzles that would benefit from an innovation, but don't necessarily feel that you have to make a breakthrough right away. That way, you can take your time and wait for an "aha" idea.

Most inventors use this technique of rotating among multiple puzzles or problems. They may give the impression that they're always completing a project, but actually, they're harvesting the ones that bore fruit and abandoning others that didn't. Give yourself some flexibility by looking into more than one puzzle, problem, or possible invention, and pushing ahead on whichever one seems to be moving forward most easily.

Eat Ideas for Lunch

Try this procedure for working out a solution to a problem or coming up with a clever idea to take advantage of an opportunity:

1. **Invite a creative friend to lunch at a diner or other informal restaurant where scribbling ideas on a large pad of paper won't elicit too many stares.**

2. **Explain the ground rules to your friend: You're both to brainstorm about the topic of your choice, and you have to suggest an idea to earn the right to take a bite.**

3. **Order sandwiches or salads, because hot entrees may grow cold before you fill your pad with ideas!**

You'll need to pick up the tab, of course, but in exchange, you get a brainstorming partner for however long it takes to fill a piece of paper with ideas and eat your lunch. If you don't follow this three-step process, you'll find yourself chatting with your friend about other things and forgetting to focus on the brainstorming topic. That's why you have to establish, and follow, a strict idea-for-a-bite rule!

What if you get through your sandwiches and still don't have the breakthrough idea you need? There's only one thing to do: Order dessert.

Work on Your Self-Talk

Those little voices inside your own head determine success and failure to a large extent. You're not crazy to listen to them; in fact, that's the sanest thing you can do. Pay special attention to the way you explain notable events to yourself. Notable events are, generally speaking, either notably good or bad.

If you think about bad events as being your fault, you're setting yourself up for pessimism and blocking your creative genius. Watch out for self-blaming, and if you start to do it, make a point of listing the external factors that contributed to a bad event. Rather than blame yourself entirely for having an automobile accident, for example, remind yourself that it was dark and icy, that the roads hadn't been properly sanded, and that the other driver was going way too fast.

Watch out for overgeneralizing a bad event too; that tendency also depresses your creative impulse. Rather than conclude that you "can't manage money well" after investing in a retirement fund that does poorly, tell yourself something productive like "I won't repeat the specific investment strategy I used in that case, because it didn't work well."

When it comes to good events, do the opposite: Generalize, and take the credit! Yes, you're brilliant; that's why you made that big sale. And if you can make one big sale, you can make many. You have the potential to be the top salesperson in your entire industry! This kind of positive self-talk actually does help increase your optimism and drive, giving you energy for creative problem-solving.

Creativity and innovation are tightly tied to mood. Hopefulness and optimism produce innovation. Work on your state of mind first, and the innovative behavior you want will naturally follow.

For more information on how to get your self-talk right, see Martin Seligman's classic books *Learned Helplessness* and *Learned Optimism* (Knopf Doubleday) and his summary of his findings, *Authentic Happiness* (Simon & Schuster), or do the exercises in the "Transforming Negative Talk" booklet, available at Trainer's Spectrum (`www.tspectrum.com/communication_negtalk.htm`).

Correct Your Mental Biases

It's hard to see problems and projects 100 percent clearly when you're human (which I assume that all my readers are). Humans have these big brains that are good at thinking but have some curious blind spots built into them. We have certain biases that lead us to make incorrect assumptions. Here are some of the biggest and most persistent mental biases:

- ✔ **The belief that correlation implies causation:** If two things are associated or occur together, we naturally assume that one is causing the other.

  If people who smoke cigarettes also tend to suffer from heart disease, for example, we leap to the conclusion that smoking causes heart disease and that to prevent heart disease, people need to stop smoking. In fact, research partially confirms this conclusion; smoking does increase the risk of heart disease. But it's not the root cause, and if we focus only on preventing smoking, we'll never eliminate all heart disease. More to the point, it might be productive to ask, "Could something be causing both smoking and heart disease?" In other words, what if you look for a *third factor* that drives the first two?

  If you apply this thinking to the example of heart disease and smoking, you might find that certain kinds of stress cause heart disease, which might get you thinking about ways to reduce or manage stress as part of a public-health strategy. Perhaps it would be more effective to help people manage their stress than to focus on creating an antismoking campaign. Nobody's doing that, however, probably because the mental bias to see correlation as causation is a strong one.

- ✔ **The tendency to satisfice:** *Satisficing* (a term coined by 1978 Nobel laureate in economics, Herbert Simon) means to make a hasty choice among alternatives instead of looking more systematically for an ideal option. When people shop for apartments, for example, they often satisfice by signing a lease for a place that has some of the qualities they wanted but not all. Why don't they keep searching? Are they too busy or afraid that all the good apartments will be gone soon? It's not clear why people stop searching and accept a less-than-perfect option, but it's clear that we do.

Satisficing saves us time and trouble, so it's fine for minor decisions. But when it comes to deciding what business strategy to use, which job to take, or whether to stop brainstorming about a major challenge or keep looking for more ideas, you definitely don't want to satisfice. You want to *optimize* — seek the best option (or at least a really good one).

When we accept mediocre options and choices, we turn our backs on our potential to create optimal solutions and don't use our capacity for innovation. The next time you find yourself saying, "Oh, well, I guess it's good enough," stop, give yourself a kick in the rear, and ask, "Or is it? What if I pour a little more creative energy into this problem? Maybe I can find an optimal solution, not just an adequate one!"

✔ **The tendency to let groups of people reach incorrect or inadequate conclusions:** There are a lot of *group decision-making biases,* each with its own peculiar flavor:

- Groups can be too polite, with each member being afraid to say something critical about a proposed course of action of decision, even though it's not a very good one.

- Groups can defer to a dominant person rather than get into conflict with him, even though other members may have valid alternative points of view that aren't being considered fully.

- Groups tend to talk and think about what they have in common — their shared information and knowledge base — and to fail to take advantage of the unique perspectives of people whose knowledge isn't shared by the rest of the group.

- Groups, just like the people who make them up, can be quite illogical, failing to apply general principles or abstract beliefs to specific decisions.

In business, people often make key decisions in small groups — management teams, boards of directors, product development teams, and so on. I recommend reading about group decision-making biases and failures to arm yourself against the many ways in which groups so easily get things wrong.

Nurture a Secret Project

Your boss is probably never going to assign you the task of going off and thinking up something brilliant. She's going to expect you to be at your desk, logging the face time needed to prove that you're a diligent worker. The challenge you face is finding time in your overcrowded daily schedule to daydream, imagine, brainstorm, or free-associate.

In the daily press of work, you need to step back and ask really big questions, like these:

✔ What's the future of my industry, and how can I help bring it about?

✔ What's the biggest, most challenging problem in our business right now, and how can I help solve it?

✔ What needs inventing right now, and why don't I just sit down and invent it?

Why indeed? If you tried to sit down and think about ideas for an important invention, your boss would notice that you weren't shuffling papers or punching the keypad of your computer and would tell you to stop napping and start working.

For many of us, it's unfortunately necessary to sneak the time needed to do any major creative thinking. Adopt a special, personal project or problem to stew on and don't tell your boss or co-workers about it unless you begin to see some practical solutions that you can propose. Until then, keep working in secret, between boring routine tasks, and keep your notes filed away in some private place. Oh, and don't feel bad about this particular bit of dishonesty. It's to everyone's ultimate good for you to try to come up with a brilliant breakthrough idea. After all, *someone's* got to.

Cross-Train in Art

It takes years to get really good at something as difficult as drawing, playing guitar, flamenco dancing, or cooking gourmet meals, but even if you never achieve full mastery, the journey offers many benefits. Studying and practicing anything artistic are great ways to get in touch with and strengthen your creative self.

Join a creative-writing group, for example. Please! If you're not actively exercising your imagination, you aren't going to come up with any brilliant ideas or inventions. It's just as plain and simple as that. The arts, which are by nature extremely creative, offer a great way to train the same mental muscles that you need to be a brilliant innovator at work.

Do Art Projects with Your Kids

Here's an interesting addendum to my tip about using the arts to build your innovation skills: Young people used to do a lot more art in the course of their academic careers. It was common to include arts in the curriculum in many schools, and it was also common for many children to take music lessons and to draw, paint, act, work with clay, or make jewelry and crafts for fun. Now schools are cutting back on arts funding to concentrate on science, math, and reading skills, while at home, children watch TV or play computer games.

What's lost by not having children engage in artistic expression every day? Certainly, the arts are poorer, but even more important, the imagination is poorer. What we learn from the arts about creative thinking, problem-solving, and expression translates strongly and directly into our working lives. If you have children at home, you may want to consider doing arts or crafts with them so as to share the benefits and to help prepare them to be innovative thinkers and doers in their adult working lives.

Start or Join an Inventors' Club

Many groups of people meet regularly to share ideas and support one anothers' efforts to invent cool things or to commercialize their cool inventions. Like-minded people are always helpful and inspiring to be around, and where can you find more innovators in one place and time than at an inventors' association meeting? Do a search for inventors' clubs or associations near you, or go to the United Inventors Association Web site (www.uiausa.org) and look at its list of links to local clubs for contacts near you.

If a club isn't near enough for you to attend meetings easily, consider starting your own. People in other associations and clubs can give you advice about organizing your own inventor's group. You might start with the Houston Inventors Association, which posts a helpful article, "How to Start an Inventors Club," on its Web site, www.inventors.org/invclub/h2start.htm.

If you have a great idea or design of your own that might be unique and worth patenting, don't share it with members of an inventors' club — not until you've actually filed for and received the needed patent protection. Otherwise, a more experienced inventor might beat you to the patent punch.

Chapter 22

Ten Tips for Better Implementation of Your Ideas

• •

In This Chapter

▶ Anticipating problems

▶ Building a strong team to maximize your chances of success

▶ Keeping clear records of your spending and your work

▶ Handling the conflicts and stresses of innovation

• •

*T*he best ideas and plans don't amount to successful innovations unless they're implemented well. Implementation is as important as creativity — sometimes more so.

Disorganization, disappointing initial results, or unanticipated flaws in the design or plan can derail many projects before they've really had a chance. Follow these tips to reduce the pain and suffering — and the high failure rate — of implementation.

Develop Your Team First

You have a great idea or plan, and you're eager to implement it. I would be, too! However, a plan is only as good as the people who are expected to execute it. Before you start to work on your development or implementation activities, take a little time to form a strong team by following these guidelines:

✔ **Make sure that you have the right group — a team with the needed expertise and capacity.** You don't want to have to change personnel or add more people because you failed to anticipate your staffing needs. The right group should be working together from the get-go to have a smooth, easy implementation.

✔ **Talk about everyone's quirks, rough edges, and pet peeves.** Teams that share their requirements and concerns upfront are better able to work together because they know not to push one another's hot buttons.

A certain amount of accommodation is always needed, and it's better to know about personal styles and needs upfront than to discover them later, when people have bitter complaints and are too angry to discuss things with level heads. (Consider taking a personality test such as The Big Five self-assessment, available at www.tspectrum.com, and comparing your results to help understand differences and how to accommodate them.)

✔ **Make the ground rules clear.** Be explicit about what constitutes doing a fair share and who's expected to do what. You get the RED (rules, expectations, and demands) out of group dynamics by discussing these items. Anyone who can't live with them should have the option of opting out *before* he or she becomes integral to the work and hard to replace.

✔ **Develop a sense of belonging by giving the team a strong identity.** Brand the team with a name that everyone likes, give it a logo, and make sure that everyone is onboard with a big-picture vision of what you want to accomplish. Innovation should be exciting, so take time to articulate an enthusiastic view of what the team is trying to accomplish.

✔ **Be sure about the purpose and focus.** Don't pull a group together to do one thing and then change your mind and tell it to do something else. Changing the purpose undermines your credibility as an innovation leader and hurts team morale. Do your strategic planning first so that when you charter a team, you'll be clear about the project and can give team members clear instructions.

With these tips in mind, you can form a strong team that bonds around a motivating development goal. That's what most innovations need to succeed.

Plan for the Worst

As the old saying goes, what can go wrong, *will* go wrong! Here are some of the things that can go wrong as you try to implement your innovation:

✔ Costs spiral out of control, and you have to give up before completion.

✔ Others sabotage the project because they think it will compete with their own projects or threaten their departments or budgets.

✔ A key assumption (about technology, more often than not) proves to be incorrect, and you have to go back to the drawing board to try to save the project with another approach or invention.

✔ Key people leave, taking some of the necessary knowledge with them and leaving the remaining team members unable to complete the project.

✔ Everything's going fine, but a key source of funding or overhead support dries up, leaving you short of the resources needed to complete the project.

✔ The innovation proves to be a success, but there's conflict about who developed it and who owns the intellectual property.

When you're developing your ideas, you need to be a confirmed optimist with a positive, creative outlook and a deaf ear to critics and naysayers. But as soon as you finalize a design or plan and begin to implement it, you need to switch mental gears and become a cautious pragmatist with a pessimistic streak.

After roughing out your plans, take at least a full day for your team to brainstorm things that can go wrong with the plan. Make a thorough, pessimistic list; then sort it according to how fatal to the project each problem would be and how likely it is to occur. Very fatal, fairly likely problems deserve immediate planning to prevent them, and if you have to budget time and money for prevention, by all means do. It's reasonable to include some preventive work for several of the major problems that could be fatal to your project. If you work within a large organization, for example, you may need to spend some time building political support to minimize the chance that others will sabotage your project.

Other potential problems may not need any immediate action because they haven't actually occurred (yet . . .), but you should develop contingency plans for as many problems as you can. That way, you've already thought about how to shift course and work around various problems, should they occur. If you're counting on a particular technology becoming commercially available in time for you to purchase a part for your new product, give some thought to alternative designs that don't rely on the new technology. If the technology is late to market, you'll be stuck without a key part for your product unless you have a backup plan in mind.

A well-planned development project includes some contingency plans for what to do when various things go wrong. It's a bit like bringing your umbrella to work: If you make contingency plans, you'll most likely be pleasantly surprised and will never need to use them.

Account for Each Project Separately

From the first time you purchase anything, the innovation should be a separate accounting entity. Give it a project name and code (if you're using a computer-based accounting system), or simply start a set of files or books for it that you can enter into an accounting program or electronic spreadsheet later. Whatever you do, just make sure that you track time, money, and the use of supplies or assets day by day, over the entire life of the project.

By accounting for each development project separately, you'll know what you're spending, how much you've invested, and what you'll need in returns to make the innovation profitable. Also, it'll be easier to project future expenses, which is a good idea when you update your plans.

What if the project fizzles and you never implement the innovation? All the costs are potential tax deductions, provided that you accounted for them clearly from the beginning.

Also, if you're an entrepreneur and hope to develop your invention to the point at which you can attract outside investors, you'd better have accurate, detailed records of what you've invested in it to date. Without those records, you'll have a hard time showing how much your own investment is — and won't get paid back for it with an appropriate share of equity.

Document Failures

It's human nature to want to forget failures and mistakes. In innovation, however, it's amazingly helpful to have detailed records of anything that goes wrong. Most projects suffer setbacks. The projects that ultimately succeed are the ones in which the development team learns from setbacks.

To learn from experience, you have to document and study it. Figure out what went wrong and why. Clarify what processes or materials you used and what alternatives you could try next time. Good records allow you to evaluate the innovation intelligently and learn rapidly from experience.

What if you reach an impasse, or something goes so terribly wrong that you have to abandon the project? You still need to document the problem before you close the project down. It's amazing how many innovations proved to be a little ahead of their time. In a few years, revisit old failures to see whether technology has caught up with them and you can now find a good solution to a problem that seemed insurmountable before.

Differentiate Owners from Workers

I used to help Silicon Valley entrepreneurs write their business plans when they were ready to approach venture-capital firms for major funding. In 90 percent of the ventures I saw, there was conflict about who ought to get a share of equity when the venture funding came in or when the company went public or was acquired by some major industrial, electronic, or pharmaceutical firm.

In the early days of a new venture, the lines between founders and employees blur easily. Some people may think that they're working at reduced salaries in exchange for a chance to profit from the venture when it succeeds, but if they don't have formal, written documents proving that they own shares, they won't get a dime when the next round of investment comes in. What they may get instead is an aggressive lawyer who will harass the founders or owners and quite possibly scare investors away. Nobody wants to invest in a startup team whose members are lawyered up and angry at one another.

A similar problem arises with many patent filings. Who are the inventors? Is a lab assistant an inventor, or was she just doing work for hire? She may think that she contributed an important idea to the final design, but the senior scientists may disagree. Then there's the question of how the inventors assigned the rights. Did they develop their patentable invention while working for an employer that thinks it ought to control the rights, or did they come up with the key ideas on their own time?

To prevent confusion and conflict about ownership and intellectual-property questions, clarify every role from the very beginning. Most people who will contribute to your project will be employees or contractors working on a work-for-hire basis, and the terms of their employment ought to specify that they won't have any legal interest in the innovation. (See Chapter 17 for more information about managing your intellectual property.)

Communicate

If you're developing a prototype product all by yourself, all you need to do is make sure that your patent attorney knows what you're up to. But usually, innovation involves a growing number of people as the project progresses. Any new development, whether it's a patentable product, a new business process, or an exciting new ad campaign, is going to require cooperation within a core project team, as well as periodic contributions from an ever-expanding circle of occasional contributors.

Communication is key to keeping all the contributors on track and avoiding errors, confusion, and rework. I can guarantee that no two members of your team see the project exactly the same way or have exactly the same ideas about how to complete it, what the specifications should be, or any other details. Unless you make everyone talk regularly, in detail, about what they've been doing and what they plan to do next, things will go wrong.

Although constant communication can seem to be boringly detail oriented, hold weekly (at least) project meetings — in person if possible, or by videoconference or teleconference — to go over who's doing what. I guarantee that every meeting will uncover at least one point of confusion or misunderstanding that you'll be glad you cleared up.

Avoid Burnout

Take a break. You deserve it. Even if you don't think that your results are sufficient to earn you a break, I'm sure you *need* one. People suffer burnout when they're working on the scale-up and implementation of innovations. Burnout is a common problem because the work creates a sense of urgency.

Innovating is exciting and tense and can be very rewarding emotionally, but it can also be highly stressful. Manage your health, and keep your energy up so that you have the strength and resilience to see the project through to the end, even if unexpected problems arise and the timeline has to be pushed back. Good emotional health is essential to successful innovation.

Resolve Conflicts (Don't Avoid Them)

Disagreements can and should arise during development and implementation. There are difficult decisions to be made, and you often have to make them under time and cost pressures. The core team of innovators has an emotional stake in making the idea work. People get more emotionally involved in innovation than in regular work, and the result is conflict.

People use a variety of styles or approaches to deal with conflicts. Avoidance, accommodation, competition, and compromise are four of the most common styles (see Chapter 13). A development or implementation team needs to use a fifth style for resolving conflict: collaboration. To collaborate effectively, each party to the conflict needs to share concerns honestly, clearly, and fully, with no holding back, no politicking, no deception, and no overasking in the hope of winning ground from more-accommodating teammates.

A collaborative approach is important in innovation teams because it produces the highest-quality solutions to conflicts. It also preserves and in most cases improves the working relationships within the team. In other words, it's good for both the team and the project for team members to collaborate by communicating fully and honestly about any concerns or disagreements.

For more information on how to negotiate a high-quality, collaborative solution to disagreements within your development or implementation team, see Chapter 13 or consult *Mastering Business Negotiation* by Roy J. Lewicki and Alexander Hiam (Jossey-Bass); or study *The Conflict Master Course: Turning Conflict Into Cooperation*, a workshop published by Trainer's Spectrum (www. tspectrum.com).

Know When to Persevere

If your basic assumptions about your innovation hold true, but you run into practical difficulties that slow you down, it's usually a good idea to persist. There are good reasons to pull the plug on a project, but there are plenty of bad reasons too.

Don't give up prematurely! Every innovator runs into some unforeseen difficulties during development, scale-up, or implementation. Things rarely work out as easily as you hoped. If the project is fundamentally on track and the basic idea is valid, however, don't allow a few practical problems to derail it.

What if you're going over time or money budgets? Well, that could prove to be fatal, but it doesn't always have to be. There can be alternative ways to fund a project. Also, you can always revisit the forecasts and see whether the work you've done allows you to make a better-looking forecast for future returns. If so, an increase in investment may be justifiable. It's worth running the numbers again, anyway.

Many projects go through several rounds of effort and funding before finally breaking through to commercial or practical success. Yours could be one of those projects that needs the team to regroup, reassess, and then reinvest in another round. Be careful not to pull the plug prematurely. Nobody said innovation was easy!

Know When to Quit

Every innovative plan, design, or project rests on a few key assumptions. When a key assumption proves to be flawed or just plain wrong, it's time to admit defeat and close the project before any more effort or money is wasted on it.

It's hard to admit that you're wrong. It's disappointing to quit. Winners never quit, or so the old saying goes. But that's not a good rule for innovators. A better saying is this one: If you can't win this game, try to win the next game. Innovators who are smart enough to walk away from a loser quickly are able to get started on a new project quickly too, which greatly increases their odds of success.

What are your key assumptions? What do you need to be right about for your project to be worthwhile? Make a short list of critical assumptions and then see whether they prove to be correct. If not, pull the plug on the project at once and begin searching for your next big idea.

Index

• A •

activity, 21
ad campaign, 71
adopter, 262–264
adventure, 34–37
Adventure Careers, 33
age
  as career change barrier, 35
  fastest-growing age groups, 42
All-Biz Web site, 172
Allen, Kathleen (*Entrepreneurship For Dummies*), 282
American Red Cross, 284
analogy
  coming up with, 211
  as invisible activity in presentation, 210–211
  presentation, 207, 210–211
angel investor, 307–308
appendix, 305
application, trademark, 283
art project, 329–330
The Art of Thought (Wallas), 47
assessment
  complexity, 220
  leadership style, 56
  personality, 95
  self, 332
  StratLead Self-Assessment, 56
  value, 277
attendee
  brainstorming, 104–106
  cost-cutting session, 236
audience, presentation, 200–202
auditory signature, 215–216
Authentic Happiness (Seligman), 327
authorization, 259
avoider versus engager, 223

• B •

back story, 34
background, presentation, 216
back-tracker, 184
Ballbarrow invention (Dyson), 188
banner ad, 272
bar chart, 209
barrier
  career change, 34–36
  creativity, 14–16
  financial, 35
benchmarking industry innovation
  businesses to watch for, 176–177
  competency alignment, 179
  job candidate interview, 177
  positive approach to evaluation, 178–179
  upstarts and startups, 175–177
  what businesses are boasting about, 178
bestseller, as new product, 176
best-selling product, 88
beta testing, 266–267
bias, 327–328
Big Five self-assessment, 332
billboard, 272
blame, 163, 326
blogging, 270
blue ocean strategy, 81
blue-water brainstorming, 81–82
body language
  during brainstorming session, 110–111
  contraction type, 320
  expansion type, 320
  expressing optimism through, 63
  in meeting, 319–320
  during presentation, 216–217
  withdrawal type, 319
boosting your career
  commission-based job, 314
  doing what you love, 313–314

boosting your career *(continued)*
  enthusiasm, 312
  parallel career paths, 314–315
  problem-solving, 312–313
  risk taking, 311
  stepping up, 311
  through championing, 316
  through education, 315
  volunteer work, 315–316
booth space, 171
boundary management, 254
brainstorming. *See also* meeting
  about this book, 3
  asking for examples about, 118
  attendee, 104–106
  blue-water, 81–82
  body language during, 110–111
  braindrawing, 116
  brainwriting, 114
  breaking into smaller groups, 128
  cause-effect diagram, 115
  clarification of instructions, 120
  closed-end questions, 109
  closed-minded thinking, 102, 105
  for combination ideas, 186–187
  common thinking traps, 110
  core methods of, 112–116
  cost-cutting session, 240–241
  creative chitchat, 138
  creative distance, 107
  creative facilitation, 101
  creative friction in, 106
  creative process planning, 106–108
  criticism in, 110
  critiquing results of, 122–124
  cycling between private and
      group work, 141
  design fixation, 126–127
  with diverse group of people, 81
  encouragement during, 117
  excluding people from, 105
  facilitator, 105
  facilitator roles in, 108–111
  familiarization with challenge
      at hand, 111
  first-round question-based research, 124

fishbone, 115–116
focus-shift question, 126
freeing the imagination for, 118
free-minded activity, 137
group creativity, 102–104
group dynamics, 101
group size, 105
habitual gestures in, 111
index card, 137
individual, 141
initial briefing, 112–113
initial retreat for, 107
"interesting questions to study" chart, 124
inviting questions for consideration, 104
length, 107–108
list, 205
listening skills, 109
making a case to explore fresh ideas, 103
mind mapping, 116, 133–137
mixing traditional and creative elements, 81
multiday, 108
negative dynamics in, 109–110
nominal group technique (NGT), 137–139
nonverbal behaviors, 110–111
note taking, 106, 132
orientation, 112
Osborn brainstorming rule, 113–114
participant, 118–120
pass-along, 114–115, 139–141
payoff analysis, 168
people with creative chemistry, 104
people with fresh perspective in, 106
persisting long enough, 122–125
positive attitude during, 103
positive reinforcement during, 119
power of incubation, 107
power of team thinking, 137–141
practice for, 119
for presentation, 204–206
problem-solving, 164–165
production blocking, 138
qualifying adjective, 109
random word technique, 116–117, 141
refocusing, 125–126
reframing, 102
researching before, 107

round-sticker method, 122–123
rush to judgment trap, 110
selecting people for, 103
setting the tone, 112
shape, 131
sharpening the view with narrower
    definitions, 127–128
sketching design for, 130
small-scale model, 132
social loafing, 105
solution, 226–228
stage fright, 119–120
sticky notes for, 132
storyboard, 131
struggling with ideas during, 117
suggestion system for, 104
supplier, 181
visual reference material, 129
visual thinking, 129–130
warm up, 112–113
wrap up, 117
brand identity, 282
brand name, 276
Branding For Dummies (Chiaravalle
    and Schenck), 282
B2B (business to business), 69
Buchaca, John (*Patents, Copyrights, &
    Trademarks For Dummies*), 276
budget, 235
build the team stage, 251
BuildingGreen Web site, 172
burnout, 335–336
business plan
    appendix, 305
    cash-flow project, 303–304
    clarity of the concept, 298
    company description, 301
    concept length, 298
    cover page, 299
    credit history, 305
    description of, 79
    documentation, 305
    executive summary, 299–300
    financials, 304
    funding need, 303–304
    market analysis, 300

    marketing and sales summary, 302
    organization and management, 302
    product description, 301
    quality of business concept, 298
    record keeping, 305
    résumé, 305
    service or product line presentation,
        302–303
    table of contents, 299
    team strength, 298
    title page, 299
business recreation strategy, 80–82
business strategy, 86
business to business (B2B), 69
Business Wire Web site, 178
Bvents Web site, 172

• C •

calmness, 222
caption, 74
career. *See also* boosting your career
    about this book, 2
    as adventure, 34–37
    career change barrier, 34–36
    hobby as, 24
    shadow, 315
career path
    downward move, 36
    entrepreneurial options, 44
    freelance and consultative work, 43–44
    growing through current employer, 36–37
    inventing your next job, 42–44
    lateral move, 36
    momentum, 36
    moving toward growth, 40–42
    opportunistic moves, 36–37
    parallel, 314–315
    proposing new position for yourself, 43
    short-term and volunteer projects, 37
    transferable skills and experiences, 37–39
    utilizing personal and professional
        networks, 37
CareerBuilder Web site, 36
carrying cost, 35

case history, 211–212
cash-flow projection, 303–304
cause-effect diagram, 115
challenge, 325
champion recruit, 268, 316
change management
  disloyalty in, 95
  openness to new ideas, 94
  painting a clear picture about, 95
  personality assessment, 95
  resistance to change, 94–96
  skepticism, 96
  snapback behavior, 97
  strategy, 94–97
  transition process, 96–97
Chaordix Web site, 153
Charmasson, Henri J. A. (*Patents, Copyrights, & Trademarks For Dummies*), 276
chart, 209
charter the team stage, 251
Chiaravalle, Bill (*Branding For Dummies*), 282
Chinese divination symbols, 156
choreographic works, 276
clarity of the concept, 298
clean-slate approach, 233–234
clip art, 216
closed-ended question, 109
closed-minded thinking, 102, 105
cluster analysis, 136
coach leadership style, 54–56
coaching/developmental leadership style, 57
collaborator versus competitor, 223
combination
  brainstorming for, 186–187
  candy bar example, 185–186
  classic, 185–186
  copycat product, 193
  display board, 196
  Dyson example, 188
  examples of, 184–185
  genetic, 183
  need-driven invention, 193
  oxymoron invention, 192
  power of, 183–184
  problem theme, 190–191

problems with solutions, 189–191
relevance paradox, 194
resourcefulness in searching for, 191–193
unusual forms, 195
weak signal, 194–195
word-play invention, 192
commission-based job, 314
communication
  innovation process plan, 250
  keeping on track through, 335
  marketing, 69
  project promotion, 259
company description, business plan, 301
comparative analysis, 165
Compendium Institute Web site, 136
competence
  benchmarking industry innovation, 179
  core competency, 93
  creativity and, 30
  transferable skills and experiences, 37–38
competitor offering, 77
competitor verus collaborator, 223
complaint, 143–144
complementary strategy, 92
confidence, 15, 35
conflict
  beginning dialogue in, 222
  best way to view, 221
  calmness during, 222
  collaborative approach to, 336
  competitive negotiation, 224
  competitor versus collaborator, 223
  complexity assessment of, 220
  engager versus avoider, 223
  facilitating brainstorming during, 228
  honesty in, 226
  judgment in, 227–228
  natural collaborator, 223–224
  open-mindedness in, 224
  outcome, 220
  positive focus, 229
  problem-solving team, 225–226
  reframing, 221–222
  respectful listening, 222
  safe to share idea acknowledgment, 227

setting good example of teamwork during, 225–226
solution brainstorming, 226–228
style, 223–224
transition process, 226–228
turning into opportunity, 219–222
win–win solution, 228–229
The Conflict Master Course: Turning Conflict Into Cooperation workshop, 336
constraint, 73
construction business, 172
consultant, 43–44
consultation
  employee, 49
  supplier, 181
contest
  crowdsourcing, 151
  e-mail, 150
contraction type body language, 320
copycat product, 193
copyright
  how to, 280–281
  as intellectual property, 279–281
  legal advice, 280
  U.S. Copyright Office Web site, 280–281
  Web site, 280
  works for hire, 281
core competency, 93
corporate strategy, 86
cost cutting
  attendee, 236
  brainstorming methods, 240–241
  clean-slate approach, 233–234
  consequences, 242–243
  cost accounting, 239
  creative determination, 231–232
  documentation, 243–244
  employee incentive for, 235
  finding losses, 239
  frost effect avoidance, 231–233
  implementation, 241–244
  informing those who will be affected from, 242
  learning from others, 236–239
  negative side effect, 242, 244
  perverse effect, 243

pessimism, 232–233
progress report, 243
proposal evaluation, 241
repetitive service and quality problem, 236
savings creation method, 239–244
self-efficacy, 231
spending category identification, 233–234
take-away idea, 236
tracking and managing, 244
unexpected benefit, 242
cost estimation, 277
cost, patent, 287–289
cover page, business plan, 299
creative brief
  creative input, 73
  goal setting, 72
  the message, 73
  schedule and constraint, 73
  strategic playing field, 72
  target customer profile, 72
creative chemistry, 104
creative determination, 231–232
creative dissatisfaction
  cost of not innovating, 170
  informed choice, 168
  intuition applied with logic, 170
  opportunity cost, 170
  opportunity recognition, 169–170
creative distance, 107
creative facilitation, 101
creative friction, 106
creative process, 106–108
creative searching stage, 51, 81
creative thinking process (Poincaré), 47–48
creativity
  about this book, 3
  ad campaign, 71
  avoiding isolating situations, 27
  balancing tight and loose activity, 21–22
  barriers to, 14–16
  becoming a leading innovator, 29–31
  being aware of your strengths and weaknesses, 15–16
  challenging yourself, 24
  competence and, 30
  controversial issues, 12

creativity *(continued)*
  creative departments, 13
  creative force, 12
  creative style, 15–16
  crossing boundaries for good ideas, 173–175
  in daily routine, 21–23
  daydreaming, 22
  diverse experiences as, 25
  energy, 30–31
  generating more ideas, 12–14
  holding out for more options, 13–14
  imagining innovation to meet daily need, 12–13
  learning from innovation mentor, 27–28
  marketing, 71–75
  mentor, 16, 27–28
  mind and body exercise, 23
  open-ended questions as, 27
  Personal Creativity Assessment, 15
  as powerful personal asset, 12–16
  pursuing interesting questions, 22–23
  recognizing great ideas, 13
  right-brain activities, 11
  seeking broader experience, 24–29
  seeking the company of innovators, 26–27
  stepping up to development teams and roles, 30–31
  supporting inquisitive behavior, 27–28
  surrounding yourself with creative people, 26–27
  taking personal risk, 24–25
  thinking outside of the box, 174–175
  thinking under pressure, 13
  through visual image, 16–18
  warm-up exercise, 73
  workspace needs, 18–20
creativity enabler, 16–17
credibility
  as career change barrier, 35
  in presentation, 200
credit card, 35
credit history, 305
criticism
  in brainstorming session, 110
  as creativity barrier, 15
cross-training, 175, 329
Crowd Fusion Web site, 176

crowdsourcing
  contest, 151
  for new ideas, 151–153
  resource, 153
customer
  feedback, 144–145
  focus group, 144–145
  survey, 146–147
customer–embraced strategy, 86
customer profile, 72
customer value, 87

• *D* •

daydreaming, 22
de Jong, Jeroen P.J. (*European Journal of Innovation Management*), 49
decline stage, product category, 89
delegate leadership style, 54–56
delegational/trusting leadership style, 57
demographic and geographic growth trends, 41–42
Den Hartog, Deanne N. (*European Journal of Innovation Management*), 49
design
  launching the project, 258
  presentation, 214
design fixation, 126–127
design flexibility, 249
development
  and implementation network, 256–257
  innovation process plan, 248
Dewey, John
  Dewey Decimal System, 163
  How We Think, 163
  problem-solving method, 163–165
diagram, redesign, 146
diffusion
  adopter, 262–264
  aiming for sophisticated buyer, 268–269
  basic description of, 261
  beta testing, 266–267
  champion recruit, 268
  diffusion curve, 264
  early day personal media emphasis, 269–271

free sampling, 272–273
inflection point, 271–272
length, 264–265
media mix, 268–272
strategic parameter, 265–266
diffusion expert (Rogers), 267
dinner/lunch meeting, 325–326
Directory of Venture Capital (Lister and Harnish), 306
The Directory of Venture Capital & Private Equity Firms (Grey House Publishing), 306
disagreement. *See* conflict
discovery
launching the project, 258
as leadership skill, 64
discrimination, 35
display board combination, 196
diversity
as creativity practice, 25
lack of, 26
team, 252–253
documentation
business plan, 305
cost cutting, 243–244
failure and mistake, 334
intellectual property, 292
downward move, 36
"dumb questions," 23
Dyson, James (Ballbarrow invention), 188

• *E* •

earnings estimation, 277
economic growth, 1
elder wisdom, 154–155
e-mail
contest, 150
creative conversation in, 150–151
getting recipient's attention through, 149–150
for pass-along brainstorming, 140–141
request for creative suggestion using, 148–149
soliciting ideas through, 83
employee
consultation, 49
reward, 50

employer, growing through current, 36–37
Employment Spot Web site, 36
encouragement, 117
energizer role, 253
energy cost, 234
engager versus avoider, 223
enthusiasm, 312
entrepreneurship
angel investor, 307–308
basic description of, 295
deciding whether to proceed, 296
how to develop, 44
intellectual property protection, 297
load, 308
research, 296
venture-capital, 305–306
Entrepreneurship For Dummies (Allen), 282
European Journal of Innovation Management (de Jong and Den Hartog), 49
EventsEye Web site, 172
executive summary, business plan, 299–300
exercise, 23
exhaustion, 15
expansion type body language, 320
expense
carrying cost, 35
credit-card debt, 35
health, 36
housing, 35
expert help, 181–182
explanation, 259
external communication, 254

 • *F* •

Facebook, 151
facilitator, 105, 108–111
facility cost, 234
fact-finding phase, 164
facts, in presentation, 208–209
failure, 334
feedback
about leadership, 59
customer, 144–145
from leadership, 49
financial barrier, 35
financial reward, 50
financial risk management, 60

financials, business plan, 304
finish the work stage, 251
fishbone brainstorming, 115–116
Fisher, Roger (*Getting to Yes*), 227
Five Ps framework
  people, 76
  placement, 76
  pricing, 75
  product, 75
  promotion, 76
flexibility, design, 249
flowchart, process design, 147–148
focus
  as leadership skill, 64
  team development, 332
focus group, customer, 144–145
focus-shift question, 126
font, 216
forced-choice question, 54
foreign patent protection, 289
free sampling, 272–273
freelancing, 43–44
FreeMind software, 136
funding need, business plan, 303–304
FundingPost Web site, 307

● *G* ●

genetic combination, 183
geographic and demographic growth
  trends, 41–42
Getting to Yes (Ury, Fisher, and Patton), 227
giving up, 336–337
Global Positioning System (GPS), 184
goal setting
  creative brief, 72
  examples of, 46
  finding abnormal ways to accomplish, 69
  innovation process plan, 249
  as leadership skill, 46–48
GPS (Global Positioning System), 184
graph, 209
graphic works, 276
greed, 86
Greenbuild International Expo, 172

group decision-making bias, 328
group dynamics, 101
growth
  in current organization, 41
  encouraging your own, 40–41
growth stage, product category, 89

● *H* ●

handout, 213–214
Harnish, Tom (*Directory of Venture Capital*),
  306
Hartman, Ross (naval architecture firm), 38
Harvard Business Review article (Kim and
  Mauborgne), 81
health
  health insurance cost, 234
  as money saver, 36
Hiam, Alexander
  Marketing For Dummies, 151, 266, 300
  Marketing Kit For Dummies, 282, 300
  Mastering Business Negotiation, 336
  Mentoring for Success, 59
hobby, 24
honesty, 226
hopefulness
  approaching problems with, 162–163
  as positive attitude, 62
hostility. *See* conflict
housing expense, 35
How to Write a Great Business Plan
  (Sahlman), 297
How We Think (Dewey), 163
humor, in presentation, 207–208

● *I* ●

I Ching, 156
idea generation (Osborn), 3. *See also*
  creativity
IdeaConnection Web site, 153
illumination, 48
imagination. *See* creativity; intuition
iMindMap Web site, 136

implementation
  complexity of, 247
  development network, 256–257
  group rule, 332
  innovation process plan, 248–252
  launching the innovation, 257–260
  partnership, 257
  planning for the worst, 332–333
  project promotion, 259–260
  rate of adoption projection, 260
  team development, 331–332
  team innovation, 251–256
incubation
  brainstorming session, 107
  as part of Poincaré thinking process, 48
index card, 136–137
individual-creative role, 252
individual-logical role, 252
informal champion recruit, 268
initiation, 248
InnoCentive Web site, 153
innovation
  about this book, 3
  development, 248
  integration, 248
  mentor, 27–28
innovation process plan
  benefit emphasis, 250
  communication, 250
  design flexibility, 249
  four-step diagram, 248
  goal, 249
  implementation team, 250–251
  initiation, 248
  introduction, 248
  monitoring the result, 250
innovation-oriented leadership, 53
innovative cycle, 16
inquisitive behavior, 27–28
inspiration
  customer complaint as, 143–144
  customer focus group as, 144–145
  customer input for, 143–146
  customer survey as, 146–147
instruct leadership style, 54
instructive/directive leadership style, 57

integration, 248
intellectual property
  audit, 293
  basic description of, 6, 275
  brand name, 276
  choreographic work, 276
  copyright, 279–281
  cost estimation, 277
  documentation, 292
  earnings estimation, 277
  entrepreneurship, 297
  graphics work, 276
  innovation-oriented, 293
  investment estimation, 277
  motion picture, 276
  musical work, 276
  patent, 285–290
  pictorial work, 276
  protective measures for, 292–293
  sculptural work, 276
  secret formula, 276
  SWOT analysis, 278
  symbol, 277
  tracking protective steps taken, 278–279
  trade secret, 290–292
  trademark, 281–285
  value assessment, 277
  what merits protection, 276–277
  written work, 276
intellectual stimulation behavior, 49
internal communication, 254
International Registration of Marks,
    Madrid System, 283
interview
  looking for evidence of innovative
    contribution in, 177
  résumé, 38
introduction
  innovation process plan, 248
  introduction stage, product category, 89
intuition
  along with logic, 170
  basic description of, 153
  elder wisdom, 154–155
  I Ching, 156
  invention, 155–156

intuition *(continued)*
  naturalistic decision-making (NMD), 154
  nature as, 154
  New Age approach, 153
  soothsaying technique, 155–156
  tarot card, 155–156
invention
  need-driven, 193
  word-play, 192
inventors' club, 330
inventory cost, 234
investment estimation, 277

• J •

judgment, 227

• K •

Kim, W. (*Harvard Business Review* article), 81
knowledge diffusion behavior, 49

• L •

laboratory, 20
lateral move, 36
lead user, 146
leadership
  delegation, 49
  demonstrating commitment to
    innovation, 48–50
  discovery, 64
  employee consultation, 49
  feedback about, 59
  feedback from, 49
  focus, 64
  getting to know yourself as, 51–55
  goal setting, 46–48
  innovation-oriented, 53
  innovative leadership checklist, 49–50
  intellectual stimulation behavior, 49
  knowing when innovation is required,
    50–51

knowledge diffusion behavior, 49
  maintenance-oriented, 52
  mentor, 59
  positive attitude, 61–63
  problem-solving, 64
  putting all skills together, 63–65
  recognition from, 49
  risk management, 60–61
  role-modeling behavior, 49
  seeking varied experiences, 59–60
  skill, 59–61
  support, 49
  as universal trait in any career, 45
  vision, 46–48
  visualizing possibility for, 46–50
leadership style
  adjusting to creative context, 58
  adjusting to fit any situation, 54–56
  assessment, 56
  coach, 54–56
  coaching/developmental, 57
  delegate, 54–56
  delegational/trusting, 57
  instruct, 54
  instructive/directive, 57
  knowing which style to use, 55
  relate, 54
  relational/concerned, 57
leadership volume, 51
Learned Helplessness (Seligman), 327
Learned Optimism (Seligman), 327
leverage, 258
Lewicki, Roy J, (*Mastering Business
  Negotiation*), 336
licensing, 93
life-cycle, product, 88–89
line graph, 209
listening skills, 109
Lister, Kate (*Directory of Venture Capital*), 306
loan, 308
logic, 170
logo, 214, 277
loose activity, 21
loss, minimizing the, 168
lunch/dinner meeting, 325–326

• M •

Madrid System for International
    Registration of Marks, 283
maintenance cost, 234
maintenance-oriented leadership, 52
major problem, 324–325
market analysis, business plan, 300
marketing
  abnormal ways to accomplish goals, 69
  ad campaign, 71
  assessing and violating the norm, 68–70
  caption, 74
  communication, 69
  competitor offering, 77
  creative brief, 72–73
  creativity, 71–75
  Five Ps framework, 75
  free sampling, 272–273
  narrowing your focus, 75–77
  as power impact, 67–68
  salespeople, 70
  social norm, 69–70
  strategy, 68, 86
  visual stimulus, 74
  YouTube, 69
marketing and sales summary, 302
Marketing For Dummies (Hiam), 151, 266, 300
Marketing Kit For Dummies (Hiam), 282, 300
mass mailing, 272
Mastering Business Negotiation (Lewicki
    and Hiam), 336
maturity stage, product category, 89
Mauborgne, R. (*Harvard Business
    Review* article), 81
meeting. *See also* brainstorming
  asking for multiple alternatives in, 322
  asking for original information
      and ideas in, 317
  body language in, 319–320
  brainstorming, 321–322
  controlling topic in, 320–321
  length, 321
  location, 322
  lunch/dinner, 325–326

  with mentor, 29
  problem resolution, 318–319
  reorganization, 318
  "sideways thoughts" board, 319
  spoiler, 321
Mehrabian, Albert (*Nonverbal
    Communication*), 320
mental bias, 327–328
mentor
  creativity, 16
  innovation, 27–28
  leadership, 59
  meeting with, 29
  mentoring others, 29
  personally inspired, 28
Mentoring for Success (Hiam), 59
mind and body exercise, 23
mind mapping. *See also* brainstorming
  as brainstorming technique, 116
  cluster analysis, 136
  combining research with, 134–135
  index card, 136
  mind map drawing, 133
  producing insight and proposal from,
      136–137
  software, 135–136
Mindjet MindManager Web site, 136
mistake, 334
Mom Invented Web site, 153
momentum, 36
monitoring, 50
Monster Web site, 36
motion picture, 276
music
  musical works, 276
  in workspace, 20
MySpace, 151

• N •

National Venture Capital Association
    (NVCA) Web site, 306
naturalistic decision-making (NMD), 154
nature, as intuition, 154
naval architecture firm (Hartman), 38

need-driven invention, 193
negative dynamics, 109–110
negotiation, 259
news business, 176
NGT (nominal group technique)
 generating ideas using, 138
 for group-decision making, 137–138
 increasing productivity of group using, 139
 taking votes using, 138
NMD (naturalistic decision-making), 154
Nonverbal Communication (Mehrabian), 320
note taking, 106, 132
NovaMind Web site, 136
NVCA (National Venture Capital
  Association) Web site, 306

• O •

open-ended questions, 27
open-mindedness, 224
opportunity cost, 170
Opportunity Knocks Web site, 36
optimism
 approaching problems with, 162–163
 as positive attitude, 62
 pragmatic approach to, 62
 through body language, 63
organization
 business plan, 302
 how this book is organized, 4–6
 presentation, 200
organizer role, 253
orientation
 brainstorming session, 112
 leadership, 52–53
Osborn, Alex
 brainstorming rules, 113–114
 idea generation, 3
outline-oriented presentation, 207
out-of-date strategy, 86
overcommitment, 85
owner and worker differentiation, 334–335
oxymoron invention, 192

• P •

parallel career path, 314–315
partnership
 implementation, 257
 strategy, 92–93
parts purchase cost, 234
part-time project, 37
pass-along brainstorming
 changing dynamics using, 139
 e-mail version of, 140
 instruction, 114–115
 passing tough questions using, 140
 storytelling during, 140
patent
 abstract, 287
 checking references in, 287
 cost, 287–289
 foreign patent protection, 289
 full-text search post-1976, 286
 as intellectual property, 285–290
 licensing agreement, 290
 provisional, 289–290
 searching existing, 286–287
 uniqueness, 285
 usefulness, 285
 worth of applying for, 288–289
*Patents, Copyrights, & Trademarks
  For Dummies* (Charmasson and
  Buchaca), 276
Patton, Bruce M. (*Getting to Yes*), 227
payoff analysis
 boosting through creative techniques, 167
 brainstorming, 168
 maximize the profit, 168
 minimize the loss, 168
 payoff table creation, 166–167
 quality improvement, 168
performance management, 254
persistence, 323–324
personal creativity. *See also* creativity
 fastest-growing age group, 42
 fast-growing cities, 41–42
 geographic and demographic growth
  trends, 41–42

Personal Creativity Assessment, 15
personal growth
  in current organization, 41
  encouraging your own, 40–41
persuasion, 207
pessimism, 232–233
phase-shifting, 83
photograph, presentation, 209–210
pictorial works, 276
pie chart
  portfolio representation, 85
  in presentation, 209
placement (Five Ps framework), 76
plan. *See* business plan
Poincaré, Henri (creative thinking
      process), 47–48
point of view, 206
policy, 15
portfolio
  need for, 84
  pie chart representation, 85
positive attitude
  during brainstorming, 103
  hopefulness and optimism as, 62
  leadership, 61–63
  pragmatic approach, 62
  ripple effect from, 62–63
  through body language, 63
positive reinforcement, 119
PR Newswire Web site, 178
practice, 119
pragmatic approach to optimism, 62
preparation
  analogy, 207
  as part of Poincaré thinking process, 48
  presentation, 203
presentation
  analogy, 210–211
  audience, 200–202
  auditory signature, 215–216
  authoritative source, 207
  background, 216
  bad example of, 215–216
  body language during, 216–217
  brainstorming for, 204–206
  chart, 209

credibility in, 200
design, 214
excitement in, 202
five tools of, 207
font, 216
framework, 206–207
fresh perspective in, 204
good example of, 215
good presentation importance, 199
graph in, 209
handout, 213–214
humor in, 207–208
insight, 202
list, 205
logo, 214
organization, 200
outline-oriented, 207
persuasion in, 207
photograph, 209–210
point of view, 206
preparation, 203
professionalism in, 200
quotes in, 209
relevance, 207
research, 203
slide, 213–214
sources and facts, 208–209
stage fright, 201
statistics in, 209
storytelling in, 211–212
structure, 201
style, 213–216
text, 214
thesis statement, 205
video in, 209–210
visual aid in, 209
white space, 215
press release, 178
pricing (Five Ps framework), 75
problem
  approaching with optimism and
      hopefulness, 162–163
  circling the wagons reactive
      approach to, 163
  creativity prompts, 162
  misdiagnosed, 164

problem *(continued)*
  postponing decisions based on, 161
  survival exercise, 160–161
  think-of-uses-for-brick test, 162
  turning into innovation opportunity,
    159–163
problem theme, 190–191
problem-solving
  best alternative approach, 165–166
  boosting your career through, 312–313
  brainstorming, 164–165
  comparative analysis, 165
  defining the problem, 163–164
  Dewey's method of solving, 163–165
  fact-finding phase, 164
  as leadership skill, 64
  payoff analysis, 166–168
  solution set, 164–165
  team, 225–226
process design
  flowchart, 147–148
  redesign, 146–148
product
  best-selling, 88
  copycat, 193
  Five Ps framework, 75
  life-cycle, 88–89
  rating, 90–91
  underperforming, 84–85
product category, 88–89
product description, 301
product line, 88
product or service line presentation, 302–303
product video, 271–272
product-based strategy, 88–91
production blocking, 138
production stage, 51, 81
professionalism, 200
profit
  maximizing the, 168
  product rating, 90–91
profit margin, 90
progress report, cost cutting, 243
project
  accounting for each project separately,
    333–334
  underperforming, 84–85

project promotion
  authorization, 259
  communication, 259
  explanation, 259
  negotiation, 259
  support, 260
projection, 260
promotion (Five Ps framework), 76
proposal. *See* presentation
proprietary brand, 281
provisional patent, 289–290
provocation, 149
PRZoom Web site, 178
publication
  The Art of Thought (Wallas), 47
  Authentic Happiness (Seligman), 327
  Branding For Dummies (Chiaravalle and
    Schenck), 282
  *The Directory of Venture Capital & Private
    Equity Firms* (Grey House Publishing),
    306
  Directory of Venture Capital (Lister and
    Harnish), 306
  Entrepreneurship For Dummies (Allen), 282
  European Journal of Innovation Management
    (de Jong and Den Hartog), 49
  Getting to Yes (Ury, Fisher, and Patton), 227
  Harvard Business Review article (Kim and
    Mauborgne), 81
  How to Write a Great Business Plan
    (Sahlman), 297
  How We Think (Dewey), 163
  Learned Helplessness (Seligman), 327
  Learned Optimism (Seligman), 327
  Marketing For Dummies (Hiam), 151, 266,
    300
  Marketing Kit For Dummies (Hiam), 282, 300
  Mastering Business Negotiation (Lewicki
    and Hiam), 336
  Mentoring for Success (Hiam), 59
  Nonverbal Communication (Mehrabian), 320
  *Patents, Copyrights, & Trademarks
    For Dummies* (Charmasson and
    Buchaca), 276
punctuated equilibrium, 51

• Q •

quality improvement, 168
question
    closed-ended, 109
    "dumb," 23
    focus-shift, 126
    forced-choice, 54
    open-ended, 27
quitting, 337
quote, 209

• R •

random word technique, 116–117, 141
rating, product, 90–91
recipe, 276
recognition, 49
record keeping, 305
redesign, 146
Redux Web site, 177
reframing
    brainstorming, 102
    conflict, 221–222
    strategy, 86
relate leadership style, 54
relational/concerned leadership style, 57
relevance paradox, 194
reorganization meeting, 318
research
    before brainstorming session, 107
    combining with mind mapping, 134–135
    entrepreneurship, 296
    presentation, 203
reseller, 92
résumé
    business plan, 305
    example of, 39
    looking for evidence of innovative
        contribution in, 177
    for nontraditional interview, 38
    rewriting, 38
    in tabular format, 39
    traditional, 37
return on investment (ROI), 167

reward, 50
risk management
    ability to manage, 61
    financial, 60
    leadership, 60–61
    technological change, 60
risk taking
    boosting your career through, 311
    calculated, 24
    as creativity practice, 24–25
Rogers, Everett M. (diffusion expert), 267
ROI (return on investment), 167
role-modeling behavior, 49
round-sticker method, 122–123
rule, 332
rush to judgment trap, 110

• S •

Sahlman, William (*How to Write a Great
        Business Plan*), 297
salary cost, 234
sales and marketing. *See* marketing
salespeople, 70
Sargent-Welch Web site, 176
satisfice term (Simon), 327
SBA (Small Business Administration), 304
schedule, 73
Schenck, Barbara Findlay (*Branding For
        Dummies*), 282
sculptural works, 276
S-curve, 271
secret formula, 276
secret project, 254–256, 328–329
secret, trade, 290–292
self-awareness, 253
self-blame, 326
self-censorship, 15
self-determination, 24–25
self-doubt, 15
self-efficacy, 231
Seligman, Martin
    Authentic Happiness, 327
    Learned Helplessness and *Learned
        Optimism*, 327

selling, 308
service or product line presentation, 302–303
shadow career, 315
shape-brainstorming session, 131
shipping cost, 234
short-term project, 37
shyness, 15
"sideways thoughts" board, 319
Simon, Herbert (satisfice term), 327
site. *See* Web site
skepticism, 96
sketching, 130
skill, leadership, 59–61
skunkworks, 254–256
slide, presentation, 213–214
Small Business Administration (SBA), 304
small-scale model, in brainstorming
    session, 132
smart mob, 151
snapback behavior, 97
social loafing, 105
social media, 269
social norm marketing, 69–70
social-creatives role, 252
social-logicals role, 252
software, mind mapping, 135–136
solution brainstorming, 226–228
solution set, problem-solving, 164–165
soothsaying technique, 155–156
spending category identification
    budget, 235
    combined savings, 235
    energy cost, 234
    facility cost, 234
    health insurance cost, 234
    inventory cost, 234
    maintenance cost, 234
    parts purchase, 234
    repetitive service and quality problem, 236
    salary cost, 234
    shipping cost, 234
    telecommunications cost, 235
    travel cost, 235
    vehicle cost, 235
    water cost, 235
spoiler, 321

stage fright, 201
statistics, in presentation, 209
sticky note, 132
Stone, Charles A. (Stone and Webster
    consulting firm), 313
storytelling, 211–212
storyboard, 131
strategic alliance
    licensing, 93
    mixing traditional and creative elements,
        81–82
    relevance of, 79
strategic phase, 51, 81
strategic plan, 79
strategist, 79
strategy
    based on greed, 86
    based on real points of interest, 86
    blue ocean, 81
    blue-water, 81–82
    business, 86
    business recreation, 80–82
    change management, 94–97
    complementary, 92
    corporate, 86
    customer embraced, 86
    customer value in, 87
    e-mail, 83
    influencing from bottom up, 83
    levels, 86–87
    lower-level, 86
    marketing, 68, 86
    mattress war example, 87
    out-of-date, 86
    partnership, 92–93
    phase-shifting, 83
    product-based approach, 88–91
    reframing, 86
    strategic innovation cycle, 81
    suggestion box, 83
    underperforming project and product,
        84–85
StratLead Self-Assessment, 56
streaming video, 270
strengths, weaknesses, opportunities, and
    threats (SWOT) analysis, 278

structure the work stage, 251
studio, 20
style. *See also* leadership style
  conflict, 223–224
  presentation, 213–216
style sheet, 282
suggestion box, 83, 104
Super Eco Web site, 176
supervision, 15
supplier
  brainstorming, 181
  consultation, 181
  evaluation of, 179–180
support
  lack of, 15
  project promotion, 260
survey, customer, 146–147
survival exercise, 160–161
suspending judgment, 227
SWOT (strengths, weaknesses,
      opportunities, and threats)
      analysis, 278
symbol, 277

● *T* ●

table of contents, 299
"take-away idea," 236
tarot card, 155–156
tax identification number, 282
team development
  boundary management, 254
  build the team stage, 251
  charter the team stage, 251
  diverse contribution, 252–253
  energizer role, 253
  exploration task, 252
  external communication, 254
  finish the work stage, 251
  finisher role, 253
  focus, 332
  individual-creative role, 252
  individual-logical role, 252
  internal communication, 254
  member and leader development, 254
  organizer role, 253

  performance management, 254
  secret project, 254–256
  self awareness, 253
  sense of belonging, 332
  skunkworks, 254–256
  social-creative role, 252
  social-logical role, 252
  structure the work stage, 251
  team formation and maintenance, 254
  team leader role, 254
  team vision, 254
Team Leadership Inventory (Trainer's
      Spectrum), 254
Team Roles Analysis assessment, 252–253
technological change, 60
telecommunications cost, 235
TESS (Trademark Electronic
      Search System), 284
text, presentation, 214
thesis statement, 205
ThomasNet News Web site, 178
tight activity, 21
title page, business plan, 299
Toastmasters Web site, 201
toothbrush invention, 262
trade secret, 290–292
trade show
  booth space, 171
  how to find, 172
  which to attend, 173–174
  wrong, 173–174
Trade Show News Network (TSNN)
      Web site, 172
trademark
  application, 283
  brand identity, 282
  brand management, 281–282
  criteria for, 282–283
  increasing your chances for approval of,
      284–285
  as intellectual property, 281–285
  proprietary brand, 281
  rights establishment, 284–285
  tax identification number, 282
Trademark Electronic Search System
      (TESS), 284
Trainer's Spectrum Web site, 59, 254, 327

training, 175, 329
transferable skill, 37–39
Transforming Negative Talk booklet, 327
transition process
  change management, 96–97
  conflict, 226–228
travel cost, 235
TSNN (Trade Show News Network)
    Web site, 172

• *U* •

underperforming project/product, 84–85
uniqueness, 90–91
United Inventors Association Web site, 330
unusual combination form, 195
Ury, William L. (*Getting to Yes*), 227
U.S. Copyright Office Web site, 280–281
U.S. Patent and Trademark Office, 283, 285

• *V* •

value assessment, 277
vehicle cost, 235
venture-capital, 305–306
verification (Poincaré thinking process), 48
viability, 179
video
  in presentation, 209–210
  product, 271
  streaming, 270
vision, 46–48
visual aid, 209
visual reference material session, 129
visual stimulus marketing, 74
volunteer
  boosting your career through, 315–316
  as career opportunity, 37

• *W* •

Wallas, Graham (*The Art of Thought*), 47
water cost, 235
weak signal, 194–195

Web site
  about this book, 2
  All-Biz, 172
  Bevent, 172
  BuildingGreen, 172
  Business Wire, 178
  CareerBuilder, 36
  Chaordix, 153
  Compendium Institute, 136
  copyright, 280
  Crowd Fusion, 176
  Employment Spot, 36
  EventsEye, 172
  FundingPost, 307
  IdeaConnection, 153
  iMindMap, 136
  InnoCentive, 153
  Mindject MindManager, 136
  Mom Invented, 153
  Monster, 36
  National Venture Capital Association
      (NVCA), 306
  NovaMind, 136
  Opportunity Knocks, 36
  PR Newswire, 178
  PRZoom, 178
  Redux, 177
  Sargent-Welch, 176
  Super Eco, 176
  ThomasNet News, 178
  Toastmaster, 201
  Trade Show News Network (TSNN), 172
  Trainer's Spectrum, 59, 254, 327
  United Inventors Association, 330
  U.S. Copyright Office, 280–281
  World Intellectual Property Organization
      (WIPO), 283
Webster, Edwin S. (Stone and Webster
    consulting firm), 313
white space, 215
win–win solution, 228–229
withdrawal type body language, 319
WordArt, 216
word-play invention, 192
worker and owner differentiation, 334–335

workspace
  computer desktop, 20
  items needed in, 19–20
  laboratory, 20
  music in, 20
  studio as, 20
World Intellectual Property Organization
    (WIPO) Web site, 283
written works, 276

YouTube, 69, 270

Notes

Notes

Notes

Business/Accounting & Bookkeeping
Bookkeeping For Dummies
978-0-7645-9848-7

eBay Business
All-in-One For Dummies,
2nd Edition
978-0-470-38536-4

Job Interviews
For Dummies,
3rd Edition
978-0-470-17748-8

Resumes For Dummies,
5th Edition
978-0-470-08037-5

Stock Investing
For Dummies,
3rd Edition
978-0-470-40114-9

Successful Time
Management
For Dummies
978-0-470-29034-7

Computer Hardware
BlackBerry For Dummies,
3rd Edition
978-0-470-45762-7

Computers For Seniors
For Dummies
978-0-470-24055-7

iPhone For Dummies,
2nd Edition
978-0-470-42342-4

Laptops For Dummies,
3rd Edition
978-0-470-27759-1

Macs For Dummies,
10th Edition
978-0-470-27817-8

Cooking & Entertaining
Cooking Basics
For Dummies,
3rd Edition
978-0-7645-7206-7

Wine For Dummies,
4th Edition
978-0-470-04579-4

Diet & Nutrition
Dieting For Dummies,
2nd Edition
978-0-7645-4149-0

Nutrition For Dummies,
4th Edition
978-0-471-79868-2

Weight Training
For Dummies,
3rd Edition
978-0-471-76845-6

Digital Photography
Digital Photography
For Dummies,
6th Edition
978-0-470-25074-7

Photoshop Elements 7
For Dummies
978-0-470-39700-8

Gardening
Gardening Basics
For Dummies
978-0-470-03749-2

Organic Gardening
For Dummies,
2nd Edition
978-0-470-43067-5

Green/Sustainable
Green Building
& Remodeling
For Dummies
978-0-470-17559-0

Green Cleaning
For Dummies
978-0-470-39106-8

Green IT For Dummies
978-0-470-38688-0

Health
Diabetes For Dummies,
3rd Edition
978-0-470-27086-8

Food Allergies
For Dummies
978-0-470-09584-3

Living Gluten-Free
For Dummies
978-0-471-77383-2

Hobbies/General
Chess For Dummies,
2nd Edition
978-0-7645-8404-6

Drawing For Dummies
978-0-7645-5476-6

Knitting For Dummies,
2nd Edition
978-0-470-28747-7

Organizing For Dummies
978-0-7645-5300-4

SuDoku For Dummies
978-0-470-01892-7

Home Improvement
Energy Efficient Homes
For Dummies
978-0-470-37602-7

Home Theater
For Dummies,
3rd Edition
978-0-470-41189-6

Living the Country Lifestyle
All-in-One For Dummies
978-0-470-43061-3

Solar Power Your Home
For Dummies
978-0-470-17569-9

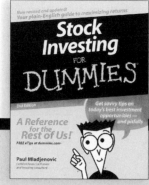

Internet

Blogging For Dummies,
2nd Edition
978-0-470-23017-6

eBay For Dummies,
6th Edition
978-0-470-49741-8

Facebook For Dummies
978-0-470-26273-3

Google Blogger
For Dummies
978-0-470-40742-4

Web Marketing
For Dummies,
2nd Edition
978-0-470-37181-7

WordPress For Dummies,
2nd Edition
978-0-470-40296-2

Language & Foreign Language

French For Dummies
978-0-7645-5193-2

Italian Phrases
For Dummies
978-0-7645-7203-6

Spanish For Dummies
978-0-7645-5194-9

Spanish For Dummies,
Audio Set
978-0-470-09585-0

Macintosh

Mac OS X Snow Leopard
For Dummies
978-0-470-43543-4

Math & Science

Algebra I For Dummies,
2nd Edition
978-0-470-55964-2

Biology For Dummies
978-0-7645-5326-4

Calculus For Dummies
978-0-7645-2498-1

Chemistry For Dummies
978-0-7645-5430-8

Microsoft Office

Excel 2007 For Dummies
978-0-470-03737-9

Office 2007 All-in-One
Desk Reference
For Dummies
978-0-471-78279-7

Music

Guitar For Dummies,
2nd Edition
978-0-7645-9904-0

iPod & iTunes
For Dummies,
6th Edition
978-0-470-39062-7

Piano Exercises
For Dummies
978-0-470-38765-8

Parenting & Education

Parenting For Dummies,
2nd Edition
978-0-7645-5418-6

Type 1 Diabetes
For Dummies
978-0-470-17811-9

Pets

Cats For Dummies,
2nd Edition
978-0-7645-5275-5

Dog Training For Dummies,
2nd Edition
978-0-7645-8418-3

Puppies For Dummies,
2nd Edition
978-0-470-03717-1

Religion & Inspiration

The Bible For Dummies
978-0-7645-5296-0

Catholicism For Dummies
978-0-7645-5391-2

Women in the Bible
For Dummies
978-0-7645-8475-6

Self-Help & Relationship

Anger Management
For Dummies
978-0-470-03715-7

Overcoming Anxiety
For Dummies
978-0-7645-5447-6

Sports

Baseball For Dummies,
3rd Edition
978-0-7645-7537-2

Basketball For Dummies,
2nd Edition
978-0-7645-5248-9

Golf For Dummies,
3rd Edition
978-0-471-76871-5

Web Development

Web Design All-in-One
For Dummies
978-0-470-41796-6

Windows Vista

Windows Vista
For Dummies
978-0-471-75421-3

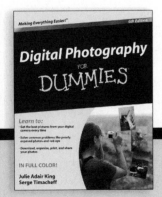

DUMMIES.COM®

How-to?
How Easy.

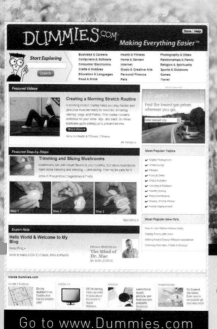

Go to www.Dummies.com

From hooking up a modem to cooking up a casserole, knitting a scarf to navigating an iPod, you can trust Dummies.com to show you how to get things done the easy way.

Visit us at Dummies.com

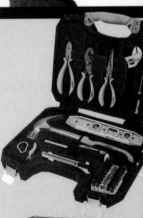